PRIVATE POWER, PUBLIC PURPOSE

Thomas d'Aquino

THOMAS D'AQUINO

PRIVATE POWER PUBLIC PURPOSE

ADVENTURES IN BUSINESS, POLITICS, AND THE ARTS

SIGNAL

McCLELLAND
& STEWART

LIBRARY AND ARCHIVES CANADA CATALOGUING IN PUBLICATION

Title: Private power, public purpose : adventures in business, politics, and the arts / Thomas d'Aquino.
Names: d'Aquino, Thomas, author.
Description: Includes bibliographical references and index.
Identifiers: Canadiana (print) 20220415129 | Canadiana (ebook) 20220415145 | ISBN 9780771000737 (hardcover) | ISBN 9780771000744 (EPUB)
Subjects: LCSH: d'Aquino, Thomas. | LCSH: Businesspeople—Canada—Biography. | LCSH: Directors of corporations—Canada—Biography. | LCSH: Philanthropists—Canada—Biography. | LCGFT: Autobiographies.
Classification: LCC HC112.5.D37 A3 2023 | DDC 338.092—dc23

Jacket design by Andrew Roberts
Jacket photograph by Jean-Marc Carisse
Typeset in Palatino Nova Pro by M&S, Toronto
Printed in Canada

Published by Signal,
an imprint of McClelland & Stewart,
a division of Penguin Random House Canada Limited,
a Penguin Random House Company
www.penguinrandomhouse.ca

1   2   3   4   5   27   26   25   24   23

Penguin
Random House
Canada

For Susan,
My North Star.

CONTENTS

INTRODUCTION

Private Power, Public Purpose is based on the underlying premise that humans are invested with power: the power to think and to act, and, in the best of all possible worlds, to act for the benefit of others and society as a whole. The more power one has, the more consequential becomes its exercise. History teaches us that power often corrupts and, wielded with malice, can do great harm. Those who possess great power face a formidable test of character. Abraham Lincoln summed it up with the words "Nearly all men can stand adversity, but if you want to test a man's character, give him power." Leadership, then, must be judged by how power is exercised and for what purpose. This is a book about power and purpose. It is also about responsibility, with leadership being a common theme throughout.

As fortune would have it, for a good part of my life considerable power was invested in my role as a business leader—power that to the best of my abilities I sought to exercise with great care, sometimes with success, sometimes not. In the main, this memoir tells that business story with perspectives as well on political power and the power of philanthropy in the arts.

Issues, people, and events form the backbone of this memoir. It covers a transformative period in Canadian economic and political history beginning in the 1960s and leading up to the present day. Significantly, it chronicles a fundamental transition in the culture of business in Canada—a transition in which I was privileged to play a central part.

This memoir speaks to the origins of the greatly enhanced role for Canadian business in the shaping of national public policy, beginning with the creation of the Business Council on National Issues (BCNI) in the late 1970s. I led the BCNI— subsequently known as the Canadian Council of Chief Executives (CCCE) and today as the Business Council of Canada (BCC)—from 1981 to 2009. During my years at the Council's helm, I worked with over one thousand chief executives and entrepreneurs as well other leaders in Canada and internationally. Their engagement, support and our collaboration form a crucially important part of the story I tell.

Public policy figures prominently throughout this book, and the policy domains covered are many. They include competitiveness, fiscal policy, trade, taxation, employment, labour relations, inflation, energy, the environment, corporate governance, and foreign policy and defence. Intimate insights are offered on the great policy debates of the day, including free trade, national unity, defence policy, and the environment. I describe in considerable detail my activities as a business ambassador and my work on five continents.

While hugely stimulating, my job as the "CEO of the CEOs" was not always an easy one. Being an activist surrounded by powerful people led inevitably to charges of excessive influence. I took no comfort in being decried as "Canada's de facto prime minister" and write candidly of how I countered this perception by employing every diplomatic tool at my disposal and partaking eagerly in respectful public debate. That did not stop death threats, an invasion of my office by masked intruders, ugly attacks in print and in person, and a burning in effigy on the streets of Ottawa. But I soldiered on, convinced that the responsible exercise of power aimed ultimately at promoting the public good would lead to a more prosperous, inclusive, and compassionate country.

The overarching theme of this book is leadership and what it means to me. I write about leaders from the worlds of business, politics, public policy, and the arts who have inspired me. No one has inspired me more than my wife, Susan, who for more than a half century has travelled my journey with me while pursuing her own remarkable career in the public service of Canada. My book is dedicated to her.

It begins with my happy childhood growing up as the son of Italian immigrant parents in the beautiful Kootenay region of British Columbia and traces my formal and informal educational journey, concluding with studies at the University of London. My return from England and work in Montreal leads to my years on Parliament Hill serving cabinet minister James Richardson and Prime Minister Pierre Trudeau. My early entrepreneurial years are chronicled in London, Paris, and Ottawa, followed by my three decades as the founding CEO of the Business Council of Canada and my work as a corporate director with several global enterprises. I turn to the arts and philanthropy in the latter part of this memoir with a prominent mention of the National Arts Centre and detailed insights on the National Gallery of Canada, where I served as a founding director of its foundation and chair for eighteen years.

Part memoir, part history, and part political and economic commentary, this memoir concludes with an epilogue titled "Reaching for Gold"—a challenge to Canadians to marshal our collective talent and resources to make Canada the best country in the world in which to live, work, invest, and grow.

ROCKCLIFFE PARK
OTTAWA

1

BEGINNINGS

This would be a very different story if a young man standing on the ramparts of a town in eastern Sicily had not exclaimed *"basta!"* ("enough!"). My father, Cateno, born in 1901, was on leave in picturesque Taormina from his Carabiniere troop. It was the early twenties and Sicily was immersed in conflict. Communists and fascists were in violent confrontation in the streets, and civil order was severely threatened. My father was proud of being a Carabiniere. Created by King Victor Emmanuel of Savoy in 1814, the Royal Carabinieri Corps played an important role in the evolution of Italy. More than a national gendarmerie, it was organized as a military force and to this day is considered part of Italy's armed forces. My father's hope that Italy, emerging from the bloody conflict of World War I, would see positive and real change sweep across the land had been shattered. He once told me of an incident on the outskirts of the ancient city of Syracuse where his commanding officer issued an order: "In the face of a mortal threat, shoot first; ask questions later." My father had sworn allegiance to the king of Italy and saw communists, fascists, and other radicals as dangerous. With the formation of the National Fascist Party in 1921 under the leadership of Benito Mussolini, and with fascist gangs increasingly asserting themselves in the streets with calls for a takeover of power in the country, he made what he often referred to as the "most painful decision of his life"—to leave his family, friends, and the camaraderie of the Carabinieri behind and reach out for a life in the New World.

In early 1924, he sailed for Canada and upon arrival immediately headed west, where he had heard that fortunes were to be made in mining for silver and gold. He settled in Trail, a small industrial city in the Kootenay region of southeastern British Columbia, no doubt attracted by its significant Italian community. The core of the city's economy was the giant Consolidated Mining and Smelting Company (today's Cominco), where workers enjoyed one of the highest per-capita incomes in the country. An enterprising and independently minded person, my father was soon involved in several businesses, including real estate. Later, he would own a hotel in the city, and eventually he built what would become the Trail headquarters of Eaton's department store, which he leased to the company.

Back in Italy, a beautiful widow with two young children had returned to her birthplace near Lucca, in the heart of Tuscany. Born in 1906, née Anni Mandoli, she had spent a few heartbreaking years in Trail, lost her husband to liver failure, and returned to Italy to live with her family. With Europe moving ever closer to war, she responded to a proposal from my father to come back to Canada and marry him. By her own admission, it was not love at first sight. But life with him offered the promise of stability for her and the children. With mixed emotions, she returned to Trail and they were married. Not long after, my mother, known as "Annie" to her friends, brought me into the world. It was November 3, 1940. Canada was at war and Europe was engulfed in conflict.

Our character is often deeply influenced by our parents and I am no exception. My father was an assertive and driven man who at times could unleash a terrible temper. Although he was capable of compassion, and indeed I can recall many instances where he generously reached out to others in need of help, he was, in the general parlance, "tough." When it came to me, his only child, he was stern and unbending, and I was required to live by a code of his making. Despite the discipline he demanded of me, I never doubted his love. My mother, on the other hand, was warm, immensely kind and loving, and deeply sensitive. She always saw the good in people. A devout Roman Catholic, she attended daily early-morning services for a good part of her life and, in her later years, would visit the local hospital every day to give comfort to the sick. My father respected our local priests and gave money to the church but rarely attended services. As a young man, he had bravely railed against what he called "the suffocating oppression of the church" and remained unrepentant of it all his life. Our family life was enlivened by the goings-on of my half-brother and -sister who, being teenagers when I was born, brought both joy and trials into the home. They were always loving and protective of me and we remained close all our lives.

When Italy, in alliance with Nazi Germany, entered the war in June 1940, my father was distraught. It was "the most catastrophic blunder imaginable," I recall him telling me in later years. It should be said that a large photograph of King George VI and Queen Elizabeth taken on their 1939 visit to Canada hung prominently in our living room. On occasion, when I was very young, my father would ask me to stand beneath the picture and sing "God Save the King" and "O Canada" for our friends. There was never any question about the loyalties of the d'Aquinos. But love of the ancestral motherland, its history and culture, never faded in those early years. Italian was the language spoken in our household, and my parents saw to it that it was "proper" Italian and not a dialect. Most Italian immigrants I knew spoke a regional dialect, and few of their children attempted to converse in Italian at all. My mother was especially proud of my facility in the language, claiming, with some justification, that our Italian was the purest—the language of Dante and the Renaissance. In Tuscany, there remains fervent debate among the Florentines, the Sienese, the Pisans, and the Lucchesi as to who commands the most perfect of Italian accents. My mother never gave ground on the matter, saying that the finest Italian was definitely spoken in Lucca.

My father would always remind me of the significance of our family name. "You carry the name of Christendom's most important philosopher and jurist," he would say. "Always honour your name." He was speaking of the Dominican friar Saint Thomas Aquinas, of course, whose name was Tommaso d'Aquino. Born in 1225 in Roccasecca, Italy, near the town of Aquino (Aquinum in the ancient Roman period), Aquinas came from a noble Longobard family going back to the eighth century. To make his point, my father gave me a book when I was in my early teens by English writer and theologian G.K. Chesterton. Of Thomas Aquinas, Chesterton wrote he "was born in the purple, almost literally on the hem of the imperial purple; for his own cousin was the Holy Roman Emperor. . . . He was Italian, and French and German and in every way European." The historical weight and significance of my name has never been lost on me. From time to time, when travelling in Europe, and especially Italy, mention of it would provoke disbelief. On one such occasion, when I was crossing the border from France into Italy, a customs officer asked my name. When I responded, he bellowed, "And I'm Napoleon Bonaparte!"

Shortly after the end of the war, my family moved to the nearby community of Nelson, where I began my schooling and quickly made friends, some of whom remain close to this day. Nestled in the mountains and bordered by an arm of beautiful Kootenay Lake, Nelson was a prosperous community with forestry, mining, and railway transportation forming the heart of its economy. It boasted fine heritage buildings, excellent schools, and a community ethos where culture and learning were highly prized. The mountains, rivers, and streams offered excellent hiking and fly-fishing, and there was rarely a weekend in the non-winter months when I would not go off into the mountains in search of the perfect trout pool. In winter, excellent downhill and cross-country skiing was readily accessible. Nearby, the majestic Kokanee Glacier was a big draw for those of us who liked to hike.

Nelson was settled primarily by British immigrants and its population consisted mainly of people of European stock. When I was growing up there, Indigenous people and visible minorities were few and far between. There were churches aplenty, with faithful Protestant and Roman Catholic congregants. At school, I had one Jewish classmate, his faith something I was unaware of for many years. The community was free of ethnic tensions, and I never sensed any form of discrimination linked to my Italian heritage.

The academic training I received at the local schools—Hume, Trafalgar, and L.V. Rogers—was excellent. Nelson scholars each year placed high in the provincial rankings. Sports, including hockey, lacrosse, soccer, baseball, and basketball, were important parts of our lives, as were plenty of cultural activities. While at Trafalgar, I was elected president of the student council and I remained active in extracurricular activities throughout my years in Nelson. When I delivered the valedictory address at my high school graduation in 1958, I remember speaking of the challenges and opportunities that lay ahead. I spoke of the Soviet Union's recently launched Sputnik satellite, the opening salvo in the space race, and warned that the future of the democratic world hinged on our ability to harness science to maximum advantage.

If communing with nature, fly-fishing, cultural activities, and sport remain at the centre of my most enduring memories of my early years, there is one other pursuit that has made a lasting impression: gardens and gardening. Passionate about his flowers, vegetables, and fruit trees, my father expected me to pitch in and to do the work to a high standard. When I protested that I would rather play baseball, he would remind me of one of my mother's favourite quotations: "One is nearer to God's heart in a garden than anywhere else on earth." For the past four decades, gardens and gardening have occupied an important place in my life and Susan's. In my case, it all began in my father's garden, and now, when I am pruning our hedge, fertilizing our perennials, or edging our flower beds, I often think of him watching over me and insisting on what he would call *"un lavoro perfetto"* ("a perfect job").

I was excited about entering first year at the University of British Columbia (UBC) in Vancouver in the autumn of 1958. The university's enormous campus, set by the ocean and backdropped by mountains, is one of extraordinary beauty. This is what I drank in every day there. I lived in one of the men's residences, conveniently located next to the women's residences, and eagerly embraced my new-found freedom. While I was given a generous allowance by my father, it was conditional on following a strict budget and accounting for all my expenditures on a monthly basis. The most enduring memories I have of my undergraduate years are the endless hours of argument and counter-argument with my fellow students, often going late into the night, helped on by generous lashings of malt whisky. Largely oblivious to life's dangers, we thought of ourselves as young lions. And for good reason. We were living in the best of times, awash in economic opportunities. Jobs were sure things then. Only the spectre of nuclear annihilation gave us pause.

Fraternity life attracted me. I joined the Zeta Zeta chapter of Psi Upsilon, a non-sectarian fraternity with a literary bent founded at Union College, Schenectady, New York, in 1833. Like many young people, I found myself searching for role models and was very much taken by the fraternity alumni who had excelled in their military, academic, and business careers. While fraternities still exist on campuses today, they smack of elitism to many, but at the time they were much more common. In its defence, fraternity life taught me the importance of comradeship, trust, and loyalty—essentials in the shaping of lifelong friendships. It also introduced me to a degree of diversity I had not known. Among my contemporaries were individuals of Chinese and East Indian descent and different faiths. Today, the fraternities have in fact gone much further in embracing diversity, reflecting a Canada very different from the one of a half century ago.

In September 1959, my father died suddenly. That such a powerful force in my life should be taken away in the blink of an eye was a terrible blow. We had our clashes and were fundamentally different people, but losing him felt like the ground falling away. It was not something I was even slightly prepared to deal with. My grieving mother and family insisted that I return to UBC soon after the funeral, and in mid-September I did so. It was perhaps too soon, all things considered, and a difficult year followed. I found it hard to concentrate and my social life took a frenetic turn. I spent far more time partying than I should have, mostly because I needed an escape. And my father's passing demonstrated how quickly and without reason one's days on earth can end. I did, however, manage to keep up with my classes and passed all my subjects. Still, there was an emptiness where my father had been, and I decided that wherever he was, he would want me to push forward.

My remaining years as an undergraduate at UBC were enormously satisfying and, I would say, productive. Campus life was endlessly energizing. Impressive professors immersed me in fields that I came to love and helped shape and deepen my thinking. I took up debating and sharpened my skills by presenting arguments both on serious subjects and outlandish ones to boisterous student audiences. It was possible then if not now to have great fun debating either side of "Be It Resolved That Gentlemen Prefer Blondes," "Frailty Thy Name Is Woman," and "Chastity Is Outmoded." It became increasingly clear to me over this time that the study of law was in the cards for me and I was ready for it.

Something momentous happened early in my final undergraduate year at UBC: a chance meeting with a smart, enchanting, beautiful young woman named Susan Peterson. A Montrealer in her first year at UBC, she brought an air of quiet sophistication to the campus, I thought. I was beguiled.

The following September, I attended my first year of law school at Queen's University. As I was about to leave Vancouver for Kingston, Ontario, Susan decided at the eleventh hour to switch from UBC and continue her undergraduate work at Queen's—a serious step in our deepening relationship. I had found a place to stay in Kingston; Susan, to her mother's relief, was safely tucked away in the women's residence. As I sat through my early lectures on constitutional law, contracts, criminal law, torts, and property law, I knew I had made the right decision. While I was by no means certain I would ultimately practise law in the conventional sense, I was convinced that training in the law would prepare me for any number of professional pursuits. Academic achievement was taken seriously at Queen's, and there I met a number of inspiring thinkers in the disciplines of economics, law, business, political science, and history. One of these was David Dodge, who would go on to become a highly respected deputy minister of finance in Ottawa and governor of the Bank of Canada. Dodge and I would collaborate closely in the years to come on key fiscal policy issues. Thoughtful and measured, he was someone I would count among the most influential economic thinkers of his time. Our friendship endures to this day.

While our time at Queen's was enjoyable, Susan and I both agreed that UBC and Vancouver had more to offer. So following a summer in Montreal, back to Vancouver we went to resume our studies. Upon arrival in Vancouver, I met, by chance, a fellow law student by the name Joe Clark and we decided to share an apartment. Little did I know that one day he would serve as Canada's sixteenth prime minister and that our paths would cross often in the decades to come. As for Susan and me, it became increasingly clear over the ensuring year that we were bound for marriage. We set the date for August 25. The venue was to be Montreal.

On a sunny day in the spring of 1965, we both graduated from UBC. I bid farewell to my fellow graduates with my address as "class historian." I saluted the "revolutionary" "Report of the President's Committee on Academic Goals," which said the criteria by which UBC's achievements would be judged were "the fostering in the student of a permanent spirit of enquiry and creativity, engendering in him or her powers of sound judgment, and developing the cultural resources of society." These were worthy goals then and, in my view, remain so today for all institutions of learning. In my address, I went on to bemoan that the Canadian flag, adopted by Parliament in 1965 after a period of acrimonious debate, was "raised at this university unceremoniously." To me, the raising of the new Canadian flag merited national jubilation. There was far too little of that. This critical observation spoke to my deep love of country, which has stayed with me all my life. I also took the opportunity to salute one of my heroes, Winston Churchill, "giant of the twentieth century," whose death earlier that year was widely mourned. My admiration of Churchill remained a constant in my life, his speeches and writings commanding more of my time than those of any other leader of the twentieth century. Of his many qualities, it was his courage and pluck that attracted me most.

When Susan and I got married, the wedding was composed of many moving parts that somehow, but not without effort, magically fell into place. Susan was of English and Scottish extraction on her mother's side, Swedish and Danish on her father's. They were second-generation Canadians hailing from Winnipeg. I, of course, was of Italian extraction. My parents were deeply conservative and "old school," and I was raised in the Roman Catholic faith. Susan's parents were Protestants. My widowed mother represented our family at the wedding, and while she carried it all off with her usual positive view of things, I know what a shock it was to learn I was getting married in an Anglican church. This was somewhat tempered when she came to understand, several years earlier, why I had decided to leave the Roman Catholic Church and, with Susan, opt for confirmation as an Anglican. My quarrel with the church was intellectual: I could not accept the doctrine of papal infallibility and Vatican conservatism on matters such as mixed marriage or the celibacy of the priesthood. Our wedding was a beautiful ecumenical affair with all the ceremonial ritual of the Anglican high church. The Roman Catholic choir that sang the wedding mass was one of Montreal's finest. My dear mother captured the moment when she told me she felt very much at home.

Following our wedding, we headed back to Vancouver and the next phase of my law studies. Admission to the British Columbia bar required a year of articling with a law firm, which I was very lucky to do at Davis, Hossie, Campbell, Brazier and McLorg (later known simply as Davis & Company), one of Vancouver's most respected firms. The work was demanding and competitive—but I enjoyed every moment. That said, I was also an outspoken advocate for better working conditions and higher pay for us "lowly clerks." We were paid $75 per month! That aside, the partners were remarkably supportive, although I'm sure I tested their patience more than once. When I was called to the bar, in October 1966, I was startled to see more than half a dozen partners show up at my calling ceremony. When I expressed my surprise and gratitude, one of them, Boyd Ferris, said tongue-in-cheek, "You've done well, young Tom, but you've also been a bit of a rabble-rouser. We just want to be sure you are leaving town!"

I did leave town. The world awaited, and Susan and I chose to go to London, where I had decided to pursue a master of laws degree. London at the time, in my mind, was pretty much the centre of the world, a place where everything seemed to be happening at once.

I found a modest furnished flat—always cold in the winter months. Susan and I survived thanks to an electric blanket that came with it. We could only afford to heat the flat for a short time each day, and in winter, the water in the toilet sometimes had a thin layer of ice in the mornings. Susan found a job with the hotel division of the Rank Organization and assumed the role of principal breadwinner. She kept us going, along with some help from her family and mine.

My year studying at the University of London was hugely rewarding. With classes at University College and the London School of Economics, and with the library at the British Museum close by, the intellectual stimulation was non-stop. My studies were also of practical relevance. Courses on comparative constitutional law, undoubtedly dry to some, prepared me for the great constitutional debates Canada would soon face. The course on administrative law sharpened my understanding of government accountability and due process. The lectures on international law and company law honed my thinking on the issues I would eventually tackle in the business world. One of my close friends and classmates in London was a fellow Canadian, Phil Elder. He and I shared a deep concern about the growing cracks in the Canadian federation, and in 1967 we organized and co-chaired a conference in London focusing on our country's constitutional future. Attended by Canadians and British colleagues, its tone left no doubt that serious unity challenges lay ahead.

That year in London was a voyage of discovery for Susan and me and launched us on our way to becoming enthusiastic anglophiles. British history, British architecture, the enchanting towns, villages, gardens and landscapes, British literature, British museums, and so much more came to be woven into our very beings. Our discovery of brass-rubbing led us on weekends to out-of-the way churches dotted here and there in the countryside to take imprints on our hands and knees of ancient brasses memorializing men and women who had made their mark over the centuries in many different ways in their communities and country. This practice is no longer permitted, and we still treasure the rubbings we have and the beautiful churches and villages they led us to. Among the most celebrated of the military brass rubbings in our collection are from the effigies of Sir John d'Abernon, England's earliest surviving memorial brass (1277), Sir Roger de Trumpington (1289), and Sir Robert de Bures (1331).

It is, of course, always fascinating how one can meet others by chance in a new place and they become part of one's life. On a late-night pub crawl with friends from university, I met a Scotsman who, it turned out, lived just down the road. David Durie, a graduate of Christ Church, Oxford, had joined the civil service and was living, as we were, on a modest salary. Our lasting friendship with David and his wife, Susie, began with an invitation to a haggis dinner on Robbie Burns day. With his fine sense of humour, David tried to convince us that the haggis was an elusive animal—with two legs shorter on one side than on the other—that his father had trapped on a Scottish moor. David went on to a distinguished civil service career and ultimately was appointed governor of Gibraltar.

When our year in London was coming to an end, we vowed to come back to live and to work. But for the moment, we prepared for our return to Canada.

When Susan and I arrived in Montreal in the late autumn of 1967, the mood in the country was wonderfully upbeat. The centennial year, crowned by Expo 67, was accompanied by a burst of pride and shared patriotism. Pleased to be returning there, and surrounded by friends and family, we quickly settled in and started new jobs— I as a legal adviser to the Canadian Air Line Pilots Association, and Susan with the National Film Board. At the same time, I could see that Canada was entering a period of significant change, although I did not know the direction it would take. But I had a strong feeling that the 1960s-spawned upheaval playing out in the United States would inevitably reach across the border. The early months of 1968 were indeed to become a harbinger of change. A political revolution was in the making.

2

SERVING THE PRIME MINISTER

On February 16, 1968, Minister of Justice Pierre Elliott Trudeau announced his candidacy for the leadership of the Liberal Party of Canada. While I had met Trudeau and some of his early key supporters, such as fellow British Columbian Gordon Gibson, Quebec lawyer Marc Lalonde, and Quebec organizer Pierre Levasseur, I was still surprised when the telephone rang asking if I would join the leadership campaign team. I agreed, subject to my employer in Montreal, the Canadian Air Line Pilots Association, offering me a leave of absence. My boss thought it was an excellent idea, and Susan was all for it. So off to Ottawa I went, taking my first step directly into the world of federal politics.

My interest in politics began at an early age. Growing up in Nelson, I had occasion to meet a succession of mayors and local representatives sitting in the British Columbia Legislature. This was not as surprising as it may sound, for Nelson was a small community of some seven thousand people. I remember how impressed I was when I met the formidable Bert Herridge, the Co-operative Commonwealth Federation and later New Democratic Party member of Parliament for Kootenay West. English born, erudite, and a fine speaker, he became known as "the Squire of Kootenay West" and served in Parliament for close to twenty-three years.

Despite all that, to the best of my knowledge, my parents voted either Conservative or Liberal. Socialism was not looked upon with affection in my household.

Local and provincial politics interested me less than national politics. I remember going to listen to Prime Minister John Diefenbaker when he visited nearby Trail and sitting just below his speaking platform. Seeing "Dief the Chief" in full rhetorical fury made a strong impression, but something else that happened on that occasion left perhaps an even more lasting impression, especially for a young boy. Seated in the audience was a group of Doukhobor protesters, local folk of Russian origin who were self-proclaimed pacifists. At a certain point in the speech, the all-woman group rose in unison and shed their clothes. The audience gasped, but Diefenbaker was quick to respond. "I will not be intimidated," he exclaimed. "I have seen those things before."

I was already fascinated by the history and politics of both the ancient and modern world, and in particular the struggle among great powers in peace and war. With a deep appetite for historical texts, and encouraged by my father, I would read aloud to him on Sunday afternoons. My only foray into student politics was my successful run for the presidency of the Trafalgar Junior High School student council, but by the time I entered first year at UBC, I had some knowledge of thinkers such as Plato, Aristotle, Aquinas, Machiavelli, Locke, Montesquieu, Rousseau, Hegel, Marx, and Lenin.

At university, as a keen debater and president of the debating union, politics was never far from my mind. Following Oxford Union rules, I relished the thrust and parry around resolutions such as "Canada deserves its own flag"; "No truck or trade with the Yankees"; "Quebec separatism must be opposed"; "Better peace-keepers than warriors"; "The Canadian West is being exploited by the East"; and "Canada must renounce nuclear weapons." My political views were maturing, but I had no partisan affiliations.

So here I was in 1968, with no shiny Liberal Party credentials, off to support a man who had captured my imagination with his invocations of the "just society." While some considered Trudeau a parvenu, the fact that Prime Minister Lester Pearson had given him a supportive nod said something to me. The leadership campaign itself was intense and exciting. I was thrown into policy analysis, some wordsmithing, and lots of organizational work. Trudeau performed with a style that tantalized and provoked. The signs of "Trudeaumania"—the teeming crowds, flashing cameras, screaming young women—were everywhere. The array of competitors for the Liberal crown was formidable: experienced and respected figures such as Paul Martin Sr., Robert Winters, John Turner, Allan MacEachen, Paul Hellyer, Eric Kierans, and Joe Greene. In the end, at the leadership convention on April 6, following seven and half hours of voting, Trudeau prevailed on the fourth ballot. As I stood in the brightly lit convention hall in Ottawa, I could feel the electricity. The earth as we knew it had moved. An advocate of the so-called new politics had triumphed and the era of Trudeau, the "philosopher king," was about to begin.

Following the convention and a round of enthusiastic celebrations, I returned to my job in Montreal as I had promised I would do. Driving back, with the first signs of spring along the highway, I was elated. I felt that in some small way I had contributed to a political transformation. I also weighed my options. Should I continue with my legal career? Teach at law school? Seek my fortune in business? I had even toyed with the idea of running for office myself one day, and my close-up look at the Trudeau leadership campaign made me think it might be worth a try.

In the wake of the April 6 triumph, and then Trudeau's swearing in as Canada's fifteenth prime minister, I knew that a federal election was not far off. When I heard that the date had been set for June 26, I felt I was missing being part of a history-making event and longed to become involved. But my professional commitments in Montreal kept me focused on my job. After all, I could not possibly ask for a second leave of absence. So I sat out the election in Montreal.

As I expected, Trudeau won a convincing majority; the country appeared to be in his thrall. What I was not expecting was a call from James Richardson, who had recently been appointed to the Trudeau cabinet and would go on to become minister of supply and services. He was a scion of an old Winnipeg-based family that had built its fortune in the grain trade. He had left the post of chief executive in the family company in order to run for Parliament in 1968. Now he was looking for an executive assistant to take charge of his office, and he invited me to meet with him in Ottawa.

At first I was skeptical, clinging to the notion that I had to get on with building some solid private-sector credentials. Furthermore, I had no connections to Richardson's home base of Winnipeg. When we met, though, I was taken by his idealism. He was a true believer in the maxim that serving in public office was the noblest of pursuits. He had given up the reins of corporate power for what he felt was the common good, not an easy decision for a man of privilege charged with perpetuating a family dynasty. I was also struck by his ambition to bring to the Trudeau team a business perspective, emulating the tradition of the highly influential wartime economic czar C.D. Howe. Richardson made no secret of his affection for Western Canada and the need for the West to have greater influence in national policy. At the conclusion of our conversations, I was offered the job, and told him I would accept.

Susan greeted me upon my return to Montreal and agreed to all that this would entail, beginning with a move to Ottawa. This was easier said than done. I had to explain my decision to my employers, who were disappointed but understanding. In turn, Susan would have to cut her ties with her employer, the National Film Board of Canada. Susan and I were happy in cosmopolitan Montreal, where she was born, and we worried we would miss the company and support of her parents. But they reminded us that Ottawa was not far off, and, being Winnipeggers themselves, they liked the idea that I would be working for Jim Richardson.

With little delay, we took up our new residence in the Island Park Towers, overlooking the Ottawa River and a short distance from Parliament Hill. Susan enrolled in a master of arts program in philosophy at Carleton University, and I took on my new duties working from the minister's office in the Centre Block of the Parliament Buildings. Having a keen interest in both history and architecture, I was thrilled to be situated at the House of Commons, with the Senate and the magnificent Library of Parliament only steps away.

The work was arduous but invigorating. Part of it required me to stay on top of Jim's needs as a minister, including his preparations for cabinet and cabinet committees and the daily question period in Parliament. Part of it related to his departmental responsibilities as minister of supply and services; the remainder involved his constituency commitments as the member of Parliament for Winnipeg South. This meant multitasking: running an efficient office, providing political intelligence, offering policy advice, writing speeches, and overseeing the minister's relations with his constituents. It also required close contact with other ministers' offices and the Prime Minister's Office (PMO). Here, the relationships I had developed during Trudeau's leadership campaign proved helpful and opened doors that otherwise may not have been so accessible.

I often travelled to Winnipeg with Jim, and in addition to meeting many of his constituents, I was privileged to connect with a number of prominent Winnipeggers whom I would later come to know well—among them Izzy Asper, Sandy Riley, Arni Thorsteinson, Jack Fraser, Albert Cohen, Arthur Mauro, and the young Gerry Schwartz and Jim Carr. Schwartz would go on to become one of Canada's most influential entrepreneurs, and Carr a senior minister of the Justin Trudeau cabinet.

In those early days I also met two members of Jim Richardson's family with whom I would work in later years: his daughter, Carolyn Hursh, with whom I served as a fellow director of the Calgary-based Max Bell Foundation and who would later serve as chair of the board of the family enterprise; and Jim's nephew, Hartley Richardson, who eventually served as the company's chief executive officer. Hartley and I would become friends and colleagues with close associations through what today is the Business Council of Canada and the National Gallery of Canada.

Jim Richardson was always a supportive boss. With his family in Winnipeg, he and I would often dine together on weekdays in the Parliamentary Restaurant and return to the office and chat well into the night. He was learning the ropes and so was I— and there was much to learn. Because his home in Ottawa was the Château Laurier, only a few steps from Parliament, he dispensed with the use of the chauffeured car provided as a matter of course to cabinet ministers. To my surprise, he insisted I take charge of the car, along with its driver, the affable Sgt. Stubinski. I attempted to return the car to the Crown, only to be told it was not possible. So, for the better part of a year, I endeavoured to keep Stubinski fully tasked, including driving me to and from work. I must admit, I enjoyed the perk immensely but tried not to get too used to it.

23

—

In June 1969, less than a year into my job with Jim, I was asked by a member of the prime minister's staff if I might be interested in joining the team. Considering how little time I had spent in my present position, my first reaction was to hesitate. Yet I had always made it clear to Jim that my principal interest was national policy, and now here was my chance. We had a heart-to-heart chat about it, and in the end Jim generously supported my decision to take the job. With his blessing, I moved into the PMO as a special assistant with primary responsibilities for policy analysis and speechwriting. Jim Richardson was a gentleman, and I was indeed fortunate to have had him as my first boss in Ottawa, despite it not lasting that long. In addition to introducing me to the regional politics of Manitoba, he deepened my appreciation of the West's importance in the federation. A bonus of working with Jim was to hear his views on business and family enterprise, subjects that would be at the centre of my life for decades to come.

I was to begin my new responsibilities on September 2, but first I needed to brush up on my French. I was assigned to a deep immersion course where my one and only classmate was the leader of Her Majesty's Loyal Opposition, the Honourable Robert Stanfield. I was quickly impressed by Stanfield's intelligence and quiet sense of humour, if not his facility for French. A couple of weeks in close quarters with him, and I was struck as well by his deep integrity. He spoke of politics and the country in a way that hit home. That initial bonding led to a lifelong friendship spurred on by the fact that my former UBC roommate Joe Clark was Stanfield's executive assistant at the time.

One of the first things I did in my new job was send a note to the prime minister and his senior staff that I rather cheekily titled

"The Tortoise and the Hare." In it, I outlined Stanfield's major strengths and warned that Trudeau, the hare, should not take the Tory tortoise for granted. While I received a couple of polite acknowledgements, no one took my cautionary note seriously—until the election of October 1972, when Stanfield came within a few votes of unseating Trudeau.

Most of the prime minister's senior staff were original Trudeau loyalists who had already been battle-tested for more than a year. Among the senior players were Marc Lalonde as principal secretary, Ivan Head as foreign policy adviser, Jim Davey as program secretary, Pierre Levasseur, in charge of the recently created regional desks, Roméo LeBlanc as press secretary, Timothy Porteous as chief speech writer, and Gordon Gibson as the prime minister's first executive assistant. They were an able group I came to respect highly. I worked closely with my francophone fellow speech writers, notably the cerebral Jean LeMoyne and Trudeau's old friend Roger Rolland. Rolland was the office jokester who could be counted on to inject humour into any conversation, often tinged with a touch of gossip.

I was delighted with my spacious office, with its original fireplace and high ceilings, located on the second floor of the historic East Block and only a few steps away from the prime minister's own office. My role in the PMO began—and ended—as a relatively junior member of the senior staff. While I was not lacking ambition, I came to accept my mixed collection of duties happily. I was mainly responsible for speech planning and writing, and preparing briefing notes for the prime minister on a wide variety of subjects. Whatever modest contribution to the benefit of the prime minister I may have made in the ensuing three years, the rewards for me were incalculable. Sitting near the apex of power during the better part of Trudeau's first term in office was akin to watching, and sometimes participating in, a series of high-powered dramatic plays on the national and international stages. In addition to the political upheaval sweeping the Western world, it was a time of intellectual ferment and radicalism driven by a profound desire for change.

Trudeau had raised expectations of a new way of doing politics. I keenly worked on some texts about participatory democracy, in which citizens were to have a greater say in the shaping of decisions, only to see the discussion dwindle into irrelevance. Giving meaning to this bright ideal proved too difficult when at the same time power was increasingly being centralized in the Prime Minister's Office. The role of the Liberal Party, as a consequence, was significantly weakened.

The degree to which the arrival of Trudeau in Ottawa shook the status quo was illustrated to me in a chance encounter with Paul Martin Sr. Martin was a respected elder of the Liberal Party whose son one day would become prime minister. As I was walking toward the East Block, I came upon Martin walking in the opposite direction. He stopped me and asked, "Don't you work for Trudeau?" I acknowledged that I did, whereupon he invited me to walk with him. He politely asked how I was enjoying working for the prime minister. Then he said, "Times have changed. In the world of politics I grew up in, you worked hard, made your way up the ranks, served in cabinet if you were fortunate, and then you might have a shot at the top job. Trudeau, on the other hand, came out of nowhere and in a few short years he became leader. It will never be the same again." He was right, of course.

The time I served the prime minister was marked by an intense whirl of policy conferences and fascinating encounters with political personalities and leading intellectual gurus. I got to know some of the brightest mandarins serving Trudeau, most of them concentrated in the expanding Privy Council Office. To my mind, the most significant policy initiatives of Trudeau's first term were the reorganization of the central machinery of government, the reform of the Criminal Code of Canada, the foreign and defence policy reviews, advancing bilingualism by means of the Official Languages Act, and giving birth to multiculturalism. For all that, Trudeau's first mandate was marked by the failure to come to terms with the problems bedevilling the economy. The greatest challenge of all, though, was confronting Quebec separatism and the 1970 October Crisis resulting in the imposition of the War Measures Act. Let me say something about each of these.

Soon after becoming prime minister, Trudeau had enacted a far-reaching reform of the Criminal Code. Notably, the bill decriminalized homosexuality and permitted abortion under certain conditions. It regulated lotteries, tightened the rules for gun possession, and introduced new offences related to drinking and driving. Trudeau defended the bill by saying famously that "there's no place for the state in the bedrooms of the nation," and "what's done in private between adults doesn't concern the Criminal Code." This was heady stuff and pure Trudeau!

Also well under way by the time I joined Trudeau's staff was the new government's foreign and defence policy review. Here I witnessed a struggle that was not entirely to my liking. The prime minister was determined on a change of course that in effect repudiated "Pearsonian diplomacy" and retreated from Canada's defence commitments in Europe. Ever since the 1956 Suez Crisis, I had been a strong supporter of Canada's carefully groomed middle-power role, and my allegiance to the North Atlantic Treaty Organization (NATO) was forged by the realities of the Cold War. When it came to the threat posed by communism and the Soviet Union, I was unreservedly a hawk. Also troubling to me was what I perceived to be a degree of disdain for the Anglo-dominated external affairs establishment shared by the prime minister and his closest foreign policy adviser, Ivan Head. Mitchell Sharp, the secretary of state for external affairs, whom I came to know well in later years, was sidelined by Head on numerous occasions. So were disgruntled senior departmental officials, who believed their experience and expertise were being undervalued. When, in June 1970, the Department of External Affairs published six illustrated booklets encapsulating the new foreign policy, the old gave way to the new. Canadian foreign policy was to be driven primarily by the national interest. I felt at the time that we were stepping back from the global stage and that Canada was being diminished as a result. Not that my views mattered, as I was not in any way engaged in the foreign policy review. But the surprise and broad disappointment that struck many senior members of the public service took a long time to dissipate. At least Canada was not going to withdraw from NATO, though it reduced its troop commitment and renounced its nuclear role.

The Official Languages Act came into force only days after I joined the prime minister's staff. The bill gave the English and French languages equal status in Canada's government and in all the services within its jurisdiction, including the courts. It was adopted in the House of Commons with the support of all parties, even though official bilingualism was a divisive issue in many parts of the country. I supported the legislation as an overdue recognition of the rights of French-speaking citizens and, in my own thinking, as a reflection of who we are as a nation. The Official Languages Act was to me the spear tip of Trudeau's vision of Canada, the vision that had prompted him and fellow Quebecers Jean Marchand and Gérard Pelletier, known collectively as the "three wise men," to come to Ottawa in 1965. Having carefully studied Trudeau's texts on the role of French Canadians in Canadian society, I felt I understood the powerful forces driving the desire to recognize "the French fact" at the national level. I travelled to my native British Columbia to defend against accusations that Trudeau was "forcing French down our throats." Later, in the lead-up to the 1972 federal election, it became clear to me that Trudeau and his government had not done a good job explaining the Official Languages Act. Nevertheless, I believed then and still believe today that it was the signature initiative of Trudeau's first term in office. Regrettably, it did little to dampen nationalist fervour in Quebec.

On October 8, 1971, the prime minister announced in the House of Commons a "policy of multiculturalism within a bilingual framework . . . as the most suitable means of assuring the cultural freedom of Canadians." I was aware of the evolution of this idea, which had been discussed at the cabinet committee level and by the full cabinet the previous month. The day following the announcement in the House, Trudeau spoke about multiculturalism in one of his signature speeches in Winnipeg, before a jubilant meeting of the Ukrainian Canadian Congress. This was a speech I helped craft, and I welcomed the initiative. The policy of multiculturalism made perfect sense to me and elegantly managed to untangle the country from the notion of official biculturalism and the concept of two nations. I was also strongly in accord with the prime minister's conservative interpretation of multiculturalism's meaning: that it was largely symbolic and conferred no specific group or economic rights. Regrettably, over time this idea gathered momentum as a politically driven issue, burning up public funding and acquiring institutional status, and its own ministry.

In October 1970, Canada recognized the People's Republic of China and suspended diplomatic relations with the Republic of China (known today as Taiwan). I took great interest in this milestone initiative inspired by Trudeau, whom we on the staff looked upon as a "China hand." Though not involved, I considered it a smart and brave step, especially given that it was opposed by the United States. The Nixon administration followed suit not long after, but Canada's initiative won us favour with Chinese leaders for decades to come. I traded on Canada's early recognition initiative to some advantage during my later frequent visits to China. What surprised me most at the time was how little space Trudeau's bold China policy occupied in the Canadian national discourse.

No issue engaged my intellect and captured my emotions in those years more than the October Crisis in 1970. On the sixteenth of that month, I accompanied the prime minister on the short, brightly lit walk on Parliament Hill from the Centre Block to his office in the East Block. We were surrounded by soldiers in battle gear carrying automatic weapons. I asked myself if this could really be happening here in Canada. Like most Canadians, I had never seen armed troops in our streets. In silence, we climbed the stairs to the prime minister's office, where he was to deliver the historic address invoking the War Measures Act.

The terrorist Front de libération du Québec (FLQ) had been pursuing their often deadly operations since the early 1960s, including an escalating series of bombings in Quebec, which by 1970 had claimed six lives. Now they had kidnapped British diplomat James Cross and deputy premier of Quebec and minister of labour and immigration Pierre Laporte. The deteriorating situation in the province, punctuated by growing political unrest in Montreal, had already prompted Quebec premier Robert Bourassa to call for the assistance of the army. Few people expected the next dramatic step.

The television cameras were at the ready when Trudeau sat down, a yellow flower in his left lapel, with his notes on a lectern on his desk and the Canadian flag to his right. Under the lights, his face was ashen. Trudeau's words were sombre and uncompromising.

Having contributed to the contents of the address, I felt a shiver go up my spine and pride at the sangfroid with which the prime minister defended Canadian democracy that night. "Persons who invoke violence are raising deliberately the level of hate in Canada," said Trudeau. "They do so at a time when the country must eliminate hate and must exhibit tolerance and compassion in order to create the kind of society which we all desire. . . . Canada remains one of the most wholesome and humane lands on this earth. If we stand firm, this current situation will soon pass. We will be able to say proudly, as we have for decades, that within Canada there is ample room for opposition and dissent, but none for intimidation and terror." These words remain fixed in my mind to this day.

The debate about the wisdom of invoking the draconian War Measures Act continues even now. In the prime minister's defence, I will say this: based on my observations and proximity to the events, I believe Trudeau, an ardent civil libertarian, acted reluctantly but correctly. In Quebec, there were open calls for insurrection and rumours of possible mass bombings, and respected intellectuals called for compromise with the terrorists. In this confused and uncertain situation, the unknowns trumped the knowns. The reality is that the prime minister, members of his cabinet, and the top echelons of the security establishment simply did not know what might happen next.

The callous murder of Laporte that followed the next day caused a collective intake of breath. Disbelief and anger overwhelmed me. To many who had found it difficult to come to terms with the imposition of the War Measures Act and its suspension of civil liberties, the actions of the Trudeau government now seemed justified. The prime minister's response to the murder was filled with fury. "There are few occasions when an entire population of a country shares a single emotion and senses a deep unity in the face of events," he said. "This is one of those occasions. . . . The men responsible for these crimes are not representative Canadians. They are members of a hard core devoted to a single purpose— to inspire within all of us fear and hatred, and in this atmosphere to destroy our nation. They are beneath contempt."

And then came the words that proved prophetic: "The FLQ has sown the seeds of its own destruction." My modest contribution to the shaping of this historic address were those few words, which I offered up in the belief that the national revulsion, including in Quebec, at what the FLQ had done would doom the revolutionary movement dedicated to violence. But while dreams of revolutionary overthrow had been crushed, support for the separatist cause in Quebec nevertheless grew over the next decades.

The Constitution was never far from Trudeau's mind during his first term. When he was justice minister, he had published a government statement titled "A Canadian Charter for Human Rights." A year later, he set out the federal position on constitutional change in a document titled "The Constitution and the People of Canada." Given my own deep interest in constitutional affairs, I devoured these documents and looked forward eagerly to the meeting of the first ministers planned for Victoria in June 1971.

British Columbia premier W.A.C. Bennett hosted the meeting. The premiers and Trudeau meant to draw up plans to deal with the patriation of the Constitution, an amending formula, and provincial or regional representation in the House of Commons, the Senate, and the Supreme Court. Like so many closely following this file, I had high hopes that the Victoria meeting would result in a historic breakthrough. But Quebec's premier Bourassa, spurred on by his social welfare minister's hawkish demands for more concessions for his province, withdrew his support at the eleventh hour and scuttled the entire project. This forecast how difficult it would be in the years to come to obtain a national consensus. Trudeau was bitterly disappointed.

I was to become friends in later life with Claude Castonguay, the Quebec minister who gave voice to these hawkish demands at the meeting, when he became active in the Quebec business community. Always thoughtful, to me he was the quintessential nationalist and an uncompromising advocate of the right of the Québécois to be *maîtres chez nous*. My conversations with Castonguay helped me better understand the roots of Quebec nationalism: the desire to have Quebec recognized as a nation, the thirst for greater autonomy and fullest possible exercise of the province's powers under the Constitution.

Among all of Trudeau's impacts on national policy-making, one of the most significant but little known is the change he made to the machinery of government. This was a matter about which he knew relatively little, but of one thing he was certain: he was determined to bring order and discipline to decision-making and put an end to what he considered was the chaos of the Lester B. Pearson years. Trudeau set out to restructure the organization and operations of the cabinet and cabinet committee system, with detailed planning and analysis being removed as responsibilities of the cabinet and assigned to committees. He was aided in this task by one of Ottawa's most senior mandarins, clerk of the privy council and secretary to the cabinet Gordon Robertson. As a mentor and tutor, Robertson taught me a great deal about the culture and operations of the federal public service, something that would come in very useful later. Also deeply involved in shaping this transformation was Michael Pitfield, an assistant secretary to the cabinet and confidant of the prime minister. Pitfield eventually succeeded Robertson as clerk, in which position he would exercise great influence, causing him to be resented by some of his long-serving public service colleagues.

In conjunction with the restructuring of the cabinet and cabinet committees, the PMO was considerably expanded. Under the watchful eye of Marc Lalonde as principal secretary, by 1970 the office employed some eighty people, double the number it had in the Pearson years. In addition to supporting the multiple responsibilities of the prime minister, the staff was expected to be his eyes and ears. Trudeau did not want to become a captive of the bureaucracy, and our job in part was to offer him countervailing advice. I was perfectly placed to understand how this newly created machinery worked. In 1974, two years after leaving Trudeau's staff, I published an academic paper titled "The Prime Minister's Office: Catalyst or Cabal?" It made the case for the way the office had evolved and explained the reasons behind the changes. While the paper was generally well received, opponents of the growth of prime ministerial power were not convinced. Serious debate still swirls around the concentration of power in the PMO that accelerated under Trudeau and continues unabated to this day.

The power and influence Trudeau exerted in his early years have been chronicled by a number of biographers. In my experience, Trudeau was dispassionate in his demeanour, although I never doubted he harboured well-concealed emotions of considerable intensity. This was particularly so at the time of the FLQ crisis. And no doubt he suffered terribly from the difficulties surrounding his marriage to Margaret. But in the moments when I saw him, he seemed cool, at times detached, and always in control. His intellect was a powerful political advantage. As prime minister, he was invested with great powers, such as the power to appoint ministers and to fire them. At the height of Trudeaumania, he could count on the enormous political advantage of his mass appeal. But his intellect was his ace card. His cabinet ministers were in awe of their cerebral leader, though most of them were more experienced politically. He was described by his critics as arrogant. His arrogance, though, was not of the swaggering type. In reality, he was quite shy and not very often at ease with people. He was not a "retail politician" the way his son Justin is.

I, like others in the PMO, knew little of Trudeau's personal life other than his public appearances with dazzling women like Barbra Streisand. His secret marriage to the strikingly beautiful Margaret Sinclair came as a stunning surprise to us. As staffers, we toasted with relish his marriage and the birth of Justin little more than nine months later because we could see first-hand how genuinely happy Trudeau was. We had no idea then that the match would face a tumultuous future.

By 1972, the prime minister's popularity had eroded dramatically. The days of Trudeaumania were gone. Polls showed that Canadians were deeply concerned by the state of the economy; inflation was out of control and unemployment stood at over 6 per cent. Opposition leader Robert Stanfield was beginning to draw blood with his attacks. Meanwhile, Trudeau's critics on the left, led by the eloquent David Lewis of the New Democratic Party, charged that he was bowing to "corporate welfare bums" and ignoring the dangerous rise of foreign control of the Canadian economy. This criticism was supported by former Liberal cabinet minister Eric Kierans and a host of economic nationalists, including Walter Gordon, who had favoured Trudeau in 1968. Trudeau responded by launching an election campaign under the banner "The Land Is Strong." I was not comfortable with a campaign that relied heavily on a defence of the Liberal record, especially when it became clear that people's economic concerns were paramount. The electorate was looking for solutions. Nevertheless, I pitched in, buoyed by the energy that permeates political campaigns. My contribution focused on speech writing and preparing briefing notes. The pace was frenetic.

I enjoyed one memorable break from the election fever when I was asked to accompany former prime minister Pearson to the first game of the historic Canada-Soviet hockey series in Montreal on September 2. After Phil Esposito and Paul Henderson scored in the first six minutes, Pearson was ecstatic, and so was I. But the tide turned, and the Russians won the game by a score of 7 to 3. Undaunted, Pearson predicted that Canada would win the series. Happily, he was right. As I drove back to Ottawa that night, I reflected on Pearson, who I barely knew—on his great service to our country, on his pivotal role in solving the Suez Crisis, earning him the Nobel Peace Prize, and on how, for a brief shining moment, he brought Canada into the international spotlight as a respected middle power. What troubled me, however, was how Trudeau, in my view, had not paid him the deference he deserved as a former prime minister and statesman—and as the man who stepped forward to help pave Trudeau's way to the highest office in the land. Sadly, less than four months after our memorable night at the Montreal Forum, Pearson died.

The campaign ground on. Polling reports, buttressed by senior campaign officials such as Torrance Wylie and Senator Richard Stanbury, suggested that the Liberals had a good chance of forming a majority government. Significantly, Trudeau was polling more favourably than Stanfield. But by the last week of the campaign, the prospects of victory were considerably more uncertain. On election night, October 30, Trudeau edged out Stanfield by a mere two seats: 109 to 107. Dejection reigned that night at Ottawa's Skyline Hotel, where we watched the returns. The hare had won, but the tortoise had come uncomfortably close.

—

I had started to make plans to return to the private sector as early as the autumn of 1971. With the election likely coming in 1972, I'd figured I would stay put until after that and then move on. While I considered possibilities in Canada, both Susan and I wanted to return to London. By the summer of 1972, I had accepted an offer to work with the international management consulting firm Spencer Stuart. Susan, who had completed her master of arts at Carleton and was lecturing in philosophy at the university, was very pleased to be accepted to do doctoral work at the University of London.

Following the election, and preparing to leave for my new job in London, I embraced my colleagues one last time and thanked them for their camaraderie. I shook the prime minister's hand tightly and thanked him for having provided me with the experience of a lifetime. Trudeau spoke a few brief words of appreciation and wished me well. When I walked away, I looked back at him and heard him say to the small group of people surrounding him, "We are going to carry on." Disappointed as he certainly was in such a narrow election victory, his posture was one of defiance. I knew he was far from done.

If I were to choose the best four years of the past half century to have served in government, it would be 1968 to 1972. It was a time when the national government, led by a dashing, contrarian intellectual, ushered in far-reaching change. The public service attracted the best and the brightest. Faith in what government could achieve was strong. Trudeau's political court was described in some circles as "Camelot North," picking up on the Kennedy legacy, which still burned brightly in America. Yet I put aside any thoughts of returning to the political realm. I had seen the rough-and-tumble of politics up close—the jockeying for position and favour and power, the endless compromise, the heavy personal sacrifices. Though I had no idea what particular road I might eventually take, I knew I would find a way to serve my country in some other way—as an independent thinker, as an influencer of public policy.

I was privileged to cross paths with Prime Minister Trudeau in office and in private life in the years to come. The last time I saw him at a private event in Montreal was when his health was in decline. It was painful to see. It was as if the light had gone from his eyes. It was not long after that I joined with throngs of mourners at Notre-Dame Basilica in Montreal in September 2000 to bid this giant of a man a final farewell. As I think back on one of the few occasions when I saw him relaxed and happy, an Expos versus Chicago Cubs baseball game comes to mind. It was September 6, 1984, and he, his three boys, chief justice of Canada Brian Dickson and his wife Barbara, and Susan and I were guests of U.S. Ambassador Paul Robinson. Trudeau was free of the burdens of office, he was with his boys whom he adored, and he clearly was enjoying the moment. When I asked him about his life outside of politics, he said, "I have had a good run and I don't regret a thing. But Tom, don't think about a political career unless you have one hell of a lot of stamina and guts too." I told him that active politics was behind me now and that working for him had shown me why.

3

BOLD AMBITIONS AND
A PAIR OF RUNNING SHOES

My career in business began in earnest when we arrived in London, just days following the election in Canada. There, I began work with Spencer Stuart, an international management consultancy with offices in Europe and the United States. My interest in business issues was kindled in 1966 and 1967 at the London School of Economics (LSE), where I studied company law. While my master of laws program encompassed comparative constitutional and international law, it was at the LSE that I first cut my teeth on the history and evolution of the joint stock company. This theoretical understanding of the company and its role in society helped shape my broader grasp of business and capitalism for years to come. It also helped, of course, that by then I was familiar with the writings of economists such as Adam Smith, Thomas Malthus, John Stuart-Mill, Karl Marx, and Friedrich Hayek.

Exposure in small doses to the business environment also came while articling in the mid-1960s with the Vancouver law firm Davis & Company. Sitting in the background as a junior clerk while senior lawyers discussed the problems of the day with major corporate clients, notably in the forest products and mining sectors, gave me a taste of what my own corporate practice might one day look like once I was called to the bar.

My time in Ottawa working as executive assistant to James Richardson further exposed me to the world of business, this time tangentially. Richardson had been serving as chair and chief executive officer of his family company when he made the decision to opt for a life in politics. Although Richardson came to Parliament as a novice, Trudeau quickly appointed him to his cabinet. I was struck by Richardson's idealism and his desire to emulate the approach that C.D. Howe had brought to his service in government. During the twelve months I served with him on secondment from my legal job in Montreal, our conversations about political issues sometimes strayed to his life in business, and in particular to the family business. Our discussions gave me the first inklings of how competitive the world of large enterprise really is and how demanding the role of a chief executive officer can be.

Very much aware of what London had to offer from our student years there, Susan and I returned to the city with great excitement. London, after all, was a major centre of global finance and commerce, and the firm I was joining served some of the world's largest multinational companies. What mattered as much to us was that, as one of the world's great cultural capitals, London offered us a rich trove of splendid museums, art, music, and theatre. We jumped in with both feet.

We quickly found a wonderful furnished flat at 21 Hyde Park Square, minutes away from Hyde Park and a comfortable fifteen-minute walk to my offices at Brook House, on Park Lane. With large windows overlooking the garden in the square below and attractive local pubs only minutes away, our new accommodations thrilled us. From day one, Susan and I were warmly received by the partners and associates of the firm. I was the only foreigner on the team and discovered that my Canadian nationality was a definite plus. They wanted to make us feel welcome and they did a splendid job of it.

In its day-to-day work, the firm focused on company restructuring, often prompted by a merger or acquisition. Its clients included some of the most respected British banks, insurance companies, and manufacturers, and the entry point with most of our clients was at the chief executive or board level. I later learned that this high-level corporate engagement and its accompanying culture was excellent preparation for what eventually would become the mainstay of my business career.

My welcome to the firm came with some advice on what every "well-bred gentleman" needed to know: where to have my shirts and shoes made (on Jermyn Street at Turnbull & Asser and Crockett & Jones, of course); who should make my suits on Savile Row; and where to purchase my wines (no establishment other than Berry Bros. & Rudd, on St. James's Street, established in 1698, would do, and within weeks of our arrival in London, I was introduced to the firm's chairman, Anthony Berry, who was delighted to open an account for me). A hard lesson in gentlemanly attire came early and abruptly when I walked into my firm's boardroom wearing a blazer, only to have one of the partners sniff, "Are you off to Henley Regatta today?"

At Spencer Stuart it was my good fortune to meet Sally Erle-Drax, a lively young lady from Kent who had superb secretarial skills, a wide circle of friends, and knew how to cook. Her first bit of advice to me was "tweeds and brown shoes for the country, navy or grey suits for the city, but never brown shoes with a business suit!"

The business of business in London taught me a great deal in a short time about the vital importance of relationships. I also saw at close hand how corporate power is wielded at the board level and by senior management. One avenue of learning was the weekly management luncheon, when past and present members of the British establishment were invited as special guests—among them captains of industry and government leaders. All discussions were deemed to be "off the record." I felt privileged to be part of these exchanges, where discussion of the most pressing and controversial issues were complemented by a hearty meal taken with fine wines and cigars. I sometimes think back to those lunches: what a contrast they were to my usual soup and sandwich habits of today!

Performing business analysis, drawing up restructuring plans, and conducting executive searches for senior managers were commonplace at Spencer Stuart. The premium product among our services was leading-edge management theory and practice. Some of my senior colleagues were good at this and were well connected to leading management gurus in Britain, the Continent, and the United States. One idea that emerged at the time, and decades later would become part of the corporate canon, was the social responsibility of corporations. Having its origins in the United States in the 1950s, the practice of corporate social responsibility, known as CSR, had by the 1970s become embedded in management discourse as voluntary action aimed at recognizing corporate responsibility beyond responding to the enhancement of shareholder value. In London, I had the privilege of engaging in some of the earliest CSR audits of major companies. The practice was to evolve significantly in the 1980s and beyond, driving companies to reach out to a wide variety of stakeholders. My early work in the field helped shape my attitudes in the 1980s, when I took up a leadership role with Canada's chief executives.

A lot of the work I did while at Spencer Stuart was wonderfully engaging. One of the most memorable client encounters I had was early on, when I was introduced to Maurice Eisenchteter. This stern Frenchman was managing director of Maison Geisweiler, a winery located in Burgundy's Nuits-Saint-Georges. At first seemingly reluctant to deal with a young Canadian novice, he was mollified by my readiness to engage him in French. He said he might be prepared to have me serve as an adviser, but only if I came to Burgundy, visited the vineyards, and met the master of the cellar—and if I "passed certain tests."

How could I refuse? Susan and I travelled to Dijon; our host was most insistent that my wife accompany me. After some three days of "work," consisting of briefings, copious wine tastings, and fine meals with Eisenchteter's family, we passed the "test." Eisenchteter arranged for me to be invested as a Chevalier de Tastevin at a colourful ceremony at the twelfth-century Château de Vougeot. We worked closely together for several years, and our families shared a friendship that endures to this day. This chance opportunity also prepared me for a lifelong involvement in the world of wine. Maurice helped me along with my "education" in Burgundian wines by sending me periodic shipments of some of the great wines of the region—among them Chambertins, Richebourgs, Romanée-Contis, and Montrachets.

I was struck by the many talented and interesting people who worked at Spencer Stuart. Its chair was Peter Brooke (Baron Brooke of Sutton Mandeville). When on assignments, if we had some free time on our hands, he enjoyed talking to me about the state of British politics. I learned a great deal from him and sensed he was destined for high office. I was not mistaken. He eventually went on to serve in the cabinets of prime ministers Margaret Thatcher and John Major, as chair of the Conservative Party, and as member of Parliament for the Cities of London and Westminster.

A well-connected and colourful man was Sir Eric St Johnston. A retired colonel and former chief inspector of constabulary and head of Scotland Yard, Eric was in modern parlance a "rainmaker" for the firm. Among his other duties, he organized the weekly luncheons that attracted such an impressive representation of the who's who of Britain. When I inquired of a colleague why these distinguished people appeared so keen to accept Eric's invitations, he paused and said with a smile, "It's simple, Tom. Eric has all the files!" Kind and generous to Susan and me, Eric frequently had us as guests at his country house in Great Rissington, in the beautiful Cotswolds.

Another weekend outing at a colleague's country house in Sussex was a near calamity. Our host, Christopher Wysock-Wright, invited me to ride with the Southdown Hunt. It was a foolish mistake on my part. Good horsemanship requires practice and skill, neither of which I possessed, but I said yes anyway. My exuberant mount was aptly named High Boy. Shortly after the hunt was under way, with High Boy at full gallop, the slippery ground gave way and I flew off the horse. Bloodied and bruised, I struggled back into the saddle and, along with my gracious host, repaired to a nearby pub. Still mounted, we were served generous shots of ginger whisky as an anaesthetic.

Our friendship with another colleague, Tim Scriven, and his wife, Valerie, were marked by happier occasions. On one such occasion, Tim invited me to a splendid dinner hosted by the Worshipful Company of Salters in the City of London. The Salters, incorporated by royal charter in 1394, knew well how to celebrate, as my terrible state the next morning attested. Valerie Scriven was the granddaughter of Sir Austen Chamberlain, foreign secretary, Nobel Peace Prize winner and half-brother to Neville. While there was little affection, it seemed, between the two sides of the family, Valerie on one occasion many years later made a point of inviting her cousin from Neville's side of the family to a dinner she had for Susan and me at her country house in Shropshire. I avoided raising the matter of appeasement over dinner, even though I have always been of the view that Neville Chamberlain had not been dealt with entirely fairly by historians (above all else, he was seeking to avoid a war with Germany but crucially also, when Britain was not prepared for conflict, playing for time).

While in London, we were fortunate that Canada's high commissioner to the United Kingdom was the affable Jake Warren. Head of post from 1971 to 1974, Jake and his wife, Joan, could not have been more generous. Susan and I were frequent guests at their residence on Upper Brook Street, and they ensured that we received invitations to garden parties at Buckingham Palace and to special occasions such as Trooping the Colour. One special dinner at their residence was in honour of HRH Princess Anne. When we arrived, I was startled to be grabbed by the arm by Joan and led quickly to sit on a sofa next to Anne, whispering to me along the way that the princess was not being very communicative. What on earth would I talk about? I wondered. Horses, of course! Susan and I had recently returned from the Grand National, where we witnessed the spectacular win of the champion steeplechaser Red Rum. At my mention of Red Rum, the princess lit up. The hitherto taciturn royal and I launched into an enthusiastic conversation.

Life in London was rewarding. Susan attended lectures at the Courtauld Institute, and after working hours and on weekends we were frequent visitors to the fine museums situated throughout the city. London's cultural treasures fuelled our passion for history and architecture. Our thirst for collecting drew us almost weekly to attend auctions at Christie's, Sotheby's, and Phillips. We could not get enough of the excitement that came with bidding and the suspense as we waited for the auctioneer's hammer to drop.

My work in London led to an unexpected turn of events in late 1973, when I was invited to join our firm's practice in Paris for a time. In part, this was driven by my reasonably good facility in French.

I departed for Paris on short notice. As in London, I was received warmly by my business colleagues. The work was similar to what I was doing in London, so the transition was relatively easy.

Upon arrival at Orly Airport, knowing it might be difficult to find a place to live in Paris, I went directly to see an apartment I had seen advertised for rent in the *International Herald Tribune* during my short flight. To my delight, and the great surprise of my French colleagues, I was able to secure a lease for the small smartly furnished flat. It overlooked the gardens of the Palais-Royal, a seventeenth-century former royal palace originally built for Cardinal Richelieu. From our balcony, I could see the famous gardens where Louis XIV played as a child. Our walks in the gardens were a constant reminder of the rich history of a place that for centuries had played a central role in the life of the French capital.

Indeed, history surrounded us. The Louvre was right across the street. Susan quickly signed up to study art history at the École de Louvre, complementing her studies while in London at the Courtauld Institute. We drank down every good thing Paris had to offer. Our stint in London and Paris was preparing us for a lifetime of appreciation and engagement in the visual arts.

The culture of the firm in Paris was quite different from that in London. A memorable example came one morning in August 1974. An urgent message interrupted our boardroom meeting. Hearing that President Richard Nixon had just resigned, managing director Jean-Michel Beigbeder let out a loud guffaw. "*Ridicule!* Imagine the most powerful man on earth resigning because he lied to the American people." I protested and maintained that this was democratic accountability in action. He would have none of it and accused me of being hopelessly naïve. Beigbeder said he had no doubt that my former boss Prime Minister Trudeau likely told many lies, "as all politicians do." I stood my ground. Politics in Canada, I told him, would exact a heavy price should a prime minister be found to have lied to the Canadian public. Canada aside, I had no idea that one day an American president would become a standard-bearer of mendacity.

Earlier that summer, Susan and I decided to return to Canada at year's end, somewhat earlier than expected. It was a difficult decision. We were living a full life in the London-Paris axis. We seriously believed we could make a good life for ourselves in Europe, with London as our base. But for all the stimulation and the pleasures we were enjoying, and all the friends and colleagues who had become part of our lives, we knew we were Canadians first. We wanted to build the rest of our lives in Canada. And this meant that I should not delay one moment longer going home to start my entrepreneurial career.

We returned to Ottawa in early 1975. The relocation was a shock: Ottawa in January, as anyone who has visited there at that time of the year knows, can be a bracing experience, and leaving London and Paris behind required quite an adjustment. Having lived in Ottawa several years earlier, though, we recognized the positives: the vibrant political culture, the company of cerebral public servants, and the many ambassadors and senior diplomats active within the capital. Ottawa was blessed as well with the new National Arts Centre, with its rich offerings of music, theatre, and dance. And only minutes away were the winter and summer pleasures of abundant wilderness.

The first priority was to move into our new home, a condominium recently completed by our friend, the developer Bill Teron, alongside the Rideau Canal. The building had admirable architectural qualities with excellent views of the city. For a brief while it was also to serve as my office. We had in addition a place in Montreal we had owned for some time: a fine old stone house in Vieux-Montréal, at 445 rue St-Paul est. Built in 1740, it was just up the cobblestone street from the historic Notre-Dame-de-Bon-Secours and the Marché Bonsecours. It was to serve us as a comfortable weekend retreat. My hope was that it would also serve as my business pied-à-terre in Montreal.

With our residences in Ottawa and Montreal in order, I quickly turned to the all-consuming task of building my business from the ground up. I had a clear vision in mind. I wanted to create Canada's first multidisciplinary public policy advisory firm that would target primarily chief executives of large companies as clients. Drawing on my legal, financial, and public policy experience, I made it my goal to provide my clients with strategic insights on how to be successful players in the public policy space. For these executives, this would involve dealing with governments of all stripes, but it would also draw into the calculation their relationships with ever-broadening numbers of stakeholders and interest groups. My work in Europe on corporate social responsibility projects was a fresh, relevant, and innovative asset to have under my belt. Highly regulated companies were at the top of my target list.

When I incorporated my first company, Intercounsel Limited, my twin priorities were to reach out to potential clients to initiate badly needed revenue flow while at the same time building myself at least the kernel of a credible team of experts. I moved on both fronts, establishing at the outset a working relationship with respected economist Wayne Clendenning and Carleton University's professor of public policy and administration Bruce Doern. My outreach to the clients I wanted was audacious, to say the least. After careful research, I drafted tailored letters to close to one hundred chief executives of major companies headquartered in Toronto and Montreal. At this early stage, I had not yet hired any support staff, so Susan agreed to type the letters one at a time, each with a carbon copy—a laborious task.

With a large mailing at the ready, Canada Post workers picked that very moment to go out on strike. We had no idea how long it would last. So I reached for my running shoes and promptly booked a flight to Toronto. My old friend Bob Armstrong met me at the airport and ferried me into the city. There, with Bob on standby, I hand-delivered some sixty letters to the corporate head offices on my list. The following day, I travelled to Montreal and repeated the exercise with the rest of my letters.

To my great surprise and relief, within a matter of weeks I received a telephone call from Clarence Shepard, the chief executive officer of Gulf Canada, the Canadian subsidiary of one of the world's largest multinational oil companies. He asked me whether I might have time to meet him at Gulf Canada headquarters in Toronto. "Yes, sir!" I replied, trying hard not to sound overly eager. Twenty-four hours later, I was on my way to Toronto. The meeting went well. Shepard appeared to be genuinely impressed by the multidisciplinary model of services I was offering. A lawyer by background who had spent time in Ottawa as chief commissioner of the federal Board of Transport Commissioners, Shepard was savvy. He was also a thoughtful and gentle man whom I came to admire greatly. This first among my client relationships also tested my thesis that one should never undervalue one's worth in professional terms. I proposed a high annual retainer-based fee, and Shepard accepted. We were good to go, and a large weight was removed from my shoulders.

Buoyed as I was by my first success, I was then invited to Montreal to meet the chair, president, and chief executive officer of the Royal Bank of Canada, Earle McLaughlin. I reported to Susan, "I have been summoned by God!" I met McLaughlin in the bank's massive boardroom at Place Ville-Marie—just the two of us. A kind, silver-haired man, he was considered one of Canada's most influential business leaders. I passed muster and was engaged to advise the bank on public policy–related issues and strategies. As you will read later, McLaughlin would play a key role in the next phase of my business career. But his signing on as my second client had a huge impact that would open more opportunities than I could have even hoped for.

With two key client relationships now secured, I pressed on, and before long I was able to engage several other important advisory relationships. Notable among them was New York–based Time Inc., the powerful media conglomerate that exercised an outsize influence in Canada through its signature publication, *Time* magazine. Another American-based advisory relationship I secured was with Virginia-headquartered Mars Inc., the iconic global manufacturer of confectionery, pet food, and other food products. It was one of the largest private companies in the United States, with a growing footprint in Canada. In my role with Mars, I monitored the London-based International Cocoa Organization. As a leading chocolate manufacturer, Mars had a special interest in the organization's work, and it was felt at Mars headquarters that a Canadian lawyer would be best suited for the job. Along with other lawyers from around the world, I was also engaged in advocacy work on behalf of Mars, seeking to make the case that the company's confectionery products were in effect nutritious food products rather than chocolate-coated candy. The Canadian government was not buying the idea. I recall finance minister Michael Wilson saying with a chuckle, "Tom, I like Mars bars, but you cannot convince me that they have the nutritional qualities of an apple or a serving of cabbage."

The Mars organization was impressive, and so was its leadership. I met Forrest Mars Jr. only once, on my first visit to Mars headquarters. His words were brief: "If you do good work, you will be well paid. If you disappoint, draw your own conclusions!"

To serve what had quickly become a thriving business, I opened an office in downtown Ottawa in a new building then known as the Inn of the Provinces. I furnished it in part with antiques and works of art that Susan and I acquired during our stay in England and hired an assistant recently arrived from England named Norma Jones, who proved to be competent and disciplined. She stayed on board for the early stage of my business operations and then was succeeded by Patricia Longino, who was from Nova Scotia. Patricia would work with me for the next thirty-one years in a number of roles. Able, energetic, and loyal, she proved to be an indispensable part of my success.

Between 1975 and 1981, my business revenues were strong, my national and international networks were expanding, and my client base grew to include Japanese, British, Dutch, and Italian companies. The mix of services I offered, with the assistance of my team, proved sustainable. A good deal of the advice was strategic, with a focus on solving business problems that arose from government policies and regulations both in Canada and abroad. Some of the advice centred on coaching CEOs and boards of directors on how to position their companies in a rapidly changing environment where stakeholders were becoming more assertive. And some of my work involved providing advice on specific business transactions, including mergers and acquisitions. The unique cross-disciplinary approach at the heart of Intercounsel's rationale was working. My engagement in Canadian public policy issues was deep, aided by my intimate knowledge of the workings of the federal government. The Trudeau government dominated these years, with the exception of the eight-month interlude during which Joe Clark served as prime minister. I knew both leaders well, having served Prime Minister Trudeau for three and half years, and having roomed with Joe Clark while we were both studying law at the University of British Columbia.

The demands my hectic business activity placed on me were made more tolerable by the fact that Susan was deeply engaged in her own work. Shortly after our return from London, former diplomat Peter Dobell invited her to work at the Parliamentary Centre for Foreign Affairs and Foreign Trade. An organization of Dobell's creation that exists to this day as the Parliamentary Centre, it provided advice and support to committees of the federal Parliament. Susan went to work assisting the Special Joint Committee of the Senate and the House of Commons on Immigration Policy, which held hearings across the country and which led to the groundbreaking Immigration Act of 1976.

Susan's next job proved invaluable in her professional formation. She responded to an invitation from Robert de Cotret, chief executive of the Conference Board of Canada, to join the board's staff as a senior research associate. De Cotret, who entered federal politics in 1978 as a Progressive Conservative, went on to serve as minister of industry, trade, and commerce in the short-lived Clark government. The in-depth research that Susan did on how Canadian boards of directors function was the first of its kind in Canada. Based on confidential interviews with fifty directors, including many chief executives, her study, "Canadian Directorship Practices: A Critical Self-Examination," identified the thirst for change in corporate governance practices. This thirst at the board level in Canada was useful intelligence for me, and I put it to good use in my Intercounsel practice.

With my practice booming, with Susan happy in her work, and both of us feeling comfortable in Ottawa, I was ready for whatever lay ahead. To say I was eager would be an understatement. Little did I know that just over the horizon awaited a new client relationship that would be transformative to my business and to my life.

4

WAKING THE SLEEPING BUSINESS LEVIATHAN

In 1977, I was invited to be an adviser to the Business Council on National Issues (BCNI), a newly formed national association of chief executives. I was excited at the prospect. Even though it was an association, the opportunity to work directly with the nation's CEOs offered enormous potential. I began my relationship with the BCNI by offering perspectives and briefings on the federal government's policy agenda.

The BCNI had its beginnings in 1976. Two men played a key role in its launch: the retired chief executive of Imperial Oil, William Twaits, and Alfred Powis, the chief executive officer of Noranda Mines. The ingredient that proved a powerful catalyst in the BCNI's creation was the introduction by the Canadian government of wage and price controls, Canada's only experience with such controls in peacetime. Administered under the Anti-Inflation Act of 1975, the controls were to last until 1978 and were meant to deal with exceptionally high inflation rates. The Trudeau government's salary and price freeze was controversial, to say the least. When the controls were originally proposed by leader of the Opposition Robert Stanfield in the 1974 national election, Pierre Trudeau mocked him memorably with, "Zap, you're frozen!"

When Trudeau was returned to office, he promptly did a *volte-face* and introduced the same kinds of controls. Stanfield, whom I had got to know quite well since first meeting him in 1969, never forgave Trudeau. Nor did other members of Stanfield's Progressive Conservative Party.

Canada's business community expressed deep concerns about the controls, believing the measure to be an overreach by an inter-ventionist-minded prime minister. Powis and Twaits respected the country's principal business organizations, the Canadian Chamber of Commerce and the Canadian Manufacturers' Association, but thought they were not well prepared to deal with such serious threats to the market economy. The two executives concluded that Canada needed a cohesive organization of senior leaders composed of the chief executives of its largest companies. After studying various models in other countries, they soon concluded that the Business Roundtable, founded in the United Sates in 1972, could be adapted to the Canadian environment.

The BCNI began to take shape around a set of key principles. It was to be a non-partisan, membership-based organization with affiliation limited to chief executives. It was to be served by an exec-utive committee and a policy committee. The Council would have a policy orientation, and its work would be driven by member-based task forces. Late in 1976, the Council selected as its executive direc-tor William Archbold, a Princeton graduate and former marketing vice-president of Imperial Oil.

Powis and Twaits reached out to the heads of the country's largest enterprises, and by the time the BCNI held its first general meeting in Toronto in April 1977, its membership had reached over ninety. Some of the more prominent leaders were Paul Lehman of Alcan; Earle McLaughlin of the Royal Bank of Canada; Paul Desmarais of Power Corporation; Peter Gordon of the Steel Company of Canada;

Cedric Ritchie of the Bank of Nova Scotia; Robert Scrivener of Northern Telecom; Ian Sinclair of Canadian Pacific; Sydney Jackson of Manufacturers Life Insurance; Albert Thornbrough of Massey-Ferguson; James Black of Molson Companies; Gordon Fisher of Southam Press; Roy Bennett of the Ford Motor Company of Canada; Fred McNeil of the Bank of Montreal; Dean Muncaster of Canadian Tire; and Richard Thomson of the Toronto-Dominion Bank. The initial members were a fairly balanced mix of manufacturers, energy producers, and companies in the financial services sector. A sign of the times, there was not a single female member. Astonishing as it sounds today, no woman was leading a major Canadian enterprise in the 1970s.

The BCNI went through some growing pains in its first few years. While it produced several studies, it did not seize on any bold priorities or engage prominently in national policy debates. In 1977, when I was invited to be an adviser to the Council, I set out to see how I could help it find its way.

Encouraged by some Council members to become more deeply involved, I decided to pitch the idea of a major study on parliamentary reform. This idea was way out of the box, and I knew that the CEOs would think it was unconnected to traditional business concerns such as fiscal, trade, and regulatory policy. My rationale for the initiative was that a healthy parliament must be the cornerstone of accountable and effective government, and ultimately a stronger country. All were necessary conditions for a dynamic economy. I believed that the involvement of senior Canadian business leaders in such a public-spirited undertaking would signal that the BCNI was genuinely interested in public policy and serving the national interest.

The chair of the Council's task force on government organization, Steele Curry, liked the idea. Curry was the chief executive of

Revelstoke Companies and a Council vice-chair. Task force member Gerald Heffernan, the highly respected chief executive and founder of Co-Steel, was another supporter. With the assistance of Bruce Doern, already an associate of Intercounsel, and research associate Cassandra Blair, we launched the study in June 1978 and completed it in May 1979. Titled "Parliamentary Government in Canada: A Critical Assessment and Suggestions for Change," the study was received positively in the BCNI and beyond. Underscoring the centrality of Parliament to Canadian democracy and our system of governance, the study's focus included the accountability of the executive (the prime minister and cabinet) and the public service for policy and administration; the legislative functions of Parliament, including its committees; and aspects of government financial accountability and the budgetary process.

The study garnered the favourable attention of my friend Joe Clark, who was shortly to be sworn in as Canada's sixteenth prime minister. Its advisory group no doubt helped burnish its credentials, among them Progressive Conservative Robert Stanfield, New Democratic Party architect David Lewis, and the House of Commons clerk, Alistair Fraser. Significantly for the BCNI, it had made its debut on the national scene with a thoughtful, non-partisan, and timely initiative to its credit.

With the study completed, I returned full time to my clients, and over the next year I offered my support to the BCNI whenever I could. But despite the success of the study, my concerns about the Council's effectiveness continued to deepen. Believing that the organization had huge, largely untapped potential, and with the quiet encouragement of a few senior BCNI members, most notably Steele Curry, I decided to stir the pot. I sent a note to the Council's leadership, which I titled "Waking the Sleeping Leviathan."

I was acutely aware that I was making a risky move. The Council's leaders were the titans of Canada's corporate establishment. These were "top-down" leaders, for the most part, who were not used to being challenged when they gave an order. What I was doing in my note, and in the conversations with which I supported it, was to suggest to them that their organization had, since its creation, little to show in the way of results. Furthermore, I was saying that the BCNI's productivity was unimpressive and its effectiveness in public engagement equally so. To my way of thinking, it lacked a cohesive agenda and was far too timid.

I was soon summoned to a meeting of the Council's leadership to explain myself. I walked into a room at the Mount Royal Club in Montreal to face a rather intimidating group that included Powis and Twaits, Ian Sinclair, Earle McLaughlin, and Paul Desmarais. I knew as soon as I saw them that I was going to be seriously challenged. While I was confident of my position, I also realized that I could just as well be fired. Should I throw caution to the wind or opt for diplomacy? I chose boldness.

I began by explaining that public attitudes forged in the 1960s and carrying over into the 1970s were rapidly changing. Authoritarian thinking and structures were being questioned. The old-boy way of doing things would increasingly come under fire, and a push for greater inclusiveness was inevitable. In such an environment, "big business" could not count on getting its way. The symbiotic relationship between business and government forged in the Second World War and its aftermath was effectively dead, I argued. Drawing on my recent experience in London, where I was an early participant in corporate social responsibility studies, I went on to say that Canadian corporations would have to recognize that enhancing shareholder value could no longer be the only focus of chief executives and shareholders. Broader stakeholder and societal concerns would have to be taken into account. The BCNI's response to this challenge, I said, should be to repurpose itself to ride the wave of change as a leader in helping to shape the national policy agenda.

In the context of the times, it is fair to say that some of my ideas were revolutionary, if not heretical. Sinclair, who relished his reputation as a kind of bull moose, challenged me vigorously. Social change? The demise of the old-boy way of doing things? "Hell," he snorted, "I can pick up the phone and call Pierre any time I want. Earle can do the same, including the minister of finance or the governor of the Bank of Canada." I countered that while he may indeed have the prime minister's phone number, these personal relationships had counted for little when Trudeau decided to impose wage and price controls over the objections of business. In the broader context, I argued that the voice of business was largely absent in post-1974 national policy, when the Trudeau government lurched leftwards and embraced a nationalist and interventionist agenda.

I walked out of the Mount Royal Club feeling quite pleased that I had spoken my mind. I was confident I was right. I was not confident, however, that my client relationship with the BCNI would survive.

I was not fired. Over the coming months, I continued to work with Council members and executive director William Archbold and his small team at BCNI headquarters in Toronto. Bill could not have been more helpful, and in a series of conversations with various Council leaders, it became clear to me that something was in the offing. In the meantime, the Council's founders and co-chairs, Alfred Powis and William Twaits, had passed the baton to Jack Barrow, former chair and chief executive officer of retailer Simpson-Sears. In early January 1981, Barrow invited me to meet with him and the Council's vice-chair, Steele Curry. Peter Gordon, of the Steel Company of Canada, was also in attendance. They asked for my conditions if I were to be appointed to the helm of the BCNI. I said to myself, Damn the torpedoes, full speed ahead, and gave them a list of conditions I knew they might well consider outlandish. I would need to be appointed the Council's first president; I would take the job for a limited time; the headquarters would need to be moved to my offices in Ottawa; I would wish to appoint my own Intercounsel staff to replace the current Toronto staff; and I would wish to retain select Intercounsel clients for a time and be able to serve them.

I believed that the last condition would likely be a deal breaker. But having spent six years building Intercounsel from scratch, I was not prepared to sacrifice the company or my team for what in my mind was a start-up with an unknown future. Keeping Intercounsel and its clients for at least three years was a form of insurance should the Council venture fail.

Most significantly, I also insisted that the Council's low-key modus operandi would have to change. The Council needed to become an active player on the national policy scene, and we should aspire to be the most influential voice of business in the country. After a moment of silence, Barrow asked if anyone had any objections to my conditions. There were none. I was offered the job on the spot with a commitment to meet all my conditions. I was elated, but also— I must confess—hugely surprised.

I returned to Ottawa, advised my stunned Intercounsel team of what was about to unfold, and invited each of them to continue to serve in their new capacity as BCNI staff. Everyone was on board. The transition would take place almost immediately, and the new signage for the office was soon in place. Meanwhile, I made a number of calls on BCNI leaders, beginning with Powis and Twaits, who generously gave me their blessings. When I advised my former boss Prime Minister Trudeau of my appointment, he quipped, "Tom, I hope you will run this organization of big shots as the BCNI and not the CNIB!" I also reached out to my most important clients, beginning with the Royal Bank of Canada. The bank's chief executive, Rowland Frazee, who had succeeded Earle McLaughlin in 1979, was pleased to hear of my appointment. At our meeting, I quietly planted a seed in his mind—that I hoped one day we might work together at the BCNI if he were to take on the job of chairing a newly invigorated Council. That dream eventually came true in 1983.

Susan welcomed my appointment, but she worried that my candle, already alight at both ends, might burn out too quickly. A significant surprise was just around the corner with Susan's career too. She had been asked to join the Privy Council Office, the federal government's most important central agency tasked with serving the prime minister. Her remarkable public service journey was about to begin just as my odyssey at the BCNI was getting under way. We could not imagine what lay ahead, but we knew for certain it would be exciting.

The decision to embrace the new challenge offered me by the BCNI required me to pause and reflect on the role of the law in my career. I had already put my legal training to use in setting up my private firm. In my Intercounsel marketing, I always emphasized that my advice to clients would be delivered through a prism that encompassed the law, economics, finance, and public policy. This multidisciplinary approach is what made Intercounsel a pioneer in the Canadian consulting space. In part, I was influenced by the role of Washington, D.C., law firms with which I had worked extensively since setting up Intercounsel. Their role in public policy and regulatory matters had been established for some time, and the partners in these law firms included some of the capital's most legendary characters.

Until I signed up with the BCNI, I had kept the idea in the back of my mind that one day I might return to Vancouver to practise law.

I had also remained engaged academically, teaching a course at the University of Ottawa's law school titled "The Law of International Business Transactions." I enjoyed my role as an adjunct professor and the opportunity to introduce students to a dimension of law studies that got little attention at Canadian universities. The course work, coupled with exposure to issues in international trade law, kept me on my toes and proved helpful as I delved deeply in the years to come into matters related to international trade.

Of the many legal relationships that shaped this period in my career, among the most memorable was my association with senator George van Roggen. George and I hit it off the moment we met. A Vancouver lawyer and stalwart Liberal with right-of-centre leanings, George began to work with me on a number of corporate files. He was appointed to the Senate in 1971, and in 1974 he assumed the chair of the Senate Committee on Foreign Affairs. Notably, his committee conducted a study on Canada–United States relations that included a key recommendation supporting the negotiation of a free trade agreement with the Americans. This recommendation was endorsed by the Senate in 1982 and was adopted by the Royal Commission on the Economic Union and Development Prospects for Canada in 1985. George was an influence on my own early activism in support of Canada–United States free trade. Indeed, on frequent occasions, over steak and a good bottle of wine, I would toast him as the "grandfather of free trade"—a compliment that he richly enjoyed.

A giant of the law and a friend and mentor to me during this time was Supreme Court of Canada justice Willard "Bud" Estey. Bud lived just across the street, and on weekends we would talk for hours about the law and politics. He had a superb mind and strong opinions, which he did not hesitate to express. He encouraged me to retain my active status as a member of the British Columbia bar—something I did, remarkably, for more than four decades. But a return to law practise was not to be. The heady environment offered by the BCNI became the centre of my world.

Speaking of law and close legal associations in my early Inter-counsel days, the name of Michael Kelen figures prominently. Kelen, an Ottawa lawyer who had cut his teeth at the Department of Justice, worked closely with me at Intercounsel. He was helpful to me in my dealings with private clients and would go on to be appointed to the Federal Court of Canada. To this day, he remains a trusted advisor and close friend.

In 1977, Susan and I made an important decision that was to have a profound effect on our lives. We purchased from architect Hart Massey, Vincent Massey's son, a mid-century modern house that he designed and had built for himself in 1959 on McKay Lake in Rockcliffe Park, Ottawa. Massey was greatly influenced by the work of famed architect Ludwig Mies van der Rohe. Susan and I engaged in a meticulous restoration of the house and created abundant gardens that we added to over time. We have lived there ever since, and the house was designated a National Historic Site in 2018. Apart from its virtues as a private place of beauty and repose, it has served as a welcome gathering place—*un point de rencontre*. Here we have hosted family, friends, and colleagues, political leaders, government officials, ambassadors, business associates, artists, heritage activists, fellow gardeners, and even ardent fly-fishers.

There are many fascinating stories associated with our house and the celebrities who have visited over the years. One such story is centred on a particular canoe with a royal connection. Being on an environmentally protected lake only a few miles from downtown Ottawa prompted Susan and me to seek out renowned canoe builder Ted Moores and his partner, Joan Barrett, of Bear

Mountain Boats. In 1981, Moores presented us with a fine eighteen-foot cedar-strip craft. Shortly after we received the canoe, Prime Minister Trudeau telephoned.

"May I come and see your canoe?" he asked.

"Of course, Prime Minister," I said. "When would you like to stop by?"

"Saturday morning," he replied.

Susan and I were out of Ottawa, but I made arrangements and Trudeau did indeed inspect our canoe. Then, in a second call, he asked if Moores could build a canoe for the government of Canada. He needed it quickly, because he aimed to present the canoe to Prince Charles and Lady Diana as a wedding gift from Canada.

Impossible, I thought, given the time it took for Moores to painstakingly build his extraordinary creations. But when I spoke to Moores, he graciously said he might be able to deliver a nearly completed craft he was building for a client. He and Joan explained the situation to their client and were indeed able to arrange to deliver the finished canoe to the Canadian government destined for the royal couple.

5

REDEFINING NATIONAL BUSINESS LEADERSHIP

The room at Montreal's Château Champlain was packed. I was barely six weeks into my new job as president of the Business Council on National Issues, and on this day, April 15, 1981, I was meeting the full Council membership for the first time. I was also about to present my inaugural address, which was to outline my vision of the BCNI's future. In attendance were the leaders of a good number of Canada's largest enterprises, most of them two decades older than I was, a confraternity of mainly men who knew each other and were confidently entrenched in their positions of power and influence. It was my task to win their trust and open their minds to a whole new way of thinking of themselves and their responsibilities as agents of change.

I set the scene by outlining the challenge that lay ahead: "Canadian society is facing profound change, and traditional values and ways of thinking are being rapidly overturned. In economic terms the disincentives to wealth creation are growing in number, and one of the casualties of this phenomenon is business itself, which is the subject of widespread suspicion and negative public attitudes." Some in the audience were acutely aware of the growing alienation many Canadians were feeling toward business. Others, if not oblivious, believed that "business as usual" would in the end prevail. But I pressed on. "Our economy is mired in a deep recession, and alienation between people and institutions, and among provinces and regions, grows deeper. And politically, our house is in disorder. Public confidence in our political process and in our political leaders is depressingly low. The current constitutional stalemate demonstrates how hopelessly divided we are about how we should reform our fundamental institutions."

I then laid out the tenets that were to govern the Council's strategy for decades to come. I said that our leadership would be defined by "shaking ourselves loose once and for all of the self-imposed conventions and constraints that have shackled us in the past. The most fundamental of these constraints has been the lingering doubt in the minds of some of our business leaders about the appropriateness of speaking out on issues of significance to a large number of Canadians. That doubt should be banished forever. As citizens you have the right to speak out and be heard. As business leaders you have a responsibility to contribute to dialogue on public policy concerns, drawing on your experience and special perspectives."

I criticized "the reluctance to enter the public policy debate ready to use to the fullest extent necessary the talent, time, and financial resources to make a decisive impact on the debate . . . even today in the face of life-or-death issues facing business." I went on to warn that "business in Canada will continue to fight a rearguard action at best as its interests are increasingly eroded by a combination of public and governmental pressures," and I called for "a quantum leap forward in the readiness to use the very considerable resources of business to fight for the issues we believe in . . . and win."

In calling for a fundamentally different approach to business advocacy, I underscored two additional points. The first was the failure of business to engage long-term in advancing its case: "Business participation in public policy debate is characterized most often by short, intense flourishes of energy that die long before an issue is resolved." I did not know that this problem would largely persist to the present day, the result of companies and their leaders having to focus on their daily business operations. As I write, I still hold the view that this failure to engage over the long term remains a fundamental weakness in contemporary business advocacy. My second additional point was the advantage of acting pre-emptively: "Rarely do public policy issues leap onto the national horizon without warning. Despite this, business most often responds after the fact. Whenever possible, we must be prepared to act pre-emptively and develop our position in such a way that we genuinely influence the substance of the emerging issue and the manner by which it is introduced."

As I addressed the group, I was taking the measure of the room. I was relieved to see a considerable number of heads seemingly nodding in approval. But before tackling some of the specific business at hand, I set out to lock in the philosophical rationale for this dramatically new approach to the Council's mission, saying, "I know that some of you . . . question whether an aggressive use of corporate resources towards the study and resolution of national issues is legitimate." I followed with a rhetorical question: "While it is true that business leaders cannot presume to speak for shareholders and employees, do they not have a responsibility to help foster the form of social and economic organization that generates wealth most efficiently and thus provides the means for improving the well-being of all?" My own response was unequivocal: "To me this philosophical rationale lies at the heart of our mission. It has been observed often enough that social conflict is lessened by widespread confidence that economic growth will provide the means for achieving a more generous distribution of economic benefits."

If there was a sense of urgency in my messaging, there was good reason. Raging around us were terrible economic conditions. We were in the midst of a global economic recession that had carried on from the 1970s—the deepest recession of the postwar period. Canada was being hit especially hard with high inflation, soaring interest rates, and unemployment. In August 1981, the Bank of Canada rate hit an astounding 21 per cent, and the inflation rate exceeded 12 per cent. Deficits were on the rise and the tax burden was increasing. Real GDP declined 5 per cent between June 1981 and December 1982. Innovation and productivity had fallen into a deep chill.

Interventions from the floor focused on the "anti-business *dirigiste* policies" of the Trudeau government. The National Energy Program (NEP), introduced in 1980, came under heavy fire; Western-based chief executives complained about the deep regional alienation it was causing. Our discussions took on a philosophical tone, with approving observations about the leadership of Prime Minister Margaret Thatcher, elected in 1979, and Ronald Reagan, who had become president that January. These sentiments, born of frustration and fear in the face of the Canadian government's interventionism, were aligned with my own view that the Council should become the tribune of a counter-revolution in economic thinking. Open markets, freer trade, and smarter regulation was to become our rallying cry. Not a mere aping of Thatcherism but rather a made-in-Canada approach that would take into account our unique circumstances. To my relief, my debut with the Council in Montreal offered proof positive that I was not embarking on this journey alone.

As sometimes happens at an event that can only be characterized as serious and sombre, there was one moment of unexpected amusement. Having completed my remarks to an enthusiastic round of applause, I walked to the back of the hall to greet Howard Lang, the chair and chief executive of Montreal-headquartered steel company Canron. Howard was the father of an old friend, Christopher Lang, and he and his wife, Helen, had an attractive farm in Knowlton, in Quebec's Eastern Townships, where Susan and I were frequent guests.

As I greeted Howard and other colleagues with whom he was speaking, I was astonished to hear him say, "Well, today we heard from Tom, and I'm pleased he is fully dressed. The first time I met him was when my wife and I returned to our farm a day earlier than expected. My son had hosted a party, and I found a far from sober Tom sleeping under my dining room table. Clearly, he is a reformed man!" One of Howard's colleagues quipped, "Tom, I'm pleased to hear that you know how to have a good time. You sounded pretty bloody serious up there." We all had a good laugh, and I was reminded of this story more than once in the years to come.

What was unusual about the Château Champlain meeting was the sheer ambition of the agenda we embraced. I spoke about the need for BCNI leadership in the areas of constitutional reform, energy policy, fiscal and monetary policy, economic and industrial policy, social policy, including retirement income and pension reform, defence policy, and the strengthening of Canada's governmental institutions. I'm not patting myself on the back here, but such broad policy engagement by business was unheard of in Canada, and indeed in any other part of the world. Founding Council chair Alfred Powis took me aside and asked if I was proposing that the BCNI establish itself as a shadow government. No, I answered, simply a knowledgeable and responsible contributor to how we as Canadians shape our lives. Powis's comment haunted me in later years when, to my great regret, the Council's critics charged that it indeed had become a parallel government and I the country's "de facto prime minister."

—

The next morning, I sat down with my team and laid out the challenge. There was excitement around the table, but could we deliver? My first priority was to put in place an organizational structure that would serve as enabler and catalyst: a policy committee that would also serve as a board of directors; a system of CEO-led task forces that would engage in the detailed policy and research work; and a lean headquarters staff that would power and support all Council operations. With the blessings of the Council's chair and executive committee, this new structure was quickly put into place. My second priority was to reach out personally to as many Council members as possible. Prominent among them were CEOs Rowland Frazee of the Royal Bank of Canada, Jean de Grandpré of Bell Canada, Gerald Heffernan of Co-Steel, Gordon Fisher of Southam, David Culver of Alcan, Cedric Ritchie of the Bank of Nova Scotia, Walter Light of Northern Telecom, Michel Bélanger of the National Bank of Canada, Peter Bentley of Canadian Forest Products, and Darcy McKeough of Union Gas. My third priority was to build the strongest possible team at Council headquarters. I was off to a good start, because I already had a trusted group in place recruited to my consulting company. We need to be smart, small, and nimble, I told them, and above all we must know policy—how to think about it and how to shape it. And being well connected was a definite plus. I emphasized the importance of strict non-partisanship in our work. On this point I was emphatic. I told the team that any breach would result in dismissal, an action I was compelled to take only ever once.

I had another important job to do. Council founders William Twaits and Alfred Powis alerted me to the fact that the creation of the Council had raised concerns among long-established national business organizations that they would be displaced by this new

CEO-based group. The Canadian Manufacturers' Association had been operating since 1871, and the Canadian Chamber of Commerce dated from 1929. I quickly reached out to the heads of these two organizations. I pledged to work closely with them and underscored the advantage of having their respective chairs sitting as members of the Council's policy committee. Building links with influential sectoral and regional business organizations was also very much on my mind. Among them were the Canadian Bankers Association, founded in 1891, the Business Council of British Columbia, established in 1966, and the Conseil du patronat du Québec, founded in 1969. In the case of the Conseil, I pressed early on to invite its chair to join our policy committee. This served exceptionally well, especially when our two organizations were able to cooperate closely on challenging national unity issues that later came to the forefront.

With the Council's organizational structure in place and business links forged, I reached out to the country's political leadership. In the months that followed, I called on cabinet ministers in Ottawa and on premiers across the country. I sensed there was genuine interest in what we at the BCNI were creating. That being said, the level of acceptance in left-of-centre circles, including the New Democratic Party and organized labour, was modest at best.

In discussing outreach strategies with my Council colleagues, I placed heavy emphasis on the importance of the federal public service. While serving on Parliament Hill from 1968 to 1972, I learned how influential government officials are in forming and executing good public policy. Deep, respectful, and trusted engagement with senior officials would be essential to the long-term success of our organization. This conviction guided my actions in the decades to come and, as I shall explain, rewarded both me and the Council handsomely. (I believed then as I do now that a highly professional and politically neutral public service is one of Canada's enduring competitive advantages. This is a point I made in an academic paper published in Canadian Public Administration in March 1984 titled "The Public Service of Canada: the case for political neutrality.")

Forging essential relationships across the country involved, of course, the media. It helped that I was a passionate advocate of a free and independent press. It also helped that I gave notice I would follow an "open book" policy in my interactions with journalists.

As the record of four decades of extensive engagement with the media would prove, the Council and I attracted a great deal of attention both in the press and in electronic media—most of it positive and, I would add, the vast majority of it in my view fair.

Despite quite literally thousands of media mentions tied to my Business Council role between 1981 and 2009, this memoir makes sparse mention of journalistic commentary. I am comfortable leaving that to the public record.

Now, as we set out on our mission, it was time to plunge into the development of the Council's policy agenda and to harness the talent and resources of my CEO colleagues.

6

FACING UP TO THE ECONOMIC CRISIS

The spring of 1981 was a sombre time for Canada. With myriad economic woes facing the country, I rallied my Business Council colleagues and we went to work confronting a herd of apocalyptic horsemen. Midway through Pierre Trudeau's last term, Canada was suffering the simultaneous impacts of high inflation, record high interest rates, soaring unemployment, and escalating deficits. Meeting in Toronto, my colleagues and I worried about potential public disorder if some means was not found to inject a sense of hope. Gordon Fisher, who at the time was chief executive of Southam, put it starkly: "We must fight with the strength of our ideas to rebuild Canadians' confidence in their economic order, or face the destruction of all that we stand for." Gordon and I quickly developed a close relationship. Silver-haired, intellectually nimble, and articulate, he was highly influential in Council circles in those early days.

The public discourse was unsettling to say the least. In many quarters, big business was seen as the bad guy. More broadly, capitalism was under attack, with prophetic warnings that the system would not survive without wrenching changes. Lester Thurow, a popular economist at the time, said that he saw no prospect for a burst of intellectual creativity that would help manage our economies toward simultaneous full employment and price stability. We at the

Council countered the gloom with a message of hope and resolve.

Early in 1982, we tabled a ten-point program for recovery. It called for concrete steps to fight unemployment and inflation, achieve voluntary restraint in bringing inflation down, tilt the tax system toward investment, create a climate of confidence in support of economic growth, resolve outstanding federal-provincial disputes, reduce barriers to trade within Canada, ease the burden of regulation, reassess universality in certain social programs, and reform some of the institutions of government. While I was pleased with the strong consensus among my colleagues on this ambitious framework for recovery, I knew the real test lay ahead. Could we translate our wish list into action? Here is where our task force structure proved to be a formidable asset. No less than seven task forces were at work, all chaired by Council CEOs: national finance, under Darcy McKeough of Union Gas; competition policy, under William McLean of Canada Packers; industrial development and international trade, under Alfred Powis of Noranda; energy policy and natural resources, under Donald McIvor of Imperial Oil; social policy and retirement income, under Syd Jackson of Manufacturers Life Insurance; government organization, under Gerald Heffernan of Co-Steel; and defence and foreign policy, under Peter Cameron of Canadian Corporate Management.

These task forces varied in size from four or five participants to ten or more. Supporting them was an around-the-clock endeavour hugely challenging me and my team. As I was the lead pen on the writing of task force reports and the Council's chief strategist and public communicator, the Council's work occupied my time seven days a week and most evenings. Fortunately for me, Susan was herself deeply occupied in her job at the Privy Council Office, and the time we managed to spend together, while limited, was never wanting for subjects to talk about. More often than not, we tumbled into bed exhausted but could hardly wait to see what the next day would bring.

The task force reports were generally well received in business, government, and policy circles. (I will refer to a number of them in future chapters.) Importantly, the people who worked on these task forces bonded and built lasting relationships that would serve the Council well in the decades to come. Ted Newall, the chief executive of DuPont Canada and later Nova Chemicals, once explained his task force "education" as follows: "Working in these various policy areas helps me better understand subjects that I often know little about. It also allows me to make a contribution to the shaping of public policy. Not bad, I'd say, for a guy who started out as a nylon salesman."

TALKING ECONOMICS WITH TRUDEAU

On July 8, 1982, Council chair Jack Barrow, Royal Bank CEO Rowland Frazee, and I met with Prime Minister Trudeau, finance minister Allan MacEachen, and economic ministers Donald Johnston and Bud Olson. I greeted the prime minister warmly. Barrow opened the meeting by lauding the government's efforts at fighting inflation, but he registered his disappointment with its high-taxation and investment-inhibiting policies. Underscoring the confidence lost between government and business, he said that as a first step we had to consult more regularly and rebuild a climate of trust between the council and the government. The council, he continued, needed to ask for a stronger reaffirmation of the government's faith in the private sector and for a framework of consistent policies that would be more positively disposed toward business. After all, he said, it was business that had to shoulder the major burden of turning the economy around and putting Canada back to work. Barrow then made the following appeal: Trudeau's government could help best by unleashing the private sector and by convincing Canadians and the world that the country would survive this recession and return to a position of even greater economic strength.

The meeting lasted three hours, but I did not sense that we were really getting through. Donald Johnston, who at the time was the president of the Treasury Board, offered some conciliatory words, but the prime minister was unmoved. Warm greetings aside, the tensions at the meeting reflected the overall business-government chill that prevailed during the remainder of Trudeau's time in office. As I left the meeting, I thought back to the election night ten years before, when I said *au revoir* to Trudeau and he wished me well. I had no idea then that I would be walking out of his office a decade later in circumstances that gave me no comfort.

During this challenging period, I was active in communicating the Council's priorities on public platforms across Canada. My insistence on drafting my own speeches did not make life easy. I got into the habit of doing most of my writing early in the morning following a 5 a.m. wake-up and finishing in the evening before bedtime. I used my public appearances to tell my audiences candidly that Canada was in deep trouble. That said, I still made every effort in most of my speeches to try to raise morale, to offer up ideas and solutions, and to marshal a broader societal response to the crisis.

There were dark moments, such as in 1982, when I stood in Canada House in London and presented an address that I titled "Canada: Is Paradise Lost?" Invoking John Milton's great epic, I equated the Canada familiar to us with paradise. It was "a land of unending promise, a place where material progress and the betterment of the human condition are as certain as the sunrise." But "suddenly our sense of certainty has vanished," I continued. I outlined the depressing facts: the unemployment rate at 10.9 per cent, the sharp drop in corporate profits, high rates of inflation, punishing interest rates, soaring deficits, and basement levels of business and consumer confidence. Then I moved to rallying mode. I pointed out that some commentators believed a severe recession might not be entirely a bad thing, because it would help reshape Canadian society, "force us to work harder, to demand less of others and more of ourselves, to link our personal ambitions more closely to the needs of the country as a whole. 'Crises,' they say, 'will bring out the best in us.'" I reminded my audience of what the poet Horace told his fellow Romans long ago: "Adversity reveals genius, prosperity conceals it." I then laid out the Council's fundamentals for recovery and reconstruction, drawing on our ten-point program. While I stressed the responsibilities of business in realizing Canada's economic recovery, I was firm on government's responsibilities, advocating that it move away from its growing penchant for intervention in the economy and its restrictions on investment.

TAMING INFLATION

Of the many addresses I gave during the recession, perhaps the most provocative and controversial was in January 1983 at the Empire Club in Toronto. I called it "The Bishops' Reflections on the Economic Crisis: A Business Response." I was responding to a recent report of the Social Affairs Commission of the Canadian Conference of Catholic Bishops called "Ethical Reflections on the Economic Crisis." The bishops lamented the human cost of the recession and, unusually for them, strayed into the domains of policy and even partisanship. They took the position that reducing unemployment was far more important than fighting inflation. Their report argued for an industrial strategy involving more government intervention, and they voiced reservations about the capitalist system.

Several of my colleagues wondered if my decision to reply was a good idea. Darcy McKeough asked me, "Isn't it a bit risky going up against the anointed of God?"

He did have a point. Given all his years serving as a formidable force in the Ontario Legislature, McKeough had a great deal more political experience than I did. Still, I stuck to my guns and offered what I believed was a sensitive rebuttal acknowledging how profoundly troubled the business leadership of Canada was in the face of the impact of the current recession. I took pains to cover all the major points the bishops had raised. Given the ravages of inflation on Canada's citizenry, that was where I decided to place my emphasis.

> The bishops argue that we should recognize unemployment rather than inflation as our top priority. We believe that the fight against unemployment and inflation are inseparable, that inflation is the greatest underlying threat to jobs and to income security. We believe that inflation has contributed significantly to the current economic crisis of Canada and the world. I find the connection between unemployment and inflation an easy one to trace, and really do not understand why the bishops fail to acknowledge it. For jobs to be created, economic production must increase; for production to increase and growth to resume, interest rates must come down—then people will spend and businesses will invest; for interest rates to come down, inflation must fall. To wage war against unemployment with little regard for inflation is to strike at one link in an interconnected chain, to treat an effect rather than the cause.

My address caused quite a stir in the media. The lead editorial in the *Globe and Mail* voiced reservations, claiming that the Business Council was short on an "immediate and concrete alternative."

Amusingly, a cartoon appeared in the francophone press with an image of my namesake, Saint Thomas Aquinas, lecturing the bishops. Not so amusing were the calls I received from some devout Roman Catholic friends who wondered, as Darcy McKeough had, why on earth I would dare to take on the bishops.

Given the centrality of the debate raging over inflation, it is worth noting that the Council in fact had intervened some months before, and with genuine creativity. We had proposed a national program of voluntary restraints aimed at letting Ottawa avoid resorting to mandatory wage and price controls. Members of the Trudeau government signalled to me that the idea was of interest, but would we help to sell it? We said we would. The government followed up by announcing the Private Sector 6 and 5 Committee, whose job it was to persuade business to get on side to reduce inflation levels to 6 and then 5 per cent over the next two years. The government turned to the indomitable Ian Sinclair of Canadian Pacific, to chair the committee. Among those chosen for the committee were our own council's chair, Jack Barrow, as well as Cedric Ritchie of the Bank of Nova Scotia, Harrison McCain of McCain Foods, and Ted Newall of Du Pont Canada. Known as the "gang of eight," the committee's members made their voice heard, and we at the Council amplified their message. From its high point of 12.5 per cent in 1981, inflation fell to 4.3 per cent in 1984. While a number of factors were responsible for the decline, the Council's support, and that of the business community broadly, made a significant contribution.

BROKERING AN EAST-WEST ENERGY DEAL

In the midst of the economic gloom, Canada found itself struggling with federal-provincial tensions. Unresolved constitutional issues were weighing in, as Alberta and the federal government confronted one another over resource and energy jurisdiction. The turbulence only increased in 1980, when finance minister MacEachen introduced the National Energy Program (NEP) as part of his federal budget. MacEachen stated his rationale for the legislation as follows: "The new energy policy limits the rise in prices of oil and gas to domestic consumers and thus continues to protect us from the violent shocks of OPEC price increases. It strengthens our specific measures to promote the most economical use of energy and in particular the displacement of oil by other fuels. It provides new impetus to the development of new sources of supply, through direct government programs and through new incentives of particular value to Canadian-owned producers."

The NEP and the constraints it imposed on petroleum-producing provinces in Western Canada triggered anger and alienation, and Prime Minister Trudeau became a target of vilification. Historians would later point out that the NEP provided the fuel behind the rise of the Reform and Canadian Alliance parties, leading eventually to the creation of the Conservative Party as we know it today.

This backdrop gave impetus to a unique and ultimately far-reaching initiative on the part of the Business Council. Deeply concerned that the energy impasse would further divide the country and worsen Canada's economic woes, I joined the Council's finance task force chair, Darcy McKeough, in hatching a plan in the spring of 1983. Why not use the good offices of the Council to convene a gathering of CEOs of oil-producing and oil-consuming companies and endeavour to offer up policy options to governments that might resolve the crisis? The most daring part of the plan was to invite premiers Bill Davis of Ontario and Peter Lougheed of Alberta to participate, along with Jean Chrétien, minister of energy, mines, and resources, representing the federal side. McKeough, a friend of both premiers, got the ball rolling by presenting the idea to

Lougheed. Lougheed said he was open to the idea so long as Davis was onside. My job was to persuade Chrétien to engage and to pull together the relevant CEOs. Chrétien obliged, and so did an impressive number of my colleagues.

I will never forget my first encounter with Peter Lougheed. I called on him at his Calgary office to explain how the process would work. He looked at me and said, "If you're running this thing, why should I trust an Easterner like you?" I was startled for a second or two until I recovered and replied, "Premier, where I grew up, over the mountains to the west, we considered people like you as Easterners." That surprised him, and Lougheed smiled. It was the beginning of a long and remarkable friendship. Only a few years later, we would be close collaborators on the Canada–United States free trade initiative and on other national issues, including the constitutional file.

Our energy initiative proceeded like clockwork. We all agreed that the exercise should not be announced to the world until we had brought it to its conclusion. It involved two summits: one on November 6 and 7, 1983, held at the Niagara Institute, at Niagara-on-the-Lake; and a second on June 4 and 5, 1984, at the Millcroft Inn, at Alton, Ontario. The summits involved forty-six participants, including premiers Davis and Lougheed and their respective energy ministers and senior officials. On the federal side, Jean Chrétien participated in the first summit and was represented at the second by his deputy minister, Paul Tellier. A total of thirty chief executives took part, representing both producers and consumers. Among them were Charles Baird of Inco, Michel Bélanger of the National Bank, Steele Curry of Revelstoke Companies, William Daniel of Shell Canada, Rowland Frazee of the Royal Bank of Canada, Peter Gordon of the Steel Company of Canada, Jean de Grandpré of Bell Canada, Dean Muncaster of Canadian Tire, Howard Macdonald of

Dome Petroleum, Darcy McKeough of Union Gas, Rad Latimer of TransCanada PipeLines, Don McIvor of Imperial Oil, Arne Nielsen of Canadian Superior Oil, Alfred Powis of Noranda, David Mitchell of Alberta Energy Company, Ted Newall of Du Pont Canada, Roger Phillips of IPSCO, Cedric Ritchie of the Bank of Nova Scotia, and John Stoik of Gulf Canada.

Following a productive first round of deliberations at Niagara-on-the-Lake, Don McIvor and I were charged with drafting a report for tabling and discussion at the second summit, scheduled for the following June. The second summit was equally productive and led to our drawing up a final report that we announced publicly on October 3, 1984. Remarkably, details of our deliberations were never leaked; our announcement caught the media by surprise. Titled "The Energy Imperative: A Perspective in Canadian Oil and Gas Policy," the thirteen-page report recommended the early deregulation of oil prices with a residual safety net to protect the economy from extraordinary swings in international crude prices; deregulation of natural gas prices as expeditiously as was practical; a lowering of federal taxes and provincial royalties; resource taxation based on profits rather than revenues; exploration and development incentives, if necessary, based on a profits tax system rather than grants; and an improved balance between Canadian participation and the need for continuing foreign investment.

Brian Mulroney had just taken office as prime minister in September. In opposition, he and the Progressive Conservative Party had been highly critical of the NEP, so we expected an openness, at the very least, to our ideas. Sure enough, the new government took note of our initiative, and in November the new minister of energy, mines, and resources, Pat Carney, sent me a letter inviting us to meet her to discuss our report. A month later, we met with her and finance minister Michael Wilson. Carney's deputy minister was there as well: it was once again Paul Tellier. His attendance was helpful to us, as he had been a participant in the two summits. I was joined by Don McIvor, Darcy McKeough, and Arne Nielsen. We came away from the meeting feeling euphoric. It was clear the government was listening and that major change in national energy and resource policy was on its way.

Buoyed by the encouraging news, I took the opportunity not long after the meeting to outline my thinking at the Strategy for Energy Policy conference at the University of Calgary. I opened my address by pointing out how timely the conference was, preceding as closely as it did a First Ministers' conference, the National Economic Conference, and the first budget of the Mulroney government. I went on to say that "oil and natural gas are a particular source of strength. And yet, in the past decade in particular, confused and conflicting objectives and policies—imposed largely by governments—have resulted in a failure to capitalize fully on this strength. Our citizens, our governments and our industries have fought one another about how our oil and natural gas resources could be developed and their benefits shared."

Pointing to the changing circumstances, I said, "The recent federal election and change in government have clearly altered the environment within which energy policy is being forged. Key members of the cabinet fully recognize the important linkage between a healthy resource sector and a healthy competitive base." Following an outline of the Business Council's position emerging from our two energy summits, I concluded, "Canada is facing some very tough challenges in an increasingly competitive world. Our immense resource base is no longer our guarantee of a position in the front ranks of world economic leadership. Some of our mainstay industries such as mining and forest products are in trouble and the return to competitiveness is not going to be easy. All the more reason to take maximum advantage of the resource trump cards we have. Energy is one of those trump cards."

On June 1, 1985, the federal government and the oil-producing provinces signed the Western Energy Accord, which dismantled in large measure the National Energy Program. The new accord reflected a great deal of the Council's thinking; my colleagues were extremely pleased. This was a perfect example of how to effect policy renewal in the national interest, with two energy summits involving the participation of two premiers and the federal minister responsible for energy policy, the engagement of chief executives from producing and consumer industries from the east and west of Canada, rigorous analysis supporting the reasons for change, and the delicate diplomacy needed to shape the new consensus.

While I was jubilant about the policy outcome, my greatest satisfaction came from a belief that we had contributed to an easing of East-West tensions—a goal never far from my mind in the decades to come.

BUILDING BRIDGES TO LABOUR

The economic-driven tensions during the years 1981 to 1985 played out as well in the business-labour domain. For me, it was a story of hope and disappointment. When I was appointed president of the Business Council on National Issues, I made an overture to Dennis McDermott, the president of the Canadian Labour Congress. A seasoned, English-born labour activist, McDermott had taken up his post in 1978 after leading the United Auto Workers in Canada. There was no dialogue between organized labour and the business leadership of the country at the time, so I was wasn't surprised that McDermott had little interest in talking to me.

Labour's relationship with government was no better. In 1981, McDermott organized a one-hundred-thousand-person protest against the economic policies of the Trudeau government. Undeterred by the cold shoulder McDermott gave me, I struck up what would evolve into a trusted relationship with Shirley Carr, his executive vice-president, who in 1986 would become the first female president of the Canadian Labour Congress. The two of us committed ourselves to trying to shift the ground in the business-labour relationship, with Carr's overall objective being to ensure that labour would have an equal voice with business and government in shaping national economic policy. She confessed to me that part of her motivation was to "catch up to you guys," by which she meant matching the growing influence of the Business Council.

Carr had for some time been seeking support for the idea of an autonomous government-funded labour advisory body. We at the Council had been promoting a similar idea in the form of a productivity council. I approached Carr about the idea of a single body promoting our joint objectives. It was not an easy sell, as the word *productivity* was generally toxic in labour circles. But I argued that if we could reach agreement we might succeed in revolutionizing the business-labour relationship, a boon for both sides.

It helped that a productivity centre was already in the cards, thanks to an undertaking in finance minister Marc Lalonde's first budget, in 1982. Following consultations with Lalonde, Carr and I were asked to head a steering committee and bring forward recommendations. We pitched for the joint body, and the government agreed. Thus the autonomous Canadian Labour Market and Productivity Centre was born, in January 1984, with a generous financial endowment. In the lead-up to its launch, we dealt with a series of ministers responsible for employment, industry, and labour, including Lloyd Axworthy, John Roberts, Ed Lumley,

Charles Caccia, and André Ouellet. I had developed a good relationship with Ouellet in 1981 during discussions on competition
law reform, and I found him particularly helpful. But the real hero
of the piece was Lalonde, who, once he took over as finance minister in 1982, demonstrated that he was prepared to take risks.
His support in cabinet for the centre was decisive.

Carr and I were appointed as the centre's first co-chairs, heading
up a board composed of an equal number of representatives from
business and labour. We recruited staff and got down to work on a
variety of issues crucial to our constituencies.

In those early years, we would spend endless hours debating the
role of capital and labour. At first I was hopeful that this new initiative was going to make a real difference. I genuinely believed
that suspicion and ideological combat could be replaced by a new,
groundbreaking spirit of cooperation. But the years to come saw
a growing ideological chasm in national politics, in part driven by
the fierce debates over deficit reduction, tax reform, and free trade.
I watched sadly as this ideal faded.

By the time Carr was elected president of the Canadian Labour
Congress, the labour movement had made a sharp turn left-
ward, influenced by the charismatic leadership of Bob White. The
founding president of the Canadian Auto Workers, White, like
McDermott, was English born. He later succeeded Shirley Carr as
president of the Canadian Labour Congress, serving from 1992 to
1999. White and I crossed swords many times, but no more intensely
than during the free trade debates of the 1980s.

In one of my first jobs while a high school student growing up in
Nelson, British Columbia, my first encounter with a fellow worker
who was a union representative left an indelible impression. I was
on the midnight shift in the Canadian Pacific Railway diesel yards,
my first day of work. I had washed down a couple of locomotives

and was getting ready to go on to the next, when he told me, "Tom, have a sleep like the rest of us. That's all you are doing tonight." When I asked why, he responded, "That's the way we do things here." It took some time for me to fathom the reasoning, but I came away thinking it was not right.

MODERNIZING COMPETITION LAWS

Apart from zeroing in on the grave inflation threat facing Canada, one of the first challenges I tackled following my appointment as the Business Council's president was to take a close look at competition law. Canada's existing regime was badly outdated, and repeated attempts to enact reforms had failed, one after the other. A rash of corporate mergers had heightened concerns in consumer and small business circles that corporate concentration was hurting competition.

Attempts at reform had not been helped by what some of my Council colleagues believed was a strong bias against big business among senior officials in the federal Department of Consumer and Corporate Affairs. The department, created in 1967 to bring together under one minister federal policies regulating the marketplace, was responsible for consumer affairs, corporations, and corporate securities, combines, mergers, monopolies, and restraint of trade. A Business Council study in April 1981, which I co-signed alongside chair Jack Barrow and William McLean, chair of our task force on competition policy, prefaced the analysis as follows: "The business community generally feels that previous approaches to competition law reform were too theoretical and all-embracing, without sufficient regard for demonstrated need. The result was severe contention, much controversy and disturbance, and ongoing delay in enacting any changes."

Most of the work leading up to the study had been completed prior to my appointment. McLean, who was the chair of Canada Packers, had been assisted by prominent Toronto competition policy lawyer William Rowley. Given my legal background, I took a strong interest in the exercise, and I was aided by a fellow lawyer at Council headquarters, Peter Vivian. After carefully reviewing our competition policy file, I concluded that we were not going to make progress in advancing badly needed reforms without first rebooting the Council's relationship with the federal government. As I saw the situation, the blame lay on both sides, with suspicion and outright hostility making cooperation impossible. I set out to break the logjam. My friends warned me that my chances of success would be slim; cooperation, after all, would entail the wolf sitting down with the sheep, and there was no doubt in my mind as to who was considered the wolf.

On June 12, I met with André Ouellet, the minister of consumer and corporate affairs. In a chance meeting a month earlier, I had told him of my concerns over how toxic the relationship had become and said I had some ideas on how we might move forward. I liked Ouellet. We had first met in 1968, shortly after he was elected to Parliament, and he was someone I could reason with. I began by explaining the dramatically different approach the Business Council was embracing under my leadership. We wanted to contribute to the shaping of public policy in a responsible way and build a new business-government relationship based on cooperation and, wherever possible, consensus. Attempts at reforming Canada's competition laws would offer a real test of whether this approach could serve the public interest and work to the benefit both of business and the federal government.

I put the following proposition to Ouellet: the government wanted to enact an ambitious package of competition policy reforms, and we at the Council wanted to see best-in-class laws and regulations entrenched in sound economic policy. If we could cooperate, we could make it happen; it would be a win-win. "But there is something you and I must do first," I said. "You must ensure that your department is receptive and open-minded. I must convince my colleagues to abandon their distrust of the department and agree to negotiate in earnest." Ouellet at first seemed surprised but then quickly saw the opening I was offering. Strong opposition from the very constituency I represented had stymied previous attempts to move forward. I was promising I could turn this around. He smiled, we shook hands, and I walked back to my office. Could I really get the competition policy task force on side? I wondered. I immediately got on the telephone and spoke with Maclean, Barrow, and other key players on the file, including Peter Gordon, Jean de Grandpré, Alfred Powis, and Ted Newall. Their unanimous conclusion was "Full speed ahead. We have nothing to lose!"

Ouellet carried out his side of the bargain. There was a changing of the guard at the top of the Competition Bureau, and Lawson Hunter, a smart and energetic lawyer, was named to head the agency. Hunter quickly won the respect of my colleagues, and he and I worked well together. That being said, there was never any doubt in my mind that he was driven by principle, and he proved to be a fierce advocate of the bureau's independence. Under Hunter's watch, new legislation was developed, and the Business Council's perspectives were actively sought. In July 1982, George Post, the deputy minister of consumer and corporate affairs, announced that a new Combines Act was ready to be introduced in Parliament, and "many ideas drawn from the Business Council on National Issues will be included in the proposed amendments." Further, he said, "Amendments are needed to preserve and extend the free market system. The goal is not to attack bigness and concentration in the private sector as such, but to create more clearly defined rules for the conducting of business."

The breaking of the logjam resulted in Canada developing over time one of the world's most advanced competition policy regimes. It also proved that there was a much more constructive way for business and government to cooperate in achieving a public policy outcome that served the public interest.

DEFENDING PENSIONS FOR LOWER-INCOME SENIORS

The Mulroney government's first budget, on May 23, 1985, was of high importance. Just *how* important was communicated by the prime minister in his own words to his caucus: "The budget will attempt to deal with a miserable fiscal heritage, but it will be tough, realistic, and fair. A budget is a fifteen-day election campaign. Every step by every player is indispensable. It's the most important day of the year, and vital for a new government. It will showcase our competence, credibility and determination. It is vital for the Minister of Finance, but we must all carry the burden. It's not Wilson's budget. It's our budget."

When Michael Wilson stood in the House of Commons and tabled the budget, my Council colleagues and I were anticipating that it would introduce strong restraint measures to begin the arduous task of reining in government spending. We had been advocating this return to fiscal sanity in the lead-up to the 1984 election. When the prime minister called me on budget day and then the following afternoon, I reiterated my council's pledge to defend against the attacks we knew were coming from those who would argue that rising deficits and soaring public debt were of little consequence. Following a careful assessment of the budget's contents, I expressed the Council's strong support for its direction and some of its key provisions, such as providing taxpayers with a lifetime tax exemption on the first $500,000 of capital gains. It helped that, in our eyes, Michael Wilson commanded respect as a businessman and as someone who understood the essentials of economic policy.

As Canadians across the country absorbed the details of the budget, it seemed at first that it would win public support for its courage and soundness. But then things began to unravel, throwing the Mulroney government into crisis and presenting the Business Council with a crisis of our own. The issue that sparked the crisis was the government's decision to partially remove inflation protection from public pensions, both Old Age Security (OAS) and its top-up for lower-income Canadians, the Guaranteed Income Supplement (GIS).

While the Council was assuredly a leader among the business community's hawks in pressing for strong measures to bring spending under control, we had also argued persistently that "the war against deficits should not be fought on the backs of the disadvantaged or the poor." In my mind, this implicit social contract had to be respected to win broad public support for a long-term strategy aimed at getting Canada's fiscal house in order. When the budget was tabled, I had sensed that the government would be vulnerable on this point, but we at the Council avoided speaking out on the subject. Without knowing what was coming, in pre-budget consultations we had argued that "super-indexing" the Guaranteed Income Supplement—to protect seniors on lower incomes—would be the wisest course of action if inflation protection was to be removed from public pensions as part of restraint measures.

Attacks on the government on the OAS issue escalated rapidly, and by June 15 Mulroney came to the conclusion that the government would have to change course. An embarrassing encounter on Parliament Hill between the prime minister and an activist senior named Solange Denis put the final nail in the coffin. Surrounded by media, Denis accused the prime minister of lying, and added,

"You made us vote for you, and then goodbye Charlie Brown." The clip of this played everywhere.

The media were by then chasing me down, demanding to know whether the Council supported the government's de-indexing move. Referencing our publicly stated position that the deficit should not be fought at the expense of the poor or disadvantaged, I said we did not. This made waves. In his memoirs, Mulroney wrote, "After even the reliably right-wing Business Council on National Issues, supposedly in favour of prudent fiscal management, withdrew its support, we knew we had to act." He said how deeply this turn of events wounded him: "No issue has troubled me more since I entered politics. . . . I have reluctantly come to the conclusion that we shall imperil future prospects if we persist in supporting this measure now."

The prime minister and Michael Wilson considered their options. They rejected hunkering down in the hope that the outrage would recede. They also rejected super-indexing the GIS. Instead they chose to make a clean break and abandon the whole de-indexing measure. To make up in part for the loss to the treasury, the government announced that the surtax on large corporations would be extended from twelve months to eighteen and that the federal excise tax on gasoline would be increased by one cent per litre.

As troubled as Mulroney was by his government's all-important first budget having been so badly disrupted, he handled the setback with grace. I greatly admired him for that. On June 28, he told the media, "We are in Parliament as commoners, servants of the people. We never contended we were perfect, but we always said we would try to be fair. I think we violated that rule of fairness and we had to correct it. We acknowledged our error and we corrected it."

The repercussions of this political storm for the Business Council were far-reaching. On June 12, while I was in a meeting with the

Council's executive committee in Montreal, I received a telephone call from an enraged Michael Wilson, who accused the Council of having "f—ked this up." We had, he said, "torpedoed" the government's carefully laid out fiscal strategy. I explained our position and encouraged him to pursue the super-indexing route, to no avail. My attempts to reach out to key staffers in the PMO were flatly rejected, with Bill Fox saying he "would like to rip my heart out." Some of my Council colleagues received calls from Mulroney party stalwarts demanding that I be fired. My friend Paul Tellier, who was serving as clerk of the privy council, called to tell me that the extension of the surtax on large corporations was being dubbed in cabinet the "Tom d'Aquino tax." Despite the furor and the recriminations, the Council's chair, Royal Bank chief Rowland Frazee, and key board members lined up solidly behind me.

Looking back, I must say that this was the greatest test of the Council's independence and credentials as a non-partisan organization. Had I been fired or had the Council bowed to pressure on de-indexing, the organization would have suffered a massive loss of credibility from which I believe we would never have recovered. For some time, my relations with the prime minister remained cool, to put it mildly. But a much-appreciated late-evening call from Mulroney a couple of months later suggested that it was time to bury the hatchet and move on. The bigger reality was that his government and the Council shared a commitment to achieving transformational goals for Canada, and high on the list was the pursuit of a fundamentally new relationship with the United States. The journey to free trade had begun, and we were on the same train.

7

LEADING ON FREE TRADE

The Canada–United States Free Trade Agreement is arguably the most important economic initiative of Canada's postwar era. The major credit for making it happen lies with Prime Minister Brian Mulroney, who embraced the idea, boldly fought a general election on its merits, and was victorious. Canada's business community made a seminal contribution to this historic initiative, and as one of its most visible representatives, I took part in the high drama of this contest for the hearts and minds of Canadian voters. Its outcome hung in the balance to the very end.

Since studying the history of international law for my master of laws degree at the University of London, I have been much taken with the notion of how, from ancient times, different societies have seen an advantage in pursuing open trade. As an undergraduate, I had already absorbed the influence of classic liberal economists such as David Ricardo and Adam Smith. Then, as I began to work in the business environment in London and Paris in the early 1970s, I saw first-hand how multinational companies conducted their business across borders with relative ease. By the time I returned to Canada and set up my own company, I was an unapologetic economic liberal. And while serving as an adjunct professor at the faculty of law at the University of Ottawa in the late 1970s, I injected into my lectures on the law of international business transactions and trade my views on the benefits of liberalized trade and open commerce.

It is no surprise, then, that when I was appointed president of the BCNI in early 1981, I came to the job with a bias toward opening up the Canadian economy. I was convinced that liberalized trade with the United States would benefit Canada. My conviction was driven by a timely imperative: the need to find an answer to Canada's lagging economic productivity. Canadian companies and workers, and our country's overall competitiveness, would benefit from lowering trade barriers and easing restrictions on foreign investment. Looking southward for a mutually beneficial arrangement with our largest trading partner was the logical approach. One other factor shaped my thinking too. I saw disturbing signs of protectionism beginning to emerge in the United States, and I feared that without agreements based on rule of law, Canada would pay a heavy penalty operating in the shadow of the American economic juggernaut.

Early in my mandate, I quietly sounded out some CEO colleagues on the idea. The initial reaction was hesitation or outright opposition. The argument I heard from some key manufacturers was that Canadian companies could not compete unless they were protected by a wall of tariffs. Many of our industries simply were not prepared to contemplate risk. I was not deterred. At Council headquarters we continued to study the idea of a comprehensive Canada–United States agreement throughout 1981 and 1982, and I continued to make the case to my Council colleagues.

Chief among the hurdles we faced was the universal rejection of the free trade idea by every one of Canada's federal parties and by the Canadian labour movement. The words *free trade* were so toxic, I had to avoid using the term in public. Yet it is worth noting that even when Canada's government was wedded to economic nationalism, some members of the Trudeau cabinet with whom I was in close contact went out of their way to affirm a degree of support for limited trade liberalization via bilateral sectoral agreements—in softwood lumber, for example, or in fish. One was the energetic minister of industry, trade, and commerce, Ed Lumley. Another was the minister of state for international trade, Gerald Regan, whose interest went beyond such limited agreements.

While we were pursuing a made-in-Canada model for bilateral free trade, Ronald Reagan had already staked out a grander vision during his first presidential campaign. In 1979, he said, "We live on a continent whose three countries possess the assets to make it the strongest, most prosperous and self-sufficient area on earth. Within the borders of this North American continent are the food, resources, technology and undeveloped territory which, properly managed, could dramatically improve the quality of life of all its inhabitants." In effect, Reagan was laying out his vision for what eventually would become the North American Free Trade Agreement.

A Council dinner I hosted in January 1982 at the York Club in Toronto provided the first opportunity to test the waters with the American president's emissaries. Our guest was the recently appointed United States ambassador to Canada, Paul Robinson. Hailing from the insurance industry in Chicago, where he had been a fundraiser for the Reagan campaign, Robinson had a commanding presence. I greatly enjoyed his company, and before long we would become friends. Over dinner, Robinson expressed enthusiasm for the idea of a Canada–United States free trade agreement. A few months later, at a lunch in Ottawa, I privately raised the idea with Bill Brock, the United States trade representative. His response was as enthusiastic as Robinson's, but he added one key caveat. He told me, "Canada would have to take the initiative. Politically, this cannot be seen as an American idea." Brock was right, of course.

I had already begun to test the idea on American business leaders. I was stunned at how little interest there was. The head of the American task force on international trade of the Business Roundtable, who at the time was the CEO of Caterpillar, said in effect that there was no need for such an agreement. Some members of the House of Representatives and the Senate that I sounded out were of like mind. I was received courteously, but their focus was on countries such as Japan and their frustrations with the General Agreement on Tariffs and Trade (GATT).

When I learned that in March 1983 Vice-President George H.W. Bush was to visit Ottawa, I approached Ambassador Robinson with a bold request. "Paul, can you arrange for me and some of my Council colleagues to meet with the vice-president for an hour or so to talk about the idea of a Canada–United States free trade agreement?" Given that Bush was going to be in the capital only for the better part of a day, his time was already spoken for. Robinson nonetheless performed his magic and we got a full hour. In advance of the meeting, the Department of External Affairs reached out to me demanding to know how we managed to pull off this unheard-of coup.

We met in a private room at the Château Laurier. Ambassador Robinson, BCNI chair and Royal Bank CEO Rowland Frazee, and seven other chief executives of Canada's leading corporations were also present. Accompanying the vice-president was Martin Feldstein, chair of the Council of Economic Advisers. Four topics were on the agenda: the United States and world economies and the prospects for recovery; Canada–United States economic relations and bilateral trade; energy; and defence and strategic armaments. Each topic was to be covered with a single question to Bush.

On the free trade issue, I offered a brief summary of the Council's work to date and said, "In light of President Reagan's vision for continental free trade, what do you think about the idea of a Canada–United States free trade agreement?"

Bush responded, "Interesting, but what's in it for the United States?"

"An economy the size of California," I told him.

"I've never thought of it in those terms," he replied, and turned to Martin Feldstein. "Marty," he said, "let's have a look at this."

At various encounters I had with Bush in years to come, he said he never forgot the Château Laurier meeting. A comprehensive free trade agreement was still years in the making, but my colleagues and I concluded that, thanks to Ambassador Paul Robinson, an important marker had been laid.

As the Council's quiet advocacy of a free trade agreement continued, I made a special point of wooing the senior ranks of the public service in Ottawa. In a meeting with Robert Johnstone, the deputy minister of industry, trade, and commerce in early 1982, and in conversations with other senior officials in the ensuing months, it became clear that there was no appetite to challenge the political direction of the Trudeau government. The view among officials was clear: the country was not ready for such a bold move. One individual who would prove to be an exception was Derek Burney. He and I would in due course become close collaborators as Brian Mulroney pursued a Canada–United States free trade agreement once he became prime minister.

During this period, I remained in close touch with Premier Peter Lougheed. More than any premier at the time, the Alberta premier fully understood the Council's reasoning on free trade. As Brian Mulroney attests in his memoirs, upon becoming prime minister he turned to Lougheed for advice, and the premier urged him to take on the free trade initiative. Later, as the debate over free trade unfolded, Lougheed and I came to collaborate closely, and he became one of the country's most powerful voices for the cause. The newly elected prime minister also took advice from Joe Clark, his appointee as secretary of state for external affairs. Given my long-standing friendship with Clark, I was extremely pleased at the senior position he held in his former rival's cabinet. There, in the department that was to be renamed Foreign Affairs, he would serve with distinction.

With Mulroney's ascent to the leadership of the Progressive Conservative Party in June 1983, and to the office of leader of the Official Opposition in August, our organization turned our attention to him and the senior ranks of his party. Here we had a challenge. Mulroney had declared he was against a comprehensive free trade agreement with the Americans. Among senior Progressive Conservatives, only John Crosbie had spoken up for the idea. To support our case, we released a paper shortly after the 1984 election, recommending that Canada and the United States sign what we chose to call a "Trade Enhancement Agreement" (I jokingly dubbed it "TEA for two"). Our paper fell short of recommending the immediate start of free trade negotiations. This was my strategic decision, and so was the initiative's name. I wanted to map out a nuanced strategy in the hope of gaining broader public acceptance for the idea. When it came to our advocacy, though, we left no doubt as to where we stood on moving forward with a comprehensive trade deal. We had laid the groundwork for Canada–United States free trade.

Two important things happened in the meantime. Mulroney won a convincing majority in the general election held on September 4, 1984, and on September 17 he became Canada's eighteenth prime minister. This signalled a fresh departure from the Trudeau years and a decidedly more pro-market stance for Ottawa. The Liberal leader whom Mulroney defeated was Trudeau's successor and his party's one-time golden boy, John Turner. I had worked with Turner when he served as minister of justice and minister of finance, and I had learned to respect and like him. During Turner's brief tenure as prime minister, I reached out to him, and we had a number of conversations on economic issues and trade. To my disappointment, I saw that his pro-business attitudes had become muted as he tried to come to terms with a Liberal Party that had moved decidedly to the left. I did not yet know that the contest over free trade would fracture our relationship.

Mulroney's arrival on the scene, though, convinced me that the time was ripe to throw our full weight behind a comprehensive free trade initiative. I was reasonably certain that the new prime minister would instinctively see the advantage of moving forward.

Equally important is that the day after the election, the Royal Commission on the Economic Union and Development Prospects for Canada tabled its report. This pivotal document is better known as the Macdonald Report, after the commission's chair, former Trudeau cabinet minister Donald S. Macdonald. Its key message was that Canada should take a "leap of faith" and enter into free trade negotiations with the United States. On this point the report was in full agreement with what Rowland Frazee and I had recommended to the commission on behalf of the BCNI. In our submission of December 12, 1983, we told the commission, "As one of the few industrial countries without free access to a market of at least 50 million people, Canada is particularly vulnerable to protectionist policies. . . . We suggest that the negotiation of an across the board free trade agreement with the United States . . . be considered."

We were not mistaken in our assessment of the incoming prime minister. Buoyed by the news of the Macdonald Report, Mulroney decided to proceed, and the free trade train departed the station. We knew the ride was going to be a rough one, but we could take some justifiable satisfaction in knowing that the BCNI had played a major role in preparing the way, and that the senior business leadership of the country was solidly on side.

At the heart of advocacy lie relationships. Taking on the free trade initiative would entail nurturing vital connections in the United States. Owing to my advisory relationship with Time Inc., senior Time executives arranged for me and my Council colleagues to meet with a list of movers and shakers in Washington, D.C., in February 1985. As a token of Time Inc.'s enormous influence, we were treated to private meetings with a remarkable array of American leaders that included no less than Secretary of State George Shultz, the defence secretary, Caspar Weinberger, and key members of Congress, prominent among them Robert Dole and Joe Biden, who impressed me with his command of foreign policy issues.

The so-called Shamrock Summit between Prime Minister Brian Mulroney and President Ronald Reagan opened in Quebec City on March 17, 1985. Its centrepiece was a gala dinner at the historic Château Frontenac in honour of the president and his wife, Nancy Reagan. Prime Minister Mulroney and Mila Mulroney were perfect hosts. The highlight of the dinner was when the president and the prime minister and their wives joined hands and sang, with feeling, "When Irish Eyes Are Smiling." Some in the media and in anti-Mulroney circles mocked this familiarity; I, of course, found it charming. It telegraphed a personal relationship between the two leaders that was to become a powerful advantage in the free trade negotiations to come.

The summit, whose agenda covered a number of important bilateral issues, provided a backdrop to several constructive exchanges. At a luncheon the next day attended by the prime minister and the president and, among others, Shultz, Weinberger, Joe Clark, and

Jim Kelleher, the minister of international trade, there was excitement in the air. It was the sense that, after years of a distinct coolness in U.S.-Canada affairs, the Quebec City meetings had opened a historic chapter in Canada's relations with its neighbour.

While the free trade initiative occupied the centre of the national stage, Prime Minister Mulroney was anxious to signal that he was not taking his eye off the ball on domestic economic issues. So it was that in April 1985, he convened the National Economic Conference. Chaired by Mulroney, the conference brought together a who's who of leaders from business, labour, academe, think tanks, and the voluntary sector.

The conference was also a pivotal moment in Susan's career. She had been working in the Privy Council Office since 1981 and had been a member of its influential priorities and planning secretariat, serving three prime ministers: Trudeau, Turner, and Mulroney. Then out of the blue, she was asked to help organize the National Economic Conference, a task she happily accepted. The conference's organizing triumvirate consisted of Susan, Montreal lawyer Stanley Hartt, and the seasoned senior public servant Arthur Kroeger. Shortly after, finance minister Michael Wilson invited Susan to join his department. She was to spend the next seventeen years in the Department of Finance, serving five ministers and five deputy ministers. Susan was also the first woman to be appointed an assistant deputy minister in the department's history. In her professional life, she went by the name Susan Peterson.

Later that summer, Stanley Hartt was named by Mulroney as deputy minister of finance. I had worked closely as a lawyer with Hartt in Montreal in 1967 and 1968. Mulroney also made one other very significant public service appointment that summer. He named

Paul Tellier clerk of the privy council and secretary to the cabinet. Tellier was both a star and a friend, and his leadership at the Privy Council Office was transformative. Mulroney came to rely on him heavily, and for good reason. At the Business Council, we went through an important leadership transition as well. David Culver, chief executive of Canadian multinational Alcan Aluminum, succeeded Royal Bank of Canada head Rowland Frazee as Council chair. Frazee had been an exceptional leader and devoted comrade as the Council moved from its infancy to front-rank status among business associations.

As discussions with the Reagan administration on the free trade initiative got under way, the prime minister needed to appoint a chief negotiator. His choice was public service veteran Simon Reisman. I knew Simon well from his days as deputy minister of finance and, after his public service career, as a consultant to industry. He and his wife, Connie, were frequent visitors to our residence in Ottawa. Simon was finance and trade savvy, and a tough, take-no-prisoners negotiator. Upon hearing the news, I called him and congratulated him. His legendary poker skills, I added, would certainly be put to good use with the Americans.

Shortly thereafter I met with Reisman and fully briefed him on where the Business Council stood on the free trade negotiations. Then I did something that startled him: I handed him a black binder containing the Council's "Elements of a Comprehensive Canada–United States Trade Agreement," with thirty-two articles and seven annexes. This document, written in the legal language of a treaty, had been prepared by me and the Council's able policy vice-president, Jock Finlayson, with the assistance of Vancouver-based trade lawyer Chris Thomas. Now, as I sat across from the calm poker aficionado, I saw a look cross his face that I could not interpret. For a moment I feared I might have offended him. It wasn't a good idea to get too far ahead of Simon Reisman, I thought. But I need not have feared. The conversation was the beginning of a productive relationship between Reisman and the Council members and me that lasted throughout the free trade negotiations. Reisman's deputy in the negotiations was public servant Gordon Ritchie, also well known to me, and an excellent complement to his boss. On the American side, public servant Peter Murphy was appointed Reisman's counterpart, while Clayton Yeutter served as the U.S. trade representative. Career diplomat Thomas Niles served in Ottawa as U.S. ambassador from 1985 to 1989. He and I got along famously, punctuating our collaboration with regular games of squash at six in the morning.

As the country headed into 1987, a critical year in the negotiations, the lineup on the Canadian side buttressing Reisman and Ritchie was consolidated. Under the leadership of Mulroney, it consisted of external affairs minister Joe Clark, finance minister Michael Wilson, international trade minister Pat Carney, principal secretary to the prime minister Bernard Roy, privy council clerk Paul Tellier, deputy ministers Stanley Hartt at finance, Si Taylor at external affairs, Donald Campbell at trade, and Ambassador Allan Gotlieb in Washington. It was a very talented bunch. Derek Burney, who was part of this inner circle, was appointed chief of staff by the prime minister in February 1987, further enhancing his position of influence in the unfolding free trade saga.

With our negotiating team in place and the Americans with theirs, the negotiations had begun, but I could see the Americans were not giving the talks the attention they deserved. My concerns in part reflected the frustration that the prime minister and his inner circle were facing and not so quietly voicing. But my concerns also flowed from the lack of interest I was witnessing in discussions the BCNI was having at the political and official levels in Washington and with senior American business leaders. Canada simply was not on the radar. The friendship between Reagan and Mulroney was not paying off.

This was put to us starkly when a delegation of four U.S. senators visited Ottawa on December 9, 1986—referred to by Allan Gotlieb in his book *The Washington Diaries* as "the most important Senate delegation to ever come to Canada." Senators Lloyd Bentsen, Spark Matsunaga, Max Baucus, and John Chafee met with Council chair David Culver and me, along with several Council members, at the Department of External Affairs. The centrepiece of the meeting was a brief presentation I made summarizing why, from a business perspective, the free trade agreement was a win-win for both the United States and Canada. I stressed the importance to both countries of an effective dispute-settlement mechanism and why it was so vital to Canada that culture, including our vulnerable cultural industries, be off the negotiating table. The senators were noncommittal on dispute settlement and did not seem to comprehend our concerns about culture. My colleagues and I came away from the meeting agreeing that much more needed to be done to bring the Americans along—especially given that the deadline for reaching an agreement was not far off.

We had seen evidence of the American lack of interest a month earlier, when we met a senior group of Business Roundtable chief executives in New York City. Present were Roger Smith of General Motors, John Akers of IBM, John Creedon of Metropolitan Life, James Robinson of American Express, and Edson Spencer of Honeywell. I had arranged the meeting with my counterpart, the Roundtable's president, William Lurie, and we had brought a strong Canadian team consisting of Council chair David Culver of Alcan, Alfred Powis of Noranda, Claude Castonguay of the Laurentian Group, Ted Medland of Wood Gundy, Steele Curry of Revelstoke

Companies, Ronald Mannix of Manalta Coal, Ted Newall of DuPont Canada, and Gerald Heffernan of Co-Steel. In a letter to Prime Minister Mulroney, this is how I summarized the meeting:

> While we made some headway in persuading them that an agreement must at the very least significantly circumscribe the application of U.S. trade laws insofar as Canada is concerned, there was strong resistance to our arguments. . . . The American chief executives demonstrated little understanding or sensitivity towards the issue of cultural sovereignty—a subject which we addressed clearly and vigorously. . . . I fear the cultural sovereignty issue more than any other has the potential to torpedo the bilateral initiative. . . . Clearly, the American chief executives have considerable expectations of what an agreement will yield on the investment front. Unlike many Canadians, they believe that trade and investment are inseparable and that important Canadian concessions will have to be made on the investment front in return for satisfying Canadian demands . . . for example, immunity from U.S. trade laws.

I concluded my note with the following warning: "The most important message (and soundest advice) I received at the meeting was that the Americans will not take us seriously in the negotiations unless we are tough, consistent and decisive."

With the prospects for an agreement looking increasingly troubled, and with protectionist sentiments in Canada rising, I decided over Christmas that we needed to launch a broad-based initiative aimed at "winning hearts and minds." I outlined my thinking over lunch at the Toronto Club in February with David Culver, Darcy McKeough,

Ted Newall, and the most recently elected member of the Business Council's executive committee, the cerebral National Bank chief executive Michel Bélanger. I proposed we create a non-partisan coalition of prominent Canadians not limited to business leaders. This was an idea that Culver and I had discussed in January. Later that same day in Toronto, the policy committee of the Business Council met and gave the idea its strong support. The name I proposed for the new organization was the Canadian Alliance for Trade and Job Opportunities.

The most daring proposition I tested on my colleagues was that Peter Lougheed and Donald Macdonald be invited to co-chair the Alliance. To my mind, the synergy was perfect: two well-known Canadians, Lougheed the recently retired premier of Alberta and Macdonald of royal commission "leap of faith" fame, one a Progressive Conservative from the West and one a Liberal from Ontario, both highly respected, both among the foremost advocates of a free trade agreement with the United States. Simon Reisman and Gordon Ritchie joined us for dinner that evening, and while we signalled that a new initiative was in the works, we did not let our guests from the government know of the bold move we were about to take. I telephoned Lougheed and Macdonald the following afternoon and both agreed to take on the challenge, subject to my providing necessary details.

I followed up with Lougheed and Macdonald in a letter providing the details:

> The campaign will encourage among the public at large a better appreciation of the importance of trade to our prosperity as a country, and it will communicate the advantages in terms of jobs and economic growth of a soundly negotiated agreement between Canada and the United States. . . .

The campaign will be independent and non-partisan, and conducted on an arms-length basis from the federal government. . . . [It] could very well have two phases—one leading up to the tabling of the draft agreement in early October 1987, and the other in the post October 1987 period when the debate in Canada on the merits of the agreement is certain to be intense.

On this last point I was prophetic.

While Business Council support would be crucial to the success of the Canadian Alliance, Culver and I decided that it should nevertheless be headquartered at Alcan offices in Montreal and that Culver should chair the executive committee. McKeough and I would serve on the committee, with McKeough having primary responsibility for fundraising while I dealt with relations with government and special interest groups. The principal source of staff support for the day-to-day work of the Alliance would rest with my team at Business Council headquarters.

Culver and I swiftly reached out to Council members and attracted a good number of recruits. We also managed to raise significant financial support for the Canadian Alliance. Lougheed and Macdonald took front stage from the moment of launch, on March 19, and in due course thirty-five organizations took up active membership.

By September 1987, it became clear to Brian Mulroney that the free trade negotiations were stuck. He writes in his memoirs that, after eighteen months of negotiation, "the United States was neither sensitive to the political risks facing my government nor committed to act on what I considered as the sine qua non for success: relief from capricious U.S. trade remedies." Since the early 1980s, the Business Council had been immersed in the problem of exempting

Canadian exporters from the punitive remedies that American courts imposed when a U.S. firm could persuade the court that the foreign rival was an unfair competitor. Binational panels for dispute settlement, free from political interference and the American court system, had been referenced countless times in BCNI position papers and were a highlight of the many speeches I had delivered since 1983. Furthermore, dispute settlement in international trade was one of my specialties in the courses I taught at the University of Ottawa law school. For years, I had argued that any bilateral deal with the United States ultimately would be judged by how effectively both countries would be prepared to cede authority to binational panels.

The fact that the Americans were not listening had already been clearly communicated to my colleagues and me at a meeting in Washington on July 8. The legendary Robert Strauss, one of Washington's uber-insiders, helped me organize the meeting. In short order, Strauss arranged for an influential list of senators and members of Congress to meet with our Canadian delegation. Our team was composed of Canadian Alliance co-chairs Peter Lougheed and Donald Macdonald, David Culver, and chief executives Michel Bélanger of the National Bank, Alfred Powis of Noranda, Allan Taylor of the Royal Bank of Canada, and Bill Stinson of Canadian Pacific. The purpose of the meeting was straightforward: we wanted to hear first-hand from this powerful group whether there was any room for negotiation on dispute settlement.

Our presence in Washington also had a touch of diplomatic drama. The night before our meeting with the American legislators, I had convened a dinner at the Four Seasons Hotel with Allan Gotlieb as our guest. Gotlieb argued that our meeting with the Americans was ill-timed; he cautioned us to go gently with our hosts. I knew that our skilful ambassador was renowned for keeping a finger on the American pulse, but I had to disagree. With equal force, I told him that this was no time to go soft. Then I looked around the table. I wasn't the only one who was steaming at being told to exercise restraint at this critical moment. More discussion followed, and finally Donald Macdonald exploded, "Goddamn it, Allan, whose side are you on?!" Don stood up and left the dinner table.

Gotlieb was shaken. I hurried after Macdonald and persuaded him to return to the table, where we resumed our discussions. My colleagues and I pressed the point that the time for unambiguous straight talk had come. Traditional Canadian politeness and appeals to a special relationship had not yielded results.

The next day, we walked into a room where senators Lloyd Bentsen, John Danforth, and John Chafee and representatives Tom Foley, Bill Frenzel, and Sam Gibbons were waiting to hear what we had to say. One after another, they protested that independent binational panels for settling trade disputes were not on, because they would impinge on U.S. sovereignty. Congressional approval could never be won, they declared. We did not mince words in our response. Without some coming to terms on this issue, the free trade pact was dead in the water and a historic opportunity would be lost. This did not seem to concern the Americans, who believed that Canada would settle for a lesser deal because the Mulroney government wanted it so badly. The one exception on the American side was Sam Gibbons, who seemed to open the door slightly on dispute settlement. In the coming weeks, we discovered how helpful he would prove to our side.

We left Washington disheartened but more resolved than ever to rescue the initiative. On the flight back to Canada, courtesy of Allan Taylor and the Royal Bank airplane, Peter Lougheed looked at me and said, "Tom, it's now or never. We are on the brink of losing this deal."

—

We turned our attention once again to the private sector, stepping up our efforts to work with influential American power brokers and business leaders. It was at this time that the Business Roundtable finally began to engage in earnest. This was largely due to American Express chief executive James Robinson III, who became an effective advocate for the free trade agreement. And here is where relationships count for so much. Robinson and David Culver were good friends, and David was on the board of American Express. The Robinson connection served both countries well in the run-up to the 1988 federal election.

My colleagues and I worked feverishly in the background. I went so far as to draft some language on dispute settlement that Robinson and colleagues could test out with Peter Murphy and his team of American negotiators behind the scenes. On September 23, Canada played its final gambit. On Mulroney's instructions, Simon Reisman walked away from the table. In the frantic final days, Mulroney's threat to place a direct phone call to Ronald Reagan worked, and Derek Burney and the Canadian team in Washington received a grudging confirmation from James Baker, secretary of the treasury, that Canada had won the day on dispute settlement. This led to an agreement in principle on October 3, 1987, just hours away from the deadline that both countries had set.

It was an enormous victory, but our jubilation was short-lived. Back home, the opposing Canadian sides on free trade girded for battle in the lead-up to the most divisive single-issue federal election in Canadian history. The Canadian Alliance for Trade and Job Opportunities engaged vigorously. No small number of its supporters and critics alike credit it and the combined efforts of the business community led by the Business Council with tilting the election of 1988 decisively in favour of the free trade option for Canada.

The Alliance's fact-based advertising no doubt moved voters—but as someone who was active at the very heart of the campaign for free trade, I believe it was simply our arguments that won the day. Our opponents proclaimed their fears; we spoke confidently about Canada's future. The unprecedented surge of business support we attracted from across the spectrum was rooted in an honest conviction that the agreement would lead to more jobs and growth. In the end, our position was the more credible one.

In the crucial months leading up to the election, the Business Council faced a number of challenges. One was to ensure that the free trade agreement did not become undone by the clash of political parties and ideologies. Another was to conduct a campaign in support of free trade that was steadfastly non-partisan. Given the growing divide in the country and the passion with which the "Mulroney deal" was attacked by a coalition of nationalists and protectionists, we soon found that operating above the fray had become impossible. Still, we made every effort to do so. Under the non-partisan leadership of Progressive Conservative Lougheed and Liberal Macdonald, the Canadian Alliance for Trade and Job Opportunities took its message to all parts of the country. My team at the Council put all our efforts into supplying the Alliance with evidence-based arguments. Likewise, at the Council itself we drew on the perspectives of our member companies to make the case in the most specific terms that the free trade agreement would stimulate growth, jobs, exports, and innovation. In turn, we encouraged our member companies to tell their own stories to their employees, their customers, and their various stakeholders. Buttressing these efforts was a coalition of like-minded academics that I had carefully assembled.

For me, the final unfolding of the free trade journey had all the thrills of a roller-coaster ride. By the time 1988 came around, my personal experience in advocating for free trade was already rooted in some five years of intense engagement. In just a few years, I had given hundreds of speeches and media appearances across Canada and the United States. Now, with the prime minister's call for a November election, I found myself constantly on the road. Of my many addresses in 1988, one of the most memorable was a speech I presented to the annual meeting of the American Bar Association in Toronto in August. I gave it the title "The Canada–United States Free Trade Agreement: Myth and Reality," and I received a standing ovation. I used it to lay out a point-by-point rebuttal of what I considered were the principal myths advanced by the anti-free trade lobby: that Canada was turning its back on the General Agreement on Tariffs and Trade; that Canada did not achieve improved access to the U.S. market; that the agreement was worthless without trade law exemptions; that Canada was up for sale; that the Canada–United States Auto Pact would be undermined; that Canadian energy and water were at risk; that Canadian agriculture would suffer; that Canada's culture would be destroyed; that Canadians would experience serious job losses; and that Canadian sovereignty was undone.

But all this exposure carried with it a cost. The principal tribunes of the left, such as labour leader Bob White, publisher Mel Hurtig, journalist Linda McQuaig, and activist Maude Barlow—with the backing of the *Toronto Star*—were merciless in their attacks on me and the Business Council. The Council was complicit in a plan to sell the country to Americans for the benefit of big business, they argued, and I personally was leading the charge. Canada's social programs would be gutted and our culture dumped down the drain. Intimidation of political opponents is not a new thing, and

Washington, D.C., is not the only North American capital to have seen it. Here in Ottawa, a group of protesters wearing battle fatigues and masks stormed the Business Council offices. I was burned in effigy in front of the Château Laurier, and a truckload of cow dung was dropped on the driveway of my home. One death threat was made, and then others. The threats kept coming. I never accepted that I should have a security detail, although that was the advice I was given. I did not take the death threats seriously. I freely admit, though, that the highly personal attacks in the media hit home and caused me sleepless nights, but I was determined to soldier on, convinced of the rightness of our cause.

In the summer months of 1988, Alliance and Business Council advocacy focused on outreach to the provincial premiers. Some of these were on side and others not. I made a point of trying to meet with most of the premiers in person and found that British Columbia's Bill Vander Zalm, Alberta's Don Getty, and Saskatchewan's Grant Devine were enthusiastic supporters of the deal. Quebec's Robert Bourassa was firmly committed, backed up by a fully engaged business community, including a sizable number of Quebec-based Business Council colleagues. In the Atlantic provinces, New Brunswick's Richard Hatfield had pledged his province's support. Ontario presented the greatest challenge. As early as January 12, 1987, when my Council colleagues and I met with David Peterson at Queen's Park, he had raised concerns about potential job losses in the manufacturing sector, the risk of jeopardizing the Auto Pact, and the erosion of Canada's cultural sovereignty. Given the growing partisan divide on the issue, I knew that Liberal politics were also in play. I liked David and was not prepared to give up on him. As the national debate intensified, though, his position hardened, despite the overwhelmingly pro–free trade stance of the Ontario business community.

—

One of the biggest surprises in the unfolding drama was the announcement by federal Opposition leader John Turner that if he were to form the next government he would tear up the free trade agreement. I thought this was a serious strategic error that in the end would undermine his ambitions to defeat Brian Mulroney. It was clear to me that Turner had capitulated to the powerful forces of the left in the Liberal Party. On a personal level, I was disappointed in the path taken by a man who was a respected minister when I was a young staffer in Prime Minister Trudeau's office. A political veteran and Bay Street lawyer who for many years had taken pride in his economic acumen and business savvy, he had now thrown in his lot with anti-free trade militants. In a conversation with Turner in August, I expressed my dismay and gave him notice that the following day the Business Council would issue a public rejection of his position under the headline "Mr. Turner, We Beg to Disagree." A once mutually respectful relationship had hit rock bottom.

While the position taken by the Liberal Party was our main concern, we did not ignore the New Democrats. Earlier that summer, on June 6, David Culver and I and several of our colleagues hosted NDP leader Ed Broadbent at Ottawa's Rideau Club. The discussion was cordial, but Broadbent did not retreat from any of the views he had been setting out before the Canadian public. His conviction was deep that the free trade agreement would undermine Canadian sovereignty, and he left no doubt that he meant to campaign against it with all his strength.

I kept in close touch with our American allies that summer. That June, in Chicago, I had an opportunity to speak with secretary Jim Baker and thank him for his part in bringing in the free trade agreement when the U.S. side looked to be immovable. In Toronto the next day, my Council colleagues and I hosted Jim Robinson of American Express and stressed the importance of now shepherding the agreement through to full implementation in both countries. A welcome distraction from the campaign was a meeting I hosted in Toronto with Helmut Kohl. The German chancellor was in Toronto for the fourteenth G7 Summit, along with the other leaders of the member states. I congratulated Kohl on his address to Parliament the day before and briefed him on Canada's agreement with the United States, stressing that this was not an attempt to create a "fortress North America." Kohl had his own opportunity to make history, and showed that he well knew how to handle it, a year and a half later with the fall of the Berlin Wall.

Another summer surprise was a call from Brian Mulroney in August advising me that he was appointing Donald Macdonald as high commissioner to London. While I was delighted with the news, it also meant that we needed to move quickly to recruit Macdonald's successor as co-chair of the Canadian Alliance for Trade and Job Opportunities. Following consultations with Peter Lougheed and David Culver, I reached out to Gerald Regan, the former Liberal minister of state for international trade. While serving in the Trudeau cabinet, Regan had signalled to me his interest in pursuing an arrangement with the Americans that went beyond sectoral trade agreements. Regan happily accepted the invitation. My Council colleagues and I feted Donald Macdonald appropriately with a celebratory dinner at the Toronto Club in September. I presented him with a bespoke bowler hat and a fine English umbrella. Shortly afterwards, Don and his wife, Adrian, departed for London, without a worry for the rain.

Besides the hundreds of speeches and media appearances I'd been making to champion the cause, I also took the stage for many debates as well. One of the most memorable of these was held in Toronto on two successive evenings, October 17 and 18. Hosted by the CBC's gracious and sharp Barbara Frum and televised nationally, it pitted Peter Lougheed and me against two arch-rivals, Bob White and Maude Barlow. The contest took place in the historic St. Lawrence Hall. Built in 1850, this National Historic Site was the venue where leaders such as John A. Macdonald, George-Étienne Cartier, George Brown, and Thomas D'Arcy McGee had spoken to the people of Toronto. The resolution up for debate on both evenings was "Be It Resolved: The Free Trade Agreement Is Good for Canada." Both sides acquitted themselves well. Lougheed and I spoke confidently about Canada's future under the agreement. Barlow and White countered with the argument that Canada could not possibly compete with the Americans under this deal and warned of the erosion of Canada's culture and its social programs. Following the second debate, Derek Burney phoned me and exclaimed, "Congratulations, Mike Tyson!" I did not feel Peter and I had delivered any knockout punch to our opponents, but I believe we made a showing that the heavyweight champion would not have been ashamed of.

One other debate in those final months stands out in my memory. It took place at Ottawa's Château Laurier on November 7, two weeks before voting day. My opponent was none other than Mitchell Sharp, one of the most highly respected members of the Liberal Party establishment. The moderator was Gordon Robertson, a former clerk of the privy council and secretary to the cabinet. The room was packed with mandarins and former luminaries of Canada's public service. Some of them had been architects in the building of postwar Canada—an extremely discerning crowd to say the least. Mitchell was a friend, and so was Gordon; I will have more to say about them in the coming chapters. The occasion, therefore, called for respect and a certain degree of restraint. Nevertheless, I pressed my points home and came away feeling I had won over this cerebral and influential audience.

The eleventh hour had arrived. The polling was showing that the Mulroney campaign was facing significant difficulties and the future of the free trade agreement was hanging in the balance. In the last week of October, as part of a last-ditch attempt to win Canadians over with a non-partisan, fact-based approach, I had begun drafting the content of "Straight Talk on Free Trade." This was to be an insert in major Canadian publications, and it would be given massive distribution. Following sign-off with Lougheed, Regan, and Culver, and under the auspices of the Canadian Alliance for Trade and Job Opportunities, distribution in the country's newspapers and other media outlets began in the first week of November. We held our breath. At this point all bets were off.

On November 9, I hosted a dinner at my home. Present were Derek Burney and Ambassador Tom Niles. We were convinced the free trade agreement was in mortal peril. But the final days of the campaign saw an extraordinary turnaround.

On November 21, 1988, in what has been described as the "great free trade election," the Progressive Conservatives, led by Brian Mulroney, won 169 of the 295 seats in Parliament. The Liberals took 83 seats and the New Democratic Party took the remaining 43. Mulroney's clear majority in the House meant that the painstaking deal signed more than thirteen months earlier was now guaranteed its passage into law.

The free trade agreement would survive after all. The night the results came in, and in the days after, there were congratulations all around—far too many calls to remember in the euphoria of the moment. I went to bed on election night feeling that a journey that had commenced in the early 1980s had finally come to its proper end. I was proud that Canada's business community had played a major role in writing Canada's history.

The final victory in the free trade saga owed its success to the creativity, ingenuity, commitment, and passion of a remarkable group of friends and colleagues. Some of our opponents had gone so far as to question our patriotism, but to my mind these were patriots one and all. To honour them and to demonstrate the Business Council's gratitude, I hosted a celebratory dinner at the Rideau Club in Ottawa on December 20. Prime Minister Mulroney, ministers Michael Wilson and John Crosbie, Peter Lougheed, Senator George van Roggen, chief negotiator Simon Reisman, and ambassadors Gotlieb and Niles were present. So were senior officials, who included Derek Burney, Gordon Ritchie, and Donald Campbell. Business Council chair David Culver was at my side, and so were business colleagues Laurent Beaudoin, Michel Bélanger, Peter Bentley, Jack Fraser, Darcy McKeough, Ted Newall, and Alfred Powis. There was much merriment and toasts aplenty—and deep, heartfelt emotion. As we shook hands and bid farewell that fine December evening, we knew that a good deed for Canada had been accomplished and that history would tell that our cause was noble and just.

8

FIGHTING FOR NATIONAL UNITY

The atmosphere in the ballroom at the InterContinental Hotel in Toronto on the evening of October 30, 1995, was tense. Together with some 150 of my Business Council colleagues—chief executives from across Canada—we had gathered for our autumn meeting. But this was no ordinary meeting. It was referendum day in Quebec, and our minds were focused on one thing only: Would Canada as we knew it survive? Present with us were Ontario premier Mike Harris and a collection of guests who had fought the good fight in support of national unity. The question put to the citizens of Quebec that day was deceptively complex: "Do you agree that Quebec should become sovereign, after having made a formal offer to Canada for a new economic and political partnership, within the scope of the Bill respecting the future of Quebec and of the agreement signed on June 12, 1995?"

My anxiety during the weeks leading up to referendum day had not let up for a minute. The polls showed that the independentist forces in the province, led by the Parti Québécois government of Jacques Parizeau, with the crucial involvement of Bloc Québécois leader Lucien Bouchard, had real momentum. The morning before the vote, Susan and I woke up to a chilly, windy day in Ottawa. We looked at each other and both of us were overcome. Would we lose this beautiful country? we asked ourselves. Later, with a large Canadian flag in hand, we marched across the Alexandra Bridge spanning the historic Ottawa River to join hundreds in a pro-Canada rally at the Museum of Civilization. We shouted our support for *un Canada uni* and joined in a boisterous singing of our national anthem, composed by Calixa Lavallée over a century before.

At our dinner in Toronto the following evening, we watched a video I had arranged extolling the beauty of Canada, from sea to sea to sea, before we turned our attention to the large television monitors in the room to follow the referendum coverage. I was in touch with colleagues in Montreal during the vote count, including Paul Desmarais Sr., and my counterparts at the Conseil du patronat du Québec, led by Ghislain Dufour. We knew it was going to be extremely close.

When it was announced that the independence option was likely to be defeated, albeit by the narrowest of margins, there was a mighty shout in the room and we broke into a spontaneous chorus of "O Canada." As I looked at my colleagues, I saw some with tears running down their cheeks. I wiped away my own tears and felt a great release in my chest. The unity struggle had weighed heavily on my emotions for months. I simply could not abide a breakup and had convinced myself that, faced with a referendum loss, I would fight on, confident that millions of Canadians, including Quebecers, would in the end never allow such a tragedy to unfold.

It was indeed the closest of calls. At 93.52 per cent, the voter turnout was the largest in Quebec history. The "No" option carried by a mere 54,288 votes—50.58 per cent. The rending of Canada had been staved off. The following morning, National Bank of Canada chief executive and Business Council vice-chair Michel Bélanger travelled from Montreal to Toronto to brief us on the outcome. Highly respected in Quebec, Bélanger served as chair of the Quebec Liberal Party's referendum committee. I was in close touch with him in the months leading up to the vote and he was always a source of sound advice. His message to us that morning left no doubt in our minds: Canada had averted a major crisis, but there was much work to be done.

One of the unique characteristics of the Business Council during my thirty-year tenure there was its engagement in areas of policy that were considered far afield from traditional business concerns. It was taken as a given that fiscal issues, trade, taxation, and competitiveness would be at the core of our mandate—not so constitutional matters. When I took on the job at the Council, one of my goals was to engage Canada's business leadership in helping strengthen the bonds of the Canadian federation. My logic was simple: a well-functioning and well-governed federation respectful of the rule of law was an essential foundation of a strong economy. I confess that my own strong personal interest in the country's constitutional affairs and my background in constitutional law were driving forces.

I came to understand the importance of Canadian unity in early adulthood, when I first studied the texts of our country's historians and political scientists. As a child, I was fascinated with the courageous exploits of Canada's early explorers. They had faced unimaginable odds as they mapped a vast territory known only to the First Nations, who had inhabited the land since time immemorial. In my student years, I crossed the continent a dozen times, seeing firsthand Canada's regions and communities. To me, it was a marvel. I believed that Canada was the most blessed of countries, bound together by its federal political system. Plumbing the depths of federalism became an obsession—a favourite subject in my political science and legal studies.

I understood early on that in the give and take of the federalist system there were inevitable tensions, both economic and cultural.

I remember a teacher in sixth grade explaining why those of us who lived in the Canadian West, which he described as the "hinterland," had to pay more for automobiles and washing machines that were manufactured in Ontario. When I asked for a fuller explanation, he simply said, "Because they are protectionists." Little did I know then that a good part of my adult life would be dedicated to fighting protectionism.

During my earliest visits to Montreal in the 1960s, I saw for the first time the cultural strains there. I found a French-speaking majority not at ease with an anglophone minority that historically had wielded great economic influence. I saw a people bridling at the power of the Roman Catholic Church. I studied the Quiet Revolution and the aspiration of the province's majority to be *maîtres chez nous*. I admired the leadership of Premier Jean Lesage, whose election in 1960 heralded profound changes in the politics and economics of Quebec. These two realities—how to accommodate the West and Quebec in the Canadian federation—became the touchstones of my own personal contribution to the enduring fight for national unity.

My exposure to Quebec's aspirations moved from the conceptual to the real during my time working for Pierre Trudeau. I had witnessed first-hand the failure of the constitutional talks in Victoria in 1971. I had observed with astonishment the 1980 Quebec referendum led by the charismatic René Lévesque. I remember on a rainy April 17 in 1982 sitting on the lawn of Parliament Hill when Canada's Constitution was patriated. There I watched as the proclamation that brought the Constitution Act into being was signed by Queen Elizabeth II, Pierre Trudeau, justice minister Jean Chrétien, and registrar general André Ouellet. Canada had formally assumed authority over its constitutional affairs. The British North America Act, which had been the guidepost for all my constitutional studies in years gone by, was renamed and amended. It entrenched Canada's new Charter of Rights and Freedoms, a guarantee of the rights of Indigenous peoples of Canada, and a formula for amending the Constitution.

As an observer of this historic event, I was elated. I felt that Canada had finally come of age and that we were exercising sovereignty in the fullest sense. Our residual dependence on the United Kingdom had finally come to an end. However, having followed the complex and controversial negotiations over patriation, I was especially uncomfortable with Quebec refusing to accept the outcome. And as it turned out, the patriation decision, which Premier Lévesque argued was a betrayal of Quebec, would blow wind into the sails of Quebec separatists for years to come.

The milestones marking the Business Council's engagement in Canada's constitutional affairs are the Meech Lake Accord in 1987, the Charlottetown Accord in 1992, the Quebec referendum of 1995, and the post-referendum initiatives culminating in 1997. Before becoming prime minister in 1984, Brian Mulroney had promised that if elected he would make every effort to bring Quebec into the Constitution "with honour and enthusiasm." The possibility of achieving this looked brighter when Robert Bourassa was re-elected premier of Quebec in 1985, defeating Parti Québécois premier Pierre-Marc Johnson. I was jubilant at Bourassa's victory; on a personal level, though, I liked Pierre-Marc Johnson, and he and I later became friends and collaborators on a number of policy fronts, including trade and the environment.

Early in 1986, the new Quebec government's minister of intergovernmental affairs, Gil Rémillard, tabled Quebec's five conditions for a return to Canada's constitutional family: recognizing Quebec as a distinct society; strengthening the province's role in immigration; giving Quebec a role in the selection of the three judges from Quebec that sit on the Supreme Court of Canada; permitting Quebec to opt out of federal spending programs in areas of exclusive provincial jurisdiction; and restoring the Quebec veto on constitutional amendments affecting Quebec's interests. By August 1986, Canada's premiers had agreed unanimously to engage with Quebec on the five proposals with a view to bringing about "Quebec's full and active participation in the Canadian federation." A year later, an agreement was reached by all eleven heads of government at a meeting at Meech Lake, north of Ottawa. It became known as the Meech Lake Accord.

With the long lead time given for each province to accept the accord, it was not surprising to me that by 1989 it had begun to unravel. Well before 1989, Pierre Trudeau, no longer in political office, had begun to sow seeds of doubt. In May 1987, he launched a vitriolic attack on the accord, referring to its authors in the most disparaging of terms: "The Right Honourable Brian Mulroney, PC, MP, with the complicity of the ten provincial premiers, has already entered into history as the author of a constitutional document which—if it is accepted by the people and their legislators—will render the Canadian state totally impotent."

While my Council colleagues and I were deeply preoccupied between 1987 and 1988 with the final stages of the Canada–United States free trade negotiations, we never lost sight of the significance of the Meech Lake Accord. After years of constitutional discord, and with a pro-federalist government now sitting in Quebec, we welcomed the consensus reached at Meech Lake in the hope that constitutional uncertainty would be banished forever. Our concern about the accord's possible unravelling was reflected in a statement I made on November 7, 1989: "Intergovernmental cooperation and a strong commitment to national unity are more essential now than ever. Canada is in the midst of adapting to a rapidly changing global economic environment and to the Canada–United States Free Trade Agreement. At a time like this, there is a clear need to strengthen the bonds of nationhood and to focus on what matters most to Canadians—a strong and prosperous national economy within a stable and effective federal state."

In the meantime, a change took place at the helm of the Business Council. David Culver retired as chief executive of Alcan and, in his place as chair, the Council elected Ted Newall, the Saskatchewan-raised chief executive of DuPont Canada. Later, in 1991, Ted became chief executive of Calgary-based Nova Corporation. He had already won his spurs in Council circles. An astute businessman, Canadian nationalist, and self-confessed policy wonk, he served the Council with distinction. As had happened with his predecessors Rowland Frazee and David Culver, Newall and I came to establish a special bond, and we were supported by a powerful executive committee: Peter Bentley of Canfor, Vancouver; Claude Castonguay of the Laurentian Group, Montreal; Jack Fraser of Federal Industries, Winnipeg; Gerald Heffernan of Co-Steel, Toronto; James Smith of Domtar, Montreal; and Allan Taylor of the Royal Bank of Canada, Toronto.

With the Meech Lake Accord in trouble, I was determined that we play a helpful role. At the same time, I realized that engagement by an independent, broad-based group might amplify our efforts, as had been the case with the Canadian Alliance for Trade and Job Opportunities during the free trade debate. I came up with an idea and reached out to two of my most trusted friends: Gordon Robertson, former clerk of the privy council and secretary to the cabinet, and Jake Warren, former deputy minister of industry, trade, and commerce, high commissioner in London, and ambassador to the United States. Their standing in Ottawa was second to none, and both were deeply concerned about the constitutional disarray facing the country. The three of us met in November 1989 and agreed to create an advocacy group to be called Canadians for a Unifying Constitution. When I proposed this name I thought it somewhat unwieldy, but Gordon and Jake liked it. We soon sent out letters of invitation to a group of prominent Canadians from across the country and set the public launch for January 22, 1990.

When we met at the Château Laurier, the atmosphere was electric. We were heartened by the enthusiastic reception of our invitation. Jean-Luc Pepin, who had been co-chair of the Pepin-Robarts Task Force on Canadian Unity, agreed to act as moderator. The media response to the launch was positive, and the fact that four former French-speaking members of the Trudeau cabinet were among our supporters caused a stir. On March 15, 1990, Gordon, Jake, and I presided at a second news conference and presented a booklet titled *Meech Lake: Setting the Record Straight*, a question-and-answer analysis of the accord. Its authors were the distinguished academics Peter Russell, professor of political science at the University of Toronto; professors of political studies Richard Simeon and Ronald Watts, at Queen's University; professor of law Jeremy Webber, at McGill University; and professor of law Wade MacLauchlan, at Dalhousie University. As Gordon Robertson attests in his excellent *Memoirs of a Very Civil Servant*, "We had five thousand copies printed, a second printing of ten thousand on 3 April, and a third of five thousand on 23 April. We were in active correspondence with the prime minister, premiers, and any others who were in a position to promote agreement on the accord."

Our final burst of advocacy took the form of full-page advertisements in Toronto's *Globe and Mail* and Montreal's *La Presse* in June. I reached out to my Council colleagues for financial support for the

ads and I crafted the content for them. We called on the prime minister and premiers to "find a way to keep our country whole" and
appealed, "You hold in trust our heritage: Tomorrow's promise lies
in your hands."

As I look back at the remarkable coalition Gordon, Jake, and I
put together with the support of close to 150 prominent Canadians,
I had no doubt the fight was a good one and the cause was noble.
Coupled with my advocacy at the Business Council, it was one of
the most exhilarating periods of my life. I was driven by the belief
that our country hung in the balance. That is what motivated me to
show up at the many debates, speeches, and media interviews. The
camaraderie was nourishing, and the passion and patriotic fervour
we shared charged our spirits.

On a parallel track, the Business Council pursued an energetic set
of pro-unity initiatives. At the beginning of January 1990, I put out
the following statement: "The vast majority of Canadians want
Canada to stay together and they want it to work. They want jobs
and economic prosperity. They want their political leaders to act
sensibly and responsibly to ensure that these ends are achieved.
We appeal to all First Ministers, therefore, to resolve the current
constitutional impasse and to spare no effort in the search for
solutions in the national interest." On April 12, Council chair Ted
Newall and I appeared before the Special Committee of the House
of Commons on the Companion Resolution to the Meech Lake
Accord. Our message to the parliamentarians was this:

> The dominance of passion over reason in the Meech Lake
> debate, and the preoccupation with politics over economics,
> has made Canadians forget just how much we have accom-
> plished together as a strong, stable and unified country.

We are one of the most prosperous societies in the world. During the last decade, Canadians working together have achieved a rate of growth second only to Japan. Our job creation record is the highest in the industrialized world. We are a great trading nation, a member of the world's most exclusive economic club, the Group of Seven. These are no small accomplishments. They reflect the contributions of our forefathers—English and French speaking, and of many other cultures—who built this country, overcoming what at times seemed like impossible odds. We are the trustees of this great country they helped to build. Are we now going to be undone—as some are predicting and some others clearly hoping—by a constitutional quarrel?

On May 18, in a memorandum addressed to first ministers, including Brian Mulroney, Robert Bourassa, John Buchanan, Grant Devine, Gary Filmon, Don Getty, Joseph Ghiz, Frank McKenna, David Peterson, Clyde Wells, and William Vander Zalm, I said the following:

On April 20, I wrote to each of you, on the Council's behalf, warning that evidence is mounting rapidly that the failure to resolve our constitutional differences is resulting in detrimental economic consequences for Canada. Since writing to you, I regret to say that these economic consequences have become increasingly apparent and are now assuming alarming proportions. The most concrete manifestations are reflected in decisions of investors in Canada, and more ominously from abroad, to downgrade Canadian investment potential. At a time when Canadian producers, consumers and workers are facing a significantly tougher economic climate, the constitutional impasse is adding a dangerous dimension to our economic problems.

During these highly charged months, my colleagues and I were also in close touch with individual premiers, and I was communicating regularly with Stanley Hartt, the prime minister's chief of staff, and Paul Tellier, the clerk of the privy council.

My hopes, and those of my Council colleagues, were shattered on June 23. The Meech Lake Accord died and with it the possibility of lasting peace in the nation's constitutional affairs. I received a much-appreciated call from Prime Minister Mulroney thanking me and the Council for our efforts. I in turn saluted his courage and leadership throughout the ordeal. I was also pleased to receive a call from Premier Bourassa expressing appreciation for the Council's constructive role in the debate. To him I offered my deep regrets and sorrow. I concluded the call with the words *"Monsieur le premier ministre, c'est pas fini."*

In his memoirs, Brian Mulroney offers a lengthy and convincing account of the reasons for the failure of the Meech Lake Accord. Eleventh-hour stumbles in Manitoba were a contributing factor. So was the reluctance of Clyde Wells of Newfoundland, who in my mind did not deal transparently with the prime minister. The anti-Meech campaign of Pierre Trudeau certainly hit home with some senior Liberals and the public more generally. But the principal villain in the piece, in my mind, was Lucien Bouchard. A long-time friend of Mulroney, Bouchard was showered with opportunities from his generous benefactor. In 1985, Mulroney appointed him ambassador to France. Before Bouchard's departure, the prime minister telephoned me and asked if I would meet with Bouchard and brief him on some economic and business matters. He was, after all, taking on a demanding job with no diplomatic or business experience. Bouchard and I had a perfectly civil conversation at my office and I was struck by his courteous manner, and during several visits I made to Paris between 1985 and 1988, he was welcoming and generous with his help.

In the national election of 1988, Mulroney was instrumental in helping Bouchard win a seat in the House of Commons. He appointed him to his cabinet as minister of the environment and political minister for Quebec. Yet despite the two men's long friendship and the political largesse from which Bouchard benefited, he abandoned Mulroney to take up the cause of Quebec independence as leader of the Bloc Québécois—one of the most stunning acts of political treachery I have observed in my lifetime. Beyond Bouchard's flirtations with separatists in Quebec while he was serving in the Mulroney cabinet, I had received reports of his behind-the-scenes criticisms of the Meech Lake Accord, which he purported to support, and of a united Canada. One such report came from my Council colleague Peter Bentley in Vancouver. After attending a meeting with Bouchard, Bentley telephoned me to say, "Bouchard is openly criticizing the prime minister and his constitutional negotiations behind closed doors. Warn the prime minister. He should be fired."

Pity the prime minister did not discover Bouchard's deceptions earlier. When he finally fired Bouchard, it was a shattering experience for Mulroney. A trusting friend, he had been repaid with a craven act of disloyalty. By coincidence, Bouchard and I were attending a conference on the environment in Bergen, Norway, days before he travelled to Paris and sent the now infamous message of support to the Parti Québécois leadership on the tenth anniversary of the 1980 Quebec referendum. The message was the final straw. Bouchard was clearly aware of its implications.

The failure of the Meech Lake Accord had precisely the impact many of us had predicted and feared. The outrage in Quebec was monumental. It did not seem to matter that eight out of ten prov-inces and the vast majority of Canada's population were in favour. The defeat played into Bouchard's plans. On June 15, 1991, the Bloc Québécois parliamentary party was officially born under his leadership as a member of Parliament who had been elected as a Progressive Conservative. In the years ahead, armed with messi-anic zeal, Bouchard would pose an existential threat to Canada. Mercifully, his efforts in the end were thwarted. As I reflect on the Meech Lake debacle, I cannot help but think of Jean Charest, who fought valiantly for the accord from beginning to end. A proud son of Quebec and great Canadian patriot, Charest would go on to lead his province as a distinguished premier from 2003 to 2012.

As if this maelstrom gripping the country was not bad enough, Canada was now facing a full-scale recession. The slowdown, which swept across much of the Western world, was caused by a combina-tion of central bank restrictive monetary policy, the 1990 oil price shock, the wind-down in Cold War defence spending, and a chill in new construction. I will turn to these challenges in a later chapter. Suffice it to say that Canada was experiencing a double whammy, one political and one economic. This prompted the Council's next major initiative on the national unity front.

On September 5, 1990, I wrote to my Council colleagues warning that "centrifugal forces in the country abound and, in the face of this, an unpopular and demoralized federal government is seemingly plagued by crisis after crisis. At peril is not only the cohesion of the nation but potentially our economic cohesion as well." I outlined a strategy for responding to the crises, beginning with a major study of post-Meech Lake constitutional options. Over the summer, I had reached out to professor Ron Watts, the highly respected director of the Institute of Intergovernmental Relations at Queen's University, and invited him and a multidisciplinary team of economists, political scientists, lawyers, and constitutional scholars to conduct the study on the Council's behalf. Gordon Robertson agreed to serve as an adviser. With the blessings of my colleagues, I assumed direction of the project. The Council's press release on September 5 announcing the initiative laid out the two-phase process: "First, the consideration of broad strategic options; and second, the elaboration of these options with the aim of producing recommendations by early January 1991. The principal findings of the study will be discussed on January 16, 1991, at a special Council symposium in Toronto on Canada's constitutional future." Our public announcement caused a stir. That business leaders would undertake an initiative of such ambition and urgency was unusual. It also signalled a pervading concern about the state of the country.

Even though I had imposed a brutally demanding timetable on Watts and his team of thirteen, they met the deadlines. The January 16 symposium took place as scheduled at the King Edward Hotel in Toronto. It was a full day of presentations, with the engagement of seventeen of Canada's leading scholars. The symposium was co-chaired by Bill Stinson, chair and chief executive officer of Canadian Pacific, and Guy Saint-Pierre, president and chief executive officer of SNC-Lavalin Group. I moderated the symposium. The event was attended by 125 Business Council members and a distinguished array of special guests from across Canada. Watts kicked off the deliberations with a paper looking at possible future institutional structures. The eight models he presented ranged from status quo federalism to Quebec's complete economic and political separation.

The overarching conclusion of the symposium was that Canada was salvageable and that the federation could be made to work. The quality and timeliness of the papers supporting our deliberations were such that I invited Watts and the Institute of Intergovernmental

Relations to co-publish them with the Business Council in a book. With the cooperation of University of Toronto Press, we were able to do this with unusual speed. Thus appeared *Options for a New Canada*, an early and influential entry into the next phase of Canada's constitutional dialogue.

Following on the heels of the symposium, the Council created a task force on the Canadian Constitution to develop a Council position to be presented at our annual meeting. Three executives agreed to co-chair the task force: Jack Fraser of Federal Industries, Guy Saint-Pierre, and Bill Stinson. Task force members were Angus Bruneau of Fortis, Arden Haynes of Imperial Oil, Ron Mannix of Manalta Coal, David Morton of Alcan, Bertin Nadeau of Provigo, and Alfred Powis of Noranda. With no time to lose, we quickly went to work on developing our position—research and writing were coupled with an intense period of consultations.

I was in close touch with Michel Bélanger, who was now co-chairing the Commission on the Political and Constitutional Future of Quebec, established by the Quebec National Assembly on the recommendation of Premier Bourassa. Interestingly, Bélanger's co-chair was Jean Campeau, a declared sovereigntist. Our task force met with Bourassa, who greeted us warmly but left no doubt in our minds about the strength of the backlash he was coping with. Not long after, I had a long telephone call with Prime Minister Mulroney and briefed him on our work on the national unity front. We also spoke of the challenging economic circumstances facing the country, a timely exchange given that Michael Wilson was presenting the federal budget the following day.

The next day, Council chair Ted Newall and I met with Ontario's premier, Bob Rae. We brought him up to date on our work and sought his advice. Newall and I then rushed back to Ottawa in time for the federal budget lockup. One person I made a point of keeping apprised of our work during this period was Paul Desmarais Sr. His significant influence in Quebec's business and political circles made him a powerful ally. In a note to Desmarais on February 21, I said, "The next year or two will be marked by uncertainty, and at times, no doubt, high drama as our political leaders struggle to resolve the constitutional impasse. In the meantime, the economic life of the country must go on, post-recession confidence levels must be rebuilt, investors must be reassured, and economic reforms must continue."

As the Council task force travelled across the country, the concerns of Western Canada were never far from my mind. In our advocacy in support of the Meech Lake Accord, we had drawn attention to the growing alienation in the Prairies and British Columbia and called for Senate reform as a means of "redressing the imbalance in the federation." To better understand the aspirations of Western Canadians, I consulted regularly with Peter Lougheed. His wisdom and advice were indispensable.

As promised, the Business Council's position on Canada's constitutional future was ready for our April 10 annual meeting. Titled "Canada and the 21st Century: Towards a More Effective Federalism and a Stronger Economy," it underscored that Canada was at a crossroads. Our paper made the case for revisiting the distribution and sharing of powers under the Constitution in order to make our federalist system work better. We argued for the reform of federal institutions, including the Senate, believing that an elected Senate with an effective array of powers and representational weighting could provide a stronger voice to Canadians living in the West, the Atlantic provinces, and the North. We concluded with a strong appeal to match constitutional reform with a bold vision for economic renewal. Our goal was to make Canada the strongest economic performer among the leading industrialized nations, the G7, by the year 2000.

In September 1991, the Mulroney government tabled a fresh consti-tutional position in a document it called "Shaping Canada's Future Together: Proposals." In his memoir, Gordon Robertson made the vital link between our Business Council initiative and this lead-up to the Charlottetown Accord.

Early in 1992, the Business Council responded publicly to the fed-eral government's proposals in a news release. "The political malaise gripping Canadians has driven many to think apocalyptically, and to denigrate our past successes and future potential. We reject this view," we wrote. "Political change is eminently manageable and our differences can be resolved. The constitutional issue should not be thought of as a crisis, but rather as an opportunity to correct some historic grievances, to strongly affirm who we are as Canadians, and to modernize the institutions of government." We went on to address our economic concerns: "The very painful effects of the cur-rent recession aside, Canada faces profound challenges in virtually every aspect of our economic life. We need to rebuild the compet-itiveness of our industries, ensure that Canadians can continue to count in the future on abundant jobs and good incomes, and tackle head-on those problems that are sapping our economic strength."

We concluded with an endorsement of the federal government's position and called for a rapid resolution, including a reinforce-ment of Canadian values and characteristics, primarily through the means of a "Canada clause" in the Constitution; a recognition of Quebec as a distinct society within the Canadian Charter of Rights and Freedoms; a recognition of the right to self-government of Aboriginal peoples of Canada subject to the Canadian Charter of Rights and Freedoms; the reconstitution of the Senate of Canada into an elected body with enhanced representation from parts of

Canada other than Ontario or Quebec, and in particular from the West; a more effective federal system with an appropriate balance of power and influence between the central government and the governments of the provinces, with the overall objective of establishing more efficient and accountable government for Canadians; and a strengthened economic union in Canada with the constitutionally guaranteed freedom of the flow of labour, capital, goods, and services, and appropriate mechanisms for vastly improved intergovernmental cooperation and macroeconomic management.

Two weeks later, Bill Stinson, Bertin Nadeau, and I presented our views to the Special Joint Committee of the Senate and the House of Commons on a Renewed Canada, co-chaired by Gérald Beaudoin and Dorothy Dobbie. The prime minister was pleased with our vigorous public defence of the accord. At the PMO, there was an important changing of the guard. Hugh Segal was appointed chief of staff, a move that I believed would serve the prime minister well. Smart and well connected in the Progressive Conservative Party, Segal clearly had Mulroney's confidence.

With the Council's position now strongly embraced by the membership and shared with the Canadian public and key constituencies, we marched forward toward the national referendum on the Charlottetown Accord, scheduled for October 26, 1992. Across the country, an elaborate array of public consultations were taking place at five conferences sponsored by the federal government. We hoped Canadians would rise to the occasion, set political and regional differences aside, and vote to affirm the accord. In the months leading up to the referendum, I gave speech after speech, including one to the Chambre de commerce de Montréal on March 31, which I titled "Suicide or Renaissance: Canada at the Crossroads." The audience applauded most strongly when I made the economic case for why Canada needed to achieve peace on the political front. It was clear that economic anxieties in the country were running deep and that people were tired of the constitutional squabbling.

I also was in regular touch with the first ministers, sending them notes of encouragement on May 25 and July 20. While the Council was unflinching in its support of the accord, as the referendum approached I made a major effort to seek a strengthening of the economic union provisions in the accord. On August 26, I wrote to the prime minister,

> While we support the constitutional package as a whole, it will not surprise you to hear of our deep disappointment with the refusal of first ministers to amend section 121 to include a constitutional guarantee for the free movement of people, services and capital as well as goods. This course of action, to our surprise, was taken despite the strong and long-standing appeals of virtually all members of the business community, a large number of informed Canadians, and the vast majority of academics on the subject. I appreciate that you and several Premiers did argue strongly for sensible changes and that your views did not prevail. The resulting setback will not sit well with the business community nor will this failure to seize a historic opportunity to serve Canada's economic interests.

As he had done with the Meech Lake Accord, Pierre Trudeau intervened yet again in strong opposition to what the first ministers were proposing. At a dinner in October at the Maison du Egg Roll in Montreal, Trudeau attacked the "doddering fools meeting in Charlottetown." His dissection of the accord received nationwide attention. Gordon Robertson was outraged and challenged Trudeau publicly in a letter that appeared in the *Globe and Mail*. "I accused the former prime minister of using his great intellectual talents, not to help the people of Canada to understand the provisions of the Charlottetown Accord, but to mislead them, and set out in detail where his alleged facts were wrong," he later stated.

I too was greatly disturbed by Trudeau's intervention and added my criticism in the form of an opinion piece in the Montreal *Gazette* on October 13, 1992, beginning on a personal note:

> Pierre Trudeau's discourses at la Maison du Egg Roll reminded me of how much has changed in the twenty years since I left the former prime minister's staff. The Right Honourable gentleman who still commands my respect spoke of the Charlottetown Accord from a position seemingly frozen in time. . . . Mr. Trudeau suggests that the Accord is little more than a hodge-podge of petty demands hurriedly cobbled together by political opportunists. Such is not the case. The Accord represents the distillation of a massive exercise in public consultation and intergovernmental negotiation. It incorporates a much broader and more inclusive vision of Canada than any constitutional initiative to date. It responds with generosity to the aspirations of our first peoples, to the French-speaking collectivity in Quebec, and to the desires of citizens across the regions of the country for a stronger voice in our federal institutions.

At the Business Council's autumn members' meeting in Toronto, we took stock of the situation. The economic threat of continued political disunity was a dominant concern. The Royal Bank of Canada's chief executive, Allan Taylor, expressed his nervousness in a presentation he made with the bank's economist Ed Neufeld. I much admired Taylor, who played such a constructive role on the Council's executive committee. Other presentations struck the same note. But at that point we were still hoping that the referendum would deliver a majority vote for the "Yes" option. The evening before, we had hosted Joe Clark, the minister responsible for constitutional affairs, who delivered a passionate defence of the accord. We in turn saluted my old friend warmly. As a key member of the Mulroney cabinet who had served with distinction as secretary of state for external affairs, the former prime minister had worked hard to help develop a national consensus. In expressing our gratitude, I presented him with a caricature print by "Spy" of Sir Wilfrid Laurier, his distinguished predecessor, who also had fought hard for national unity. The print came from my personal collection. I was more than pleased to give it to Clark with a smile, reminding the Tory minister of Laurier's "impeccable Liberal credentials."

When it came in on October 26, the referendum result was decisive. Of the ten provinces, only the three least populous gave a clear "Yes" majority: New Brunswick, Newfoundland, and Prince Edward Island. Ontario opted for "Yes" by a razor-thin margin. The Northwest Territories also voted "Yes." The remainder of the country voted "No," Quebec voting against the accord by a significant majority. The overall result was 54.4 per cent "No" and 44.6 per cent "Yes."

Professor Watts summed up the reasons for the failure of the Charlottetown Accord, and I agree fully with his assessment. "In the hurly-burly of the referendum debate," he wrote, "the larger vision embodied in the Charlottetown Consensus Report was lost in the media and partisan preoccupations with specific provisions and with concerns about the extent to which each particular group had or had not achieved all its own specific aims. . . . In the end, the political leaders found that in trying to accommodate every group, they had drafted a document that, because it required so many compromises, made more enemies than friends."

The outcome, of course, was a huge disappointment to me and my Business Council colleagues. I offered my colleagues a blunt reason for the failure: the whole accord was too damn big and ambitious and, as a result, it offered too many targets.

I spent hours on the telephone that night before collapsing into bed at two in the morning. I spoke with, among others, Gordon Robertson and Council chair Ted Newall. I told them that the country was now certain to face an emboldened threat from Quebec separatists and that the national unity crisis was far from over. I also said to Newall that I could not have been more proud of the contributions of our fellow business colleagues. While our private-sector leadership had been decisive in the great free trade debates of previous years—a subject of huge economic consequence for Canada— our deep engagement in the fight for national unity spoke to an even higher purpose: patriotism and love of country that was plain for all to see.

On November 18, I received a touching note from Joe Clark. "A great debt is owed to you personally for the way the business community was mobilized in this campaign," he wrote. "A number of members of the BCNI were disposed naturally to be helpful, but there is no doubt that you drove them to extra efforts, and I particularly appreciate that."

In the face of both the Meech Lake and Charlottetown failures, the dire prophecies of Gordon Robertson and so many of us were realized. Quebec separatists made their bid for independence in the near-death referendum of 1995. But in the meantime, post-Charlottetown, the work of the Business Council in the fight for national unity was not over. The most significant political event that followed the Charlottetown referendum was the 1993 election of a new federal government under the leadership of Jean Chrétien.

His coming to office as a Quebecer and committed patriot was enormously challenging in the wake of the constitutional failures of the late 1980s and early 1990s. Chrétien was already a veteran of the unity battles surrounding the sovereignty-association referendum in Quebec in 1980 and the patriation of the Constitution in 1982. Upon his election, I pledged the cooperation of the Council to work with him and his government on both the unity and economic priorities facing the country.

In April 1995, there also was an important transition in the leadership of the Business Council. Ted Newall retired as chair, and Guy Saint-Pierre was elected his successor. Saint-Pierre and I quickly developed a close rapport. He was of quiet demeanour, intelligent, and considerate. An engineer by profession, he also served in Canada's armed forces as an officer in the Corps of Royal Canadian Engineers. As president and chief executive officer of SNC-Lavalin Group, he commanded a place of influence within the Quebec corporate establishment. In addition, he had valuable political experience, having served as minister of education and minister of industry and trade in the Quebec Liberal government of Robert Bourassa. The first francophone to assume the post of Council chair, he benefited us with invaluable insights and relationships in Quebec throughout the Council's engagement on the constitutional front.

The next step in the Council's constitutional odyssey came the day following the close win by the federalist camp in the 1995 Quebec referendum. Jean Chrétien's government lay traumatized by the uncomfortably close call. Federalist forces within Quebec were exhausted and demoralized. Attitudes across Canada toward Quebec were hardening. Political leaders were running for cover. And sovereigntist leaders in Quebec were promising certain victory next time. At a meeting with my colleagues in Toronto in October, we passed a unanimous resolution to continue our work in the search for a resolution of Canada's unity problems.

I immediately set out to assemble a team of knowledgeable Canadians from across the country to assess the situation and to decide where to go from here. Following six weeks of intensive study and consultations, I tabled a report with the Council's policy committee. Among my recommendations, I urged the federal government and the nine pro-Confederation premiers, in alliance with federalist Quebecers, to seize the agenda. They must quickly push forward political reforms that would respond to Quebec's concerns and more broadly set in motion changes that would be beneficial to the country as a whole. My colleagues embraced this strategy and we launched the Confederation 2000 initiative, aimed at helping to build a new consensus for political change in Canada. Circumstances were not on our side, however, for early in the new year, Lucien Bouchard would be sworn in as premier of Quebec, succeeding his comrade-in-arms Jacques Parizeau.

At this point, an interesting convergence of interests brought Stéphane Dion and me together. Dion had caught my eye among the experts I had assembled to help come to terms with Canada's constitutional issues. A bright and passionate professor teaching at the University of Montreal, he had clear ideas and asserted them readily. At a meeting of advisers at the Château Laurier in Ottawa in January, Dion took his leave early, saying he had an important appointment. It turned out that the appointment was with Chrétien, who urged him that same day to join the cabinet and stand for Parliament. Years later, Dion would tell the story that at my meeting he had been so concerned with the depressing deliberations, he was convinced he should accept the prime minister's offer to serve the country rather than remain an academic in Montreal. "Were it not for Tom," he told his listeners with a touch of humour,

"I would not be in politics today." Dion was appointed to the cabinet in January and went on to distinguish himself as Chrétien's minister of intergovernmental affairs and an effective critic of Lucien Bouchard's Parti Québécois government.

The Council's Confederation 2000 conferences took place in March and May 1996, and assembled over a hundred opinion leaders from across Canada. I invited three highly respected co-chairs for the conferences: lawyer Yves Fortier of Montreal, Peter Lougheed of Calgary, and economist Judith Maxwell of Ottawa. In addition to his distinguished career as a lawyer, Fortier, whom I had known since the 1960s, had served as Canada's ambassador to the United Nations. I had always valued his counsel on matters pertaining to Quebec. Lougheed, a long-standing and trusted friend, could always be counted on to offer a thoughtful perspective on the unity question. And Maxwell brought solid economics credentials to the exercise. The conferences were an assembly of the most talented Canadians of their time. The conference report, "Today and Tomorrow: An Agenda for Action," received wide acclaim. Part of the reason for this was the practicality of its recommendations. It eschewed another attempt at a grand bargain in favour of incremental change; we thought it unwise to resort to constitutional amendments in the near term. Our report produced a consensus on the rebalancing of federal-provincial responsibilities, federal spending power, the social and economic union, and the recognition of Quebec within Canada.

By early 1997, I had become convinced that any next step in the pursuit of a new consensus for political change in Canada would have to directly involve Canada's nine pro-Confederation premiers. I came up with the idea of a "premiers-led initiative." Following our 1997 conferences, small teams of Council colleagues joined me in calls on individual premiers. Our message was straightforward:

Ottawa alone could not solve the unity problem, but the nine premiers acting in concert could provide a powerful catalyst for change. We insisted that the window of opportunity for their collective action was narrowing, given Bouchard's agenda, and that the focus of their efforts should not include constitutional steps, as the climate for these had soured.

The June 1997 federal election returned the Liberal government of Jean Chrétien with a reduced majority, and the Bloc Québécois, led by Gilles Duceppe, was supplanted as the Official Opposition by Preston Manning's Reform Party. I had known Preston for many years, going back to the 1970s, and we had remained in touch. His father, the legendary former Social Credit premier of Alberta, Ernest Manning, had offered helpful advice when I was working on parliamentary reform issues in 1979. The elder Manning was sitting in the Senate at the time.

Soon after the election, recently elected Council chair Al Flood and I dispatched a letter to the newly re-elected prime minister, opening the final chapter in the Business Council's decade-long engagement in shaping Canada's constitutional future. Flood, who was serving as CEO of CIBC, engaged with enthusiasm. We wrote that we supported the intent of the legislation passed by Parliament to recognize Quebec's unique place within Canada. We approved of federal efforts to improve the structure of the federation through a rebalancing of powers and responsibilities. And we endorsed the government's attempt to clarify the legal status of Quebec separation through its reference to the Supreme Court of Canada. But we went on to say that Ottawa alone could not solve the problem, and we appealed to the prime minister that he give his "heartfelt support to any worthwhile initiative that may emerge from other levels of government."

Following up on calls on individual premiers in July, the executive committee of the Business Council addressed a memorandum to the premiers and territorial leaders urging them collectively "to launch a series of initiatives aimed at bolstering the federation" and proposing that they adopt a common declaration as a means of moving forward. As a matter of courtesy, I sent a copy of the memorandum to Lucien Bouchard. We knew that some of the recipients expected that the Council would offer a framework for moving forward and bravely decided to try our hand at shaping one based on the following assumptions: first, that the proposals should not be overly ambitious; second, that they should steer clear of any immediate constitutional initiatives; and third, that they should seek to bridge the disparate and in some cases deeply conflicting views of the key pro-federalist actors in the country.

Our memorandum followed an interesting path to its final draft. I sat down at the beginning of July and drafted a framework in the form of a declaration that the premiers and territorial leaders might adopt. The declaration listed three principal headings: "Equality within Canada," "Quebec within Canada," and "Making Canada Work Better." In the drafting stage, I consulted with members of the Business Council's executive committee, who were solidly on board. I also consulted with Stéphane Dion. He and I spoke on the telephone a number of times, and I travelled to his cottage to walk him through the final text. Given the sensitive language surrounding the recommendations concerning Quebec and our decision to characterize Quebec's society as "unique," in place of the more controversial word "distinct," I also took some soundings in Montreal. Former Quebec premier Daniel Johnson was helpful, as was journalist turned politician Claude Ryan. To my surprise, we were not discouraged from proceeding with the word "unique."

Among the premiers, the most important player in this initiative was Frank McKenna of New Brunswick. He was the incoming chair of the Council of Premiers and was to host his counterparts in Saint Andrews in the coming weeks. I had long been a big fan of McKenna, who had been serving successfully as premier for a decade. Young, smart, and articulate, he was always supportive of the Council's work, be it on economic and trade issues or the national unity question. I had alerted McKenna to our premiers-led initiative, and he welcomed it.

Our executive committee addressed its July 15 memorandum to him, to share with his colleagues. The memorandum consisted of the declaration for adoption by the premiers and territorial leaders, and a covering note signed by me and chair Al Flood, together with Guy Saint-Pierre, Peter Bentley, Ted Newall, Jean Monty, and David O'Brien. Monty and O'Brien were the two most recent additions to the Council's executive committee; Monty had recently been named chair and chief executive officer of BCE, and O'Brien had served as president and chief executive officer of Canadian Pacific Railways since 1995.

Early Friday morning, August 1, I awoke to a welcome lead editorial in the *Globe and Mail*. Titled "Reopening the Unity File," it said, "Someone had to break the eerie silence that followed federalism's razor-thin victory in the 1995 Quebec referendum. The Business Council on National Issues has finally done so, producing a document that is sober, thoughtful and intelligent. It does not offer a solution to every tension rippling through the federation, but it does bring courage and creativity to bear in an area where both have been in short supply of late."

Our initiative was welcomed at the Saint Andrews meeting. It formed the basis of what became the "Calgary Declaration" at a follow-up meeting of premiers in Calgary on September 14, 1997, signed by all Canadian premiers and territorial leaders, with the exception of Premier Bouchard. (In an interesting side note, Gordon Robertson wrote that the Calgary Declaration "disproved the oft-made allegation of Premier Bouchard that English-speaking Canada was incapable of forging a consensus on the future of Canada and Quebec's role in the federation.") The declaration was also positively received by the Canadian public. According to an Angus Reid opinion poll conducted in November 1997, 62 per cent of Canadians supported the declaration's principles. And in Quebec, according to Radio-Canada, 80 per cent of residents considered the declaration "acceptable." In separate conversations I had following the signing with Frank McKenna and Saskatchewan's Roy Romanow, both told me of their strong appreciation of the Council's work; Premier Romanow believed that the Calgary Declaration would be "a candle in the window to Quebec"—a poignant image, I thought. With the signing of the Calgary Declaration by the first ministers, the Council's decade-long constitutional odyssey had come to an end. I believe we did our part to help save a country that in our view was too good to lose.

9

CHAMPIONING GLOBAL ECONOMIC DIPLOMACY

Among the most enriching of my life experiences has been the opportunity to travel the world as a business spokesman and meet people of many different nationalities. I have had the privilege of addressing audiences in over one hundred cities in some forty countries. Economic diplomacy comes quite naturally to me, in part because I enjoy it so much. When I took on the post of president of the Business Council, one of my goals was to see Canadian business leaders greatly expand their outreach to counterparts in other regions of the world. In the early 1980s, the Council's geographic focus outside Canada was on the United States, key countries in Europe, and Japan. This began to change as globalization accelerated in the late 1980s. Barriers between countries began to fall rapidly, spurred on by the expanded flow of goods, services, capital, and technology and the establishment of global supply chains. Economic transformation was matched by political change on a scale that was breathtaking. What better examples than the collapse of the Soviet Union, the reunification of the two Germanys, and China's historic reopening? In this new world, economic diplomacy took on a special significance.

I was introduced early on to the importance of diplomacy when I served in the Prime Minister's Office in the late 1960s. Consulting with Canada's ambassadors and their staffs was part of my job when preparing briefing notes and speeches for Trudeau. Invitations from foreign ambassadors to receptions and dinners in Ottawa were plentiful. These were opportunities for establishing networks and picking up intelligence that from time to time proved useful. To Susan and me, they also offered a window on the politics, economics, and culture of foreign countries. While, by the nature of their work, diplomats come and go, a good number became long-standing friends.

It was in those early years, and later when I took up my Business Council duties in 1981, that I was introduced to some of Canada's legendary diplomats. Among them were Lester Pearson, Arnold Smith, Jules Léger, Charles Ritchie, Marcel Cadieux, Edgar Ritchie, and Jake Warren. Warren, who served as Canada's ambassador to the United States and high commissioner to London, became a close friend and was particularly helpful to me in navigating the diplomatic waters in Ottawa and our embassies abroad. In addition to retired ambassadors, I came to know many who were engaged in Canada's foreign service, and they provided invaluable assistance when I was travelling to various parts of the world. Key among them were members of the Trade Commissioner Service, which was first established in 1894 and today encompasses a network of a thousand trade professionals working in Canadian embassies, high commissions, and consulates located in 161 cities around the world. Nurturing relationships with ambassadors and trade officials at home and abroad became a touchstone of my work in the international business domain. While some of my business colleagues were skeptical of the value of diplomatic connections, I never was. Time and time again, our political and trade diplomats helped advance the Business Council's international agenda in significant ways.

While my business engagement in Europe was regular and intense over some four decades, it is not my focus in this chapter. That said, I led Business Council missions to most of the countries that today make up the European Union, and I was a frequent speaker on platforms in Britain, Germany, France, Italy, Spain, Switzerland, and the Netherlands. I was comfortable in my dealings in European capitals in part because I felt a close kinship with Western Europeans. This is not so surprising given that European history, values, culture, and laws were so rooted in my educational formation.

With my efforts to build closer bilateral relations between Canada and other countries, the dream of a deeper Canada-Europe economic alliance was never far from my mind. I vividly recall deep discussions on this as early as 1980 with my old friend, Ambassador to the EU, Richard Tait. In due course, I became an enthusiastic advocate of the Comprehensive Economic and Trade Agreement (CETA), an ambitious transatlantic free trade agreement between Canada and the European Union, which was signed in October 2016. Of strategic importance, CETA has yet to meet its full promise but offers boundless opportunities for Canada-European cooperation.

JAPAN

I first set foot in Japan in the early 1980s at the invitation of the Japan External Trade Organization. Unusually, my participation required a commitment of more than two full weeks. It consisted of briefings from senior government officials, meetings with business leaders and think tanks, and visits to key cities. Susan accepted an invitation to join me on the trip, and our request that visits to cultural sites, museums, and famous gardens be added to our itinerary was happily accepted by our hosts. Canada's ambassador in Japan at the time, Barry Steers, and his wife, Martha, were most welcoming. Steers remained an invaluable resource to me on Japanese affairs for the remainder of the decade.

The visit launched my business association and love affair with Japan and set the stage for many return visits. In David Culver, president and chief executive of Alcan, I had an excellent mentor. Culver, who had visited Japan for the first time in 1957, was well experienced in navigating the complexities of Japanese society and had learned how to nurture business relationships there. In 1976, Culver had been appointed by minister of industry, trade, and commerce, Jean Chrétien, to serve as the Canadian co-chair of the Canada-Japan Business Committee, the principal vehicle for business cooperation between the two countries. Culver involved me in the committee, which complemented my work at the Business Council on Canada-Japan relations. This proved to be especially synergistic during his tenure as Business Council chair.

Following Culver's retirement as co-chair of the Canada-Japan Business Committee in 1989, the Business Council became the principal Canadian channel of senior-level bilateral engagement with the Japanese. Our counterpart was Japan's pre-eminent business association, the Keidanren. Our goal was to deepen Canada's ties with what was then the second largest economy in the world, the dominant economic power in Asia, and a vibrant democracy. Our relationship with the Keidanren was cordial and productive, but despite vigorous efforts in the 1980s and 1990s, we could not persuade our Japanese counterparts or successive Japanese governments to consider developing a much closer relationship with Canada based on free trade principles. They were unflinching in their commitment to multilateralism.

In October 1990, and again in May 1991, Culver and I led Business Council missions to Japan. At the 1991 meeting in Osaka, in the company of an impressive array of Japanese business leaders, we tabled a well-researched paper titled "Beckoning Opportunities: Towards a Stronger Canada-Japan Relationship." It was our most ambitious pitch to date. Notably, Toyota chair Shoichiro Toyoda and Sony co-founder and chair Akio Morita appeared interested in what we had to say. Culver and I were especially appreciative of the charismatic Morita's supportive intervention. Thanks to Culver, I had met Morita on a number of occasions, and to this day treasure an advanced version of the Sony Walkman he gave me as a gift during one of my visits to his office.

We never gave up on the Japanese and continued with our advocacy. We were encouraged by the heads of the major trading companies, in particular Mitsui and Mitsubishi, and by Masaya Miyoshi, the president and director general of the Keidanren. The highly respected and astute Miyoshi helped me navigate my business involvement in Japan while teaching me how to partake of the delicacy fugu, the blowfish which, if improperly prepared, is lethal to diners. He and I survived a number of encounters with fugu with the aid of substantial helpings of sake.

There was in due course a change of attitude on the part of the Japanese. Our persistence paid off in helping tilt their interest in Canada's direction once they were ready to question their commitment to multilateralism. In 2004, in what I called a "make or break effort," we travelled again to Tokyo to meet with senior government officials and business leaders. Accompanying me were the indefatigable David Culver, Robert Ritchie, chief executive of Canadian Pacific Railway, and Dominic D'Alessandro, chief executive of Manulife Financial. D'Alessandro's presence was especially helpful. He had joined the Council's executive committee, and Manulife

Financial was one of Canada's most significant players in Asia and our country's largest investor in Japan. The Keidanren representatives, led by Hiroyuki Yoshino, were engaged and receptive.

Shortly after our return to Canada, D'Alessandro and I wrote to Prime Minister Paul Martin and reported that the time was ripe for a fresh initiative. Martin got back to me with word that he was ready to move the relationship to a new level. During Martin's visit to Asia in mid-January 2005, he and Japanese prime minister Junichiro Koizumi signed an agreement to establish the Japan-Canada Economic Framework. Culver and I followed up with a private meeting with Prime Minister Koizumi in Ottawa in June 2006. The basis for our discussions was a memorandum we tabled addressed to the Japanese leader. It called for a comprehensive bilateral agreement that "would go beyond the elimination of tariff and non-tariff barriers to address rules of origin, customs procedures, dispute-settlement issues, standards issues, labour mobility restraints, domestic infrastructure issues, currency issues, transparency and mutual recognition of regulations, and liberalization in services." While progress in the ensuing years was slow, the efforts of the Business Council helped lay the groundwork for a solid Canada-Japan relationship that today flourishes within the embrace of the Comprehensive and Progressive Agreement for Trans-Pacific Partnership.

Of my many missions and memorable occasions in Japan, one in particular stands out: the opening of the new Canadian embassy chancery in 1991. The chancery, on Aoyama Avenue, overlooks the Akasaka Palace gardens, and the residence itself is set in one of the most splendid private gardens in Tokyo. The new building, designed by Canadian architect Raymond Moriyama, was a hit in Tokyo, and a gala was organized to celebrate the opening. In attendance were several members of the imperial family, prime ministers Toshiki Kaifu and Brian Mulroney, three former Japanese prime ministers, business leaders from both countries, and a who's who of Japanese society. Our host was Ambassador James "Si" Taylor and his wife, Mary. A small Business Council delegation travelled to Tokyo for the occasion. One of the evening's highlights was a musical performance by Canadian pianist Jon Kimura Parker on a grand piano gifted to the embassy by Alcan, thanks to Culver. Culver, who was remarkably agile at the keyboard, brought a musical close to a stellar evening celebrating Canada-Japan friendship.

The following day was sprinkled with various meetings, including a luncheon with Mulroney preceded by a 4:30 a.m. private visit to the famous Tokyo Tsukiji fish market, the largest in the world and a favourite haunt of mine when visiting the Japanese capital. That evening, Culver and I, along with Raymond Moriyama, were guests of Prime Minister Kaifu at his official residence, a building heavily influenced in design by Frank Lloyd Wright. The dinner in honour of Mulroney was an intimate affair and capped two days of productive exchanges.

My affection for Japan remains undiminished. While its economic primacy in Asia has been transcended by China, it remains one of the world's most powerful countries and an attractive partner for Canada.

My Japanese experience was not all about business, trade, investment, and public policy. To me, Japan represents so much more, historically, culturally, and spiritually. I continue to be fascinated with the dimensions of Japanese society—their approach to architecture, design of living, the calm and silence of their sacred spaces, the measured beauty and cadence of their gardens, their hugely influential art works, and even their tea ceremonies. A visit to our home in Rockcliffe Park in Ottawa reveals something of the impact of Japanese design on how we live. Our garden in particular has Japanese elements: a cascading stream and a pond bordered by carefully positioned handsome stones; a dry riverbed of stones curves beneath our cantilevered house.

Of various cultural experiences in Japan, my stay in May 1994 with Susan at Kōya-san, the mountaintop seat of the Shingon sect of Japanese Buddhism, ranks among the highest. Our friends Donald Campbell and his wife, Catherine Bergman, arranged our accommodation at one of the ancient temples. Campbell was Canadian ambassador to Japan at the time, and a very able representative. At Kōya-san, Susan and I were lost in the beauty and silence of that sacred place. Our walk through the ancient forested cemetery of Okunoin was a moving experience. The hospitality of the monks, offered with kindness and humility, was touching; partaking in their early-morning religious observances and listening to their chants transported us to another world.

MEXICO AND NAFTA

The saga by which Mexico came to join the Canada–United States Free Trade Agreement is one in which the Business Council and I were intimately involved. It began with a telephone call in the summer of 1989. On the line was one of Mexico's most influential business leaders, Claudio X. González. "We have never met," he began, "but I'm interested in how Canada managed to negotiate a highly successful free trade agreement with the United States. Would you be open to meeting me and some of my colleagues sometime soon?" "Of course," I replied, and we settled on a date in Toronto.

My colleagues and I were not prepared for the scene that greeted us at our first dinner meeting. Travelling with González were some twenty of Mexico's top entrepreneurs and industrialists, all members of what was then called the Consejo Mexicano de Hombres de

Negocios, a powerful business group now known as the Consejo Mexicano de Negocios. The articulate Gonzáles, then chair and chief executive officer of Kimberly-Clark in Mexico, spoke for the group. He asked us to lay out the strategy we had used to win Canada's free trade agreement with the Americans, which had been signed into law only a few months earlier.

I asked him the obvious question: "What is it that you have in mind, Claudio?" He responded, "We have in our new president, Carlos Salinas, a Harvard-trained Ph.D. who wants to open up our country. He wants Mexico to join the Canada–United States Free Trade Agreement."

David Culver then asked, "You mean sometime in the next decade?" González replied, "No, in the next year or two."

We were stunned. Mexico was a developing country with a largely closed economy. It had a tortured relationship with the United States. It simply did not seem feasible, politically or economically.

As surprising as this was, I did, however, have some inkling of Mexican thinking on the subject of closer continental cooperation. Some months earlier, Emilio Carrillo Gamboa, Mexico's ambassador to Canada, whom I knew fairly well, had asked me over lunch what I thought of Mexico looking northward to new economic arrangements. I said it made sense but would take time. But now, as we bid farewell to our Mexican visitors in Toronto, an enthusiastic González told us, "Stay tuned. We will be inviting you to Mexico soon to discuss how we can work together to make this happen."

The invitation came soon enough. In the middle of a cold March in 1990, a small delegation of my Business Council colleagues joined Culver and me in sunny Cancún. Over the next couple of days, we learned that Mexico indeed was moving full speed ahead. We were greeted by our Mexican business hosts and also by two senior government ministers: Pedro Aspe, secretary of finance, and

Jaime Serra Puche, secretary of commerce and industry. Aspe and Serra, both of whom I would work with closely in the years to come, advised us that President Salinas had spoken with President George H.W. Bush and that Bush had given Mexico the green light. Brian Mulroney said he first heard of the idea from Derek Burney in February 1990, when Burney had been notified by James Baker, the U.S. secretary of state. This was well after our Toronto encounter with the Mexicans the summer before. Mulroney's initial reaction, not surprisingly, was not favourable. He did not want Canada to become a spoke of an American-centred hub. But he eventually came on side: on February 5, 1991, he joined presidents Bush and Salinas in declaring their intention to negotiate a North American Free Trade Agreement (NAFTA).

The lead-up to the declaration required careful scrutiny by the Mulroney government and by the Canadian business community. My mind was made up; I had already spent months in the autumn of 1989 and winter of 1990 mulling over the pros and cons of Canadian involvement. Given that the Americans and the Mexicans were intent on signing a bilateral free trade agreement with or without Canadian participation, I believed it would be much better to be in than out. But I needed to persuade my Business Council colleagues.

I met with the Council's policy committee in Toronto and, in addition to pushing the "better in than out" argument, I outlined why I believed that the three nations could form the most powerful and competitive economic bloc in the world. I did not gloss over the risk of some trade and investment diverting from Canada to Mexico. My analysis was based in part on excellent research by Business Council staff led by our vice-president, Jock Finlayson. Members of the policy committee listened carefully. Given that the committee was made up of twenty-eight of the country's business leaders, the automotive, telecom, banking, energy, mining, transportation, engineering, consumer goods, and aerospace sectors were well represented in the discussions. We decided in principle to support the initiative and to follow up with additional company-by-company due diligence by the chief executives. Our meeting was well served by the presence of Don Campbell, then the deputy minister of international trade. Campbell was a veteran of the Canada–United States free trade negotiations. He offered us a timely perspective on the Mulroney government's intentions, and we in turn briefed him on our work. He was enormously helpful to us over the next two years on the NAFTA file until being called away in 1993 to serve as Canada's ambassador to Japan.

In April 1991, the Business Council hosted President Salinas at a dinner in Toronto. I was seated next to him. He told me he was confident that the NAFTA negotiation would proceed quickly and relatively easily. "George Bush and I have shaken hands, and what is to stop us now?" he said. I warned him about the challenges that were certain to come from Congress. I also suggested to him that NAFTA would change the face of Mexico, ushering in North American norms where none before existed. He was polite but somewhat skeptical. Years later, as his presidency was coming to an end, he said to me, "How right you were when we talked in Toronto."

Two months later, Canada's international trade minister, Michael Wilson, U.S. trade representative Carla Hills, and the Mexican trade minister, Jaime Serra, launched the NAFTA negotiations in Toronto. From the outset, Canada was very supportive of the Mexicans, and the Business Council especially so. I was in frequent communication with Wilson, Hills, and Serra, and in the early days I offered extensive advice to Mexico's chief negotiator, Herminio Blanco. At the same time, I began working with Canada's chief negotiator, John Weekes, a seasoned professional who could not have been more helpful throughout the negotiations.

The NAFTA debate sharply divided Americans, many of whom believed independent presidential candidate Ross Perot when he warned that American jobs would be "sucked away to Mexico." Bill Clinton succeeded Bush as president in January 1993, and his skill in crafting a bipartisan consensus in favour of NAFTA was impressive. There was heated debate in Canada as well, with a replay of the positions taken in the lead-up to the Canada–United States Free Trade Agreement. Again, I gave a lot of speeches in Canada and the United States, with some forays into Mexico. The BCNI case for NAFTA was based on three core principles: it opened the Mexican market to Canadian goods, services, and investment on an equal basis with the United States; it preserved and even enhanced the gains made under the Canada–United States Free Trade Agreement; and it provided a bridge to forge stronger economic ties with fast-growing Latin American markets. I also argued that the NAFTA bloc would constitute a formidable economic and competitive alliance on the global stage.

The North American Free Trade Agreement, ratified in the three partner countries, was formally proclaimed on January 1, 1994. President Clinton, having built on the good work of George H.W. Bush, signed the hard-won agreement in the United States. Today, the NAFTA countries have a population of nearly 500 million and, on the threshold of the COVID-19 pandemic, had a combined GDP of $25 trillion. Trade growth among the countries has exceeded the optimistic expectations of the agreement's architects, even though the impact on overall growth in Mexico has been disappointing. (I will have more to say later on the modified NAFTA that came into force on July 1, 2020, on the insistence of the Trump administration.)

My close association with Mexico and its political and business leaders carries on to this day. Beyond the relationship I established with Carlos Salinas, I have known and worked closely with his successors Ernesto Zedillo, Vicente Fox, and Felipe Calderón. It was a privilege to attend the inaugurations of all three. To our delight, President Fox invited Susan and me to travel with him as part of his personal entourage to several Mexican cities following his inauguration. I was also honoured to be invited to address the Senate of Mexico. Many Mexican ambassadors to Canada have provided invaluable connections to Mexico and have offered me friendship and support along the way. The cerebral President Zedillo, whom I especially admired, awarded me the Águila Azteca, the Order of the Aztec Eagle, which is Mexico's highest honour awarded to foreigners.

As for my relationships with Mexican business colleagues, they are close and enduring. They have taught me a great deal about Mexico, its history, its economy, its politics, its culture, and its psyche—both the good and the not so good. The gracious hospitality with which I have been received by many of them is second to none. Six of these business colleagues stand out: Claudio X. González , Antonio Madero, Juan Gallardo Thurlow, Pedro Aspe, Jaime Zabludovsky, and Andrés Rozental. Later on, Aspe, Rozental, Zabludovsky and I developed close relationships spanning two decades in our leadership roles at the trilateral North American Forum.

MIKHAIL GORBACHEV

During my time at the Business Council, my colleagues and I hosted kings, presidents, prime ministers, and chancellors and, at various international meetings, other world leaders. Among these encounters, a meeting with the then recently retired president of the Soviet Union, Mikhail Gorbachev, was especially revealing. The meeting took place in an Ottawa hotel on March 30, 1993, during an eight-day visit Gorbachev made to various Canadian cities. With me at the meeting were colleagues Ted Newall of Nova Corporation,

Ron Mannix of Manalta Coal, Purdy Crawford of Imasco, Jack Lawrence of Burns Fry, and David Culver. We met before Gorbachev was to attend a luncheon hosted by Prime Minister Mulroney. Travelling with Gorbachev were his translator and several members of his private foundation.

I considered, and still consider, Gorbachev one of the most extraordinary figures of the twentieth century. On his watch, the mighty Soviet Union had been dismantled, the Iron Curtain came crashing down, Eastern European countries under the Soviet yoke were liberated, and the two Germanys were united. Remarkably, this titanic shift took place with little violence. Along with millions throughout the world who had grown up with the menacing Soviet Union under Stalin, Khrushchev, and Brezhnev, I watched transfixed as the events of 1990 and 1991 unfolded. It was hard to believe that the collapse could happen so quickly and without widespread violence or civil war. It was equally hard to believe that Gorbachev survived the coup against him in the summer of 1991 while he and his family were vacationing in Crimea. Unable to contain a disintegrating and chaotic situation during which Boris Yeltsin emerged as a leading figure, Gorbachev had resigned as president of the Soviet Union and commander-in-chief on December 25, 1991.

Now here we were in a small meeting room in Ottawa, barely more than a year later. Gorbachev was both ready and willing to talk about his experience. We were mesmerized. Following my warm words of praise for his courage in having refused the demands of the coup leaders to crack down on dissent, he quickly took command of the narrative. He explained his intentions to bring about change in the Soviet Union with a view to embracing "social democracy." He made it perfectly clear that he did not wish for the dismantling of the Soviet Union but rather for a less centralized form of governance. He offered us his interpretations of glasnost and perestroika. Gorbachev was unsparing in his criticism of Boris Yeltsin, who, he believed, did not have the talent to lead a post-Soviet Russia. He offered us insights into the world leaders with whom he interacted between 1989 and 1991, notably his relationship with President Bush. And he encouraged us to ask questions, so I did: "Mr. Gorbachev, if you had to relive your experience as leader of the Soviet Union, what if anything would you have done differently?"

Gorbachev answered through his translator, and his reply was revealing. "You have a saying in English that one should not put the cart before the horse," he told us. "We have a similar saying in Russian. Thinking back, I would have pushed for more rapid change economically, but I would have been more careful about the speed of opening up politically." Interestingly, he referred to his visit to China at the time of the Tiananmen Square protests in 1989. His meeting with Chinese leaders went ahead despite the turbulence of those events; it marked a historic chapter in the evolution of Sino-Soviet relations. Gorbachev said he told the Chinese leadership that political opening and economic opening should go hand in hand. "The Chinese disagreed," he observed, and "in retrospect they were right. I believe the Soviet people were not ready for the degree of political change I wished for."

I came away from the meeting moved by Gorbachev's candour. He struck me as a well-intentioned and deeply human figure caught up in a swirl of events that were beyond his abilities to manage or to fully understand. Nonetheless, having engaged him for that brief time in close quarters, I felt I had shaken the hand of a man who had profoundly shaped world events for the better. As I said my farewell, I took a moment to tell him I had met his old friend and confidant Aleksandr Yakovlev when he was Soviet ambassador to Canada. My encounters with Yakovlev were few, and mainly at diplomatic events. The one notable exception was when we had a chance meeting on the banks of the Ottawa River below Rockcliffe Park, where both he and I lived. Accompanied by his granddaughter, he was enjoying a casual afternoon fishing for sturgeon, a fish much favoured by Russians. Gorbachev smiled and was gone. I read some time later that Yakovlev had assisted him in drafting his letter of resignation as president of the Soviet Union.

In June 1992, little less than a year before my encounter with Gorbachev, Brian Mulroney invited me to attend a state dinner in honour of President Boris Yeltsin. As the prime minister introduced me to Yeltsin, I thought of the Russian leader's bravery when he stood on a tank and defied those sent by the coup leaders to arrest him. Having listened to Yeltsin's address to the Canadian Parliament asking for financial assistance and promoting badly needed investment in Russia, I realized how difficult it would be for the new state to navigate the years to come. How much had changed since my first visit to the Soviet Union in 1974, when it was in the iron grip of Leonid Brezhnev! I could not at the time imagine that one day the democratization we all were counting on would take a different turn under the leadership of Vladimir Putin.

INDIA

No country had a greater immediate impact on my senses than India. Long before my first visit, the images of the country in my mind had been shaped by the likes of Rudyard Kipling and E.M. Forster. I imagined a vast land, a continent, in effect, encompassing many civilizations, customs, and languages. *Freedom at Midnight*, by Larry Collins and Dominique Lapierre, gave me a taste of India's struggle for independence. The central figure in these events, Mahatma Gandhi, fascinated me. In addition, my postgraduate studies in comparative constitutional laws in England in the late 1960s introduced me to the complexities of the Indian legal system. I was in awe at how such a vast emerging country could be wedded to democracy—something that remains an essential part of the modern India we know today.

When in 1994 I received an invitation to embark on a lecture tour of India, I was thrilled to be able to see the country at last. The host was the Shastri Indo-Canadian Institute, established as a not-for-profit organization in 1968 by the Canadian and Indian governments, its aim to promote research and dialogue. It was named after Indian prime minister Lal Bahadur Shastri. The institute generously extended an invitation to Susan to join me and more or less left the content of my lectures to me, on the understanding that I would address mainly economic themes. I gave the first lecture in New Delhi, followed by Bombay, Bangalore, and Madras, as they were then known—today's Mumbai, Bangaluru, and Chennai. The visit lasted ten days in all, and with my hosts' consent I was able to add to my schedule events involving the Confederation of Indian Industry (CII), India's premier business organization. Its leader was the intelligent and perceptive Tarun Das. Das and I established a solid friendship and remained in close touch for many years afterwards, as our paths crossed on both sides of the Pacific and at the World Economic Forum in Davos. Remarkably, the indefatigable Das served as the director general of the CII from 1967 to 1974 and thereafter as its chief executive until 2004. To me, no one was better connected in all of India—and in a country of close to one billion people, that was saying something.

Canada's high commissioner to India, Stanley Gooch, could not have been more helpful during my tour. In addition to offering hospitality and accommodation at the High Commission in Delhi, he facilitated calls on senior government officials in the Prime

Minister's Office and the finance ministry, and notably a visit with respected Indian National Congress veteran Pranab Mukherjee, who made a strong impression on me. Mukherjee served in a variety of senior cabinet portfolios spanning several decades, culminating in his election in 2012 as the thirteenth president of India.

My lectures incorporated a vigorous defence of market-based principles and open trade. As I was preparing my case, which was based on the simple premise that India should get aboard the globalization train, I anticipated resistance. The Indian economy, after all, was steeped in statist traditions, and there was general skepticism among the country's elites that rapid change could be harnessed successfully. I was correct in my assumptions. Apart from some in my business audiences, my listeners pushed back against my message. This was the case even though the prime minister at the time, P.V. Narasimha Rao, and his minister of finance, Manmohan Singh, were reformers who favoured India's tilt toward a market economy. Their thinking had been influenced in part by the economic crisis India faced in 1991, during which the International Monetary Fund imposed severe conditions. Singh, whom I would meet in future years, went on to be India's thirteenth prime minister, serving from 2004 to 2014.

My principal lectures in 1994 were presented in Delhi to the Rajiv Gandhi Institute for Contemporary Studies, in Bombay (Mumbai) to the SNDT Women's University, in Bangalore (Bangaluru) to the Indian Institute of Management, and in Madras (Chennai) to the Confederation of Indian Industry. En route, I gave a number of luncheon and dinner speeches at events hosted by the CII and various chambers of commerce. It was a privilege to speak from these platforms with strong audience turnout, and I gained a great deal from the discussions that followed. When I addressed the SNDT Women's University, I was mightily impressed by the large gathering of young women in their colourful saris and even more so by the vigour with which they pressed their questions. Among them, the thirst for change was much in evidence, but concern as well that a shift from India's socialist economic model to capitalism would not deliver prosperity to the broad populace. The university was founded in 1916, and I admired its motto: *Sanskrita stree parashakti* ("An enlightened woman is a source of infinite strength"). At the Indian Institute of Management, one of India's top business schools, I met some of the country's most promising future business leaders. There, I encountered few fears or doubts. The faculty and students I met believed that a market economy offered India the best prospects for growth and innovation, and they wanted to be agents of the transformation. While in Bangalore, I visited with leaders of India's high-technology industry, notable among them N.R. Narayana Murthy, the founder, chair, and managing director of technology pioneer Infosys Technologies. Also in Bangalore, I was shown a fascinating bit of history. Following a luncheon and address at the historic Bangalore Club, my host showed me a page in the club's minute book dating from 1899. There it was recorded that Winston Spencer Churchill's unpaid debt to the club of thirteen rupees was written off as an "irrecoverable sum." Churchill was in his early twenties at the time and was clearly short of funds. My lecture tour concluded in Delhi, where I was hosted by Amit Mitra, secretary general of the Federation of Indian Chambers of Commerce and Industry. In summing up my first experience of India, I told my audience, "Based on what I have seen and heard, I have little doubt that India will be a global giant of the twenty-first century. I very much want Canada to be part of India's remarkable rise."

I worked hard to help translate that wish into action, and in the decade that followed I sought every opportunity to engage with India's political and business leaders. An annual get-together at the

World Economic Forum in Davos was one useful channel. Another was the Business Council's CEO mission to India in March 2007, the first of its kind. Among my colleagues travelling with me were Marcel Coutu, Bruce Flatt, Fred Green, Jacques Lamarre, and Ron Mannix, the chief executives of Canadian Oil Sands, Brookfield Asset Management, Canadian Pacific Railway, SNC-Lavalin, and Coril Holdings, respectively. We were given the red carpet treatment in New Delhi and Mumbai, with access to the highest levels of India's political leadership. These included the prime minister and the president, and leaders of corporate giants such as the Birla Group, the Tata Group, Reliance Industries, and ICICI Bank.

Our audience at the Presidential Palace with President A.P.J. Abdul Kalam was particularly memorable. The impressive building, formerly the Viceroy's House, signalled the grandeur that was the British Raj from 1858 to 1947. The president, an effervescent aerospace scientist who had played a leadership role in developing India's civilian space program and military missile program, received us enthusiastically and with good humour.

Among the Indian business leaders who received us, no one made a greater impression on me than Vaman Kamath, the chief executive of ICICI Bank. Visionary and dynamic, he propelled ICICI into a global financial powerhouse, relying heavily on technology as a driver. He said to me, "ICICI is not a bank. It is a technology company that is involved in banking." Kamath leapfrogged over his domestic competitors by moving aggressively online and by introducing ATMs across the country. He told me with pride how ICICI reached out to India's vast rural community, tapping into the micro-banking space.

The Business Council mission returned to Canada convinced that our two countries should move quickly to deepen our economic relationship. To that end, the India-Canada CEO Roundtable, created in 2005 with the blessings of prime ministers Martin and Singh, met twice in 2007: once in New Delhi and once in Montreal. A joint venture of the Business Council and the Confederation of Indian Industry, the roundtable issued a detailed report on September 2, 2008. Titled "India and Canada: A New Era of Cooperation," it recommended that Canada and India should continue to strengthen their ties, and most particularly that they should combine their current bilateral investment protection accord "into a single, modern, high quality and comprehensive Free Trade Agreement." To my disappointment, this enterprising undertaking, representing perhaps the high-water mark of ambitions for a Canada-India economic partnership, was never consummated. When I retired as head of the Business Council at the end of 2009, I still hoped that the collective efforts of the Business Council and the Confederation of Indian Industry would lead to bigger things. That never happened, and in my view it was a lost opportunity for both countries. As I write, Canada is turning its attention to the potential of the Indo-Pacific as part of a welcome strategy in Asia that is less reliant on China.

CHINA AND HONG KONG

My first visit to the People's Republic of China was in May 1985, when Susan and I, after spending several days in Hong Kong, travelled to Guangzhou, Shanghai, and Beijing. The purpose of the trip was to gain some understanding of what was happening as the sleeping giant began to stir. My first exposure to the politics and economics of China was in 1970, while I was serving under Trudeau, when Canada and China established diplomatic relations. In 1985, China was at a rudimentary stage of economic development. The country was under the leadership of the great reformer Deng Xiaoping, the architect of the transformation that would eventually propel China to great-power status. In the cities we visited, the bicycle was vastly more common than the occasional car, and Western-style amenities were not to be seen.

Knowing these cities as I do now, I can say that I have seen staggering economic development the speed of which is unknown in modern history. Deng, a veteran of Mao Zedong's Long March, fascinated me. Here was a man who never assumed the formal role of head of government and yet had the title Paramount Leader, who admitted to making mistakes but avoided making any moves that were fatal to his ambitions. His willingness to encourage market ideas was daring and, in my view, infinitely perspicacious. Exhorting his citizens to become rich while keeping a leash on political freedoms differentiated him from the Soviet Union's Mikhail Gorbachev. Among the quotations associated with Deng is one that translates as "No matter if it is a white cat or a black cat, as long as it can catch mice, it is a good cat." As Deng so often said, his goal was to create out of communism a socialist country with Chinese characteristics.

Over the better part of the next decade, I followed developments in China closely, encouraging the expansion of our bilateral trading relationship and business investment in its fast-growing economy. In November 1994, the Business Council joined forces with Prime Minister Jean Chrétien and the first of his Team Canada missions. The prime minister, at his energetic best, was accompanied in Beijing by nine premiers, two territorial leaders, and about four hundred business people. Our stellar Business Council team was composed of fifteen leaders, among them Laurent Beaudoin of Bombardier, John Cleghorn of the Royal Bank, Dominic D'Alessandro of Manulife Financial, Hollis Harris of Air Canada, Gerald Maier of TransCanada PipeLines, Ron Mannix, then of Loram Corporation, Jean Monty of Northern Telecom, Hartley Richardson of James

Richardson & Sons, Guy Saint-Pierre of SNC-Lavalin, and Robert Wright of Teck Corporation. The Business Council delegation was the most impressive group of Canadian chief executives ever to visit China, and this was not lost on our hosts.

The prime minister and members of his mission were well received by the Chinese leadership, beginning with a dinner in Beijing on November 7 hosted by Premier Li Peng in the Great Hall of the People. The following morning, I chaired a presentation by our delegation at the annual meeting of the Canada China Business Council, a group whose chair was André Desmarais of Power Corporation. The message from us was strong and clear: the Business Council believed that China was on its way to achieving great-power status and that the potential for business between our two countries was considerable. That afternoon, the Canada China Business Council arranged for us to return to the Great Hall of the People for a private meeting with First Vice-Premier Zhu Rongji. A highly respected leader with strong economic credentials, he would go on to become China's premier in 1998. He received us warmly and welcomed questions. At one point, I asked him about the future of Hong Kong. After offering his assurances that the transition from British rule planned for 1997 would be a great success, he added succinctly, "Why would China want to kill the golden goose?" I then pressed him on Taiwan, and again his response was revealing. He said the eventual return of Taiwan to the motherland would be made easier because of the success of the Hong Kong handover. These assurances ring hollow in the light of today's crackdowns in Hong Kong and growing threats to Taiwan, but I had no doubt at the time that he meant what he said.

We soon returned once more to the Great Hall of the People, where Chrétien hosted a dinner in honour of Premier Li. Several days followed with a mixture of business meetings and visits to cultural sites in Beijing and to the Great Wall and the Ming tombs. Before leaving Beijing for Canada, I invited a former Chinese ambassador to Canada, Zhang Wenpu, to lunch. He had served in Ottawa from 1986 to 1990, and we had seen a great deal of one another at the time. During the Tiananmen crisis, he had been given the cold shoulder in Ottawa. While I was horrified by the violent crackdown, I had made a point of keeping in touch so as to better understand the Chinese government's harsh response against the country's pro-reform elements. At my invitation, he also joined my table at the dinner hosted by Jean Chrétien, where he witnessed first-hand the impressive Canadian presence in the capital. I asked him for a frank assessment of what the Chinese leadership thought of the Team Canada mission. His response did not surprise me. He said that for the entire political leadership of Canada and so many of its business elites to have travelled to China as a single delegation had made a huge impression. He added with a smile, "China could never mount such a mission. Otherwise, who would be left in charge at home?"

In the evolution of China's relations with the world, the most memorable moment I experienced was the handover of British Hong Kong to the People's Republic. The ceremonies ushering in "one country, two systems" commenced on June 30, 1997. I was privileged to be in attendance for these historic events, having received an invitation from both the British and the Chinese authorities.

That evening at the end of June, we assembled with other guests at an outdoor site overlooking the harbour. There we listened to an address by Prince Charles and witnessed a final military salute by the troops of the British garrison. Then, at an emotional ceremony close to midnight at the Hong Kong Convention and Exhibition Centre, the Prince of Wales, in the presence of British prime minister

Tony Blair and President Jiang Zemin, read a farewell speech on behalf of Queen Elizabeth. Moments before midnight, the flags of the United Kingdom and of Hong Kong were slowly lowered as we sang "God Save the Queen." Twelve seconds later, the Chinese flag was raised to the tune of the Chinese anthem, followed by an address by Jiang. Just after midnight, in a profoundly symbolic act marking the end of British rule, Prince Charles and governor Chris Patten sailed out of Hong Kong on HMY *Britannia*. A spectacular fireworks show lit up the city, and merry-making carried on through the night.

Over the course of the next decade, I visited Hong Kong often, and I kept in touch with Chief Secretary Anson Chan and Financial Secretary Donald Tsang—both highly capable individuals—and also with members of Hong Kong's business community. The last address I gave in Hong Kong in my capacity as head of the Business Council was in 2007, when I spoke of my continuing optimism for the "one country, two systems" arrangement.

I participated in a second Team Canada mission to China in February 2001. Led once again by Jean Chrétien, it was modelled on the 1994 mission but exceeded that groundbreaking initiative with an even larger delegation of approximately six hundred. One of the main purposes of my trip was to make a major presentation to an audience of senior Chinese figures in the presence of Team Canada participants. My pitch was ambitious: how to turn the attention of the leaders of a fast-growing China to the attractions of Canada as an economic partner. In the large hall, I resorted to a PowerPoint presentation in English and Mandarin. In my pitch, I was able to boast of Canada's strong performance: it had enjoyed the longest economic expansion in over three decades with twenty-one consecutive quarters of growth, low levels of inflation, an unemployment rate at a twenty-five year low, compounding fiscal surpluses with the best standing in the G7, robust trade numbers with unrivalled access to the United States market, and expanding technology credentials. Given the flood of follow-up requests I received for my speech, I felt that my message had hit home. Once again, Team Canada members were hosted at dinner by China's premier. This time it was Premier Zhu Rongji, who along with Chrétien extolled the virtues of the Canada-China partnership.

I returned to China in October 2003, unexpectedly finding myself in the company of Chrétien on his airplane en route from Bangkok to Beijing. I had been in Bangkok attending the CEO summit tied to the Asia-Pacific Economic Cooperation (APEC) Leaders' Meeting. As the meetings ended, Bangkok Airport was unable to accommodate the departure of normal civilian aircraft due to the heavy demands of the many government flights. I was due to attend a dinner in Beijing the next day in honour of Chrétien and the Chinese premier and had no way out of Bangkok. The prime minister came to the rescue, generously offering me a seat on his government aircraft. To my surprise, I was given a seat across from him and his wife, Aline. Once airborne, Mrs. Chrétien left her seat to join her granddaughter, and Chrétien invited me to join him. For most of the five-hour flight, we engaged in lively discussions about China and Chrétien's missions over the years. We also discussed domestic policy in Canada, including the economy. Interestingly, he was keen to cover the history of his relations with the business community, which at times had been turbulent. During those unforgettable hours, I saw this remarkable politician at his best—frank and provocative, and at times very funny. No prime minister before him or since has worked harder to develop Canada's relationship with China.

Back in Canada, I too was a relentless advocate of closer Canadian relations with China, both within the business community and at the political level. I believed that Canada and other Western countries needed to encourage Chinese economic development and engagement in the global economy. Better to have a China that had adopted the rule of law in international trade than a rogue power operating outside established norms. It was for this reason that the Business Council supported China's entry into the World Trade Organization. I never had any illusions that China would in the foreseeable future embrace democratic values, but my hope was that an increasingly economically empowered Chinese citizenry, with hundreds of millions drawn out of poverty, would become a powerful force for change, leading to a softening of the country's autocratic rule. Another Business Council CEO mission to Beijing and Shanghai in 2005 only strengthened my views on China and increased momentum in the bilateral relationship.

The election of Stephen Harper as Canada's twenty-second prime minister in February 2006 led to a sharp turn in Canada-China relations. No friend of the communist regime in Beijing, he harboured concerns about China's autocratic policies and its abuse of human rights. My fear was that the Harper government would set back China-Canada relations and stall the movement so many of us had worked so hard to achieve. In a letter to the prime minister in 2007, I endeavoured to make the case for why China mattered so much to Canada and briefly and respectfully walked him through the history of the relationship. "In [China's] cultural traditions, influence flows from relationships of trust and friendship that are nurtured over prolonged periods," I wrote. "Today, we in the business community are deeply worried that Canada's legacy of trust is being eroded, with serious long-term consequences for both our country's economic interests and its aspirations for leadership in spreading democratic values and respect for human rights." I assured the prime minister of the Council's intentions. "We are not suggesting that our country seek short-term commercial gain at the expense of fundamental values. We do believe, however, that Canada's effectiveness as an advocate for democratic principles and human rights in China depends on how we engage the Chinese people on the ground over the long haul and not on the volume of our public criticism of the Chinese government." I went on to say, "With every commercial transaction and relationship, we contribute to a record of a Chinese progress that is pulling hundreds of millions of people out of abject poverty. And as China grows, the expanding ranks of its new middle class are increasingly exposed not only to the world's products and services, but also to new aspirations and new ideas—a process of evolution that ultimately will transform China's society at least as profoundly as its economy."

Despite the Harper government's attitude toward China, my Council colleagues and I remained committed to advancing the two-way relationship. Two spectacular events in China at the time dazzled the world. I and others were guests of Ron Mannix at the 2008 Beijing Olympics. A stunning and creative organizational achievement involving more than ten thousand athletes, it was watched worldwide by over three billion people. With the advantage of front row seats for many of the key events in the architecturally exciting Bird's Nest stadium, we could sense the enormous pride of the Chinese people in this undertaking—and China was the winner of the most gold medals. The Beijing Olympics, to my mind, were China's "coming out party," at which they exclaimed to the world, "We have arrived!" The second grand event was Expo 2010 in Shanghai, which Susan and I attended. With the theme "Better City, Better Life" and costing some $48 billion, this powerful expression of Chinese ambition was the most expensive world's fair in history. It attracted seventy-three million visitors and hosted 192 countries.

The final address I gave on Chinese soil, as the head of the Canadian Council of Chief Executives, was in Shanghai in 2009. I was attending the annual meeting of the International Business Leaders' Advisory Council. Created in 1989 by Zhu Rongji, who was then the mayor of Shanghai—and who, of course, would go on to become China's premier—this prestigious body today is composed of some fifty business leaders of global enterprises from sixteen countries and provides advice to the mayor of Shanghai. At the invitation of Mayor Han Zheng, I gave the meeting's keynote address, titled "The Transformative Effects of the Global Economic Crisis: Implications for the World and Shanghai's Aspirations." My introductory words set the context. As we were meeting, I said, the impact of the most severe global economic crisis since the Great Depression of the 1930s continued to reverberate. One of the notable aspects of the crisis was its global reach. People, businesses, and governments in every part of the world were feeling its sting. I made the case for globalization, saying that globalization had "accelerated economic progress, lifted hundreds of millions of people out of poverty, spurred innovation and scientific advancement and brought people, cities and countries closer together—ensuring that we are better able to confront challenges that touch us all whether the challenge be a financial crisis, a devastating earthquake, a killer tsunami or a raging pandemic." I pointed out that the negative impacts of the financial crisis were still very much with us and that the world's major powers had an important role to play. In the case of China, I referred to Premier Wen Jiabao's acknowledgement a month earlier that China "is not yet steady, solid and balanced." Picking up on this, I suggested that China needed to act on a number of priorities: "Among them are the need to accelerate unfulfilled economic reforms, to deal with widespread poverty and widening income disparity, to respond to serious environmental problems, and to foster expanded domestic consumption."

Looking forward five to ten years, I outlined what I saw as five priorities for China and the world: to learn from the crisis and undertake reforms to the global financial system without destroying its market-based principles; to tackle the huge fiscal challenges that lay ahead; to confront protectionism and to restore faith in the global trading system; to deal with global economic imbalances; and to accelerate the move toward the green economy. I concluded my address by calling for a "seismic shift in the architecture of global governance," rejecting the idea of a world directed by the two superpowers, China and the United States. "While cooperation between China and the United States is essential in dealing with a host of political, economic and security issues, I believe the interests of China and the United States and the global community as a whole would be better served in a multipolar world guided by effective multilateral institutions."

Following my retirement from the Canadian Council of Chief Executives, I continued to pursue my China interests via my academic affiliations and business activities. One important channel of engagement continued through my association with Manulife Financial's board of directors, which involved periodic visits to China, where the company has extensive engagement. Another channel was my close association with a succession of Chinese ambassadors to Canada who lived a few minutes away in my Ottawa neighbourhood, Rockcliffe Park. I also continued my periodic encounters with Chinese government and business leaders at international gatherings.

Against this backdrop of my long, deep, and optimistic engagement with China, recent realities have come as a profound shock and disappointment. Since 1970, I had been an unflinching supporter of the reforms leading to a transformation of China that has electrified the world. I believed that China's road to progress through economic betterment and global engagement would serve China and the world well. I believed that the rise of an empowered middle class would inevitably lead to a loosening of the iron grip of its leaders and growing respect for the rule of law and human rights. While not expecting China to embrace Western-style values, I believed that a mutually respectful modus vivendi with the world's democracies was within reach. I am no longer of that view. The current Chinese leadership under President Xi Jinping is taking a hardline China-first approach to its international diplomacy and laying the foundations for economic and military supremacy in the decades to come. I was shocked at China's unjustifiable jailing of Canadians Michael Kovrig and Michael Spavor in the dispute over the detention of Huawei executive Meng Wanzhou. I am appalled by China's "wolf warrior" global bullying tactics. I am deeply disappointed by China's imposition of tough security laws in Hong Kong in contravention of the spirit and the legalities of the "one country, two systems" principle. Yet I shall say that my respect for the Chinese people has not diminished, and I hope that one day they will demand that their leaders deliver change and a more open society.

THE AMERICAS

I set foot on South American soil for the first time in 1992. Carlos Menem, the president of Argentina, had invited me to meet with him for a briefing on the North American Free Trade Agreement, which was to be signed by the leaders of Canada, the United States, and Mexico in less than two weeks. I was warmly received by Menem in the Casa Rosada, the country's presidential palace, with the only other person present being the president's translator. We quickly got down to business. He was most curious to know how Mexico, a developing country, had managed to gain entry to the exclusive first world Canada–United States trading partnership.

Menem was aware of my earlier intimate association with the Canada–United States free trade initiative, and now with the North American free trade undertaking that was moving toward its conclusion. He had received reports from his government and embassy officials, he told me, but he wanted to hear from an independent Canadian source. Menem was a careful listener, and after a time our conversation wandered beyond the topic at hand. He told me that Argentina could one day be an important NAFTA partner, and he optimistically assessed Argentina's economic reforms under Domingo Cavallo, his capable minister of the economy. Cavallo, whom I later met, was indeed impressive. By fixing the dollar-peso exchange rate at 1:1, he brought Argentina's inflation rate down from 1,300 per cent to less than 20 per cent in 1992, and to nearly zero during the remainder of the decade. To my surprise, Menem, no friend of the military, praised the reforms of General Augusto Pinochet in Chile, especially his success at rooting out corruption.

While in the Argentine capital, I also met with the country's highly respected foreign minister, Guido di Tella. I kept in touch with Menem and met him again in Argentina on several occasions, and also when the Business Council hosted him in Toronto, on June 2, 1994, during his state visit to Canada. Ultimately, the reforms of Menem and Cavallo, which seemed so promising, came crashing down, and Argentina's painful saga of failed dreams persisted.

Historically, Canada had not looked to the Southern Hemisphere. This had begun to change in 1990, when Canada joined the Organization of American States, an initiative of Prime Minister Mulroney. Various trade missions to the continent, including prime ministerial visits, sought to make up for lost time. It is fair to say that the results were modest. One notable exception was the decision of Canada and Chile to strike a free trade agreement. The agreement, signed in Santiago in December 1996 and implemented in

July 1997, was Canada's first free trade agreement with a nation in the Southern Hemisphere, and it was well worth the effort. Over the first decade, trade between Canada and Chile increased over 300 per cent. Moreover, Chile was setting an example among its peers in South America by implementing important reforms and managing its economy well. For this reason, I was a strong supporter in advocating for the agreement, and I pushed for closer relations between our respective business communities.

In 1995, Business Council chair Ted Newall and I met with Chilean business leaders in Santiago in the presence of President Eduardo Frei. Prime Minister Chrétien was concurrently visiting Chile and Argentina. Both Chrétien and Frei gave their blessing to an agreement between the Business Council and Chile's senior business organization, the Confederación de la Producción y del Comercio. An enthusiastic supporter of this initiative was Canadian ambassador to Chile Marc Lortie, an accomplished diplomat and good friend who would go on to serve in Paris and other senior ambassadorial posts. Before our arrival in Santiago, Ted Newall and I had been guests in Argentina of President Menem for an intimate dinner at his private Buenos Aires residence in honour of Chrétien. While the evening was suffused with camaraderie and humorous storytelling, Menem pressed Newall and me for details concerning our visit to Santiago, demonstrating his keen competitiveness with his traditional Chilean rivals.

Brazil, the giant of South America and long-considered one of the most promising of the world's emerging economies, captured my attention in the 1990s. During my visits over a twenty-year period, I concluded that despite its massive resources and large population, Brazil would be hindered in fulfilling its economic promise in large part by its political failings and suffocating corruption. So far, my assessment has proven to be correct, sadly. What better example than the misguided policies of the recent president Jair Bolsonaro?

Former Brazilian president Fernando Henrique Cardoso was an exception and generally admired for his intellect and competence. My favourite story about him involved an intimate dinner I attended in his honour in Rio de Janeiro in March 2001. I was the only Canadian present, and the timing was not ideal. Brazil was furious with Canada for our country's boycott of its beef due to concerns about mad cow disease. Given the enormous pride with which Brazilians regard their beef, anti-Canadian sentiment had risen to fever pitch. And beef was the main course at dinner! When the president and I shook hands and I was introduced as a Canadian, he said with a smile, "Given that fine Brazilian beef is on the menu this evening, I am trying to decide what would be a worse punishment: denying you our beef or compelling you to eat it." Everyone within earshot laughed. So did I, but I didn't let the moment pass before assuring him that I too was a huge fan of his country's beef.

An important chapter in my dealings with the Americas involved banker and philanthropist David Rockefeller. Among the prominent American business leaders and philanthropists I have had the privilege of knowing, he would be at the top of my list. A thoughtful, modest, soft-spoken man, his contributions to business and philanthropy are the stuff of legend. When he died in 2017, at the age of 101, he was widely mourned. The first time I met him, in Ottawa in the 1980s, he told me the story of how Prime Minister Mackenzie King played a vital role in shaping his career. As he attests in his memoirs, with his undergraduate years coming to an end, he had no clear idea of what to make of his life. His father, John D. Rockefeller Jr., a close friend of King, advised David to seek King's advice on his future career. He did so, and in the spring of 1936 he spent a weekend with the prime minister at his residence, Laurier House, in Ottawa. King counselled the young Rockefeller to pursue a career in government or international banking and to prepare the way by earning a Ph.D. in economics. Rockefeller took the advice and pursued his studies at Harvard and the University of Chicago, as King had done.

My principal connection with Rockefeller was through the Americas Society and its chair's advisory council. He was responsible for the creation of both as vehicles for promoting dialogue throughout the Americas based on democratic principles and free market economics. The focus was on Latin America, which in the 1970s and 1980s was undergoing tumultuous upheavals marked by extremism and authoritarian rule. I was honoured to be asked to join the advisory council, over which he presided as chair and, later, as honorary chair. Canadians on the advisory council were understandably in a small minority. It fell to me and my colleague André Desmarais, from Montreal, to report on political and economic happenings in Canada. These meetings offered me exposure to some of Latin America's most influential leaders and to Rockefeller's circle of friends, which included American and international political, business, and thought leaders, such as Henry Kissinger and Zbigniew Brzezinski, and progressive thinkers from throughout the region.

One memorable moment came at a meeting of the Forum of the Americas in Washington in April 1992. Over five hundred business leaders from throughout the hemisphere were present to collectively commit themselves to the goal of achieving hemispheric free trade by the year 2000. This ambitious vision did not materialize, but, to his great credit, Rockefeller was able to assemble a powerful alliance committed to advancing trade liberalization as a vehicle for economic growth and job creation in a region that had turned its back on market forces. My Mexican colleague Antonio del Valle and I were put on the list of speakers at the meeting—in part, I believe, because of NAFTA's high profile at the time. The keynote speaker at dinner was President George H.W. Bush. Before the president's address, Rockefeller kindly arranged for del Valle and me to join him and Bush for a private meeting. Bush shared with us his concerns regarding his re-election prospects in November of that year; he feared that the economic recovery, which was already under way, would not yet have registered with American voters. He said to me that "Brian" (Prime Minister Mulroney) would have a better shot in 1993, when he went to the polls, as the recession blues would have lifted by then. The president then startled the three of us by inviting us to join him on the stage while he delivered his address. So, to the sound of "Hail to the Chief," we stood as the president walked onto the stage, shook our hands, and saluted each of us from the podium. President Bush's concerns were validated when Bill Clinton won in November, denying him a second term as president.

Among the experiences I shared with Rockefeller were the travels he led to various Latin American capitals. Wherever we went, doors were opened at the highest levels on account of the Rockefeller name and his tireless efforts at relationship-building. I took the lead in organizing a trip of his chair's advisory council to Vancouver in June 2002. Prime Minister Chrétien joined us, and on behalf of the Business Council, I paid tribute to Rockefeller's extraordinary contributions with the words "The Council salutes David Rockefeller's extraordinary achievements in advancing the cause of open markets, liberalized trade, democratic reforms and social equity throughout the Western Hemisphere."

David Rockefeller's dreams of hemispheric free trade did not materialize, but not through lack of effort. A series of government-sponsored summits of the Americas were organized, the first of which was in Miami in 1994, aimed at promoting a Free Trade Agreement of the Americas (FTAA). I led the Business Council's advocacy in support of the idea. In an address I gave in Washington in 1997 to the Hemispheric Policy Forum of the Institute of the Americas, I praised the initiative as "a grand and noble idea . . . a strategic initiative whose benefits are political, social and economic . . . encompassing 3 billion people and $9 trillion in economic value."

The idea faced fierce opposition from civil society groups. Nowhere was this opposition more in evidence than at the third summit, in Quebec City, in April 2001. To those of us in attendance, it felt more like a siege, with rioters in the streets and a massive police presence employing tear gas and water cannons. To the thirty-four government leaders from the hemisphere who were present, it was a discouraging and draining experience. In the end, the FTAA failed—a grand and noble idea it was, but too complex and involving too many countries. I always harboured reservations about the FTAA's prospects for success, but I did believe that the dialogue it encouraged around the ideas of democratization, rule of law, and liberalized trade was ultimately beneficial. Throughout my involvement in the FTAA debates, one thing became clear: both public officials and private-sector leaders from participating countries expressed admiration of Canada as a successful governance model and as a practitioner of free trade in the North American context.

APEC CEO SUMMIT

A particular source of pride to me, as a champion of global economic diplomacy, has been the seminal role played by the Business Council in the launch of the first CEO summit of the Asia-Pacific Economic Cooperation (APEC). A forum for twenty-one member countries in the Pacific Rim, APEC promotes free trade throughout the region. Established in 1989 and headquartered in Singapore, it convenes annually.

"Tommy" on my first birthday, 1941.
(Photo courtesy of the author)

Mother and father. They gave me life and Canada. *(Photo courtesy of the author)*

Big sister and brother. Always there to help. *(Photo courtesy of the author)*

The greatest of adventures begins.

(Photo courtesy of the author)

Dancing with Susan at the National Arts Centre opening, 1969. *(Photo by John Evans Photography Ltd.)*

Serving the prime minister, East Block, Ottawa, 1970. *(Photo by Newton Photography)*

Early days at the Business Council with Royal Bank of Canada CEO, Rowland Frazee. *(Photo by Gilbert F.R.P.S.)*

Introducing Prime Minister Brian Mulroney. *(Photo courtesy of the Prime Minister's Office)*

Prime Minister Mulroney and the Free Trade triumph, 1988.

(Photo courtesy of the Prime Minister's Office)

Prime Minister Mulroney and Susan at the National Economic Conference, Ottawa, 1985. *(Photo courtesy of the Prime Minister's Office)*

With Prime Minister Mulroney hosting Klaus Schwab, founder of the World Economic Forum, Ottawa, 1988. *(Photo courtesy of the Prime Minister's Office)*

Exchanging a quip with Prime Minister Jean Chrétien. *(Photo by International Press Service)*

Fly fishing with President George H.W. Bush in Labrador, 2003. *(Photo courtesy of the author)*

Relaxing with the President in Labrador, 2003. *(Photo courtesy of the author)*

Treasured Council Chairmen, Alfred Powis, Rowland Frazee, David Culver, Ted Newall, and Guy Saint-Pierre, Toronto, 1996. *(Photo courtesy of the Business Council of Canada)*

Preparing to introduce President of China, Jiang Zemin, at APEC CEO Summit, 1997. *(Photo courtesy of the Business Council of Canada)*

With our troops in Germany following live fire exercises. *(Photo courtesy of the author)*

Mexican President Ernesto Zedillo, who presented me with the Aguila Azteca, Mexico's highest honour bestowed upon foreigners. *(Photo courtesy of the Business Council of Canada)*

With David Rockefeller at the New York Stock Exchange, 2004. *(Photo courtesy of the New York Stock Exchange)*

With President Bill Clinton, Susan, and Prime Minister Jean Chrétien at the opening of the United States Embassy in Ottawa, 1999. *(Photo by Jean-Marc Carisse)*

With Prime Minister of Australia John Howard at the APEC Summit, 1997. *(Photo courtesy of the Business Council of Canada)*

Above left: "Doctor of Laws" with Chancellor of Queen's University, Peter Lougheed, and Principal William Leggatt, 1996. *(Photo by Bernard Clark)*

Above right: Saluting Paul Desmarais, Sr., Montreal, 2003. *(Photo by Jean-Marc Carisse)*

Right: With Suncor CEO and Business Council Chairman, Richard George, Washington, D.C., 2005. *(Photo courtesy of the Canadian Council of Chief Executives)*

With Prime Minister Paul Martin, Toronto, 1999. *(Photo by Jean-Marc Carisse)*

With the 1997 APEC Leaders' Meeting set to take place in Vancouver, a thought came to mind: Why not invite chief executives of leading business enterprises from Pacific Rim countries to Vancouver at the same time for an APEC CEO Summit? Given the gargantuan organizational challenge this presented, with limited time to prepare, I consulted with my Business Council colleagues. The word that came back from the Council policy committee was "risky" but well worth the effort.

I then reached out to Jean Chrétien, who was to host the Leaders' Meeting, and asked for his endorsement of the initiative. The prime minister gave it without hesitation. I turned to the Pacific Basin Economic Council to explore whether it would partner with us. Its Canadian representative, business colleague Paul O'Donoghue, accepted, and he and I agreed to co-chair the CEO Summit. We also agreed that I would chair the summit organizing committee and that the Business Council would be both the organizer and the funder of the initiative. The date of the summit was set for November 22 to 24, the eve of the Leaders' Meeting, and my letters of invitation went out in January. Thirty-three of my Business Council colleagues agreed to serve as a host committee, to participate in the summit, and to provide the necessary funding. A considerable number of them had established global brands— Northern Telecom, Bombardier, Alcan, Manulife Financial, Sun Life Assurance, Power Corporation of Canada, McCain Foods, Air Canada, and the Royal Bank of Canada among them.

Despite the eleventh hour invitations for such an unprecedented meeting, an impressive two hundred chief executives and other prominent leaders came to Vancouver, most of them first-time visitors to Canada. There had never before been such an assembly. Equally impressive was the turnout of APEC leaders and senior officials who agreed to address us—more than eighty in all. We hosted six national leaders: Canada's Jean Chrétien, Chinese president Jiang Zemin, Australian prime minister John Howard, Mexican president Ernesto Zedillo, Malaysian prime minister Mahathir Mohamad, and Hong Kong chief executive Tung Chee-hwa. Other speakers included Madeleine Albright, the U.S. secretary of state, and William Daley, the U.S. secretary of commerce, and ministers representing Indonesia, Japan, South Korea, New Zealand, the Philippines, and Thailand. The agenda focused on economic performance, trade liberalization, sustainable development, technology transfer, the protection of intellectual property, infrastructure, capital markets and financing, and security issues.

There were a lot of highlights during those few days, but one anecdote especially stands out for me. As Council chair Al Flood and I were preparing to usher Jiang Zemin onstage, we were delayed several minutes. I took the opportunity to compliment the Chinese president on his efforts to communicate with me in English. To my great surprise he said, "I can recite Lincoln's Gettysburg Address. Would you like to hear it?" "Of course," I responded. And right there, in less than three minutes, he recited the 272 words of that magnificent testament to democratic principles. I have never forgotten those few moments, and as I listened to the president's address that followed, I asked myself whether deep inside he could appreciate how profoundly at odds was Lincoln's appeal to our better angels with the policies of the China he led.

As a result of the great success in Vancouver, APEC CEO Summits have become an annual event in conjunction with the meeting of the APEC leaders. I have had the pleasure of participating in numerous summits since 1997, knowing that this groundbreaking Canadian innovation has now endured over the decades.

FISHING WITH PRESIDENT GEORGE H.W. BUSH

Engagement in economic diplomacy with foreign leaders can lead to wonderful and unexpected experiences. One notable one for me was fly-fishing with former president George H.W. Bush on the rivers of northern Labrador in July 2004. The invitation came from Craig Dobbin, one of Newfoundland's most famous sons and a highly successful entrepreneur who founded CHC Helicopter, an outstandingly successful global enterprise. Craig's closest friend, fellow Newfoundlander Harry Steele, was a favourite character of mine; he also had achieved remarkable success in business. Craig and Harry were both members of the Canadian Council of Chief Executives, and I was a frequent guest of Harry's at his camp on Tom Luscombe Brook in Labrador. To me, fly-fishing for Atlantic salmon is among the greatest sports known to human kind, and the legendary rivers of Labrador are to my mind the ultimate destination.

One day Craig called and said, "President Bush is coming to my camp on the Adlatok River, and Harry and I would like you to join us. We're counting on you to keep the president engaged when he is talking politics and foreign policy and the like." I quickly understood the role I was expected to play and welcomed it. The president arrived by helicopter in the company of one of his grandsons and his secret service agents. I had already met Bush Sr. on a number of occasions, and we immediately acknowledged the connection with a warm handshake. We had a fine dinner that evening offered up by Craig's able chef, along with a choice of vintage wines. The conversation over dinner was all about the fishing and the plans for the coming days. The president and I were paired to fish together the following morning.

At 6 a.m., I awoke to find the president at my door with a cup of coffee urging me to gear up and get going. Startled, I remember saying, "I'm not in the habit, sir, of being awakened with morning coffee by the commander-in-chief! Thank you." We set off for one of the most promising salmon pools on the Adlatok. There, we saw that our ever-inventive and generous host Craig had affixed a bronze plaque on a rock face next to the pool. It proclaimed that the salmon pool we were fishing in was named the President George H.W. Bush Pool. I positioned myself on the river just below where the president was fishing. Within the first hour, and with the help of one of my favourite salmon flies, the blue charm, I brought two fine grilse to the net. Meanwhile, the president was having no luck, and I happily complied when he suggested that he and I switch pools. But first I showed him where the fish were lying and recommended that he give it a try with a blue charm. I treasure a photograph taken at that moment: the two of us together on the water. Within an hour or so, I took two more grilse and the president had not had a strike. As we made our return to the camp, he joked, "Tom, well done—but I'm going to ask Craig to change the name on the pool to the Hillary Clinton pool!"

Back at the camp, Craig awaited us, grinning nervously, wondering if Canada–United States relations were at risk. He assured the president that in the coming days, his luck would change. And it did. Following a hearty brunch, I presented Bush with a gift of salmon flies I'd had tied by a master of the art in Ottawa. I joked that the flies were a new creation and so did not yet have a name, but I thought Weapons of Mass Destruction might be apt. He had a good laugh.

Over the next days, with plenty of time between morning and late-afternoon outings, we spent many hours sitting around in Craig's comfortable chairs, eagerly listening to the president reminisce. As we listened, I thought how privileged we were to be in the intimate company of a world leader so willing to share his insights about the politics of the United States and the extraordinary global events in which he was a key player. While I had followed his career closely, I made a point before coming to Labrador of rereading *A World Transformed*, co-authored by Bush and his national security adviser Brent Scowcroft. The book, published in 1998, chronicles, among other things, the collapse of the Soviet empire, the unification of Germany, the Tiananmen Square crisis, and the Gulf War. It also offers intimate portraits of leaders that include Ronald Reagan, Margaret Thatcher, Helmut Kohl, and Mikhail Gorbachev. I was well prepared. Over the many hours in which we talked together, the measure of the man became quite clear. Here was an individual of deep experience: before serving as president of the United States, he had been a navy combat pilot, businessman, member of the House of Representatives, ambassador to the United Nations, director of the Central Intelligence Agency, and forty-third vice-president. As he spoke, words such as *honour, modesty, respect, duty, loyalty*, and *patriotism* came to mind.

During our relaxed conversations, I would intervene at times to encourage him to go more deeply into how he showed leadership and perspicacity in managing the complex issue of German unification; how, out of respect for Gorbachev, he resisted expressing any sense of triumphalism when the Berlin Wall came down; how firmly but delicately he handled the coup against Gorbachev; and why and how he limited the Desert Storm military operation to the ouster of Iraq's Saddam Hussein from Kuwait and did not bow to pressure to pursue him to Baghdad.

In speaking of domestic politics, he demonstrated what to me were time-honoured Republican values: a love of liberty, a belief in American leadership in concert with strong allies, the practise of liberalized trade, the embrace of moderate policies at home and vigorous engagement abroad. Isolationism to him was not an option. An enthusiastic supporter of the North American Free Trade

Agreement, Bush talked about the future prospects for wider continental cooperation. He spoke approvingly of the Business Council's work in deepening the NAFTA relationship following the 9/11 terrorist attacks. He expressed admiration for Brian Mulroney and asked me to explain why the prime minister's popularity ratings had fallen so low after serving two successful terms.

On a different note, I especially appreciated his perspective on family life. He told us of his good fortune to have such a devoted life partner in Barbara Bush and two sons in high office: George W., who was then U.S. president, and Jeb, the governor of Florida.

I saw the president on a number of occasions afterwards. The last time was at the conclusion of a church service on the Maine coast, not far from his residence near Kennebunkport. He greeted me from his wheelchair with a bright smile and said he retained a special place in his heart for his time on the beautiful Adlatok. The eulogies at his state funeral in Washington in 2018 said a great deal about President Bush. His extraordinary human qualities and record of service to America and the world were extolled in words of deep respect and affection by family members and old friends. Brian Mulroney spoke eloquently, recalling the close ties of friendship the president had with Canada and Canadians. It was a fitting farewell to this fine American who had called for a "kinder, gentler nation."

DAVOS AND THE WORLD ECONOMIC FORUM

In the practise of economic diplomacy, there is no better venue for "one-stop shopping" than the annual meeting of the World Economic Forum in the stunning winter setting of Davos, Switzerland. As a regular participant for close to twenty years, I have been referred to as an archetypical "Davos Man," a label that does not sit well with me. The term is credited to political scientist Samuel P. Huntington, who described "Davos Men," in a flurry of hyperbole, as "cosmocrats" who "have little need for national loyalty, view national boundaries as obstacles that thankfully are vanishing, and see national governments as residues from the past whose only useful function is to facilitate the elite's global operations."

Founded in 1971 as the European Management Forum by Professor Klaus Schwab, it changed its name to the World Economic Forum in 1987. Its motto is "Committed to improving the state of the world," and it attracts some three thousand business leaders, heads of government, creative thinkers, and other people from around the world to its annual meeting in Davos and neighbouring Klosters. One of the unique aspects of the annual meeting, which I attended for the first time in 1989, is the intimacy with which one engages in discussions in plenaries, in small seminars, in the corridors, at lunches and dinners, and at times on the ski trails. Presidents, prime ministers, chancellors, ministers, and leaders of international organizations make time to attend. The historic encounters I witnessed are far too numerous to mention, but several stand out for me: when in 1990 Chancellor Kohl and East German prime minister Hans Modrow discussed the future of the two Germanys; when in 1992 Nelson Mandela and Frederik de Klerk shook hands in the dying days of apartheid; when in 2001 Shimon Peres and Yasser Arafat talked peace; when Bill Clinton became the first sitting American president to address the forum; and when the future premier of China, Zhu Rongji, speaking in English, told us, "If you have any problems in China, call me."

The Canadian presence at Davos was never large, but it was respectable. On occasion, prime ministers and premiers saw the advantage in attending, and I had no difficulty persuading Business Council colleagues to come. Regularly, I would organize a Business Council reception and offer a briefing on the Canadian business environment. We never knew for sure who was going to show up, as we were competing with dozens of similar meetings, but we saw sufficient value in this exercise to continue with it year after year.

A highlight of my annual pilgrimage to Davos was a private dinner hosted by Canadian entrepreneur Peter Munk at his mountaintop chalet in nearby Klosters. Munk and his wife, Melanie, whom I regarded with affection, were perfect hosts. He always attracted a fascinating list of guests from around the world: government leaders, chief executives, famous authors, journalists, and even religious leaders. At one dinner, he asked me to join him at a table with a young Russian industrialist who was his business partner in a real estate project in Montenegro. I was startled to learn the Russian, who had failed in his attempts to travel to Canada, had been told, "If anyone can get you into Canada, Tom can." I took great care to explain that I had no such influence and that Canadian laws had to be respected. On another occasion, in January 1995, George Soros joined our table, where we decried Canada's dismal fiscal situation; the *Wall Street Journal* had just described Canada as an "honorary member of the Third World" and our currency as the northern peso. I quickly drafted a stern message to the finance minister, Paul Martin, on a napkin, and several of us signed it, including Peter Munk and George Soros. I forwarded the contents of the message to Martin and followed up with him upon my return to Ottawa. Weeks later, Martin tabled a tough budget with very significant cuts in spending and declared war on the deficit. Famously, he said we would eliminate the deficit "come hell or high water." To the great credit of the minister and Prime Minister Chrétien, Canada indeed began to slay the deficit and put its fiscal house in order and moved toward budgetary balance and surpluses.

I kept in regular touch with Klaus Schwab and hosted him at several meetings of the Business Council in Canada. In June 1989,

I organized an event for the World Economic Forum in Ottawa, which was attended by Schwab and some twenty-five Business Council members, together with Prime Minister Mulroney and a number of premiers. Schwab took an interest in Canada, and at one point post-9/11, with security a pressing issue, he and I discussed the idea of Canada as a possible venue to complement the Davos meetings. I recommended Whistler, Banff, and Kananaskis as options. But when I raised the subject with Prime Minister Martin and he realized the cost of securing a Canadian site, enthusiasm for the idea quickly dwindled. After the 9/11 terrorist strikes, New York aggressively pursued the idea of hosting the upcoming World Economic Forum annual meeting. This bold bid was successful, and the meeting took place from January 31 to February 4, 2002. It was a meeting like no other, with New York City and the nation still in shock, mourning, and disbelief. Manhattan was heavily guarded by an amazingly welcoming and friendly cadre of police on every corner, as was the Waldorf Astoria hotel, where most of our meetings took place. I greatly admired the courage and determination of the governor of New York and the New York City officials who wanted to show the world that the city may have been down but was far from out.

A final anecdote from Davos. In January 2004, I was flying with Bombardier chair Laurent Beaudoin at his invitation aboard the company's Global Express jet on our return from Zurich to Montreal. He had told me we would have some "interesting company" with us. The two young passengers, with their girlfriends, were none other than Sergey Brin and Larry Page, the co-founders of Google. This was before the company's initial public offering, which took place some months later. The transatlantic flight, which was to take Brin and Page on to Palo Alto after Beaudoin and I disembarked in Montreal, was fascinating. Beaudoin and I spent a good deal of time quizzing our fellow passengers on their company's brief but successful history and trying to understand the business model the two men had in mind. I sensed in both of them the excitement and uncertainty that accompanies promising start-ups. I knew the company as a search engine that had got under way in 1998 but wondered how it might expand its services in the future. Today we have the answer. As I pen this passage, the market capitalization of Google has surpassed $1.5 trillion! The encounter with Brin and Page less than twenty years ago was a "eureka" moment for me. While I did not appreciate at the time that Google, along with companies such as Microsoft, Apple, and Amazon, would become stars of what would be called in 2015 the "Fourth Industrial Revolution," it was clear that a powerful digital age was beckoning and that the traditional capitalism that had been at the centre of my business experience was heading for a massive transformation.

As I write about the World Economic Forum, I am surprised and disturbed about the conspiracy theories that are currently swirling around the organization, notably in Canada. That it attracts a wide range of leaders and professes to follow a progressive agenda are certainly true. But to attribute to it far reaching powers aimed at dominating global policy discourse and decision-making is frankly preposterous. When I see such conspiracy theories manipulated for shameless political gain, it is doubly disappointing. All the more reason to ensure that the global economic order embraces mutual respect, openness, transparency and the rule of law.

10

ASPIRING TO GLOBAL ECONOMIC LEADERSHIP

Central to my work in the 1980s and the 1990s was advancing a business and public policy agenda that would provide a solid foundation for Canada's long-term economic growth and higher incomes for all. Faced with the globalization juggernaut, the rapid advance of technology, and the global competition for talent, Canada had to move quickly or be left behind in the high-stakes game. I have already explained how we at the Business Council approached the tough challenges confronting Canada, beginning with redefining the role and responsibilities of its business leadership. We advanced proposals for tackling fiscal problems, pursuing a bold free trade agreement with the United States and subsequently Mexico and strengthening the foundations of national unity in those years when the Canadian idea was threatened by its most implacable antagonists. But there was still a great deal of work to be done.

TAX REFORM

Tax reform, never easy and rarely popular, was high on our agenda. In the address I made to the Institute of Corporate Directors in Toronto in February 1987, I explained why tax reform was so important to Canada. "A great number of Canadians believe that the tax system is unfair, complex, and burdensome. And they are right," I said. I also warned that tax reform is exceedingly difficult to achieve. Anticipating the intense debate that would be ignited by the Mulroney government's plans in this area, I said, "We should not be surprised by the controversy that will surround the government's proposals. After all, controversy and taxation are bedmates. It was this reality that prompted Edmund Burke to exclaim, 'To tax and to please, no more than to love and be wise, is not given to man.' Winston Churchill was more direct. He said, 'There is no such thing as a good tax.'"

The most important tax policy initiative of the Mulroney government was the Goods and Services Tax (GST). The GST replaced the previous hidden manufacturers' sales tax of 13.5 per cent. A value-added, consumption-based sales tax, the GST represented a major economic reform that would prove to be highly controversial when it was first implemented. The Business Council was an early advocate of replacing the manufacturers' sales tax with a value-added tax.

Our support for introducing a value-added tax was part of a broader Business Council study of Canadian tax policy initiated in 1985. At the time, Royal Bank of Canada chief executive and Business Council chair Rowland Frazee and I were of the view that advocating bold tax reform along with our pursuit of a Canada–United States free trade agreement might be overly ambitious. I consulted Gerald Heffernan, chief executive of Co-Steel and chair of the Council's task force on taxation. Following a long discussion over dinner in early 1985, we decided to test the waters and quietly raise the idea with the Department of Finance.

Marshall Cohen was the deputy minister of finance and someone I could speak with in confidence. "Don't go there" was his advice. "A consumption tax would be politically explosive and there's too much going on right now." But we did not give up. We began by building support for the idea of a value-added tax among Business Council members. It was not long before a political champion for the idea emerged in the person of finance minister Michael Wilson. In his memoirs, Brian Mulroney reveals that Wilson first proposed the idea in 1987. "Michael was adamant that we had to do this. He argued that with the huge tax reductions he envisaged in personal income taxes, the new value-added tax could be implemented in a way that was truly 'revenue neutral,' meaning that the federal government would not be extracting any more from taxpayers than it was giving up in rate concessions on the income tax side. He also felt strongly that we should implement the income tax cuts and the new consumption tax at the same time." Mulroney writes plainly of his fears over making such a move: "I knew enough about politics to predict that this innovation, however neat in its design and conception, was going to cause one helluva big political row." He was right. To Mulroney's great credit, abetted by Wilson's unflinching persistence, the two men mustered the courage to forge ahead, win caucus support, and pass the GST legislation in the House of Commons. When the Liberal-majority Senate attempted to scuttle the bill, Mulroney responded by appointing enough additional senators to outvote their opposition. Wilson could count on the strong support of the Department of Finance, where Stanley Hartt had succeeded Marshall Cohen as deputy minister. Hartt told me that at first he thought the idea of a value-added tax would be a political non-starter; it was Wilson who brought him on side once he fully appreciated his minister's reasoning.

A fierce storm of protest and country-wide opposition greeted the proposal. The Business Council waded into the battle, and once again I found myself devoting much of my time to speeches and media debates. The going was tough. In the end, when the GST became law on January 1, 1991, I was convinced that another important foundation stone of Canadian competitiveness had been secured. But the Mulroney Progressive Conservatives paid a high political price, and the effects lingered on right through the federal election of 1993.

The GST legislation did not achieve all that the Business Council had wished for. Notably, a national sales tax that fully integrated the sales taxes of the federal and provincial governments did not materialize. Yet the position that we at the Council took in the face of massive opposition helped encourage the federal government and, joined to the leadership and tenacity of Mulroney and Wilson, helped save the day for the GST.

COMPETITIVENESS

As Canada entered the 1990s, our country faced strong headwinds. The inflation of the 1970s and 1980s had driven the consumer price index sharply higher, prompting the Bank of Canada to respond. This led to a severe recession between 1990 and 1992, with high levels of unemployment and a spike in the value of the Canadian dollar. The United States fared better than we did, with less pronounced inflationary pressures. The recession of the early 1990s had a global effect; in some regions, the loss of consumer and business confidence was marked by civil unrest.

When I observed the protests descending into riots in various cities in the United Kingdom, I wondered if we might see the same in Canada. My colleagues and I were deeply concerned, and the subject of possible civil unrest came up at several of our Business Council meetings. Throughout this period, I kept in close touch with Bank of Canada governor John Crow. I enjoyed a good relationship with the tall, lean, and outspoken banker. He was not so loved by the many who charged that his anti-inflation crusade was an anti-labour gambit waged on the backs of the poor and unemployed. On one occasion, at the Château Laurier, I was chairing a meeting of the Canadian Labour Market and Productivity Centre, and Crow was speaking. One of my labour union colleagues, John Fryer, attacked Crow vociferously and suggested they settle their differences outside. I quickly brought the two to order—but only just.

As they had done in the early 1980s, the tough economic times prompted business leaders to look for effective policy solutions, beginning with our own enterprises. Our thinking at the time went something like this: the opening of the economy with free trade would bring long-term benefits; tax reform would make the country more competitive; and, painful as it was, defeating inflationary forces would further add to our competitive strength. In due course, these moves would prepare Canada for the twenty-first-century economy. But in the meantime, we asked ourselves, what could business do that would make a difference? This we knew: while our companies had to make adjustments to compete in the free trade environment we helped create, we had not done nearly enough.

On September 5, 1990, I wrote to my Business Council colleagues. "When you are asked about your principal economic concerns," I told them, "the vast majority respond 'the level of competitiveness of our businesses and of our country as a whole.' I propose that we do something about this—something significant, something that will give coherence and substance to the arguments of the BCNI and the business leaders who wish to provide leadership in advancing the case of this most important of economic issues." What I had in mind was to reach out to Harvard professor Michael Porter, who had just published a highly acclaimed book, *The Competitive Advantage of Nations*. Porter had based his analysis on a ten-nation study that included Denmark, Germany, Italy, Japan, Korea, Singapore, Sweden, the United Kingdom, and the United States. When I spoke with Porter, I proposed that he and his team add Canada to the study. We met and established the terms of reference for the eight-month undertaking. The initiative got under way in November.

The study included a statistical analysis of Canada's competitive position, an analysis of Canada's competitive infrastructure, and a case study of Canadian industries. The undertaking involved close collaboration with a group of Council chief executives led by Jack Lawrence of Burns Fry and myself, and a Council headquarters team led by Jock Finlayson. Porter's study, supported by the consulting firm Monitor, was concluded in October 1991, on time and within budget—but not without some tense moments along the way. On October 24, Porter and I released the study in Toronto and with it a summary version Jock Finlayson and I had prepared. Given the state of the economy, public anticipation was intense; we were getting requests for the study and its summary from every part of Canada.

The Porter initiative served as a catalyst for deeper and more urgent thinking about how Canadian companies could remodel themselves in the face of rapidly expanding global competition. Several months later, in an address in Montreal to the international partners of Ernst & Young, I summed up the challenge as follows: "Canada is in trouble. We are being dragged down by slow productivity growth, declining cost competitiveness, weaknesses in innovation at the enterprise level, poor business-labour relations, shortfalls in education and training, soaring public debt, and a high and rising government share of GDP."

Directing my remarks squarely at the leadership of our companies, I laid out a plan of action: we had to adopt a more intensely entrepreneurial culture and innovative management; strengthen investment performance; develop leading-edge capability to harness science and technology as a major source of competitive advantage; build strategic alliances and forge closer links with suppliers, customers, competitors, and non-business entities; upgrade and expand workforce skills training at firm and industry levels; adopt more cooperative, flexible, and participatory approaches to human resource management; build a larger presence in global markets outside of North America; and embrace sustainable development as a corporate objective.

I was equally clear about the responsibilities of governments: they needed to secure a positive economic climate, low inflation and interest rates, disciplined public-sector finances, streamlined regulations, a competitive tax system, high-quality infrastructure, and education and labour-market policies that resulted in higher standards and improved workforce skills and incentives. In the case of Canada in particular, I stressed the importance of the government role in strengthening our economic union by removing the barriers to the free movement of capital, goods, services, and labour and achieving maximum federal-provincial coordination in the fiscal, taxation, trade, and regulatory domains.

To reinforce this message, the policy committee of the Business Council issued a statement in July 1992, titled "A New Century Economy: An Agenda for Action." It elaborated on the themes and recommendations of my remarks in Montreal and concluded with a challenge: "The agenda we have put forward is not for the timid, nor for the cynics, nor for those who are seeking to roll back the forces of change. It is designed for those who see in the inevitability of change great opportunities for propelling Canada to new and higher levels of economic accomplishment and social well-being. We invite all Canadians to join forces with us in taking this journey together."

Thirty years later, regrettably little has changed. As the current national debate on competitiveness reveals, the goals by and large have remained the same. The disappointment is that relatively little action has been taken to fulfill them. Recently, at a roundtable in Ottawa, where I lamented that so many good policy solutions continue to lie fallow, one of my colleagues said, "Canadians are superb at developing sound policy positions. We are dismal failures at implementation." I could not disagree with her assessment.

THE CHALLENGE OF THE CHRÉTIEN GOVERNMENT

On November 4, 1993, Jean Chrétien, the leader of the Liberal Party of Canada, assumed office as our country's twentieth prime minister. The outcome of the general election was a political earthquake. The Progressive Conservative Party, led by Mulroney's short-term successor, Kim Campbell, was reduced to two seats in the House of Commons. Mercifully, my old friend Jean Charest was one of the two survivors. The new prime minister named Paul Martin as minister of finance. Given the dire economic circumstances facing the country in the years immediately leading up to the election, Martin faced especially tough hurdles. These were compounded by the continuing threats to national unity by separatists in Quebec.

The election of the Chrétien government raised immediate challenges for the Business Council. Chrétien and I had already clashed on what he perceived to be the Council's bias in favour of the Mulroney government's positions on free trade, the GST, and constitutional reform. Fences needed to be mended. I was optimistic that I could bring about a rapprochement. Moreover, I was convinced that the new government would, on its own, recognize the benefits of moving the party back toward its centrist roots, especially on economic matters. With his business experience, Paul Martin in the finance portfolio gave my colleagues and me hope. In addition, despite our differences, I had always found Chrétien's "little guy from Shawinigan" style disarming.

Early in Chrétien's term, Council chair Ted Newall and I went to see him. Our task was to pay our respects and to do what we could to persuade him to rethink his opposition to both NAFTA and the GST. It helped that Chrétien and Newall had a trusting relationship. The prime minister gave us a good hearing but made no promises. Meanwhile, Council members and I actively lobbied Liberal cabinet ministers, in particular Paul Martin and the minister of international trade, Roy MacLaren, to preserve the status quo on the GST and NAFTA. In time, the new government wisely came to the same conclusion on what was in the national interest.

DEFICITS AND DEBT

With NAFTA and the GST secure, our attention at the Council turned to the serious fiscal challenge facing the country. Both of Brian Mulroney's finance ministers, Michael Wilson and his successor, Donald Mazankowski, were competent and driven by a high sense of public purpose. In addition, both were fine gentlemen, and it was a pleasure to work with them. Mazankowski had served as deputy prime minister and House leader since 1986 and was aptly nicknamed the Mulroney government's "chief operating officer." The one goal that eluded them both, however, was taming Canada's deficit. This challenge fell to the new government and finance minister Paul Martin. Chrétien had an instinctive belief that runaway deficits were dangerous, and his support for Martin's anti-deficit crusade was crucial.

By 1993, deficits had been accumulating for some twenty-four years, beginning with Pierre Trudeau's first term in office. The federal debt, as a consequence, was rising inexorably. In the last year of the Mulroney government, the deficit had risen to 5.4 per cent of GDP and the national debt to over 62 per cent of GDP. By the time of the 1993 federal election, interest payments on the debt were in excess of $62 billion, and one in every three dollars the government took in was devoted to paying interest. This was not healthy from an economic point of view. Nor was it a winning situation politically. Provincial government finances were in no better shape, and the country's collective debt burden was drawing increasingly negative reviews from debt-rating agencies. The situation was so dire that rumours were rife of possible intervention by the International Monetary Fund.

Paul Martin's first budget took a cautious approach, and criticism was quick to come. We at the Business Council did not pull any punches. We were deeply concerned. Confidence levels in the economy were tanking, and a rise in interest rates wreaked damage on budget calculations. It was these circumstances that led the Chrétien government to bite the bullet and tackle the deficit. Martin had the advantage of being served by deputy minister of finance David Dodge. Smart and principled, Dodge was a plain speaker and a fine economist. He would continue to serve effectively at Finance until 1997, and from 2001 to 2008 served as the seventh governor of the Bank of Canada. I first met David at Queen's University, where we became friends. He also was Susan's boss in the Department of Finance, where he was highly respected.

In my view, free trade and the GST, signature economic achievements of the Mulroney government, were matched in significance by the Chrétien-Martin restructuring of federal fiscal policy. The 1995 budget introduced sharp cuts in government program spending for a period of two years, which led to a remarkable turnaround in the government's fiscal position. By the 1997/98 fiscal year, to strong applause from the Business Council, the federal deficit had been eliminated. This was to continue for a decade more. Canada's fiscal turnaround was enthusiastically recognized at a series of presentations I made to the annual meeting of the World Economic Forum in Davos titled "Northern Renaissance." The country's success was capturing worldwide notice. In October 1997, *The Economist* wrote of Chrétien: "No other major country's leader can boast of such fiscal virtue, or so large a swing to it so swiftly achieved."

Thanks to the Mulroney and Chrétien economic reforms, Canada was significantly better positioned as we approached the beginning of the new century. But in the Business Council's view, more work needed to be done, both by government and the private sector. We focused in particular on reducing the tax burden. In an October 1998 report titled "Tax Reduction Initiative," I announced the results of a six-month study by the Council and argued that Canada's income tax burden was so far out of line with that of the country's major trading partners and competitors that significant tax reduction had to begin at once, and that the government needed to convince Canadians that taxes were going down, that they would continue to fall year after year, and that, once cut, they would stay cut.

The Chrétien government did not disappoint. Martin saw the need and the benefits of cutting taxes, and in his budgets of 2000 and 2001 he delivered an ambitious program of tax cuts. In the meantime, we at the Business Council pressed for an even bolder approach. Paul Martin heard me say that a $100-billion tax cut would massively boost Canadian competitiveness. This led to a late-evening telephone call from the minister. He was fuming.

"Tom," he said, "what have you been smoking? Where am I going to find $100 billion?"

I stood my ground and argued that given Canada's now strong economic fundamentals, thanks to his stellar fiscal moves, a big cut phased in over time was not only affordable but would deliver major economic benefits to the country as a whole.

"Look," he retorted, "if you do not understand the arithmetic here at Finance, get Susan to explain it to you!" Before I could respond, he added, "I guess I shouldn't have said that. I know the two of you are separated by a bamboo curtain."

"More like an iron curtain," I told him.

We had a good laugh about it, but the reality was that Susan, who would serve five finance ministers during her public service career, was notoriously tight-lipped. I respected her unflinching discretion, as did others.

Martin's record as finance minister is deserving of special praise. Restoring order to federal government finances and ushering in major tax cuts are a large part of the story, but that was not all. With the assistance of an exceptionally able team of senior officials, he reinforced the central role of his department in managing the billions of dollars that the federal government transfers to provinces and territories each year. By this means, he was able to influence social policies within a national framework sensitive to the government's fiscal, economic, and political agendas. One of his innovations I admired most was his use of budgetary cushions for debt reduction. Add to these achievements the hugely consequential securing of the future of the Canada Pension Plan (CPP). In his fine memoir, *Hell or High Water: My Life in and out of Politics*, Martin says, "When we took office in 1993, we actually had two financial time bombs dropped in our laps: the deficit and the CPP." The problem with the CPP was the size of its unfunded liability and the questions surrounding the government's capacity to fund its Old Age Security requirements—a subject that had received relatively little public notice. Martin puts his finger on the matter: "The problem was, as the ratio of pensioners to workers shifted, the ability of the workers to sustain the burden was increasingly compromised." Because the CPP was jointly administered by Ottawa and the provinces and would require an increase in contributions to give it the soundness it required, negotiating the needed reforms was particularly complex and politically sensitive, to say the least. In Martin's memoir, he praises Susan, the assistant deputy minister responsible for federal-provincial fiscal relations, for the important role she played. He says, "At Finance, our approach to pension reform, which required in-depth coordination with provincial officials, was skilfully developed and led by Susan Peterson." Given the significance of the CPP reform, this was high praise indeed. Arguably, it was the crowning achievement of Susan's public service career.

CANADA HOUSE AND THE PRIME MINISTER

I was able to mix business with pleasure at a memorable event that took me to England in May 1998. Arguably our country's most famous landmark in a foreign capital, Canada House, on London's Trafalgar Square, was being reopened on May 13 after a major restoration. The Queen was to cut the ceremonial ribbon, and Chrétien was to represent the government. Having received an invitation to attend, I took full advantage and arranged for a Business Council event at Canada House, thanks to my friend Roy MacLaren, the Canadian high commissioner in London.

Her Majesty, with her usual charm and grace, performed splendidly. The Canadians present reflected on the historical significance of the occasion: the Queen was following in the footsteps of her grandfather, George V, who had opened the building in 1925. The restoration of Canada House was assisted with donations from Canadian businesses. The new quarters offered visitors leading-edge technical facilities, an auditorium, a film screening room, and a multipurpose space to showcase visual art.

In organizing the Business Council dinner, I invited on the Council's behalf a group of British business leaders as well as a number of former British high commissioners to Canada with whom I had retained a close association. Among them were Sir Brian Fall and Sir Nicholas Bayne, consummate diplomats who had served with distinction in Ottawa. I was helped in assembling the British business guests by Winfried Bischoff, the chair of investment bank Schroders, whom I knew from sitting on the bank's Canadian advisory board. Also helpful to me was Adair Turner, who at the time was the director of the Confederation of British Industry. In addition to Roy MacLaren, we were joined by Canada's minister of international trade, Sergio Marchi. The star of the evening was, of course, Chrétien, who was in an ebullient mood. My Canadian business colleagues included Al Flood of CIBC, John McNeil of Sun Life Financial, and Ron Mannix of Coril Holdings. Among our guests was also Conrad Black.

The most delicious part of the evening was the extraordinary culinary experience offered by a group of Canadian chefs, members of Canada's Culinary Olympics team. They were in London for the opening of the competition, and I, not wanting to miss out on this once-in-a-lifetime opportunity, had asked if I could hire them for the evening. They did not disappoint, with plate after plate of beautifully presented delicacies. From memory, there was salmon from Newfoundland and British Columbia, lobsters from Nova Scotia, oysters from Prince Edward Island, bison from Manitoba, elk and beef from Alberta, shrimp from Matane in Quebec, and a selection of superb cheeses. The chefs had paired the small servings with an excellent assortment of Canadian wines. It was a warm and successful evening—an occasion when Canadian excellence was on display. The prime minister was very proud. We all were.

CANADA GLOBAL LEADERSHIP INITIATIVE

Looking back on three decades of policy activism on the part of the Business Council beginning in the early 1980s, one of the most ambitious, overarching undertakings was the Canada Global Leadership Initiative, launched in April 1999. Its goal was to make Canada "the best place in the world to live, to work, to invest and to grow." In the lead-up to the launch, several Council members expressed discomfort with the title and the ambitious goals I had suggested. One went so far as to say that the title was "too grandiose and the goals pie in the sky." Fortunately, the Council's executive committee was composed of bolder thinkers. David O'Brien had been elected chair, and the vice-chairs were Jacques Bougie, John Cleghorn, Jean Monty, and Jim Shepard. O'Brien was president and chief executive of Canadian Pacific, and Bougie, Cleghorn, Monty, and Shepard were the chief executives respectively of Alcan, the Royal Bank, BCE, and Finning International. They were fully supportive of the ambition of our initiative and gave me the word: "Let's go for it."

Their enthusiasm was complemented by long-time Business Council member Ron Mannix. As an example of his passion for advancing good public policy, Ron made a generous financial contribution to the Canada Global Leadership Initiative. His gift helped expand the excellent resource base we counted on as the initiative unfolded.

In an address to the Business Council membership in November 1999, I briefed my colleagues on the progress of the journey we had launched six months earlier. In my address, which I titled "Storming the Status Quo: On the Road to Making Canada a Global Leader," I said, "Behind us lie the great struggles against rampant inflation and runaway government deficits. Behind us lies the crusade to persuade Canadians to cast off the shackles of protectionism and embrace the disciplines and rewards of the marketplace. Behind us lie two decades of divisive debate and painful adjustments that today have yielded concrete results—a Canada with remarkably improved economic fundamentals." I went on to point out, however, that while we were making progress, other countries were doing even better.

In the next segment of my address, I summed up the rationale for the Canada Global Leadership Initiative. I pointed out that while we saw progress in Canada, we saw too little creative energy, too much complacency, and too many disquieting signs. We saw public debt and taxes continue to rise. We saw a currency that had still failed to gain much respect. We saw exporters quick to profit from the lower costs a sagging currency brings but slow to invest in the productivity needed to compete over time. We saw business investment rising but our share of foreign direct investment falling, even within North America. Most telling of all, amid the longest economic expansion in North America since the Second World War, we saw real after-tax incomes of Canadians wallowing in stagnation. We saw progress all over the world, but Canadian families could not seem to capture a fair share of the benefits. And so we sounded the alarm, an alarm that a leading editorial in the *Globe and Mail* referred to as the equivalent of a 911 call to the prime minister of Canada.

We spoke out not a moment too soon. Corporate Canada was facing a wave of takeovers. The country was losing a score of head offices, and talent was being lured away by opportunities beyond our borders. Moreover, some of Canada's most impressive companies were having to come to terms with what was called "the Canada discount," attributable to a weak and declining currency, small, illiquid equity markets, fragmented securities regulation, high taxes, especially on capital gains, and a lingering suspicion of interventionist policies.

To face these challenges, we at Council headquarters engaged our members in an intense round of conversations. We organized CEO roundtables in Canada's major cities. We created an advisory board of some of the country's brightest minds. We reached out to Canada's leading think tanks. By April of 2000, we were ready to bring forward our ideas to the Canadian public at the Canada Global Leadership CEO summit in Toronto, convening the full Business Council. Guests included other business leaders, heads of business associations, federal and provincial government leaders, university presidents, respected academics, and think tank representatives. Two provocative Business Council papers were tabled: "Global Champion or Falling Star? The Choice Canada Must Make" and "Going for Gold: Winning Corporate Strategies and Their Impact on Canada." These papers articulated an unprecedented business-led call to action, with business squarely shouldering its own share of responsibility for moving forward.

To underscore how important an entrepreneurial culture is to economic success, I invited Hong Kong chief executive Tung Chee-wha to dinner the evening before the CEO summit. Tung spoke in glowing terms of Hong Kong's flourishing economy in the aftermath of the 1997 handover to China. As we listened to his impressive presentation, none of us could imagine that Hong Kong's great promise would diminish so decidedly in the years to come and that its economic paramountcy would be supplanted by Shanghai. All this is to say that politics can undo in a short time the progress of even the most dynamic of economically advanced societies.

Paul Martin reacted coolly to the hard-hitting recommendations flowing from the summit. In part, this was due to a statement in one of the Council papers accusing the finance minister of "breathtaking timidity" on tax cuts. I was responsible for those words. They were meant to have a shock effect, and they did. Martin made it clear to me that he was not pleased, but there was no doubt in my mind that I had caught his attention.

NORTHERN EDGE

Following the CEO summit, I was so profoundly stimulated by the experience—the explosion of good ideas, the fascinating rounds of cross-country discussions, the stimulation of meeting so many talented people, the vivid examples of what was working well and not so well in Canada—that I decided to write a book. Given the demands of my work schedule, Susan thought I was mad, and so did my colleagues at Business Council headquarters. Among my colleagues, there was one exception: David Stewart-Patterson. David, who was our senior associate in policy and communications, encouraged me to take on the challenge. An excellent writer with a strong intellect, David had signed on in early 1997 and would go on to serve the Council with distinction for close to a decade and a half. I invited him to co-author the book with me, and he readily accepted. Our goal was to speak to some of the principal issues emerging from the Canada Global Leadership Initiative and, in some cases, go beyond the consensus adopted by our Council colleagues. We wanted to break fresh ground, test new ideas, and push the boundaries with bold solutions. Chair David O'Brien and the executive committee gave their blessing to the undertaking and we went on to complete our book in the last six months of 2000. The title we decided on was *Northern Edge: How Canadians Can Triumph in the Global Economy*.

In preparing to write the book, we not only drew on the rich collection of ideas and research flowing from the Canada Global Leadership Initiative but also interviewed over sixty chief executives across the country. While this was a gargantuan task, it afforded us the benefit of their views in the immediate aftermath of the Global Leadership Initiative, when many of the issues were still fresh in their minds. Many of them are quoted in our book, and their comments add valuable insights.

The book's policy prescriptions remain of central relevance to today's policy discourse in Canada. For example, on the need to prepare for bad times in good times, strive for continuous improvement, grasp the significance of exponential change, spare no effort in the competition for talent, defend publicly funded education, deal with the causes of poverty, practise environmental leadership, and lead by example.

David and I were very pleased with the reception to our book in Council circles. The greatest reward is that its themes have continued to influence Business Council thinking for two decades. To show our appreciation of the Business Council's support of Northern Edge, I proposed to David that we donate to the Council the monetary advance we received from the publisher. David graciously agreed.

PAUL MARTIN AND THE G20

The G20, otherwise known as the Group of Twenty, is an international forum for the governments and central bank governors representing nineteen leading economies and the European Union. Collectively, the G20 economies account for some 90 per cent of the world's gross product, approximately 80 per cent of world trade, and the majority of the planet's population. Paul Martin has been rightly recognized as its principal architect, and this is no small achievement.

I had been a close follower of the work of the Group of Seven countries, known as the G7, since 1975, when its predecessor, the

G6, was created by France, Italy, Japan, the United Kingdom, the United States, and West Germany. Canada joined the group a year later. Like so many observers, I became convinced by the mid-1980s that the G7 could not legitimately carry out its role as a consensus forum on global economic and security concerns. The absence among its members of rising powers such as China, India, and Brazil and other key actors from the emerging world in my view would lead inevitably to a diminution of the G7's influence. To the great credit of Martin, who was serving as Canada's finance minister at the time, he took steps to do something about it.

In the spring of 1999, while sitting in the Washington office of Larry Summers, President Clinton's nominee for treasury secretary, Paul Martin proposed expanding the G7 to include major players from the developing world. Summers quickly came on side and, according to both Martin and Summers, the two of them composed a list of possible member countries on the back of a manila envelope. Thus was born the G20. Martin chaired its inaugural meeting in Berlin in December 1999. He did so again in 2000 as its host in Montreal, and continued in the chair through 2001, when India was unable to perform the role. In the meantime, Martin stepped up his campaign to elevate the G20 from a collective of finance ministers and central bankers to the country-leader level. Martin's proposal met with strong resistance, especially from G7 leaders, until the great financial crisis in 2008.

The first meeting of G20 country leaders, held in Washington on November 15, 2008, was so successful in dealing with the crisis that it was repeated in London and Pittsburgh in 2009. It was in Pittsburgh that Martin's wish was fully realized and the country leaders designated the G20 to be the premier forum for their international cooperation. It was an extraordinary feat of statecraft and one that is underappreciated in Canada. It has also spawned a business response: B20 is a group of business leaders from the G20 countries who meet annually to offer policy recommendations to the G20 leaders. From inception, I was a strong supporter of both the G20 and B20 and ensured that the Business Council weighed in with our views on the G20's deliberations.

CORPORATE GOVERNANCE REFORM

In December 2001, the corporate world was shaken by the bankruptcy filing of energy services giant Enron, a company regarded as one of the most innovative and well managed in the United States. The collapse was sudden and unexpected, and it led to huge losses in investor wealth and in jobs, undermining confidence in investment markets. Enron's reported revenues in the 1990s were in the range of $10 billion, ballooning to close to $140 billion in 2001, and I counted myself among many business colleagues who were startled by its success but openly confessed to not fully understanding the company's business model. When it was revealed that Enron had falsified its accounts and that management and accounting advisers were complicit, the cries for regulatory reform grew louder. Close on the heels of the Enron scandal was the WorldCom debacle in the summer of 2002. One of the largest long-distance telephone companies in the United States, WorldCom was discovered to have over $3.8 billion of fraudulent balance sheet entries. In due course, the company admitted it had overstated its assets by more than $11 billion, one of the most massive accounting frauds in the history of the United States.

The turbulence generated by these collapses exacerbated an already unstable economic environment precipitated by the bursting of the dot-com bubble. The bubble, generated by excessive speculation surrounding internet-related companies, was punctured in

2002 when the Nasdaq Composite stock market index plunged 78 per cent from its peak. Canada was not spared. The most severe casualty was Nortel Networks, an iconic Canadian company founded in 1895 as the Northern Electric and Manufacturing Company. At its height, Nortel accounted for more than one-third of the total valuation of all companies listed on the Toronto Stock Exchange and employed over 94,000 people worldwide, with close to 26,000 in Canada. Nortel's market capitalization dropped from C$398 billion in September 2000 to less than C$5 billion in August 2002. Its stock price cratered, and 60,000 jobs disappeared.

The company's chief executive, John Roth, stepped down in 2001. Roth had been an active member of the Business Council and clearly was stunned by Nortel's sudden fall. He did not escape withering criticism. Should he have anticipated the burst of the dot-com bubble? I can't answer that except to say this: at no time in my conversations with him did I sense he saw the coming crisis. He did, however, speak of his discomfort that the company occupied such a huge position on the Toronto Stock Exchange. The failure of Nortel in my view was the most catastrophic corporate failure in Canadian history, with far-reaching social and economic consequences. It was also a harbinger of more trouble ahead as corporate financial complexity deepened, challenging the ability of governments and regulators to anticipate or avoid financial crises.

With confidence in markets shaken and public trust in private enterprise quickly evaporating, I believed the Business Council should act. I proposed to Council chair Charles Baillie and to our board of directors that we should conduct a study of Canadian corporate governance practices and examine ways in which they could be strengthened. The full membership of the Council strongly endorsed the initiative: we were off and running. It was agreed that Baillie and I should co-chair the undertaking, and in July 2002 we launched our new project. I had an excellent relationship with Baillie, whom I had known personally for two decades. Chief executive of the TD Bank Financial Group, Baillie was liked and respected among his peers. He was erudite with a sense of humour.

In September, barely two months later, Baillie and I tabled our report, titled "Governance, Values and Competitiveness: A Commitment to Leadership." It was co-signed by six highly experienced colleagues: Robert Brown, Derek Burney, David Emerson, Richard George, and Paul Tellier, the chief executives respectively of Bombardier, CAE, Canfor, Suncor Energy, and Canadian National Railway, and by David O'Brien, former Council chair and chair of EnCana. For six weeks, David Stewart-Patterson and I had carried out an intense bout of research and consulted a good number of Council colleagues. At a time of growing cynicism directed at capitalism and corporate greed, my colleagues were strongly motivated to get their thoughts on the record.

In the meantime, political reaction in the United States was swift and sharp. On July 9, 2002, President George W. Bush travelled to New York to deliver a blistering message to corporate America: "We've learned of some business leaders obstructing justice and misleading clients, falsifying records, business executives breaching the trust and abusing power. We've learned of CEOs earning tens of millions of dollars in bonuses just before their companies go bankrupt, leaving employees and retirees and investors to suffer. The business pages of American newspapers should not read like a scandal sheet." He went on to say, "When abuses like this begin to surface in the corporate world, it is time to reaffirm the basic principles and rules that make capitalism work: truthful books and honest people, and well-enforced laws against fraud and corruption. All investment is an act of faith, and faith is earned by integrity.

In the long run, there's no capitalism without conscience; there is no wealth without character."

To the president's credit, he followed up on these moral lessons with a ten-point accountability plan for American business, aimed at confronting corporate malfeasance and improving corporate governance. He also made clear what he considered to be the direct responsibilities of CEOs. "Everyone in a company should live up to high standards. But the burden of leadership rightly belongs to the chief executive officer. CEOs set the ethical direction for their companies. They set the moral tone by the decisions they make, the respect they show their employees, and their willingness to be held accountable for their actions. They set a moral tone by showing their disapproval of other executives who bring discredit to the business world."

"Bravo, Mr. President!" I said to myself. Bush gave his speech just one day after Charles Baillie and I had started writing our report. The following day, I spoke with the American ambassador to Canada, Paul Cellucci, and praised the president's initiative.

To this day, I remain immensely proud of our Business Council report. It was substantive and hard-hitting. Its opening paragraph does not mince words. We said that Canadian corporate governance standards were among the highest internationally, and Canada's enterprises and business leaders had a strong record of integrity, which served as a competitive advantage for our country. But even in Canada, we said, there had been prominent examples of illegal and unethical behaviour, and the sheer scale of some of the most recent scandals in the United States had lessened public confidence in enterprise throughout the world. Free markets worked well in fuelling human progress, we stressed, but trust was their indispensable foundation. We made it clear we were deeply disturbed by the irresponsibility of some of our peers. And we recommended that governments prosecute violations of the law with full vigour, including confiscation of ill-gotten gains and penalties that included jail time where justified.

Our recommendations embraced best practices in the domains of executive compensation, insider trading, CEO certification of annual and quarterly reports, strict enforcement of legal penalties, sanctions with compensation, and codes of conduct. On matters of governance, we acknowledged that the prime responsibility for policy and rules lies with shareholders, boards of directors elected to represent them, and regulators, and not with CEOs. It was important to state this division of responsibilities clearly, as I was reminded by governance experts that CEOs should not be telling boards what to do. At the same time, the collective wisdom and experience of the CEOs who made up our Council membership, many of them board members in their own right, was profound. We did not hesitate to let our views be known, and we knew that we would be heard.

On board independence, we endorsed the TSX governance guidelines making it clear that a substantial majority of board directors should be independent. We recommended that the same apply to the audit, governance, and compensation committees of the board. On board leadership, we recommended that the posts of chair and CEO be separate. On the role of the audit committee, we recommended strong financial competence on the part of its members and full empowerment, including direct authority over the work of the company's external auditors. On equity compensation, we recommended that both directors and senior managers should be given incentives to focus on the sustainable growth of shareholder value. And on transparency and disclosure, we recommended maximum compliance.

We stressed that restoring public trust and meeting the highest standards of corporate behaviour should not be left to boards of directors and CEOs alone. Everybody who influences the process of corporate decision-making—shareholders, directors, executives, employees, accountants, lawyers, financial analysts, journalists, and educators, as well as government officials and regulators—should be involved.

Our report was well received in government, academic, and business policy circles, and its timing could not have been more propitious. Important to Baillie and me was the high degree of acceptance of its contents within our own family of CEOs and entrepreneurs.

On one dimension, there was some difference in our approach compared with that of our American business counterparts. The Americans rushed to implement "bulletproof laws" against corporate malfeasance as reflected, for example, in the Sarbanes-Oxley Act, enacted on July 30, 2002. This overwhelming reliance on a highly legalistic, rules-based system caused us some concern. We accepted that enforceable rules were essential, but we also argued that adherence to well-understood principles and values was also very important.

Early in 2003, I addressed a corporate governance conference in Toronto. I began with a warning: "The new expectations of corporate governance sweeping across the world are based on a simple reality—you can run but you cannot hide. Inquisitive eyes and ears of governments and regulators, analysts and money-managers, customers and NGOs, journalists, whistleblowers are everywhere. Communication is instant. Analysis follows quickly. And the market's judgment can be swift and brutal."

I pursued my theme of principles and values versus rules with the following argument: Our goal should be to do better than Sarbanes-Oxley, and that did not mean simply trying to go further down the same road. By doing "better," I explained, I definitely did not mean looser or laxer but rather achieving equal or superior outcomes in terms of good governance and sustainable growth of shareholder value and doing a better job of preventing, not just punishing, ethical lapses and legal wrongdoing.

Making the case as to why the tone at the top mattered, I went on to say, "The bottom line is that all the rules in the world will not restore public confidence. And while regulators can make new rules and shareholders can vote for new governance practices, it is CEOs who must set the tone at the top of their enterprises. And in any recipe for rebuilding public trust, there is simply no possible substitute for honesty and personal integrity. Yes, we need to do a better job of catching and punishing those who break the rules and abuse that trust. But in the age of information overload, character matters more than ever. . . . It is business leaders who must earn the public trust. . . . No government can legislate that trust. No regulator can restore it. Businesses and business leaders must earn it."

The work of the Business Council provided a channel for our country's CEO community to contribute to the reform of Canadian corporate governance. Never before had the leaders of enterprise in Canada collectively tackled corporate governance reform backed by a strong consensus. Of course, we were not the only players. A host of interested parties had their say, and many of their ideas and recommendations carried both value and influence.

Shortly before speaking in Toronto, I had been to the World Economic Forum in Davos, where the clarion call for corporate governance reform was everywhere to be heard. The reforms in the United States that followed the public outrage at the Enron and WorldCom scandals were being mirrored in other jurisdictions. The overarching message at Davos was that countries that upheld high standards of corporate governance would be winners in the race for global economic leadership. Sadly, the great financial crisis of 2008–9 proved yet again that no matter how stringent the rules, corruption and the abuse of power could still make an appearance. Canada weathered the crisis relatively well, and our financial institutions remained rock solid. Good governance helped make the difference. In the decades since, Canada's reputation as one of the world's leaders in corporate governance has served us well.

On the subject of corporate conduct, the Chrétien government introduced landmark legislation in 2003 to eliminate corporate and union donations to parties at the federal level and limit personal contributions to just $5000. (Prime Minister Harper subsequently slashed the individual limit to $1000.) I had long been concerned about such donations and their effects on the electoral process. I dreaded too the prospects of Canada following the American example where the role of money in politics in my view is profoundly corrosive. I also objected to the presumption in some quarters in Canada that corporations were fair game for party bagmen to insinuate that money will buy you influence in Ottawa. When I first heard of the Chrétien government's intentions, I strongly encouraged the government to move forward. It did and the Canadian electoral system is better for it. So is corporate Canada.

11

9/11 AND REIMAGINING NORTH AMERICA

Following the implementation of the Canada–United States Free Trade Agreement and NAFTA, I continued to give thought to how these historic achievements could be cemented and built upon. While I never supported the view that the continent could or should move toward a common market arrangement involving deeper institutional integration, I believed that the free trade model could be improved upon. As I used to say to my students at law school, "When it comes to trade agreements, think of a bicycle; if you are not peddling, you fall over. So it is with trade agreements. They need to evolve."

In discussions with colleagues in the United States and Mexico, the subject of a "NAFTA plus" was often on the agenda. Mexican president Vicente Fox, who assumed office on December 1, 2000, was an active exponent of a more integrated North America. During a visit to Toronto as president-elect, when I chaired a luncheon in his honour, he outlined a vision for the continent that went well beyond the status quo. Not surprisingly, the Chrétien government was cool to the idea, as was Washington. Sovereignty issues remained a point of sensitivity in both Canada and the United States, and despite Fox's willingness to test the waters on a NAFTA plus, sovereignty concerns were never far from the surface in Mexico as well. Notwithstanding that, influential members of Mexico's business community, notably my old friend Juan Gallardo, were keen to pursue the possibilities of it, but it never amounted to much in the 1990s.

I was of the view that the most promising avenue for improvements lay in our bilateral relationship with the United States. President Clinton, after all, was an active supporter of liberalized trade. He fought hard in support of NAFTA, and throughout his presidency continued to advocate the benefits of free trade despite vigorous opposition from some of his fellow Democrats. It helped that during his tenure the United States economy recorded robust annual growth and strong job creation. Notably, the Clinton administration was able to generate budget surpluses from 1998 to 2001, the only surpluses recorded after 1969. It also helped that Clinton and Jean Chrétien enjoyed a positive relationship. I had the opportunity to meet Clinton on several occasions, thanks in part to two very able U.S. ambassadors who served in Ottawa during his presidency. One was James Blanchard, a lawyer and former governor of Michigan. I struck up a good relationship with Blanchard shortly after his arrival as ambassador in 1993, and we remained in close touch during his tenure. The other was lawyer Gordon Giffin, who served as ambassador from 1997 to the conclusion of the Clinton presidency. Both were smart and well connected. Both were passionate about Canada and superb interpreters of the Canadian scene. Whenever I needed counsel or help in dealing with Canada-United States issues, they were always there. The Blanchards and the Giffins were frequent guests at our residence and Susan and I at theirs.

Visits to Ottawa by American presidents are customary. These are usually accompanied by state dinners and an address to Canada's Parliament. I have been privileged to meet six presidents in our national capital, beginning with Richard Nixon. The most memorable of these visits for me was President Clinton's, on

October 8, 1999. Clinton was in Ottawa for the opening of the new American embassy, and Susan and I were guests at the ribbon-cutting ceremony. Apparently, it was the first time a sitting president had opened any American embassy. Ambassador Giffin was especially proud of having pulled this off.

Following the ribbon-cutting, Clinton was scheduled to travel to Mont-Tremblant to deliver a speech to an international conference hosted by the Forum of the Federations. Knowing that this was on his schedule, I asked him at the embassy reception what his central message was going to be. He would say, he told me, that "federations were created for a reason and usually they work well. Your country is a good example." The president went on to Mont-Tremblant and stunned his audience, including Quebec separatist leaders, with a largely extemporaneous speech extolling the virtues of federalism and upholding Canada as a shining example. Understandably, his words were received with enthusiasm in federalist circles but not by the likes of Quebec premier Lucien Bouchard. When I read the transcript of Clinton's remarks, I was hugely impressed. They were learned as well as eloquent. His intervention at Mont-Tremblant was also a way of doing a favour for his friend Jean Chrétien, an example of how important personal relationships can be between leaders.

The Chrétien-Clinton relationship was well served in Washington by Ambassador Michael Kergin, who had succeeded Derek Burney. Just as Burney had the ear of Mulroney, Kergin had the ear of Chrétien. I rarely set foot in Washington without calling on Kergin for advice. Always accessible, he could not have been more helpful.

In an address I presented in Montreal on June 5, 1999, celebrating the tenth anniversary of the Canada–United States Free Trade Agreement, I identified areas where Canada and the United States might expand the benefits of the trade pact. "We must make fresh efforts to engage Americans in a common cause. For starters, we must seek every opportunity to eliminate impediments at the border, but in addition we should consider moving beyond the NAFTA rules to common standards; to non-discrimination in governmental procurement; to further liberalization in services; and yes, even to common rules about competition policies and subsidies. The effect of such a move would be to bolster Canadian growth, productivity, innovation and investment."

Shortly thereafter, there was an important changing of the guard in the United States. On January 20, 2001, George W. Bush was inaugurated as the forty-third president, with Dick Cheney as his vice-president. Susan and I were in Washington for the inauguration ceremonies, which we observed from the balcony of the Canadian embassy on Pennsylvania Avenue. I was always impressed by the pomp associated with the orderly transfer of power in the Great Republic. On inauguration morning, we watched from our windows at the Hay-Adams hotel as Bush and his entourage visited St. John's Episcopal Church, directly across the street—an oft-respected inauguration day tradition. Bush's victory over Democrat standard-bearer Al Gore was a narrow one. I had met Gore only once, when, in April 1997, he graciously invited me to join him at his table at a luncheon he hosted for Chrétien at the magnificent ceremonial quarters of the State Department. Experienced, earnest, and engaging, he would have been a worthy president, I believe.

GINGER GROUP AND 9/11
Many of my American colleagues believed that the post-NAFTA status quo was satisfactory and there was no real need to reopen the free trade agenda. One exception was Peter McPherson, the president of Michigan State University. Highly respected, he had served in senior positions in various American administrations, including

as deputy secretary at the United States Treasury in the latter years of the Reagan presidency. In the late 1990s, McPherson and I decided to form a "ginger group" of like-minded Americans and Canadians to explore how we might advance our common agenda, and we agreed to serve as co-chairs. Among the Canadians in the group were Derek Burney, former ambassador to the United States and chief executive of CAE; David Emerson, Canfor chief executive; James Gray, Canadian Hunter Exploration chair; Simon Reisman, chief Canadian negotiator of the Canada–United States Free Trade Agreement; Michael Hart, professor of trade policy at Carleton University; Stanley Hartt, former deputy minister of finance and chair of Salomon Smith Barney Canada; Angus Reid, chair and chief executive officer of Ipsos-Reid; and Paul Tellier, the president and chief executive officer of Canadian National. The Americans came to the table with an influential group including General Motors chair John F. Smith.

I hosted the first meeting of the ginger group at Ottawa's Rideau Club in September 2001. Michael Hart prepared a thoughtful briefing paper for the meeting on the future of the Canada–United States economic relationship. Hart, whom I regarded as the finest trade policy analyst in Canada at the time, concluded that "the time has come for Canada and the United States to consider jointly whether they can take steps to remove or constrain remaining barriers to cross-border trade and investment. . . . They are most likely to be resolved on the basis of a comprehensive initiative that can capture the imagination of political leaders on both sides of the border and generate the level of support necessary to overcome narrowly focused opposition." As for Mexico, Hart recommended that the Canada–United States initiative should move ahead on its own with the goal of bringing Mexico along at a later date, assuming that the results could be incorporated into NAFTA.

While most of us at the table shared enthusiasm for the idea of a fresh Canada–United States initiative, the consensus was that it would be difficult to galvanize political support for such a move among the political leadership of the two countries. The greatest obstacle, we agreed, was complacency. Part of my summation included words that haunt me to this day: "Barring a major economic or security threat to the continent that would shake us out of our complacency, the likelihood of successfully mounting a new and bold bilateral initiative is slim." It was impossible to imagine, as we said our farewells, that the next morning the world as we knew it would be changed forever.

I departed for Montreal by train early on the morning of the eleventh. In Montreal, the sky was a brilliant blue as I went off to a breakfast meeting. Moments after 9 a.m., I was called out of my meeting and told an aircraft had struck one of the towers of the World Trade Center in Manhattan. We rushed to a television set and watched in utter disbelief. I remained transfixed as a second aircraft struck the second tower. Both towers were now burning. If there had been any doubt, the second strike confirmed in our minds that this was a coordinated attack. At 9:29 a.m., President Bush made his first public statement acknowledging that the attacks were "an apparent terrorist attack on our country." Minutes afterwards, it was confirmed that a third aircraft had crashed into the Pentagon. The calls I made in the ensuing hours are a blur to me now. I spoke with Susan, of course, to family members, and friends in New York and elsewhere across the country. In addition to deep shock and sadness, anger welled up in me as I thought of the countless victims. I met my old friend David Culver for lunch at the Mount Royal Club. We tried to grasp the immensity of what had happened. I also called my office to cancel my flight to New

York City planned for Thursday of that week, where I was to attend a board meeting of David Rockefeller's Americas Society.

I rushed back to Business Council headquarters that afternoon, where I met with staff and began a round of calls with Council colleagues. I also got in touch with the Prime Minister's Office, the ministries of defence, finance, and trade, the RCMP, and various security officials. Everyone I spoke to was trying to digest what was happening. Over the next seventy-two hours, it became clear that the attacks were going to have a major impact on Canada–United States border operations and potentially far-reaching consequences for bilateral economic activity. The day following the attacks, I sent a letter to President Bush expressing both sorrow and solidarity. On September 14, Susan and I joined with one hundred thousand other Canadians on Parliament Hill mourning the great tragedy—a tragedy that took the lives of three thousand people from ninety-three countries, twenty-four of them Canadians.

Prime Minister Chrétien, American ambassador Paul Cellucci, and Governor General Adrienne Clarkson offered moving salutes to the victims. All around us, I could see people in tears as the prime minister reminded us that Canadians across the country were gathered in similar ceremonies of tribute. This spoke to me in a deeply emotional way, driving home what I always believed represented the uniqueness of the Canadian-American relationship.

While it would take several days to fully understand Canada's remarkable response to the 9/11 catastrophe, I shared a deep sense of pride in what came to be known as "Operation Yellow Ribbon." Within hours of the terrorist attacks, Canada had offered safe harbour to hundreds of American flights, thus clearing the skies over the United States from further potentially destructive suicide missions. Over 30,000 passengers and 238 aircraft were diverted to Canadian airports, as near and as far as Halifax, Gander, Vancouver, Winnipeg, Toronto, Calgary, Moncton, Montreal, Goose Bay, Edmonton, Hamilton, Whitehorse, Deer Lake, and Yellowknife. It was an extraordinary example of close collaboration between our two countries in the face of a grave emergency. It was notable that the senior officer at North American Aerospace Defense Command at Cheyenne Mountain who coordinated the initial response was a Canadian by the name of Michael Jellinek.

One of the most revealing encounters I experienced in the immediate aftermath of 9/11 was with Richard Perle, chair of the Defense Policy Board Advisory Committee in Washington. Thanks to an introduction provided by my friend Berel Rodal, Perle accepted my invitation to come to Ottawa for a dinner I hosted on October 21 and a breakfast meeting the following morning. Perle, a neo-conservative hawk, was highly influential in the Bush-Rumsfeld circle and would come to be known as one of the principal architects of the invasion of Iraq. Our dinner took place in the Hayes Suite at the Château Laurier and included Business Council chair Jean Monty; Herb Gray, the deputy prime minister; Gen. Ray Henault, chief of the defence staff; Giuliano Zaccardelli, commissioner of the RCMP; Mitchell Sharp, adviser to Prime Minister Chrétien; Berel Rodal; and business colleagues CIBC chief executive John Hunkin and entrepreneur Jozef Straus. Perle lauded Canada's military engagement in the war in Afghanistan, which had been launched a couple of weeks earlier, on October 7.

The most memorable part of the evening's discussions surrounded Iraq. Convinced that Saddam Hussein was in possession of weapons of mass destruction, Perle intimated that conflict with Iraq was inevitable. Notably, he said that the liberation of Iraq from its ruthless dictator would be enthusiastically welcomed by the Iraqi people and that Western intervention might be the first step in a grand plan to democratize the Middle East. At the meeting, none of us questioned whether Saddam was indeed in possession of weapons of mass destruction. When I asked Perle whether the United States was prepared to act unilaterally against Iraq, his answer was unequivocally in the affirmative. "Without the benefit of an allied coalition?" I asked. "A coalition of the willing would help, but sometimes allies can be a pain in the rearend," he responded. The following morning, I hosted a working breakfast for Perle at the Rideau Club; among the guests was Ambassador Paul Cellucci. As we said our farewells, I could not imagine that Iraq would come to play such an important foreign policy challenge for Canada only two years later.

Shortly after the ceremony on Parliament Hill to mourn the victims of 9/11, I spoke with Ambassador Cellucci. We had met on a number of occasions since his appointment by President Bush in April. Having cemented our relationship over a fine Italian meal shortly after his arrival, he had told me of his Italian and Irish roots and of his life in politics, notably as a governor of Massachusetts—no small achievement for a Republican in a state with strong Democrat leanings. Now our concerns quickly focused on the Canada–United States border, which was frozen in the aftermath of the attacks. That afternoon, I received a call from Pierre Pettigrew. We had worked well together since Pettigrew's appointment as international trade minister in the summer of 1999, and I found him smart and personable. I told him I was following up with the chief executives of Canadian companies heavily engaged in cross-border traffic. I pledged that the Council would spare no effort to help keep the borders as operational as possible. The following week, I spent hours on the telephone with the heads of Canadian National, Canadian Pacific, General Motors, Ford Canada, Air Canada, Alcan,

Nortel, Bombardier, and other businesses, including banks and insurance, and energy and trucking companies. All the while I remained in close touch with senior government officials, reporting the grave impact on business and urging Ottawa to join with Washington in taking rapid action to unlock the borders.

Earlier that same week, I attended a dinner at 24 Sussex Drive hosted by the prime minister. Although the dinner was in honour of the French ambassador, the impact of the terrorist attacks dominated our discussions. Among the guests were British high commissioner Andrew Burns and the prime minister's foreign policy adviser, Claude Laverdure. Pettigrew was also present, as was Gen. Ray Henault, the recently appointed chief of the defence staff. I congratulated Henault on the impressive manner in which the Canadian and American militaries were working together in the face of the crisis.

On November 1, I appeared before the House of Commons Standing Committee on Industry, Science and Technology. The title of my presentation was "Beyond September 11: Assessing the Damage, Planning for Recovery." Addressing the long lineups of vehicles at the border, I told committee members that we needed to ensure that the temporary impact of measures to ensure border security did not cause persistent structural damage to the Canadian economy and that governments at all levels and in both countries were fully aware of our shared interest in ensuring an open border.

The Chrétien and Bush administrations moved quickly. On December 12, a Smart Border Declaration was signed by Canada's minister of foreign affairs, John Manley, and Governor Tom Ridge, director of the U.S. Office of Homeland Security. Its aim was to continually improve border security, information sharing, infrastructure protection, and law-enforcement cooperation between the two nations.

The following day, I congratulated Manley and announced the Council's strong support of the declaration and the creation of a CEO action group on Canada–United States cooperation. Derek Burney and Paul Tellier readily accepted my request that they co-chair the action group. In the Council's news release, we pledged our support for rapid implementation of the thirty-point action plan laid out in the Smart Border Declaration. While recognizing the unique and pressing needs of the moment, Tellier nonetheless looked to the future: "Over the longer term, Canadians need to develop a more confident vision of who we are and what we want our country to be. We need fresh thinking and bold ideas for shaping Canada's role in North America that go beyond our current arrangements."

On a similar note, I added, "Our contributions to the war on terrorism have created an important opportunity to articulate a new vision of the relationship that will enhance Canada's sovereignty and competitiveness within a highly integrated North American economy."

When I addressed my Council colleagues in Toronto on January 15, 2002, I saluted our newly elected chair, BCE chief executive Jean Monty, and toasted the Council's newly adopted name. We were now the Canadian Council of Chief Executives—in French, le Conseil canadien des chefs d'entreprise. It was difficult to leave behind the name Business Council on National Issues. As emotional as this decision was, I led in recommending the change. I was persuaded we needed to reflect more accurately the nature of the organization and clearly identify it as Canadian.

At the January meeting, I continued to lay the groundwork for the Council's next major initiative: our effort at redefining Canada's role in North America. Our work in the late 1990s, including that of the ginger group, pointed us in the direction of a more closely knit post-NAFTA continent both in economics and in security. The 9/11 tragedy added significant impetus for the Council to pursue the closer integration we were seeking, beginning with the Canada–United States relationship. In my address to my colleagues, I stressed the need to enhance security without inhibiting the flow of people and goods across the Canada–United States border, highlighting the importance of moving well beyond the terms of current trade arrangements. I tabled some options, such as a common external tariff, to enhance the flow of goods and services which could conceivably lead as far as a full customs union, inclusive perhaps of improved labour mobility between our two countries. I suggested a less ambitious but still very significant step forward that would involve expanding the free trade agenda to include more comprehensive agreements in areas such as dispute settlement, competition policy, procurement, standards, and regulations. I concluded by saying, "What is lacking is a grand, made-in-Canada vision—a clear, bold, confident affirmation of who we are and who we want to be in North America."

With 2002 came some unexpected successions in the Council's leadership. Jean Monty retired as BCE chief executive and therefore stepped down as Council chair. This was disappointing, as we had worked exceptionally well together and I admired his drive and sharp mind. The Council board of directors elected Toronto-Dominion Bank chief executive Charles Baillie as Monty's successor. Regrettably, Baillie's term too was cut short, by his unexpected departure from TD, but not before we were able to complete the major project on corporate governance I spoke of in the previous chapter. As the Council prepared for the new year, we chose Suncor chief executive Rick George to succeed Baillie. George commanded Canada's largest energy company and was a highly respected member of the Alberta business community. He and I would go on to experience a long and productive relationship in the unfolding saga of the Council.

NORTH AMERICAN SECURITY AND
PROSPERITY INITIATIVE

In January 2003 we were ready to launch the Business Council's "big idea." My recommendation to my Council colleagues was that we name our initiative the North American Security and Prosperity Initiative (NASPI). It won strong support. The details of our initiative were outlined in a document titled *Security and Prosperity: Toward a New Canada–United States Partnership in North America.*

At our January meeting, I outlined the principal NASPI objectives, calling for action on five fronts: reinventing borders by eliminating as many as possible of the barriers to the movement of people and goods across our border with the United States and by shifting the emphasis to the protection of the approaches to North America; maximizing economic efficiencies, primarily through harmonization or mutual recognition across a wide range of regulatory regimes; negotiating a comprehensive resource security pact covering agriculture and forest products as well as energy, metals, and minerals, based on the two core principles of open markets and regulatory compatibility; rebuilding Canada's military capability both to defend our own territory and to share in ensuring continental and global security; and creating a new institutional framework based not on the European Union model but on cooperation with mutual respect for sovereignty, perhaps using joint commission models to foster coordination and to prevent and resolve conflicts. I set out a twenty-four-month time frame for moving forward with the new initiative, with the goal of winning support from the political leadership in Canada and the United States. We had to take into account the anticipated change in leadership in Canada given Jean Chrétien's retirement in late 2003. We also had to consider that George W. Bush would be running for a second term in 2004.

The launch of NASPI required both organization and financial resources. Among my Council colleagues there was no shortage of volunteers willing to give time to the initiative. The post-9/11 political and economic context added an element of urgency and importance to our undertaking. I set a fundraising target of $2 million. Over a quiet dinner at the World Economic Forum meeting in Davos later that month, Ron Mannix helped to get the ball rolling by pledging $500,000. I was startled by his generosity, but he added a demanding condition: I would have to pick up the tab for dinner. I followed by personally pledging $100,000, an unusual step that took many of my colleagues by surprise. But I was more than comfortable making this move, as I always saw myself both as Council CEO and an entrepreneurial partner in the organization. I also wanted to signal my faith in NASPI and set an example I hoped others would follow. I was not wrong in my expectations. Paul Desmarais Jr. of Power Corporation of Canada followed suit, and so did Richard George of Suncor, Tim Hearn of Imperial Oil, Hal Kvisle of TransCanada PipeLines, Gwyn Morgan of EnCana Corporation, and Rob Ritchie of Canadian Pacific Railway, all at the $100,000 level. Twenty-three chief executives from across Canada went on to add their company contributions, and before long our financial requirements were met.

At the January 2003 meeting where I had made my presentation, we were joined by Paul Martin. The finance minister gave a vigorous speech following dinner. Those of us who knew him well were conscious that this was an important moment in his political career, with succession to the leadership of the Liberal Party of Canada not far off. Canada's ambassador to the United States, Michael Kergin, provided us with updates on the fast-moving Washington scene, and American ambassador Paul Cellucci assured us of his strong support for the Council's stepped-up efforts to deepen bilateral ties.

With our bold initiative under way, I gave notice that the Council would next convene in Washington in early April, where we looked forward to building American leadership support for NASPI. In the meantime, a situation was unfolding that would place a heavy strain on the Canada–United States relationship: the impending invasion of Iraq.

INVASION OF IRAQ

The United States-led invasion of Iraq began on March 19, 2003. Two days earlier, Prime Minister Chrétien announced in Parliament that without the approval of the United Nations Security Council, Canada would not participate in the conflict. United Nations approval did not materialize, and Chrétien stood by his decision. It had ripple effects in Washington. On the evening of the seventeenth, and for several days thereafter, I received calls from American colleagues advising that the U.S. administration was surprised and displeased. Given the strong public opposition to the war in Canada, and especially in Quebec, I was less surprised by the prime minister's decision. Also, friends in Canada's military were quietly telling me that our forces were already stretched as a result of our commitments in Afghanistan.

I supported the war, a position I came to regret. My reasoning was that toppling Saddam Hussein and liberating the Iraqi people could lead to the beginnings of a democratic transformation of the Middle East. Such a step, coupled with the removal of the Taliban from power in Afghanistan, had in my mind a noble purpose. In juridical terms, it was a "just war." One misgiving that weighed heavily on me was my fear that the United States and Britain would not have the staying power to see a difficult mission through to a satisfactory conclusion—in other words, that the war would be won but the peace might be lost. I feared that the rebuilding process would prove to be too complex and costly. More fundamentally, history had taught me that "Western crusaders" are never received with open arms in Muslim lands and that a broad-based coalition with Arab nations, as was mounted in Operation Desert Storm to liberate Kuwait, would have been much more effective. The latter point is one I made to presidential adviser Richard Perle at our Ottawa meeting barely more than a month after the events of 9/11. My misgivings were justified.

The Council did not formally adopt a pro-war stance, but many of my colleagues stood in solidarity with the Americans and the British. I spoke of this in a number of media appearances following the outbreak of the war. Our views were influenced by the same rationale that underlay our North American Security and Prosperity Initiative: an emphasis on the importance of securing the continent from foreign threats and further strengthening Canada's already deep cooperation with the United States in defence. It was against this backdrop that the Council convened in Washington in April. We had a packed agenda, with briefings on the energy picture by U.S. energy secretary Spencer Abraham; on border security by U.S. homeland security secretary Tom Ridge and Canadian foreign minister John Manley; on the Iraq campaign by Richard Perle; and on the economic environment by Bank of Canada governor David Dodge and American economist David Hale. In addition to providing my colleagues with an update on our NASPI project, I chaired a panel consisting of former American ambassadors Tom Niles, Jim Blanchard, and Gordon Giffin, and former Canadian ambassador Derek Burney.

Concerns were raised in the meetings about Canada's refusal to engage in the Iraq campaign. Somehow this got back to Chrétien and his staff, who interpreted it as an attempt to apologize to the

Americans on Canada's behalf. Clearly, this was not the Council's intent, nor was it mine. In my case, despite my personal support for the war at the time, I sought to smooth ruffled American feathers by underscoring the significance of Canada's continuing engagement in Afghanistan.

Advancing the NASPI idea and building support for it remained a Council priority over the following two years. A key premise of NASPI was that the continent's economy and security were indivisible. Following the launch of the initiative, I retained two groups of academics to dig more deeply into the related economic and security issues: one to focus on reinventing the border, led by Michael Hart at the Norman Paterson School of International Affairs at Carleton University, and the other on defence and security issues, headed by David Bercuson at the University of Calgary. The Council's work garnered support from the Bush White House, where we were well introduced, and in administration foreign policy and defence circles. This served us well, given NASPI's goal of establishing a new economic and security-based framework for North America.

THE PAUL MARTIN GOVERNMENT

In the meantime, important changes were taking place in Canada. On December 12, 2003, Paul Martin succeeded Jean Chrétien as the country's twenty-first prime minister. I welcomed the transition, although I wished that the succession had gone more smoothly. I knew and respected both men. Despite the sponsorship scandals hanging over the Liberals' heads at the time of the transition, I shared a view widely held among my Council colleagues that Chrétien and Martin working together had very significantly improved the economic standing of Canada since 1995.

We were certain that the superbly credentialed former finance minister would continue to advance Canada's march toward improved global competitiveness.

The new prime minister was quick off the mark in making important structural changes. These included creating a new Department of Public Safety and Emergency Preparedness and the Canada Border Services Agency. As well, Martin created a new cabinet committee on Canada–United States relations and appointed a parliamentary secretary to focus on the bilateral relationship. One particularly welcome appointment made by Martin was to install Anne McLellan as deputy prime minister and minister of the newly created public safety department. I briefed her on the Council's NASPI project, and over the following two years she was a valuable interlocutor on security-related issues.

When the Council convened in Washington again in April 2004 to advance the case for closer continental cooperation, we were mindful that Paul Martin and George W. Bush would be meeting at the Summit of the Americas in Mexico in the weeks to come. The timing was ideal. We touched a number of bases, including discussions with the president's chief of staff, Andrew Card, and the president's homeland security adviser, Gen. John Gordon. Careful not to ignore the other side of the partisan aisle, I invited Senator Hillary Clinton to address the Council. On the urging of Clinton confidant and former ambassador to Canada Gordon Giffin, she accepted. When the senator arrived at the Willard Hotel, where we were meeting, there was electricity in the air. Interestingly, Clinton devoted part of her remarks to the subject of health care, with an honourable mention of Canada.

These discussions in Washington highlighted a number of political and economic concerns. One was the sharp political divide in the United States as the country moved toward the November elections. Another was growing protectionism in the face of American job losses to developing countries such as Mexico and China. Not surprisingly, American preoccupation about the security of the homeland was an overarching theme.

NEW FRONTIERS

The Washington meeting provided the perfect backdrop for the release of the Council's paper "New Frontiers: Building a 21st Century Canada–United States Partnership in North America." Prepared at Council headquarters after eighteen months of research, analysis, and consultations in Canada, the United States, and Mexico, the forty-three-page paper made fifteen recommendations. Building on the core objectives of NASPI, the paper expanded into areas such as tariff harmonization, rules of origin, trade remedies, energy strategy, defence priorities, and strengthening bilateral institutions such as the North American Aerospace Defense Command (NORAD). In calling for a comprehensive strategy, it also urged greater coordination in Canada across federal government departments, between federal and provincial governments, and between the public and private sectors. I was especially pleased with the enthusiastic reception "New Frontiers" received in business, government, and academic circles. Most importantly, my Council colleagues were unequivocally on board. At the end of the day, I knew that their commitment was essential to advancing our agenda in North American business circles. I was fortunate to be backed up by a strong Council executive committee consisting of chair Rick George and vice-chairs Dominic D'Alessandro, Paul Desmarais Jr., Jacques Lamarre, Gwyn Morgan, and Gordon Nixon, the chief executives respectively of Manulife Financial, Power Corporation of Canada, SNC-Lavalin Group, EnCana Corporation, and the Royal Bank of Canada.

—

On July 28, my Council colleagues and I hosted a dinner for Florida governor Jeb Bush in Montreal. While we had hosted other U.S. state governors in the past, our evening spent with Jeb Bush had special meaning. He represented a state with close connections to Canada and he was, after all, the brother of the president and the son of a past president with strong ties to Canada. The dinner was held in a private room at the Fairmont Queen Elizabeth Hotel. We warmly saluted the Canada–United States partnership and talked up business opportunities. The governor thanked us for our country's support in the wake of the 9/11 terror attacks and acknowledged Canada's commitment in Afghanistan.

The previous evening, I had attended a dinner for the governor hosted by Quebec premier Jean Charest at the historic Château Ramezay in Old Montreal. One of the topics that came up at my dinner table was whether the governor might one day succeed his brother George as president. This speculation was far from a fantasy; Jeb did indeed seek his party's presidential nomination during President Obama's second term. None of us could have imagined then that his candidacy would be upended by the likes of Donald Trump.

While concentrating on the Canada–United States relationship at the Council, we continued to nurture our relationship with Mexico. In late October 2004, we convened a Canada-Mexico "retreat" in Montreal. The retreat was an informal gathering of Canadian and Mexican leaders of which I had been part since the 1990s. It was the brainchild of my friend Mexican industrialist Juan Gallardo. In Montreal, we were joined at a private lunch by President Vicente Fox of Mexico and Prime Minister Martin. There was agreement all around that closer continental cooperation was a must and that building deeper ties between Canada and Mexico should be a high priority.

To drive home the point, Martin and Fox signed the Canada-Mexico Partnership Agreement in Ottawa, opening the door to a more formal public-private process of political and economic coordination.

On November 1, I wrote a letter of appreciation to President Fox, praising the Canada-Mexico Partnership Agreement and the dialogue which it initiated—a dialogue in which I would participate in the years to come.

At the conclusion of 2004, I was satisfied that the Council was making steady progress toward the goal of closer continental cooperation in the economic and security domains. I received a telephone call from Paul Martin on November 29, and followed up with a letter to him dated December 1 in which I summed up where I believed we stood. I referenced our "New Frontiers" initiative and saluted the recent Canada-Mexico Partnership Agreement. Looking ahead, I said,

> Two overarching imperatives will motivate our efforts and serve as a catalyst. One is the obvious need not only to make the NAFTA work better, but to transcend it. In a fast-changing world marked by new-age trade and investment agreements, and by dynamic alliances, especially among Asian and European countries, the NAFTA is increasingly showing its age and its limitations. The second imperative is the powerful challenge to North American competitiveness largely driven by Asia, with which in this continent we must come to terms. Unless we urgently combine our thinking and our resources to deal with this challenge, we will face inevitable decline. The competitive challenge to North America has profound implications for the future of some of Canada's key industries and this is a subject of priority concern to me and my colleagues at the Council.

The year 2004 heralded important elections in Canada and in the United States. On June 28, the government of Paul Martin was returned to office with a minority, and in November George W. Bush won a second term. Martin's minority raised concerns in Council circles that the momentum of NASPI might be blunted. This turned out not to be the case.

COUNCIL ON FOREIGN RELATIONS TASK FORCE

One other notable initiative on the North American agenda was launched in 2004. The Council on Foreign Relations, based in New York, sponsored an independent trilateral task force examining the continent's future. Thanks to Richard Haas, the cerebral president of the Council on Foreign Relations, this was the first time his organization had launched such an undertaking with foreign organizations as partners—the Canadian Council of Chief Executives being one, and the other being the Consejo Mexicano de Asuntos Internacionales. I had actively pursued this idea, believing that an eminent multidisciplinary group would complement the work of continental business leaders in a powerful way.

Joining me as the principal catalysts were Professor Robert Pastor of American University, and Andrés Rozental of the Consejo Mexicano, who had served as Mexico's ambassador to the United Kingdom. We agreed to serve as task force vice-chairs and as guides. I reached out to former foreign minister John Manley to serve as Canada co-chair; the Americans recruited former Massachusetts governor William Weld to serve as U.S. co-chair; and the Mexicans brought former finance minister Pedro Aspe to the table as the Mexico co-chair. Thirty-one members made up the task force—a virtual who's who of leading thinkers from across the continent.

The task force tabled its report, titled "Building a North American Community," in May 2005 and made the following key recommendations: create the institutions necessary to sustain a North American community; immediately create a unified North American Border Action Plan; develop a secure North American border pass with biometric identifiers; enhance law-enforcement cooperation; expand defence cooperation; adopt a common external tariff; develop a North American energy and natural resource security strategy; stimulate economic growth in Mexico; deepen trilateral educational ties; and establish an annual summit of North American leaders.

A reading of the Council on Foreign Relations task force report leads to two conclusions. The first is that the work of the Council's NASPI project, launched in 2003, had a significant impact on our task force deliberations and recommendations. The second is that the task force recommendations broadly matched the boldness of NASPI's ambitions. In my view, the real significance of the work of the task force is that it validated, from the perspective of a group of eminent thinkers from across the continent, what until then had been largely a Council-driven idea.

MISSILE DEFENCE

On February 24, 2005, Paul Martin announced Canada's refusal to participate in the American plan to develop an intercontinental missile defence system. This was greeted with disappointment in Washington. It was the third time Canada had turned the Americans down on cooperation in missile defence. Pierre Trudeau had done so in 1969 with regard to the Safeguard system, much to the chagrin of the Nixon administration. Likewise, when Ronald Reagan extended an invitation to Brian Mulroney for Canada to participate in the Strategic Defense Initiative, Mulroney declined. Mulroney characteristically handled the refusal, though, with a masterful stroke of diplomacy directed to the president himself: he simply picked up the telephone and explained the reasons for Canada's decision. According to Mulroney, Reagan was accepting and gracious in his response.

Given the Council's advocacy of closer defence cooperation between our two countries in the wake of 9/11, we had been nudging the Martin government toward accepting President Bush's invitation. In a surprise telephone call shortly before he announced his decision, Martin asked that I meet him in his office late that afternoon. He advised me then that Canada would decline the offer to participate in the plan. I made the strongest case I could linking missile defence to the national interest. We should not be doing this simply to make the Americans happy, I told Martin, and we certainly should not be seen to be bowing to American pressure, but our participation would guarantee Canada a voice in the deployment of the missile system. If we were absent, the system would operate in any event, but it would operate without us; decisions affecting Canada's land and airspace would be out of our hands.

At the end of an hour and fifteen minutes of lively discussion, it was clear to me the prime minister's mind was made up. One part of the calculation, and one I fully understood, was that he faced strong opposition to the idea in his caucus. I thanked Martin for taking me into his confidence and suggested that he speak directly to the president so that his decision would not take the Americans by surprise. For some reason, this did not happen. In retrospect, Martin's decision was a wise one. A study of American ballistic missile defence plans shows that there were many issues bedevilling the various programs with regard to costs and operational effectiveness.

NORTH AMERICAN FORUM

My work on North American issues in the post-9/11 period included creating the North American Forum. The forum describes itself as a private, non-partisan institution engaging senior leaders from Canada, Mexico, and the United States. It meets annually and draws on representatives from business, government, academe, research organizations, and the voluntary sector. The forum held its first meeting in Sonoma, California, in 2005, hosted by founding American chair George Shultz, former U.S. secretary of state and secretary of the treasury.

The origins of the idea sprang from a meeting I had in Leesburg, Virginia, in September 2003 with two colleagues, Canadian Berel Rodal and American Ronald Lehman II. Lehman, who was to become a cherished friend, had a distinguished career of service to three American presidents, Reagan, Bush, and Clinton, three secretaries of defence, and three national security advisers, in a variety of roles in the promotion of peace through international disarmament and non-proliferation policy-making.

At the time, Rodal was promoting the idea of a North American forum focusing on security issues in the style of the Munich Security Conference. In line with the post-9/11 work I was doing at the Council, I suggested broadening the idea to include economics, trade, energy, and the environment. We left the table in agreement, I pledged the Council's support, and we set out to recruit three eminent founding co-chairs. Lehman reached out to Secretary Shultz, I reached out to former Alberta premier Peter Lougheed, and former Mexican finance minister Pedro Aspe was recruited by Andrés Rozental. All three accepted.

Ever since, the forum has played an important role in promoting North American dialogue. It has met fourteen times since its creation, rotating among the three countries. I worked closely with

Lougheed and provided the forum with the institutional support of the Council. The World Affairs Council, based in San Francisco, and subsequently the Hoover Institution at Stanford University have done likewise for the American chair. In the case of Mexico, the forum has counted on the support of the Mexican Council on Foreign Relations. Before his death in 2012, Lougheed asked me to succeed him as Canada chair; in 2010, Shultz passed the baton to former secretary of defence William Perry, who in turn was succeeded by retired admiral Gary Roughead; and in Mexico, former ambassador Jamie Zabludovsky serves as Aspe's successor.

The annual sessions of the forum in our respective countries have produced a rich and diverse collection of ideas and insights that have helped build trust and understanding among continental thought leaders. Forum meetings, with approximately twenty-five representatives from each country in off-the-record discussions, have been instrumental in shaping constructive attitudes and policies. Presidents, prime ministers, cabinet ministers, ambassadors, military commanders, business leaders, and gifted academics have joined in our discussions of trade policy, job creation, innovation, the digital economy, advanced manufacturing, tax policy, energy research, environmental regulation, border management, migratory patterns, continental defence, and anti-crime cooperation. I had the pleasure of hosting the most recent in-person meeting of the North American Forum in Ottawa in 2018. There, I saluted one of my all-time American heroes, George Shultz. The venerable Shultz, then in his late nineties, was with us in Ottawa. He continued to offer rare insights, drawing on a lifetime of distinguished service to the United States and the world, until his passing in February 2021 at the age of one hundred. Shortly before his death, Susan and I were privileged to participate in his hundredth birthday celebration. Although a virtual experience, it was moving to hear the plaudits of so many of his admiring colleagues, including President George W. Bush, James Baker, Condoleezza Rice, Henry Kissinger, and Alan Greenspan. They were saluting an American giant who had walked among us.

The North American Forum (NAF) is now moving to a new phase. The Hoover Institution is being succeeded by the partnership of the Institute of the Americas and the School of Global Policy and Strategy at the University of California San Diego led by Richard Kiy and Caroline Freund respectively. The new U.S. chair is Ambassador Thomas Shannon Jr. In Canada, the Business Council of Canada (BCC) has assumed the lead institutional role in the NAF and I have passed on the baton as Canada chair to the BCC's Goldy Hyder. The latest in-person meeting of the Forum took place in La Jolla in November 2022. I will remain involved as Canada chair emeritus. A worthy initiative lives on as does the challenge of building a more cooperative and competitive North America.

SECURITY AND PROSPERITY PARTNERSHIP OF NORTH AMERICA

On March 23, 2005, at a summit in Waco, Texas, Prime Minister Paul Martin, President Vicente Fox, and President George W. Bush founded the Security and Prosperity Partnership of North America (SPP). Soon after, I began receiving calls from the media asking me to comment on the "surprising" similarity of this name to that of the Council's North American Security and Prosperity Initiative. While I was pleased with the parallel in the names, I was much more interested in what the leaders had in mind. It turned out that the SPP vision was as ambitious as what we at the Council had been hoping for and advocating for some time.

In Waco, the leaders set out two fundamental realities: "First, September 11, 2001 marked a new era in which economics and security have become undeniably intertwined. Second, the transformation of global trade and investment by new economic powers such as China and India has made it vital for the North American partners to work together more effectively and efficiently." The goals of the SPP were cooperation and information sharing, improving productivity, reducing the costs of trade, enhancing the joint stewardship of the environment, facilitating agricultural trade while creating a safer and more reliable food supply, and protecting people from disease.

We welcomed the emphasis the SPP was placing on economics and trade and the opportunity this offered for private-sector engagement. An idea I had been promoting since the mid-1990s in discussions with my American and Mexican business counterparts was the creation of a trilateral effort to promote competitiveness. My thesis was simple: by working closely together and combining the resources and innovative capabilities of all three countries, the North American region would constitute a formidable regional power bloc that could successfully face up to the growing Asian economic giants.

I discussed the outcome of the Waco summit with Canadian ambassador Frank McKenna in Washington. The business-minded McKenna liked the emphasis on the economy and competitiveness. As it turned out, McKenna would serve for little more than a year as ambassador, but in that short period he could not have been more helpful to me and our various undertakings at the Council.

THE STEPHEN HARPER GOVERNMENT

In January 2006, as the SPP began to take shape, Canadians went to the polls. On February 6, Stephen Harper became our country's twenty-second prime minister, heading up a minority government. The first time I had met a relatively young Stephen Harper was when he accompanied Reform Party leader Preston Manning on a visit to my office some years before. Thereafter, I had watched with great interest Harper's evolution in federal politics as leader of the Canadian Alliance, and the adept manner in which he engineered the merger of the Alliance and the Progressive Conservative Party. When he was elected the new party's first leader, in March 2004, I knew that the politics of the old order had changed.

Of all my meetings with Stephen Harper, our most intriguing private exchange was in 2004, following the June election that had returned Paul Martin to office. He invited me to Stornoway, the residence of the leader of the Opposition. As Stornoway is only a few minutes up the road from my home, I walked up. It was a sunny evening, barely after 5 p.m., and I did not know what to expect. A fascinating conversation over dinner followed, lasting some four hours. It was open, congenial, and surprisingly candid. We covered a wide range of topics, including the economy, Canada–United States relations, foreign policy and defence issues, and relations with China. I took advantage of the opportunity to brief Harper on a number of Council priorities, including the status of the North American Security and Prosperity Initiative. When I returned home, I noted in my diary, "Harper is smart, serious, intensely analytical and ambitious. I expect he will exercise strong discipline over his party and has a vision for the country at odds with conventional thinking. He should not be underestimated."

Immediately following Harper's election as prime minister, I reached out to him requesting that the Council have an opportunity to brief him on the results of a major study we were preparing to release later in February. To my surprise, his response was immediate and in the affirmative. The study was titled *From Bronze to Gold: A Blueprint for Canadian Leadership in a Transforming World*. The meeting took place at Harper's offices in Ottawa on February 15. Joining me from the Council were Richard George, Dominic D'Alessandro, Paul Desmarais Jr., Jacques Lamarre, and Gordon Nixon. We were joined by Derek Burney, who was acting as an adviser to the Harper transition. Seeing Burney in this role was reassuring. He was a seasoned veteran and understood the workings of the Prime Minister's Office. The meeting with Harper was cordial, but he signalled clearly that he intended to take Canada on a different path than that followed by the Liberal governments of Chrétien and Martin. He pointedly said that his approach to Canada-China relations would shift significantly from the status quo. I also got the clear sense that relations with the business community were going to be conducted at a healthy distance. This did not surprise or disappoint me. He was on the record, after all, about his discomfort with "business elites," and elites of any stripe, for that matter.

We shared an advance copy of *From Bronze to Gold* with Harper and stressed how important it was in our view that his new government seize the opportunity to pursue a vigorous and comprehensive pro-competitiveness agenda. Among the study's recommendations, we emphasized the need to repair the Canada–United States relationship and to move forward with the North American Security and Prosperity Initiative, launched the previous year.

The day after our meeting with the prime minister, Harper announced the nomination of former Mulroney government finance minister Michael Wilson as Canada's ambassador to the United States. My colleagues and I were thrilled with Wilson's appointment. Wilson telephoned me that afternoon and I congratulated him wholeheartedly. Given his deep experience both in government and business and his solid command of bilateral trade issues, I could not think of a better choice. Wilson was also well connected in Mexican government and business circles. He proved to be of invaluable assistance during the three and a half years he served in Washington.

Harper's debut on the continental stage as prime minister took place in Cancún, at the second summit of North American leaders, on March 31, 2006. A week earlier, I briefed him on the Council's engagement in North American affairs, from the Canada–United States Free Trade Agreement through to the Security and Prosperity Partnership. I took a page out of *From Bronze to Gold*, extolling the virtues of competitiveness, and concluded, "The United States is currently preoccupied with broader foreign policy issues, notably Iraq and the continuing war on terrorism. Mexico, for its part, is in the final stages of its presidential election cycle. Canada therefore has an important opportunity for North American leadership, and we would urge you, as the head of a new government with a fresh mandate, to make the most of the opportunity and to establish yourself as the champion of a new vision of North American cooperation."

In accordance with understandings reached at the first leaders' summit, in Waco, Texas, in 2005, private-sector leaders had been invited to Cancún. In my note to the prime minister, I explored the possibilities this opened: "A welcome new element within the SPP is the proposed North American Competitiveness Council (NACC). This new body could provide a way for business leaders from Canada, Mexico and the United States to offer their insights from the front lines of global commerce on how best to strengthen the competitiveness of all three countries through greater trilateral cooperation." I attached to the note some suggested key messages that he might wish to share with the leaders. They included building on the foundations of NAFTA; keeping up pressure for progress on the SPP; establishing a North American Competitiveness Council; considering greater cooperation in trade negotiations with non-NAFTA countries; making North America the default framework for regulation; involving all levels of government on regulatory convergence; facilitating the movement of skilled people; developing a North American energy strategy; forging a North American approach to climate change; and making the private sector a full partner in emergency planning.

Five colleagues were invited to attend the summit, among them chair and vice-chair Richard George and Paul Desmarais Jr. The Cancún summit was productive, and significantly the leaders gave their blessings to the idea of a North American Competitiveness Council (NACC).

NORTH AMERICAN COMPETITIVENESS COUNCIL

While the Canadian Council of Chief Executives maintained an active interest in the overall SPP initiative post-Cancún, we focused primarily on the NACC from 2006 to 2008. Our engagement was formalized when we were asked to provide the secretariat with support and act in an advisory capacity to the Canadian members of the NACC. The consultative reach of the NACC extended broadly in the three countries, with "hundreds of companies, sectors associations, and chambers of commerce throughout North America participating in the process."

In February 2007, NACC members submitted an initial report to the SPP cabinet ministers and secretaries of all three countries. It offered fifty-one concrete recommendations that would have a meaningful impact on improving the competitiveness of the three economies in areas including border-crossing facilitation, standards and regulatory cooperation, and energy supplies and distribution.

In August of that year, the three leaders met in Canada at the Château Montebello, near Ottawa. By then, Felipe Calderón had succeeded Vicente Fox as president of Mexico. I had met Calderón on a number of occasions in Mexico before his inauguration in December 2006. Given that Canada was hosting, Stephen Harper and senior members of his cabinet were heavily involved in the run-up to the summit. In July, the Canadian NACC delegation and I joined the prime minister and members of his cabinet at a preparatory meeting in Ottawa. The Canadian NACC CEO team included Richard George and Dominic D'Alessandro. Also with us respectively were Annette Verschuren, Hunter Harrison, Richard Waugh, Michael Sabia, and David Ganong of Home Depot Canada, Canadian Pacific, Scotiabank, BCE, and Ganong Brothers. I was especially pleased that Linda Hasenfratz, chief executive of Linamar, had also joined the Canadian delegation. The stage was set for the Montebello summit, and I was proud of the good work that Canadian government and private-sector leaders had done.

On the eve of the summit, I hosted a luncheon for President Calderón. We met at the Rideau Club, where the president gave an upbeat address while leaving no doubt about the serious challenges Mexico was facing from its pervasive drug cartels. That evening, the NACC delegations from all three countries met over dinner at the National Gallery of Canada, with Canadian, American, and Mexican ministers in attendance. The Canadian cabinet was represented by ministers James Flaherty, Stockwell Day, and Jim Prentice. As chair of the National Gallery of Canada Foundation, I was pleased to be able to showcase our national art treasure to our guests. Our visit included a walk-through of a fine exhibition of Renoir landscapes.

The following morning, on August 21, our NACC delegations met with the three leaders at Montebello. Prime Minister Harper and presidents Bush and Calderón entered the room and greeted each of us. From President Calderón I received a warm Mexican embrace. President Bush and I had a brief exchange in which I reminded him that his father and I had fly-fished together in the northern rivers of Labrador. The NACC reports were presented to the leaders, and our Canadian team acquitted themselves exceptionally well.

The communiqué issued by the leaders acknowledged the constructive work of the NACC—and this was not mere diplomatic window dressing. A comparison of NACC recommendations and the actions taken by the three governments shows just how constructive such engagement can be.

The SPP government working groups as well made significant progress on an ambitious range of undertakings. Looking ahead to the next summit, the leaders set out priorities for their respective ministers in areas including North America's global competitiveness, safe food and products, sustainable energy and the environment, smart and secure borders, and emergency management and preparedness.

The exchange between NACC representatives and the leaders produced one moment worthy of special mention. While looking at ways to resolve the continuing obstacles to the flow of goods across borders, the NACC took aim at regulatory hurdles. I was aware that my colleague David Ganong, who headed up the oldest chocolate manufacturing business in Canada, was frustrated by differing cross-border regulations concerning the colouring used in his company's popular jelly beans. To make the point that trade should not be held hostage to the tyranny of small differences, I urged him to bring his problem to the attention of the three leaders. It took some persuasion on my part, but in the end Ganong spoke up. His story captured the attention of President Bush in particular. Then and there, Bush instructed his people to investigate the matter and clear it up. The jelly bean story hit the press and even drew a mention in *The Economist*. In the next day's *Ottawa Citizen*, under the headline "Summit a Hill of (Jelly) Beans," journalist Deirdre McMurdy wrote, "Ganong made the point to leaders that streamlining the regulations for the manufacture of the candy would be a small, but metaphorically resonant, sign of their ability to cooperate on much bigger issues."

—

The third meeting of the leaders with the involvement of the NACC took place in New Orleans on April 21 and 22, 2008, hosted by President Bush. New Orleans was still recovering from the devastation of Hurricane Katrina. Surrounding us was evidence aplenty of the trauma the storm had wrought upon the city and the region. I felt a deep sadness for the city's people.

The New Orleans meeting was not as productive as its predecessor at Montebello. For one thing, the United States was in the countdown to the presidential election in November. Much more consequential, however, was the deepening gloom brought on by the Great Recession, which had begun to unfold in December 2007 and not surprisingly was dominating our discussions. Nevertheless, Bush spoke encouragingly about progress in SPP negotiations. At the reception with the leaders on April 21, I exchanged some thoughts with the president on the subject of the recession. He was obviously concerned and asked me how Canadian business was faring. I told him that the road ahead looked somewhat grim but that the Harper government and the Bank of Canada were handling the crisis well.

I returned to Canada with Dominic D'Alessandro, and we spoke of how crises were often the best test of leadership. We agreed that the global financial crisis demanded top-notch leadership from all the major economies.

PRESIDENTIAL CANDIDATE JOHN MCCAIN

On June 20, 2008, Senator John McCain, the Republican presidential candidate, paid a one-day visit to Ottawa. Thanks to David Wilkins, the American ambassador to Canada at the time, the Council was able to play a key role during the senator's visit. Wilkins had been appointed ambassador by President Bush in June 2005, succeeding Paul Cellucci. The affable lawyer from South Carolina had served for many years as the Speaker of the South Carolina House of Representatives. I quickly hit it off with the well-liked and highly respected Wilkins. The new ambassador was a friend of South Carolina senator Lindsey Graham, who in turn was close to McCain. I asked Wilkins if the Council could host a CEO round-table with McCain and a select number of my colleagues running major enterprises in Canada. His response came quickly. The meeting took place in the Sir John A. Macdonald Room at Ottawa's Rideau Club. Wilkins and Senator Graham were present. So was Ambassador Michael Wilson. Business colleagues in attendance included Elyse Allan, Ed Clark, Richard George, Blake Goldring, Linda Hasenfratz, Paul Hill, Thomas Jenkins, Michael McCain, Ted Rogers, and Louis Vachon—the chief executives respectively of General Electric Canada, TD Bank Group, Suncor, AGF Management, Linamar, the Hill Companies, OpenText, Maple Leaf Foods, Rogers Communications, and the National Bank.

John McCain outlined his vision for the United States and the world. He began by reaffirming his strong support of NAFTA, echoing what he had said to a luncheon audience at the Economic Club of Ottawa. Then he spoke about the economic crisis, America's position in the world, and the importance of getting energy policy right. McCain was refreshingly non-partisan. To the surprise of some of us, he did not offer any criticism of his rival for the presidency, Barack Obama, who was on record with his reservations about NAFTA. At one point, I asked McCain whether he had decided on his vice-presidential running mate. He was noncommittal but pointed out that the choice would have less to do with his preference and more to do with a choice the Republican Party would favour. At that moment, it would have been hard for any of us to believe that in the end the nod would go to Alaska governor Sarah Palin.

Later that afternoon, my Council colleagues and I welcomed McCain back to the Rideau Club for a reception for some hundred guests prior to winding up his whirlwind visit to Ottawa. Once again, he voiced his support for free trade, a strong economy, honest government, and a powerful America in the world. I thanked him, shook his hand, and wished him well.

As I reflected on his visit, I thought we had been in the presence of a man of great decency, a war hero who knew the meaning of honour, duty, and sacrifice—a moderate in his party. At that moment, I believed that should he win the presidency, there was hope that Republican extremism might be curbed and the traditional Republican virtues might return to the mainstream in the party. In the ensuing election, McCain lost, and the stage was set for the takeover of his party by political malcontents and extremists, and eventually their standard-bearer, Donald Trump.

PRESIDENT BARACK OBAMA

The election of Barack Obama as the forty-fourth president of the United States was an earthquake in American politics. His attainment of the highest office in the United States as the first citizen of African-American descent was a stunning achievement. I recall first hearing about Obama during a visit to Washington in 2006. He had been described to me as a "brilliant, Harvard-trained lawyer from Illinois who was making waves in the United States Senate." The next time his name came up was in a discussion I was having with former American ambassador to Canada Gordon Giffin, in the spring of 2008. At that time, like many others, I believed Hillary Clinton was the most promising contender in the Democratic Party.

Giffin, although a strong Clinton supporter, told me to keep my eye on Obama. I began to pay close attention. While I was taken by some of Obama's fine speeches, I was concerned that, if elected, he might reverse course on an North American free trade agenda that had been championed by every president since Reagan, including, notably, Bill Clinton. Obama's selection of Senator Joe Biden as his vice-presidential running mate was a positive in my mind, given Biden's long-standing experience in foreign policy.

After issuing a statement on behalf of the Council congratulating president-elect Obama, I wrote an open letter to him, the full text of which was published in the *National Post* the same day. "Perhaps nowhere on earth is the American Dream understood better than in Canada," it read. "Our people are bound together not merely by geography and history, but by common values of freedom, democracy and self-determination—the belief that individual men and women should be entitled to achieve to the fullest of their potential, regardless of the circumstances of their birth or position."

I went on to remind the president-elect of how closely tied our two peoples were through our economies, that Canadians and Americans were cousins, figuratively and in many cases literally, that we were also friends, colleagues, co-workers, customers, and business partners, and that millions of jobs depended on the goods and services that flowed back and forth across our shared border every hour of every day. I spoke of Canada as a faithful ally of the United States and of our military role in combatting the Taliban and in helping rebuild Afghanistan. I further underscored the importance of constructive global engagement and that, like Obama, Canadians believed that closer multilateral cooperation was essential to achieving enhanced international security, prosperity, humanitarian rights, and environmental protection.

I concluded by stressing the importance of cooperation in border management and in energy and the environment, and took direct aim at protectionism. I emphasized that open markets and open trade had always been vital to the health of our economies, and that history showed the folly of responding to a slowing economy by raising barriers to the free flow of goods and services.

The global financial crisis that President Obama inherited, and his desire to distance himself from the George W. Bush presidency, led to the demise of the Security and Prosperity Partnership. While my fears that the United States might back away from our progress on continental and global trade liberalization did not materialize, the grand vision inherent in the Security and Prosperity Partnership gradually faded. There was no more talk of the "North American community" that so many of us had worked toward over the previous two decades. The elaborate network of trilateral committees engaged in some three hundred areas of cooperation was dismantled. Work carried on, to be sure; important innovations that were ushered in by the SPP, such as the annual meeting of North American leaders, continued.

As I look back at my personal involvement in North American affairs since the early 1980s and the remarkable contribution of the Council, I have few regrets. The Canada–United States Free Trade Agreement was a triumph of statecraft and the foundation for the North American Free Trade Agreement, which brought Mexico into the continental economic orbit. The Council played the paramount private-sector leadership role in their realization. In turn, the Canada–United States Free Trade Agreement and NAFTA served as catalysts for other bilateral and regional free trade agreements around the world. The tragedy of 9/11 provided the impetus to move ahead, and the Business Council's North American Security and Prosperity Initiative laid out a map for the three-nation

Security and Prosperity Partnership that followed. My one major regret is that Canada, the United States, and Mexico did not embrace fully the significance of acting in concert as a regional economic power more than capable of taking on other major regional economic blocs. The SPP and its surrogate North American Competitiveness Council were meant to move the continent in that direction.

Is this grand vision dead? Certainly for the foreseeable future. The United States is deeply preoccupied with the threat to global peace arising from Russia's brutal aggression in Ukraine. China also figures prominently in the American economic and security calculus, with the future of Taiwan in the balance. The pledge of Chinese-Russian security cooperation adds to American concerns.

Domestically, supply-chain disruptions and surging inflation are major headaches for President Joe Biden. Add to these challenges the bitter and dangerous partisan divide which threatens the very stability of American democracy. And as if these were not enough, consider the powerful protectionist forces gripping American politics. In this explosive mix, there is precious little room for the dream of a North American community.

The situation in Mexico is of no help. For his part, President Andrés López Obrador has embraced an inward-looking, statist, and interventionist agenda and has rolled back significant reforms. Under his leadership, closer continental cooperation is a non-starter.

In the face of these realities and challenges, Canada has no choice but to press for relationships that are as productive as possible, especially with the United States. Our massive economic and security interests render this our highest continental priority. At the very least, NAFTA's replacement, the Canada–United States–Mexico Agreement, otherwise known as CUSMA, serves as an anchor for broad cooperation on multiple fronts. It is not inconceivable that circumstances will change and that the idea of a North American community will one day enjoy a renaissance. If and when that happens, the foundations will have been laid and business leaders will be well armed to play a key role.

12

WALKING TALL ON THE ENVIRONMENT

Growing up in Nelson, in the Kootenay region of British Columbia's southeastern interior, and regularly exploring the mountains, forests, lakes, and streams that were at my doorstep, bonded me to my natural surroundings. I hiked and fished in spring, summer, and autumn. Sleeping under the forest cover was a thrill. Skiing and snowshoeing on remote mountain trails was a favourite winter pastime, as was occasionally climbing nearby Kokanee Glacier. Casting a fly into my favourite trout pools was my idea of heaven. Given this early and intense connection to the great outdoors, it is no surprise that, in the decades in which I led the Council and engaged in advocacy on myriad policy issues, my mind was never far from the environment and the many threats to it.

At university in the 1960s, I was, like so many, influenced by the nascent environmental movement. I was a believer that Canada's natural endowments were incomparable, and that as Canadians we had a duty to the world to look after them. One of my summer jobs in student days was with the provincial fisheries hatchery in Nelson, where we introduced trout fingerlings into local lakes and streams. Giving back to nature in this way inspired me and introduced me for the first time to the idea of sustainability.

From an academic perspective, I was introduced to the growing body of environmental law and policy while teaching international trade law at the University of Ottawa in the 1970s. The exposure was no more than tangential, but it nevertheless signalled to me the growing importance of the environment in government and regulatory circles. It was shortly after taking the helm of the Business Council in 1981 and becoming involved in national energy policy issues that I truly began to develop my environmental consciousness. In due course, I found opportunities to speak about the trade policy–environment nexus. I predicted that it would become increasingly important in decades to come.

My engagement in environmental issues began in earnest after reading *Our Common Future*, otherwise known as the Brundtland Report, the 1987 report of the World Commission on Environment and Development, chaired by Gro Harlem Brundtland. As a former prime minister of Norway, with a strong background in public health and the sciences, Brundtland herself was the driving force behind the report. At the time, the Council had not yet seized on the environment as a priority issue, and frankly, what I was reading made me feel negligent. I rallied support among my colleagues for engaging on the environmental front and won over some who were hesitating. I began by ensuring that Council members were apprised of the Brundtland Report, and then we went to work. One of the first people I reached out to for advice was fellow Canadian Jim MacNeill. He had been the director of environment at the Organisation for Economic Co-operation and Development (OECD) in Paris and secretary general of the World Commission on Environment and Development. Most notably, he had been the lead author of *Our Common Future*. MacNeill agreed to act as an adviser to the Council and, importantly, as a mentor to me. I was thrilled to have at close proximity one of the world's leading experts on sustainability.

In May 1989, I announced the launch of the Council's first task force on the environment and economy. Thomas Kierans, chair of ScotiaMcLeod, agreed to serve as chair. An impressive cross-section of industry leaders signed on, including Peter Allen, Angus Bruneau, Cecil Flenniken, John Fraser, Richard Haskayne, Ron Mannix, Donald Phillips, Paul Phoenix, John Thompson, and Marshall Williams, the CEOs respectively of Lac Minerals, Fortis, Canadian Pacific Forest Products, Federal Industries, Interhome Energy, Manalta Coal, Inco, Dofasco, IBM Canada, and TransAlta Utilities. This was the first time a collectivity of Canadian CEOs had pledged to tackle the environment, and it marked the beginning of a fascinating journey.

Within days of the announcement, I delivered my first major address on the environment. The occasion was a conference in Winnipeg on sustainable development hosted by the government of Manitoba. It coincided with the establishment in Winnipeg of the International Institute for Sustainable Development. I chose a somewhat unusual title for my speech: "Environment and Economy: Until Death Do Them Part." Some in the audience were stunned by my opening comments: "At this groundbreaking conference hosted by the government of Manitoba, we are grappling with what some consider are irreconcilable forces—a wholesome environment and vigorous economic development. It is my belief that these are not irreconcilable. Far from it; they can and must be made mutually reinforcing. There can no longer be any doubt—the cost of failure will be fatal and will lead inevitably to the destruction of planetary life as we know it." I say stunned, because to most observers the Council dwelt mainly on traditional economic issues such as fiscal policy and international trade. Suddenly, the environment moved to the front ranks of our priorities, and I was using existential language to describe the seriousness of the challenge.

I focused on four points. The first was the need to embrace a new set of values and attitudes with regard to the environment. I put the following questions to the audience: "How are we going to convert our approach of the past, which has led to our current predicament, to a new, environmentally compatible one that will lay the foundation for a long-term balance between environmental and economic interests? How will we promote a much higher level of societal awareness, one that will help us better understand the implications of environmental degradation for the way in which we go about our lives?"

Next, I drew attention to the Western world's disproportionate consumption of the planet's resources. I pointed out that global sustainability would not be achieved until we came to terms with this sharp disparity. Thirdly, I lamented the curse of short-term thinking, both in government and in business, and argued that achieving a balance between protecting the environment and economic development would require disciplined long-term planning. As my fourth point, I argued that new methodologies and new tools needed to be developed to properly assess the costs and benefits of marching toward greater sustainability. I emphasized the importance of finding solutions in technology: "By leap-frogging current norms, corporations can gain financially by reducing their expenditures below what they would otherwise have to spend to catch up. Indeed, businesses can improve their competitiveness in the marketplace by positioning themselves as environmental leaders."

I concluded my remarks with a quotation that I found both instructive and moving. In a letter to American president Franklin Pierce in 1855 attributed to Chief Seattle of the Suquamish people of the Pacific Northwest, the Chief wrote, "This we know, the earth does not belong to Man; Man belongs to the earth. All things are connected like the blood which unites one family. Whatever befalls the earth, befalls the sons of earth. Man did not weave the web of life. He is merely a strand of it. Whatever he does to the earth, he does to himself." I feel I connected with the audience and that what I said about the environment resonated. I was to learn in years to come that bringing about transformational change in environmental policy is far from easy. As I left the stage in Winnipeg—which I had shared with my old friend Joe Clark—Premier Gary Filmon, leading Canadian environmental activist Maurice Strong, and several others pumped my hand enthusiastically and said, "Well done!"

With the Council now fully engaged in addressing the nexus between the environment and the economy, our efforts picked up speed. At Council headquarters, we supported the work of the Council environment and economy task force with research, and once again I went out on the speakers' circuit. In December 1989, I addressed a conference in New York City hosted by the Americas Society and made the case for a continental approach to advancing environmental sustainability in which businesses on both sides of the border would work together. I stressed not only that business must show leadership but that we must be more effective at telling our stories. I also underscored that seeking environmental solutions would require an effort at all levels of society; that business was only part of the problem and could only be part of the solution; that consumers would have to abandon their attachment to the throwaway society and demand environmentally friendly products; that investors would have to be induced to look beyond the quarterly bottom line in deciding where to put their money; and that municipalities would have to stop dumping raw sewage and untreated waste into our water systems and find new ways to reduce and dispose of garbage.

In May 1990, I travelled to Norway to attend the Bergen Conference on Sustainable Development, hosted by the Norwegian government and the United Nations Economic Commission for Europe. It was one of a series of conferences leading up to the June 1992 Earth Summit in Rio de Janeiro and was attended by the environment ministers of thirty-four countries. Travelling with me was Noranda CEO and Council colleague Adam Zimmerman. I admired Zimmerman. He had strong opinions and was not at all hesitant to make his views known. We did not see eye to eye on free trade issues and he was wary of what he called my "all in" position on the environment. We had some testy debates, but we both enjoyed the sparring and in the end always shook hands amiably. In Bergen, business representatives mingled freely with ministers. I met Brundtland and took the opportunity to congratulate her on her environmental leadership. I introduced Maurice Strong to some members of the North American and European business delegations, and I was pleased to have the opportunity to address the business sessions of the conference and lay out the rapidly developing position of the Business Council in Canada.

The central issue at the conference was climate change. The overarching message delivered by the ministers was that industrialized countries had to limit greenhouse gas emissions through more efficient and environmentally sound energy use. A large number of the industrialized countries represented in Bergen agreed they would stabilize the emission of greenhouse gases at 1990 levels by the year 2000. The United States was not part of this commitment and, as time would tell, the Bergen commitments were among a litany of failed promises. The conference lent support to two key principles: the precautionary principle and the principle of common but differentiated responsibilities of states for responding to climate change.

In November 1990, I welcomed lawyer John Dillon to our headquarters team. He was a man of quiet demeanour with a wry sense of humour. I asked him to take on the role of senior associate and general counsel with responsibility for regulatory affairs. Dillon and I became fast friends, and before long he was devoting much of his time to environmental policy. Over the years, he developed an impressive competence in environment and sustainability issues and related economic and energy matters, and he continues to serve the Council in this capacity.

One of the meetings at Bergen led to an important private-sector initiative. I introduced Maurice Strong to Stephan Schmidheiny, a Swiss industrialist who had taken a keen interest in environmental issues. The two of them got on very well—so well that Strong, who was serving as secretary general of the United Nations Conference on Environment and Development, appointed Schmidheiny as an adviser in the lead-up to the 1992 Earth Summit. In 1991, Schmidheiny went on to found the Business Council for Sustainable Development (BCSD), composed of close to fifty CEOs of major enterprises. With the blessings of the BCSD's members, Schmidheiny authored an influential book, *Changing Course*, which was presented at the Earth Summit with considerable impact. It signalled that the BCSD was solidly on board with the urgency of tackling climate change and laid out an ambitious program for business engagement at the leadership level. Ken McCready, a Business Council colleague and CEO of TransAlta Corporation, was an active member of Schmidheiny's group and helped shape his book. John Dillon and I were strong supporters of Schmidheiny and McCready and the work of the BCSD. When in 1995 the BCSD merged with the World Industry Council for the Environment to become the World

Business Council for Sustainable Development (WBCSD), I pledged the continuing support of our council. The WBCSD today represents some two hundred major enterprises and continues to pursue an active agenda. Sadly, Ken McCready died in 2011. He is rightly regarded as a pioneer in the quest to broaden international business support for sustainability.

The Earth Summit in Rio ran from June 3 to 14, 1992. I was unable to attend, so I asked John Dillon to represent the Council. The Canadian government was represented by Mulroney's minister of the environment, Jean Charest, and the Liberal Opposition by Paul Martin. Canadian Maurice Strong, of course, was everywhere to be seen. After all, the summit was mainly his creation. Schmidheiny's *Changing Course* served as the principal business thread at the conference, even though business representation was relatively sparse. As I followed the conference proceedings from afar, I continued to receive enthusiastic reports on Charest's performance. I was told he was dynamic and articulate, and that he communicated the Mulroney government's sincere desire to embrace a progressive approach to the environment.

In advance of the summit, the Council's task force on the environment and the economy tabled a strategy paper titled "Towards a Sustainable and Competitive Future." Its companion paper, "Business Principles for a Sustainable and Competitive Future," outlined a set of eight operating principles that it urged businesses of all sizes to adopt. Our work was well received at Rio and generally seen as progressive, including by some non-governmental activists.

The Earth Summit raised awareness of the sheer scale of the global environmental challenge. The ambitious agenda covered economic growth in the developing world, climate change, poverty reduction, trade policy, access to water, forests and natural spaces, toxic chemicals, desertification, pollution control, and the precautionary principle. Importantly, the summit resulted in an agreement on the United Nations Framework Convention on Climate Change, which in turn led to the Kyoto Protocol and, in due course, to the 2016 Paris Agreement. In addition, the Convention on Biological Diversity was opened for signature.

Some say that the signature agreement emerging from the Earth Summit was Agenda 21, a non-binding action plan of the United Nations regarding sustainable development. It was to be executed by the United Nations, other multilateral organizations, and individual governments around the world. Individual governments were encouraged to draw up their own Agenda 21 provisions. The bold objective of Agenda 21 was to achieve global sustainable development by 2000. We are still waiting for the nations of the world to fulfill this objective.

At the Earth Summit, debates about the relationship between trade policy and the environment intensified. At an earlier conference sponsored by the National Round Table on the Environment and the Economy in Toronto, on November 4, 1991, I had said the following: "A decade ago when I was teaching a course on the law of international trade, the relationship between the environment and international trade was barely talked about, even in academic circles. But its leap to prominence is not without controversy. Some see it as the natural emanation of the sustainable development debate; some, as a promising weapon in the rapidly developing arsenal of trade policy instruments; some, as a catalyst for competitiveness; some as an impediment to competitiveness; some as the channel for north-south cooperation; some as the bedrock of fortified trading blocs; and still others, as the cornerstone of trade policy and trade law reform."

Today, the call to impose tariffs on exports from countries with poor environmental records is very much alive.

—

When the Earth Summit was over, I called Maurice Strong and congratulated him. I also sent him a copy of a major address I presented in Montreal on June 1, just before the summit. It was titled "Business Leadership and the Global Environmental Challenge." The audience consisted of some 1,500 actuaries from forty-nine countries who were attending the twenty-fourth International Congress of Actuaries. I kicked off my remarks with a sobering message, one I would have delivered in person had I been in Rio:

> The earth's resources are being depleted with a deadly swiftness. To put it another way, we humans are living more and more off our natural capital. The interest generated by that capital, which has served us well for several millennia, no longer suffices. The weight of population growth and the effects of irresponsible consumption are behind a persistent degradation of the environment. Deserts are eating up once-productive agricultural lands. Forests in many parts of the world are being destroyed. Wetlands are disappearing. Rivers, lakes and even seas are dying. The pollution of land, water and atmosphere has led to a spread of toxic substances. Some species and vital genetic resources have been lost forever. Air pollution caused by industrial and automotive waste products is significantly reducing quality of life in major urban areas throughout the world. Water pollution is contributing to serious health problems in both urban and rural areas and is threatening food production. In the face of this catastrophic onslaught, the earth's climate is changing with potentially devastating consequences.

The balance of my address focused on the role and responsibilities of business worldwide in seeking solutions to the environmental challenge. I identified four "musts" facing business: the need to recognize that the so-called green phenomenon was not a flash in the pan but was here to stay; the need to accept that the move to a greener world offered major business opportunities; the need to accord environmental factors a prominent role in senior decision-making; and the importance of embracing environmental efficiency as a key source of competitive advantage.

I concluded my address with a tip of the hat to Maurice Strong, who was presiding in Rio. "Some say that Maurice Strong—a Canadian—is a dreamer," I said. "Others call him a prophet or a far-sighted realist. On one thing I believe we can all agree: the threat to humanity that he describes has never been clearer, and the imperative of taking collective action has never been stronger."

In the lead-up to the Earth Summit and in its wake, I was satisfied that we at the Council and in certain other business circles in Canada fully understood the importance of moving forward with a holistic approach to reconciling environmental and economic priorities. We pushed for meaningful progress in attaining higher levels of energy efficiency and in limiting emissions of greenhouse gases. It was a good start, but we all had a long way to go.

The Kyoto Protocol, adopted in 1997, was a watershed in the evolution of the Council's approach to climate change. The protocol took the form of an international agreement that extended the 1992 United Nations Framework Convention on Climate Change, committing nations to reduce greenhouse gas emissions. The commitment was based on the scientific consensus that global warming is in fact taking place, and that human-made carbon dioxide emissions are the predominant cause. The protocol was adopted in Kyoto, Japan, on December 11, 1997. The Council was one of a handful of business organizations that formed part of Canada's formal delegation, and I asked John Dillon to represent us. Canada's delegation was headed by environment minister Christine Stewart and natural resources minister Ralph Goodale. I was pleased that Goodale was attending, as my colleagues and I were counting on him to ensure that Canada would emerge from Kyoto with sensible commitments that were also fiscally responsible.

In the end, the outcome for Canada was extremely disappointing. We approached the negotiations with a great deal of goodwill and with a view that the Council, as a business pioneer in climate change, had something useful to contribute. Critical to the Council was that Canada should negotiate commitments that were carefully thought out and capable of being implemented in a way that served both environmental and economic objectives. This did not happen. At the insistence of Prime Minister Chrétien, Canada committed itself to a reduction of greenhouse gas emissions to 6 per cent below 1990 levels by 2012. Canada was not prepared for this undertaking, and it was clear to me and Council members that the target was unrealistic. Other resource-based economies, such as Australia and Norway, negotiated commitments that were far more realistic than Canada's. The Council had argued for years for a holistic approach that would bring the provinces and all other key players, including business and consumers, within one tent. To add insult to injury, the commitments embraced by the federal government ignored agreements that had been reached with the provinces a few weeks before. The result was a fracturing of any possible national consensus.

I had already informed the prime minister that I was apprehensive about Canada's level of preparedness for Kyoto. In a letter to Chrétien, I told him of the Council's concern and recommended steps aimed at protecting Canada's national interest in the negotiations. I wrote that it was important for all countries, both developing and developed, to take on new commitments to reduce climate change, and that a scheme of differentiated commitments be adopted to ensure an equitable sharing of the burden. I also asked that the government engage Canadians in an informed public debate on the scientific and economic implications of climate change and responsible policy options. We recommended as well that Chrétien create a high-level team of senior officials from the ministries of the environment, natural resources, finance, industry, and international trade led by an experienced negotiator reporting directly to him. These recommendations by and large fell by the wayside. The most disturbing aspect about the Kyoto Protocol process was how relatively little Canadians knew about what it would require to implement its commitments. To me, this was a colossal failure of public policy and a lost opportunity to build a strong national consensus that would propel Canada forward as an environmental leader.

When it became clear in the spring of 2002 that Chrétien was seriously considering ratification of the Kyoto Protocol, the Council tabled "The Kyoto Protocol Revisited: A Dynamic and Responsible Alternative for Canada." We put forward an eight-point framework for action that would enable Canada to make a meaningful contribution to addressing both the long-term global challenge of climate change and more immediate priorities such as alleviating poverty, providing clean water, and improving health care in developing countries around the world. In my view, this was a holistic and unifying strategy that would serve both the national interest and Canada's obligations toward the developing world.

Essential elements of our plan included:

- a broadly based and inclusive national process to engage Canadians in the climate debate and galvanize their support to reduce greenhouse gas emissions;
- a stronger commitment by industry, to be defined through negotiated agreements between industry sectors and governments, that would set emissions performance goals;
- a longer-term technology strategy that would place Canada at the forefront in the development and adoption of new technologies and lower-carbon forms of energy;
- coordinated actions to address greenhouse gas emissions and air pollution in cities through such means as urban planning and new government investments in urban and intercity public transit;
- a leadership role for Canada internationally in promoting a longer-term global solutions to the climate challenge that could also help developing countries to improve living standards; and
- a Canadian program on climate change and adaptation.

When the Council released "The Kyoto Protocol Revisited," we believed it offered a comprehensive strategy that could unite the country and establish Canada as a global environmental leader. Before the year was out, our hopes were dashed.

Canada's Parliament ratified the Kyoto Protocol in December 2002. In a last-ditch effort to persuade parliamentarians to postpone ratification, I addressed a meeting of MPs in Ottawa. I spoke on behalf of a coalition of business organizations, arguing that Canadians, on the whole, did not properly understand the protocol and that most of the provinces and the overwhelming majority of the business community were against it. We hoped a postponement would lead to the shaping of a dynamic and sensible strategy that would serve the national interest and be a model to the world.

In addition to fracturing the possibility of a national consensus, the Kyoto debacle was exacerbated by the conflict within the Liberal Party between Jean Chrétien and Paul Martin. Although he was no longer in cabinet, Martin voted for ratification but made it clear that he was uncomfortable with the targets Canada had embraced. By the time Martin succeeded Chrétien as prime minister, in December 2003, the debate about environmental policy in Canada had intensified. At the time of the federal election in June 2005, Canada's emissions had soared well above its Kyoto commitment. Presiding over a minority government did not make Martin's job any easier. With the arrival of Stephen Harper as prime minister in January 2006, it was clear that Canada's Kyoto commitments were doomed. At the Climate Change Conference in Bali in 2007, Canada opposed binding targets unless they were embraced by countries such as China and India. In the meantime, Conservative environment minister John Baird announced a plan to regulate industries that were heavy emitters. Interestingly, while Harper never concealed his discomfort with the Kyoto Protocol, it was not until December 2011 that his government announced Canada's formal withdrawal.

The Conservatives under Harper were returned to office with a strengthened minority in October 2008. He easily defeated Liberal leader Stéphane Dion, who had based a central part of his campaign on what he called the "Green Shift," a plan to shift the burden of taxation from income taxes to carbon taxes. I had warned Dion that such a program, which was not revenue neutral and which he was advancing in the face of a severe recession brought on by the global financial crisis, would fail because of its timing and interventionist elements. While I was mindful not to take sides in the election, I felt duty bound to offer Dion my views, which mirrored the policy position of the Council. Dion, whom I knew well and respected, was so earnest in his convictions and so driven by his idealism that I felt badly for him when he was so decisively rejected by voters.

The last major environmental policy undertaking by the Council under my leadership took place in 2007. Growing increasingly frustrated by the discord, division, and mistrust surrounding the national debate on the environment, in March 2007 we created a task force on environmental leadership. Co-chaired by Richard Evans, chief executive officer of Montreal-based Alcan, Richard George, chief executive of Calgary-based Suncor Energy, and myself, the task force aimed to break through the confusion with a clear strategy that would build the strongest possible consensus within the business leadership community and hopefully build bridges between the key political and environmental players. The thirty-three-strong membership of the task force was a formidable coalition made up of CEOs representing manufacturing, energy, chemicals, engineering, banking and financial services, consumer goods, pipelines, mining, and transportation. Our members brought a great deal of experience and depth to the table, many of us having been engaged in environmental issues for more than a decade. This task force exercise, in my view, was one of the most outstanding created by the Council, which had a remarkable record of success over the decades through its task forces. Between March and September, we engaged in extensive consultations among our members while also testing our ideas on some of the brightest thinkers in the country. We were prepared to be ambitious.

The task force met in New York City in May on the sidelines of a Council mission focusing on global financial markets. When I laid out our proposed strategy, I was encouraged by the strong appetite of my colleagues to mount a "breakthrough initiative." I described the political context as follows: "It is clear that Canadians are ill informed on the issue of climate change but interested and willing to learn. Governments, however, are playing retail politics with a long-term problem. The recently announced federal plan addressed some of the concerns raised by industry, but companies still face a highly uncertain environment. Federal and provincial governments appear to be moving in different directions, and environmental groups have generated a degree of fear that has undermined rational debate and left the public confused and with a poor understanding of the economic consequences."

We tabled our task force report on September 25, 2007. The title I proposed to my colleagues, "Clean Growth: Building a Canadian Environmental Superpower," reflected our ambition. While the global financial crisis was just around the corner, Canadian economic performance had been strong and there was exuberance in the energy and commodity sectors. We considered the economic circumstances to be propitious.

The report, carefully stitched together and tabled as a declaration, merits a reading in its entirety. It is of historic importance that we embraced carbon pricing; we were the first major business organization in North America to do so. While this had been a long time in coming, in reality Council positions going back to the 1990s had implicitly accepted the principle of carbon pricing. The declaration put forward five key propositions:

- create a coherent national plan of action, one that saw governments, industry, and consumers working together toward shared goals;

- put a strong focus on investment in the new technologies that could help Canada and the rest of the world achieve a rising standard of living with a reduced environmental impact;
- set targets that kept companies healthy and profitable and encouraged and enabled increased investment in new technologies;
- encourage businesses and individuals to change behaviour with appropriate price signals that could be strengthened through carefully designed market-based mechanisms such as emissions trading and environmental taxation; and
- champion a future international process that would ensure the participation of all major emitting countries.

We elaborated on each of the propositions in our report. Below are some points I believe drove home a strong and, in some cases, a transformational message.

We lamented that in the fifteen years since the signing of the United Nations Framework Convention on Climate Change and the decade since the negotiation of the Kyoto Protocol, Canadian public policy had been marked by grandiose gestures and sweeping promises that produced far too little real impact.

We pressed for the development of a national plan that began with open minds and constructive dialogue, pointing out that for far too long the Canadian debate had focused on the question of how ambitious our targets should be rather than on what we were prepared to do—as governments, businesses, public institutions, and individual Canadians.

We emphasized that we all contributed to the creation of greenhouse gas emissions and that nothing meaningful would happen unless we all took on our share of responsibility.

We argued that the key to a sustainable future was technology innovation and that because our country was a major energy and resource producer and exporter, we should focus our research and development on cutting the carbon intensity and environmental impact of the way we produced conventional hydrocarbon energy as well as on new low-carbon energy sources.

On the critical issue of taxation, we said if any new environmental tax were to be proposed, it must be a substitute for existing forms of taxation, not a revenue grab, and that any new tax in Canada must not discriminate against any particular sector or region and should be implemented only as part of a broader tax reform that aimed to enhance our country's economic as well as environmental performance.

We concluded that as a country, as industry sectors, and as individual enterprises, we should drive Canadian leadership by benchmarking ourselves against the rest of the world, but we also said we had to recognize that a long-term plan that included all significant players globally was the only effective solution to climate change; that Canada should champion an approach to future international agreements that ensured participation from all major emitting countries; and that in the end our country should be a model to the world in demonstrating how to align public policy to strengthen economic and environmental performance.

Our report had a far-reaching impact. Within the business community, it signalled an unprecedented degree of solidarity around a clear vision for the environment and the relationship between the environment and the economy. Leaders of all major sectors were on board. So were producers and consumers, and Easterners and Westerners. One of the most important outcomes for me was the bridging of interests on the part of resource producers in the Western provinces and manufacturers and consumers in Central and Eastern Canada. I was hopeful that this pan-Canadian alliance would set the stage for a cooperative approach to policy development for the decade to come.

At the federal level, the response from some high-placed Conservatives and Liberals was supportive—although one Conservative cabinet minister said he was worried about the Council's flirtation with carbon taxes. Two premiers with whom I had a close association, Gordon Campbell of British Columbia and Jean Charest of Quebec, signalled their approval. So did Ed Stelmach of Alberta and Dalton McGuinty of Ontario.

I was also hopeful that our vision would win support from the environmental community, with whom business had been in conflict for more than a decade. My hopes were not in vain. I was pleased to discover that environmental activist Elizabeth May, who later sat in Parliament as leader of the federal Green Party, had enthusiastically praised our report. I was more than surprised, though, when, at a conference in Toronto a short time later, the redoubtable broadcaster and environmental activist David Suzuki with whom I was sharing the platform, enthusiastically shook my hand. Both he and May were ecstatic that the Council had embraced carbon pricing. We had cut the Gordian knot!

The great promise shown by our report was thwarted, to a large extent, by the global financial crisis. Quite simply, Stephen Harper turned his attention elsewhere. Over the decade from 2010 to 2020, my dreams of Canada becoming an environmental superpower vanished. While I applauded Justin Trudeau's government signing on to the landmark Paris Agreement of 2016 on greenhouse gas emissions, mitigation, adaptation, and finance, a good part of the decade saw continuing skirmishes over targets for greenhouse gas reduction and bitter conflicts over environmental taxation. The conflict even led to producing provinces challenging the federal government's carbon tax before the Supreme Court of Canada. Pipeline construction continues to be challenged. My wish for a unified federal-provincial commitment in support of a grand national plan has failed to materialize. Tensions between Ottawa and the resource-rich Western provinces persist, as alienation in Alberta and Saskatchewan has risen to worrisome heights. On the positive side, Canadians are increasingly open to sustainability and the idea of a green future. And businesses are embracing environmental innovation; they see it as essential to their long-term competitiveness and are taking serious initiatives aimed at lowering their emissions. Companies in the resource sector have broken new ground with commitments to zero emissions by 2050. The momentum is growing.

While I would have wished for a great deal more progress toward fulfilling the ambitious goals developed by the Council over more than two decades, I take heart in our legacy on the environment. I remain convinced that the basic principles we espoused beginning in 1989 and continuing through to 2009 remain in large measure valid. They need only to be resurrected by visionary leaders— leaders who can build a new national consensus. We have a vast treasure house of resources, and we have some of the smartest innovators in the world in dealing with sustainability—we need only gifted leaders to get Canadians across the country on board with a unified vision about our environmental future. Our status as an environmental superpower remains well within our reach.

13

SALUTE TO CANADA'S ARMED FORCES

"Ken, step on the damn brakes!"

It was early in November 1982, and I was sitting in the turret of a Leopard 1 tank on a manoeuvres field at the Canadian Forces Base in Lahr, West Germany. Ken Harrigan, the CEO of the Ford Motor Company of Canada, was below me in the steering and engine compartment. Following a briefing from tank personnel, we had sped down the field and were returning to our starting point, where a dozen or so of our Business Council colleagues were standing with our host, Maj.-Gen. François Richard, commander of Canadian Forces Europe. As we approached, Harrigan mistakenly pressed on the accelerator, causing the tank to speed up and everyone in front of us to scatter. Harrigan then jammed on the brakes, bringing the massive vehicle to a dead stop and throwing me from my seat in the turret. Supposedly in charge of this exciting demonstration run, and sporting a couple of bruises on my forehead, I emerged from the turret and apologized. The experience prompted many a good laugh over a fine dinner in the officers' mess that evening.

Our reason for being in West Germany was to see our army and air force units at work first-hand. In nearby Baden-Söllingen the following day, we witnessed an impressive mock bombing run by CF-104 Starfighters that came screaming over the airfield. It was one of many such missions over the years.

In my 1981 inaugural address as president of the Business Council, I spoke of national defence and foreign policy as being among our priorities. This was novel, to say the least, and in policy terms *terra incognita* to the business community. My rationale was that a strong national defence capability was essential to the overall health of the country and that business leaders needed to know and understand this. This engagement had nothing to do with procurement or defence contracting; the focus was on policy and strategy. I am proud to say that the Council maintained an active engagement in defence policy issues for some twenty-five years, primarily via task forces made up of Council members.

My colleagues and I were fortunate to meet many of our men and women in uniform. We invariably came away impressed by their commitment, discipline, confidence, and professionalism. At the same time, we also came away with the impression that public knowledge, understanding, and appreciation of the role of our military was weak. Pursuing our work connected us with our military commanders in the field and at headquarters. The chiefs of the defence staff I came to know were very supportive of our efforts and gave generously of their time. I single out especially generals Ramsey Withers, Gérard Thériault, Paul Manson, John de Chastelain, Maurice Baril, Raymond Henault, Rick Hillier, and Walt Natynczyk. We learned a great deal from them: about the military command system, the relationship with the minister of defence and the government of the day, the constant struggle to acquire the resources necessary to do the job, and Canada's role beyond our borders. The importance and intricacies of Canada's global alliances were laid out at briefings at NATO headquarters in Brussels and at various briefings in the United States, including at the Pentagon, Andrews Air Force Base, Naval Station Norfolk, and North American Aerospace Defense Command at Cheyenne Mountain.

There were some heartwarming moments, such as being received so enthusiastically by our soldiers at our military base at Wainwright, Alberta, following a speech I gave in support of our armed forces. Some were awe-inspiring, such as traversing the vast Canadian Arctic to better understand threats to our northern approaches. Some were thrilling, such as watching dawn live-fire exercises at Grafenwöhr in eastern Bavaria, within sight of Warsaw Pact Czechoslovakia; sitting in the command centre at Cheyenne Mountain witnessing a mock Soviet missile attack on North American targets, including Cheyenne Mountain itself; or watching the launch of fighter aircraft from an American nuclear aircraft carrier in the Atlantic.

There were some amusing moments as well. Unforgettable was when my feisty Council colleague and friend Rod Bilodeau, then CEO of Honeywell Canada and a Second World War veteran, challenged American defence secretary Caspar Weinberger. The Council task force was meeting with Weinberger at the Pentagon, and the subject of Arctic sovereignty came up. Weinberger politely rejected Canada's claims and made reference to the oil tanker SS *Manhattan's* 1969 transit of the Northwest Passage without Canadian government approval. Bilodeau said, "Respectfully, Mr. Secretary, the U.S. had no business doing this. If I could not muster a warship to ward off the *Manhattan*, I would have attacked the ship in my motor boat, if necessary!"

The Council's engagement in defence issues went far beyond informative fact-finding missions to Canadian bases and military installations in Europe and the United States. For the first time in history, an association of Canadian business leaders was intimately involved in analyzing defence policy. Our first major initiative came in the form of a sixty-six page report in September 1984 titled "Canada's Defence Policy: Capabilities versus Commitments."

Following two and half years of study, the tabling of the report coincided with the arrival in office of the Mulroney government. I signed the report along with Council chair and Royal Bank of Canada CEO Rowland Frazee and Peter Cameron, chair of the Council's task force on foreign policy and defence and CEO of Canadian Corporate Management. Frazee was a Second World War veteran with battlefield experience in the European theatre. Cameron served with the 48th Highlanders of Canada, played a leadership role in Canada's reserves, and held the rank of brigadier-general. The report's assessment was dire: the armed forces had deteriorated significantly in strength and effectiveness and Canada was not pulling its weight in the NATO alliance. It went on to say that "the Canadian forces have been subject to benign neglect and an inadequacy of resources for almost twenty years." It recommended a major expansion of the defence budget over a ten-year period, with a 79 per cent increase in spending and the raising of overall troop levels to over 200,000. Recognizing the major changes in the nature of warfare, including the deployment of advanced technologies, the report called for new thinking along with increased investment in research. It also recommended that the geographical reach of Canadian forces should be extended to include the Arctic and Pacific theatres. Its criticism of Canada's naval capabilities was scathing, making the point that the country, possessed of one of the world's longest coastlines, could not possibly mount a credible maritime defence. In an address several months earlier to a meeting at the Royal Military College of Canada in Kingston, Ontario, of the Canadian Institute of Strategic Studies, I hammered the point home: "The fact that a maritime nation like Canada has only three or four destroyers capable of functioning in conditions remotely approaching modern, conventional naval warfare, no modern submarines, and no mine-sweeping capability is scandalous. So is the virtual absence of a Canadian military presence in the millions of square miles that comprise the Canadian North."

This first report set the stage for Council reports and recommendations related to defence policy over the next three decades. The themes of underinvestment in troop strength, equipment, and advanced technologies, and failure to carry our weight in our defence alliances, remained central to our advocacy and are valid to this day. A Council policy paper in 1987 titled "National Security and International Responsibility" followed our 1984 entry into the defence policy debate. In the meantime, I was active on the speakers' circuit, addressing defence policy issues from podiums in Canada, the United States, and Europe.

The fall of the Berlin Wall, collapse of the Soviet Union, and the end of the Cold War massively changed the strategic calculus for Canada's armed forces. But it turned out that the so-called peace dividend and anticipated permanence of the United States as a hyperpower dominating a unipolar world were short-lived. The shock and audacity of the 9/11 terrorist attacks on the American homeland further shook up conventional thinking, prompting Canada to intensify its focus on North American defence and security. Our Council work mirrored this shift, as I have explained in an earlier chapter of this book.

There are two subjects I feel compelled to revisit, however. One is the active roll I played, largely behind the scenes, in urging Prime Minister Martin to join the American plan for a ballistic missile defence system. My principal motivation was not to curry favour with the United States, particularly post-9/11, when Americans were feeling a heightened sense of vulnerability; it was primarily because I believed it was in Canada's national interest. Better to be part of the decision-making process than to be left out and have the Americans calling the shots even when the interception of

intercontinental missiles might take place above Canadian territory. The second subject is the wars in Afghanistan and Iraq. I supported Canada's military involvement in Afghanistan. Early on,
I also supported calls for Canada to join with the United States in
effecting regime change in Iraq. While I would defend Canada's role
in Afghanistan as serving a just cause, it was a terrible mistake to
participate in the Iraq venture. My hopes for an American-led allied
effort that would deliver transformational change in the morass that
is the Middle East were dashed, with powerful and painful lessons
learned—lessons being driven home to this day.

Canada's great sacrifices in war have always moved me. I find it
staggering that Canada, with a population in 1914 of eight million,
raised an army of some 650,000 and suffered 160,000 casualties,
with 60,000 dead. The sagas of Vimy Ridge and Passchendaele, of
the D-Day landings on the Normandy beaches in 1944, and of heroic
exploits of our army, navy, and air force in helping crush the Nazi war
machine remain vivid in my mind and inspire me. I followed closely
the efforts of our troops in Korea, in the Balkans, and in Afghanistan
and those of our much-respected peacekeepers. Since my early teen-
age years, I cannot remember once missing a Remembrance Day
commemoration or failing to shed a tear at the sound of the Last Post.

Of the many heroic exploits of our military known to me, one in
particular hits home because of its connection to my home town of
Nelson. It involved a young Nelsonite, naval pilot Lieut. Hampton
Gray who, flying some fifty feet above the water and under heavy
enemy fire, sank a Japanese destroyer—an act of daring that cost him
his life and won him the Victoria Cross.

I have read deeply of war and traced some of the greatest military
campaigns of the ancient, medieval, and modern periods. I am old
enough to have known combatants and have some understanding
of the unspeakable brutality of war. That so many young Canadians

have given their all so that we can live in peace, security, and comfort lives in my mind. For my offices in downtown Ottawa, I chose a property that faces on the National War Memorial including, I am pleased to say, a bust honouring Lieut. Hampton Gray. The final resting place for me and some of my family is in the Beechwood Cemetery in Ottawa, which also serves as Canada's National Military Cemetery.

I have spoken of the meaning of this sacrifice both at home and beyond our borders, in places like London, Paris, Berlin, Rome, Brussels, Amsterdam, Oslo, Canberra, Seoul, Tokyo, and Hong Kong. One of the most memorable was a gathering the Council hosted in Ottawa in May 2005, following the inauguration of the Canadian War Museum. The vast majority of my Council colleagues joined me, some 130 in all, in the impressive new building, which houses a quiet place of remembrance, military equipment, exhibition spaces, an art gallery, and a theatre. We were joined by politicians, the chief of the defence staff, and senior officers, veterans, military experts, and academics for a series of symposia focusing on defence policy and strategy. The minister of national defence, Bill Graham, delivered a fine keynote address over dinner. As I listened, I looked around the cavernous hall, where we sat surrounded by vintage tanks, artillery pieces, and a fighter plane dramatically suspended over our heads. I am sure we all thought of how much destruction and death they may have wreaked in their time; of our soldiers and our enemy combatants alike, of their sufferings; of the elemental tragedy of war and its unsparing effects on innocents, women, and children. Yet I chose this venue as a mark of our respect and as a reminder that war is best avoided unless there is no choice, and that an effective defence is a necessary deterrence to conflict.

Respect carries with it a duty to remember. With this in mind, and to coincide with our gathering at the Canadian War Museum, I asked Canadian military historian Jack Granatstein to prepare a paper for publication on Canada's industrial war effort during the Second World War, a subject that had never been tackled. Granatstein was an ideal choice, having also served as chief executive officer of the War Museum from 1998 to 2001. He produced an excellent piece of original research titled "Arming the Nation: Canada's Industrial War Effort, 1939–1945." It gave details on the extraordinary contribution of Canadian workers and enterprises to the Allied victory. This, coupled with the heroic efforts of our armed forces, makes for a stunningly impressive saga—a time when Canada, and all of Canada, was punching well above its weight in world affairs.

In the Council's work on defence policy over some twenty-five years, we were assisted by many knowledgeable collaborators: senior Canadian and allied military officers, retired officers, academic experts, and a host of ministers and secretaries of defence. One individual stands out: retired Brig.-Gen. George Bell, who offered invaluable advice and supportive research over a couple of decades. One organization stands out as well: the Conference of Defence Associations, headed for many years by my good friend retired Col. Alain Pellerin. With the benefit of a thirty-five year military career with experience in Canada and Europe, Pellerin tirelessly advanced the agenda of the organization. What impressed me most was the calibre of individuals he was able to attract to its board and the insightful policy work he oversaw. Among the organization's many leadership initiatives, the annual meeting it hosted in Ottawa was a must-attend event, featuring Canadian and allied military commanders and leading-edge thinking on policy and strategy. Pellerin's organization also hosted the annual Vimy Award, which recognized individuals for their exemplary contribution to military and strategic affairs. For a number of years, I was privileged to serve alongside Chief Justice Beverley McLachlin as a member of the Vimy Award selection committee.

My final address to the Conference of Defence Associations as head of the Council was in 2007, when I returned to some of the themes that had formed the core of the Council's advocacy over three decades. I saluted the extraordinary contribution of our men and women in uniform. I once again warned of the dangers of complacency, of taking our national security for granted, of the complexity of the new threats, including cyber warfare. More than a decade has passed since then, and regrettably I must conclude that as a country we remain woefully unprepared for today's threats. Since the Second World War, we have relied heavily on the security offered by the United States. That reliance will not change in the foreseeable future, but moving toward a more independent and robust posture in North America should be a high priority for the nation. This will not happen without a transformation in thinking and leadership. God forbid that it will be driven by a catastrophic turn of events that seriously imperils our security. Whatever the case, it is time for Canada to wake up.

Two recent extraordinary developments have brought our military into the spotlight. One is Russia's brutal aggression in Ukraine, implicitly condoned by the Xi Jinping regime in Beijing.

The breakout of war on the European continent has required NATO allies to revisit their defence preparedness. Significantly, it also has led previously neutral Finland and Sweden to apply for NATO membership. Canada has responded with fresh commitments to badly needed defence renewal, but in my view it has done so without the needed heft and urgency. We are still far from meeting our commitment to 2 per cent defence spending in accordance with our NATO pledge. This has not gone unnoticed among our allies, in particular the United States. Among other vulnerabilities, Canada's capacity to defend its sovereignty in the Arctic in the face of a hostile Russia is woefully inadequate. More broadly, the Beijing-Moscow alliance has grave implications for Taiwan and the future of peace in the Pacific. Canada can rightly claim to be a Pacific power, but our military capabilities deployable in the region are meagre.

The other development that has shaken our military is the cascade of sexual misconduct cases in the ranks, reaching the highest level of command. Never having served in our armed forces, I have been shocked to learn of their extent, and surprisingly so have some of the retired senior officers I know. The report of retired Supreme Court justice Louise Arbour in May 2022 detailed the causes of misconduct and tabled forty-eight recommendations for dealing with the problems. The minister of national defence, Anita Anand, and Wayne Eyre, chief of the defence staff, quickly voiced their acceptance of the report's recommendations and pledged to resolutely follow up.

I hope that the Arbour Report will trigger actions to remedy the affliction which has plagued our armed forces for too long and which has hurt morale among serving women and men. But the changes that must go deep into the culture of our military will take time, resources, and persistence to see through. Likewise, the urgent need to rebuild a dangerously weakened military into a modern, highly effective armed forces will require time, massive resources, persistence, and unshakable political will. The theme of inaction in the face of vital national concerns has been a recurring one in this memoir. In the case of Canada's armed forces, a continuing absence of commitment and meaningful action will lead to incalculable consequences for the country's future.

14

CONFRONTING THE GLOBAL FINANCIAL CRISIS

Of the many meetings of the Council membership over three decades, one stands out. It took place in New York City in May 2007. We gathered on the eighth floor of the Ritz-Carlton Hotel in the heart of the financial district. The evening before, Merrill Lynch & Co. hosted us at their headquarters and Eliot Spitzer, the recently elected New York State governor, gave us a lively and optimistic address. When I introduced the governor, I referenced his career as a crime-busting attorney general of New York and his fame as the "sheriff of Wall Street."

On May 8, as we listened to one speaker after another, the buoyant mood remained a constant. To be expected, Mayor Michael Bloomberg, whom I much admired, was the first to offer an uplifting message. Henry Kravis, of Kohlberg Kravis Roberts & Co., and Jon Winkelried, co-president of Goldman Sachs, spoke about a world awash in liquidity and the seemingly endless deal-making opportunities. As chair of the proceedings, I asked both Kravis and Winkelried at different times that morning the same question: "Looking ahead at the global financial picture, is there anything that keeps you up at night?" Geopolitical uncertainties aside, they both answered with bullish forecasts. My colleagues asked questions about the brewing problems associated with the rise in sub-prime mortgage loans, housing speculation, and household debt. The capacity of the major banks to manage growing risk also came up several times. Again, assurances were given that the financial system was strong and that it could accommodate a "soft landing."

When we left New York, many of us were far from reassured that all was well in the domain of global finance. "Too much exuberance, too much complexity. It's tough to understand what is really going on," one of my colleagues said on our flight back to Canada. Mere months after our meetings in New York, the global financial system plunged into a mammoth crisis. So much for the foresight of some of the smartest financiers in the world, I thought. So much for being able to see far-off "black swans" before they arrived.

While we at the Council had no idea how serious the situation would become, we were able to face it with a strong leadership team. In January 2007, the Council's board of directors had elected Gordon Nixon as chair. Nixon, the chief executive of the Royal Bank of Canada, succeeded Suncor chief executive Richard George, who had served our organization with exceptional commitment. I had urged Nixon to take on the post, thinking that he would be an ideal successor to George. By the beginning of 2007, I had started to think about my own succession. Just as Royal Bank chief executive Rowland Frazee was highly instrumental back in the early 1980s in helping me lay the foundations for the Council's success, Nixon, I believed, would be excellently placed to guide the transition to a new Council chief executive. In addition, I knew I could count on the Council's executive committee, which was composed of seasoned colleagues I deeply respected: Laurent Beaudoin of Bombardier, Bruce Flatt of Brookfield Asset Management, Hartley Richardson of James Richardson & Sons, Paul Desmarais Jr. of Power Corporation of Canada, and Annette Verschuren of Home Depot Canada.

JAMES FLAHERTY AND THE HARPER GOVERNMENT

We were satisfied that government finances and the Canadian economy were being competently managed by the Harper government and James Flaherty, Harper's finance minister. I liked Flaherty and his straight-talking style; my work with him and his department was grounded in mutual respect. It also helped that the Canadian economy was still performing well, despite the slowing United States economy and the credit squeeze in global financial markets. Largely driven by the boom in the resource sector, Canadian growth held steady, with strong gains in employment and robust household spending. To the surprise of many, by the end of 2007 the Canadian dollar had reached parity with its American counterpart.

Flaherty's budgets and economic statements leading up to 2008 had much to commend them. The Council strongly supported his commitment to balanced budgets and debt reduction. We also favoured innovative policies such as the introduction of the Registered Disability Savings Plan in 2007 and the Tax-Free Savings Account in 2008. We took issue, however, with Flaherty's decision in his first budget, in May 2006, to implement Stephen Harper's election promise to reduce the Goods and Services Tax (GST) from 6 to 5 per cent. Having vigorously campaigned in support of the Mulroney government's introduction of the GST, we thought that this represented a rollback of a hard-won gain. However, I lauded Flaherty's other tax reduction measures, which would help cushion the economy from the impacts of the global financial meltdown and improve Canada's competitive position in the years to come.

One of the boldest and most controversial actions taken by Flaherty early in his mandate dealt with taxation on the distributions of income trusts. Announced on October 31, 2006, the move came to be described by those affected as the "Halloween Massacre." With some 250 trusts listed on the Toronto Stock Exchange, the shock was considerable. I was not so surprised by the government's move. The popularity of income trusts in Canada had been surging, and the federal government was growing increasingly alarmed by the decline in its revenue receipts from Canadian companies. When some large enterprises signalled that they were seriously eyeing the income-trust model, BCE and Telus among them, the alarm bells grew louder and Flaherty acted. Officials at the Department of Finance were suggesting to me that the revenue loss from these two conversions alone might amount to over $2 billion. Needless to say, Flaherty came under heavy attack, but he did not yield one inch. Speaking before the House of Commons Finance Committee on January 30, 2007, the minister defended his actions by saying, "I'm not prepared to sacrifice the interests of millions of hard-working Canadians who pay their taxes and play by the rules so that a select group of special interests can enjoy a tax holiday." Basing his arguments in part on tax fairness, Flaherty went on to point out that "evidence was mounting that we were turning into an income-trust economy, an economy where tax avoidance drove business investment decisions and foreign investors stood to make significant gains at the expense of Canadian taxpayers. No responsible government could stand by and let this happen."

The Council had taken no position on the income-trust issue, and I fully understood the reasons for the government's concern. When asked by some Council colleagues for my take on what, if anything, the government might do, I warned that in my opinion government intervention was inevitable. The outrage caused by the government's actions among some investors had one regrettable consequence for me. A Toronto-based entrepreneur, who was a personal friend and Council member, protested that the Council should have intervened. Further, he charged that powerful Council members, hostile to income trusts, were quietly siding with the government.

Attempts on my part to persuade him that the government was determined to deal with what it considered a "crisis situation" were futile. He resigned from the Council and our friendship was ruptured. The loss of our friendship was painful to me. Moreover, it marked the only occasion during my long tenure at the Council that a member resigned over a policy difference.

Canada dodged the full impact of the early stages of the financial crisis. The price of oil continued to surge in the first months of 2008, and employment and output continued to expand. But to my consternation, it was not long before we began to see a collapse in oil and other commodity prices. By October, Canada was officially saddled with a recession. The sense of crisis had deepened in September with the collapse of Lehman Brothers, the fourth largest American investment bank. The potential of bank insolvency became the number one issue in the United States and in other countries. That is when the world was faced with the "too big to fail" debate and the moral hazard associated with it. During this period, I reached out on a regular basis to seek insights from my colleagues running Canada's six largest chartered banks: Gordon Nixon at Royal Bank, Bill Downe at Bank of Montreal, Gerald McCaughey at CIBC, Louis Vachon at National Bank, Richard Waugh at Bank of Nova Scotia, and Ed Clark at TD Bank Group. In my efforts to understand the crisis, it was especially helpful to me to be serving as a director of North America's largest insurance company, Manulife Financial. Elected to the board of directors in 2005, I was able to view the financial crisis up close. Manulife's formidable chief executive, Dominic D'Alessandro, under whose leadership the company had rocketed to first place among large insurers, was always available and helpful to me.

In the face of such turbulence, we were fortunate in Canada to be served by superb leaders at the Bank of Canada. In February 2008,

Bank of Canada governor David Dodge passed the baton on to Mark Carney. Dodge had acquitted himself exceptionally well as governor, just as he had done as deputy minister of finance. Carney was a worthy successor whose deep private- and public-sector experience was exactly what was needed to help guide the country through the crisis. Dodge and Carney were trusted friends, and their advice in these years was invaluable to me and my colleagues.

The tough challenge facing Canada required strong leadership on the part of the prime minister, to be sure, and Harper was not found wanting. He tackled his job with his legendary discipline and could count on the support of a talented team in cabinet. In addition to Flaherty at Finance, the ministers with whom we worked most closely in the 2007–9 period were David Emerson, Stockwell Day, Jim Prentice, Jason Kenney, Rona Ambrose, Monte Solberg, John Baird, Peter MacKay, Maxime Bernier, and Michael Chong. I had known Emerson the longest. As the chief executive officer of forestry giant Canfor, based in British Columbia, he served on the Council as a director and a vice-chair. His business credentials, his academic background, and his experience as a senior official serving the British Columbia government prepared him well for high office in Ottawa. Elected as a Liberal, his surprise jump to the Conservatives following the election of Harper in 2006 caused quite a stir but provided the prime minister with some additional star power in his new ministry.

As we lived through the dramatic months of financial turmoil, it became clear that Canada's financial institutions were going to be spared the carnage we were witnessing in the United States and beyond. None of our banks required bailouts; they continued to lend, they remained profitable, and they maintained dividend payments. Importantly, we were well served by the country's financial regulatory system made up of dedicated professionals. One key advantage over our peers was that our financial institutions were less highly leveraged than their American and European counterparts. Another was that our financial institutions were mandated to hold higher capital positions. Going into the crisis, Canada had yet another advantage that few countries possessed: our economic fundamentals were strong. We were running a consistent set of government surpluses, inflation was relatively low, and we had the lowest debt-to-GDP ratio of any of the G7 countries.

In responding to the crisis, the G20, the brainchild of former finance minister Paul Martin, came into its own. The enormity of the challenge was clearly beyond the capacities of the International Monetary Fund or the existing framework of the G20 finance ministers. Therefore, the G20 gathered for the first time the heads of government in a series of meetings in Washington, London, and Pittsburgh, which we at the Council monitored closely. The first of the summits, in Washington in November 2008, delivered a consensus on the need for large fiscal stimulus packages and monetary policy intervention. The second, in London in April 2009, focused on financial sector reform and, to further this end, established the Financial Stability Board. The third, in Pittsburgh in December 2009, committed the G20 to establishing a permanent architecture devoted "to meeting the needs of the 21st century."

While it was reassuring to me that world leaders appeared to be talking the same language about reform, I was deeply troubled by the fallout of the financial crisis. The negative impact on employment was far-reaching, and businesses large and small suffered losses for which they were not responsible. In addition, countries were saddled with sharp increases in their debt loads. Understandably, the crisis shook the faith of the public in financial institutions. It also raised doubts about the capitalist model and fostered deep resentment against what was seen as unbridled greed. In retrospect, we know that the crisis had more than one cause and there was plenty of blame to go around. A good number of banks were culpable of failing to manage risk. But there were also failures in due diligence among board directors, accountants, lawyers, and regulators. The crisis was so profound, we have been living with the political, economic, and social consequences ever since. In political terms, it served as a catalyst for populist movements in the United States and Europe. It also spawned anti-elitist sentiments and eroded trust in so-called experts. The most vivid example of this can be seen in the politics of Donald Trump.

Suffering from the continuing recession, the Canadian economy contracted by 2.6 per cent in 2009. The painful effects were evident in job losses and a drop in consumer spending. The impact on Canadian businesses, small and large, was much in evidence. At Council meetings and in my calls to colleagues across the country, uncertainty and anxiety permeated our discussions. As was the case in previous recessions I observed, the hardest pill for my CEO colleagues to swallow was having to lay people off with no clear idea when better times would return. The sense of gloom was exacerbated by poor economic performance in the United States, Canada's most important market by far. When President Obama came to office in January 2009, the American economy remained in deep recession, with falling GDP, rising levels of unemployment, and significant hikes in government borrowing. But by the end of 2009, relief at last was in sight. Obama introduced $832 billion in stimulus that, coupled with unemployment benefits, tax cuts, and infrastructure spending, helped the United States turn the corner. So did easing on the part of the Federal Reserve and other central banks and the coordinated action by G20 countries.

In Canada, the return to economic health by 2010 was swift and the numbers impressive. The Canadian economy grew by a startling 3.3 per cent that year. Virtually every sector across the Council membership was in positive territory and making significant gains, including manufacturing, construction, mining, oil and gas extraction, retail trade, finance and insurance, and transportation. The mood among my colleagues shifted and confidence levels rose. Canada was back to work.

FROM BRONZE TO GOLD

Throughout 2008 and 2009, the financial crisis and ensuing global recession commanded the attention of governments across Canada. As a consequence, work by business and think tanks dedicated to enhancing Canada's long-term economic prospects was to some extent sidelined.

At the Council, we remained active, building on the deep body of our work on global competitiveness going back more than fifteen years and initiatives aimed at bolstering North American competitiveness via the North American Competitiveness Council. A case in point was the tabling in February 2006 of our report "From Bronze to Gold: A Blueprint for Canadian Leadership in a Transforming World." Taking aim squarely at "the culture of complacency" in Canada, we called on Canadians to embrace bold new policies that included turning creative ideas into new businesses, helping immigrants do better faster, forging an environmental advantage, developing a Canadian energy strategy, investing creatively in infrastructure, cutting the cost of regulation, cutting taxes on investment, and rethinking our relationships with the United Sates and the world.

During this time, I spoke often of the long-term risks and challenges keeping me awake at night: the emergence of new economic powers such as China and India that will transform the twenty-first-century global economy and rewrite the rules of the game in almost every industry; the explosion in the application of new technologies in all areas of business and community life, sparking an epochal transformation from an industrial economy to a knowledge economy; and the demographic shift of an aging population where we go from having too many people for the available jobs to having too many jobs for the number of people who can do the work (smart immigration policies being one answer to the problem, better education and skills training being another).

With the launch of "From Bronze to Gold," and returning to the issue of complacency, the Council offered the following advice: "In the 1990s, Canadians waited for a crisis before acting decisively. Today, many Canadians feel satisfied with our country's progress, and without a sense of urgency, it is difficult to mobilize consensus around controversial issues. We would suggest, however, that the best time to contemplate fundamental change is when we can build on our strengths rather than when we have our backs against the wall."

FOREIGN TAKEOVERS

Through 2006 and 2007, one challenge momentarily shook Canada's entrenched culture of complacency: the stepped-up pace of foreign takeovers of iconic Canadian companies. The acquisition of household names such as the Hudson's Bay Company, Fairmont Hotels and Resorts, Inco, Dofasco, Abitibi Consolidated, CP Ships, Domtar, ATI Technologies, Intrawest, and Algoma Steel raised alarm and captured public attention. So did interest among foreign buyers in Stelco and Alcan, which were considered promising targets. The alarm was sounding in Council circles, and I was hearing a great deal about it. This was not surprising, as many of the companies involved were Council members and their CEOs my colleagues. My own view on this subject had been honed over many years. My concern about foreign takeovers is that they result more often than not in the loss not only of head office activity and jobs but also the support activities of accounting and law firms and financial institutions. In other words, head offices matter a great deal to the local economy. In addition, the loss of so many listed companies trading on domestic exchanges has negative consequences for the Canadian capital market. Having been intimately engaged with so many of Canada's corporate "champions" for so long, this was a subject close to my heart. There was an emotional element at work as well. I took great pride in the champions we had in Canada and had devoted decades of effort to help create an environment where more and bigger champions could flourish. The matter required urgent attention, and the Council in many respects offered the perfect forum for assessing the challenge and proposing solutions.

At a meeting of the full Council in Toronto, we debated the issue for a good part of the day. The arguments were well informed and marked by flashes of passion. I witnessed in some of the exchanges strong nationalist sentiments, with calls for intervention by Canada's Parliament. On the other side stood those who spoke up for the traditional Council leaning toward free markets. Our discussions were supported by the results of two internal surveys of the membership. The survey results and our deliberations pointed us in a direction with which I was thoroughly comfortable. We channelled our views to the Competition Review Panel, the creation of which had been announced by the Harper government in July 2007 with the mandate to review Canada's competition and foreign investment policies and explore ways to improve the country's productivity and competitiveness. In our view, the timing of the government's initiative was perfect and the panellists well chosen. Lynton "Red" Wilson was designated as the chair. His colleagues were Murray Edwards, Isabelle Hudon, Tom Jenkins, and Brian Levitt. Wilson and Levitt had led major enterprises and served on the Council for many years. Entrepreneurs Edwards and Jenkins, the prime movers at Canadian Natural Resources and OpenText respectively, were currently active in Council affairs, and the talented Isabelle Hudon was a senior executive with Sun Life Financial.

In January 2008, the Council tabled its submission, titled "From Common Sense to Bold Ambition: Moving Canada Forward on the Global Stage," with the Wilson panel. Six months later, the Wilson panel tabled its report, titled "Compete to Win." There was a high degree of synergy in the conclusions and recommendations of the two reports. I congratulated the panel, saying that its report gave Canadians a solid blueprint for action that could deliver stronger economic growth, better jobs, and a higher quality of life in the face of intense global competition. Stressing the need for urgency, I said that the sooner we acted, the sooner we would strengthen Canada's competitive position in the face of growing international risks and uncertainties. On the critical issue of foreign takeovers, I lauded the panel's position. The best defence against the disappearance of Canadian champions was to build more of them. Returning once again to the theme of complacency, I warned, despite all of the positive economic news Canadians had enjoyed in recent years, that as a country we had become dangerously complacent about a wide range of emerging challenges to our quality of life.

Zeroing in on specifics, we endorsed in particular the panel's calls for action in the areas that aligned with long-standing Council positions:

- on tax reform, lowering corporate taxes, eliminating capital taxes, reducing personal income taxes for lower- and middle-income Canadians, and harmonizing provincial sales taxes with the GST;
- on skills development, supporting excellence in post-secondary education and reforming Canada's immigration process to meet labour-market needs;
- on building global businesses, focusing public policy in support of small and medium sized enterprises that demonstrated the desire and capacity to grow internationally;
- on corporate governance, giving directors of Canadian public companies the same powers as their counterparts in the United States when assessing takeover offers;
- on Canada's economic union, eliminating all internal barriers to the free flow of goods, services, and people within three years, and harmonizing federal and provincial environmental assessment policies and procedures;
- on Canada–United States relations, embracing as Canada's top trade priority the need to move goods and people securely and efficiently across the United States border;
- on international trade and investment, setting an ambitious timeline to conclude foreign trade and investment agreements with priority countries, incorporating comprehensive business input;
- on regulation, assessing all regulations against competitiveness impacts, and harmonizing wherever possible product and professional standards with the United States; and
- on innovation and intellectual property, ensuring R&D and innovation policies supported both domestic and global investment, and that new copyright legislation, patent laws, and counterfeit and piracy laws rewarded creators and furthered competition and innovation.

If my readers who have followed the debate about Canada's long-term competitiveness have concluded by now that many of the policy issues and proposed solutions are all too familiar, you are correct. Skip forward to 2023, and you will see much that is immediately recognizable in policy circles about competitiveness and the essentials of prosperity. While it is true some major achievements were attained in past decades in the trade liberalization and tax reform domains in particular, there is still much to be done. It is reassuring that the current CEO of the Business Council, Goldy Hyder, continues to warn that one the greatest threats to Canada is "complacency" and that action on multiple policy fronts is necessary.

In current policy discussions in which I am involved—including in business, academic, and think tank circles—my clarion call remains the same. As a country, we excel at producing good policy ideas. We punch well below our weight, however, in implementing policy, in turning ideas into action. In the epilogue to this book, titled "Reaching for Gold," I endeavour to address the most pressing policy ideas that in my view are essential to moving our country from bronze to gold.

15

PASSING THE COUNCIL BATON
AND LIFE THEREAFTER

My send-off from the Business Council took place on October 26, 2009, at the National Gallery of Canada in Ottawa. Susan and I stood in the reception area and greeted some two hundred guests, among them Prime Minister Stephen Harper, two former prime ministers, premiers, chief justices, federal cabinet ministers, labour leaders, current and past bank governors, the clerk of the privy council, a number of ambassadors, and an affecting turnout of my Council colleagues.

Before dinner, we gathered in the gallery's auditorium, where I delivered my valedictory. I was overwhelmed with a deep sense of humility, gratitude, and of appreciation of the comradeship that bound us together in pursuit of what I believe were good and noble, not to mention patriotic, causes. I thought of how my mother and father would have felt had they been present. Their courageous journeys to Canada from Italy nearly a century before, their hard work, and their love and devotion had helped prepare the way for me. Above all, they would have approved of the path I had chosen—not the courtroom or high finance but helping to shape good public policy for the country they embraced and gave to me.

We left the auditorium, and side by side with Stephen Harper I walked up the red-carpeted colonnade to the Great Hall. At dinner, there were speeches from no less than Joe Clark, Paul Martin, Jean Charest, Jim Flaherty, Stockwell Day, and Mark Carney, and business colleagues Jim Pattison, Ron Mannix, Hartley Richardson, and Annette Verschuren, among others. To everyone's surprise, Harper spoke for a full ten minutes. He was generous and gracious in his praise. One sentence in particular caught my attention. He said, "You have been bold, enterprising and passionate for the causes you have embraced—usually right, frequently successful. Quite a record!"

Journalist L. Ian MacDonald attended and described the event in the *Ottawa Citizen*: "[Thomas d'Aquino's] marathon five-hour tribute evening on Monday at the National Gallery of Canada was organized a lot more along the lines of a state dinner than a retirement party. It was, in fact, a unique gathering of the Canadian establishment. . . . No one would be surprised if Democracy Watch demanded the guest list and howled at the outrage of the corporate elite rubbing shoulders with the political class—the people who own the country socializing with the ones who run it." With that, MacDonald touched a sensitive point with me. The elitist label has never sat comfortably.

PERCEPTIONS OF EXCESSIVE INFLUENCE

During my three decades as Council CEO, I had attracted a great deal of pointed and sustained criticism from the tribunes of the left. The criticisms came from numerous people who channelled their views via the media and also in a stream of books that portrayed me as the lead perpetrator of a "corporate coup" against the Canadian state. Lead among them was author and journalist Peter C. Newman, who offered a grossly exaggerated view of my influence in his widely read book *Titans*:

> Meanwhile under Tom d'Aquino's leadership, the members of the Canadian Business establishment have good reason to believe they are running the country's economy. They formulated a solid agenda, put their muscle, their brains and their dollars behind it. Then they declared war on governments and battled out each outstanding public policy issue. Without ordinary citizens becoming aware of it, Ottawa capitulated. The regimes of Brian Mulroney and Jean Chrétien came to agree that what was good for the BCNI was good for Canada. Tom d'Aquino had proven himself to be not only a brilliant political strategist on behalf of big business, but he emerged as the most powerful influence on public policy formation in Canadian history.

This same theme ran through the writings of Linda McQuaig, Duncan Cameron, Mel Hurtig, Maude Barlow, Bruce Campbell, Tony Clarke, Murray Dobbin, and others. It was a frequent refrain of the Centre for Policy Alternatives and all too often echoed in the rhetoric of the Canadian labour movement. Far from taking satisfaction from any of it, it made me feel profoundly uncomfortable, both personally and on behalf of the Council. After all, I was the chief communicator for the Council, and I did not accept for a moment that being described as the most powerful influencer in the country was a good thing. There were some insiders who said to me, "Tom, don't knock it! This image of power and success is something money can't buy."

While my Council colleagues were not particularly perturbed, the criticism did not go down well with some of those closest to me.

One afternoon, my old friend Gordon Robertson, former clerk of the privy council, asked me to come to his home. He had read an article in the November 1992 *Canadian Forum* written by Murray Dobbin. It was titled "Thomas d'Aquino: The De Facto PM." Robertson was concerned that Dobbin's article, along with similar public commentary about me, was damaging my reputation. "Tom," he said, "you are just too darn powerful and you need to tone it down."

One reality worked against me and the Council: we were often successful in our efforts to shape the public agenda. This simply added fuel to the fire. Also, my ideological opponents were flummoxed by my style. I was not some cigar-chomping caricature of a capitalist with a bullhorn in hand. I welcomed and indeed enjoyed reasoned debate. I worked hard at building bridges, employing diplomacy rather than adversarial tactics. One of my critics, journalist Linda McQuaig, put it this way: "The friendly, personable d'Aquino doesn't really seem like a businessman at all. With his relaxed manner and his talk about social problems, he comes across more like an environmental lawyer or maybe a hip advertising executive. When he really gets going, he has an almost Kennedy-esque aura."

My words came naturally. I genuinely believed that the immense financial clout of our Council members would not on its own advance our agenda, but that well-researched policy positions coupled with skilful diplomacy would. I also embraced a deeply rooted philosophical belief that capital, successfully and responsibly deployed, would lead to improved social outcomes as well as business profits. During my three decades at the Council, time and again I would identify Council positions with the national interest, be they fiscal, trade, environmental, foreign policy, defence, or constitutional. This approach was rare in Canada, and equally rare among business associations around the world. It certainly unnerved many of my critics. I have never made a secret of my views on the role of capitalism and on the importance of corporate social responsibility; they were the bedrock of my approach and the position I successfully urged on the Business Council from the very start. Those who knew me well were not surprised by the content and style of my advocacy. Simply put, one's business persona is shaped by one's moral compass. Mine was set early in life by my mother, who always reminded me of the importance of respecting and assisting the less well off. Indeed, I shall never forget her words the night before she died. "Help the poor," she said. "The rich know how to look after themselves."

CEO SUCCESSION

Succession is part of our lives. It happens in families and in every form of human organization, sometimes abruptly, sometimes planned. Often, it does not go smoothly. This is not surprising given that in the transfer of power and authority, egos often get in the way. In the political world, power struggles are common, often visible, and at times acrimonious. In the business world, overt power struggles are less common and in general less visible. In part, this is due to the high premium given to succession as the holy grail of sound management and good governance.

During my three decades leading the Council, I worked directly with over a thousand CEOs and witnessed a string of successions in many companies. In the case of Air Canada, Alcan, DuPont Canada, the Bank of Montreal, the Bank of Nova Scotia, Bombardier, CAE, Canfor, CIBC, Manulife Financial, Dofasco, the National Bank of Canada, Nortel, the Royal Bank, and TransCanada PipeLines, the turnover of CEOs at each ranged between four and seven during my tenure. By way of example, at the Royal Bank of Canada I worked with chief executives Earle McLaughlin, Rowland Frazee, John Cleghorn, Allan Taylor, and Gordon Nixon. In the case of foreign-owned enterprises such as Ford Motor Company of Canada, General Motors of Canada, IBM Canada, Imperial Oil, 3M Canada, Mitsui & Co. Canada, Shell Canada, and Siemens Canada, the turnover of CEOs was generally even higher. Within the Council leadership itself, our board of directors was constantly renewing itself; I had the privilege of working with thirteen chairs in all.

With this exposure to so many successions, I knew that one of the most important responsibilities of the Council's board of directors was to secure a strong successor to me. The recruitment process is placed, more generally than not, in the hands of an executive search firm, whether recruitment is done from outside or within. When I signalled that I wished to take my leave of the Council no later than December 31, 2009, I took an unconventional step. I offered to nominate several worthy potential successors on the understanding that if this initiative did not have a satisfactory outcome, the Council's board of directors would resort to traditional recruitment methods. With the blessing of the Council's directors, chair Gordon Nixon and the executive committee agreed to proceed with my proposal. Following up, I quietly reached out to four individuals well known to me who I believed possessed high potential for the job. All four were exceedingly able, had proven track records, and were highly respected in their milieus.

On March 10, nine months before my departure, I joined former Council chair and then honorary chair Richard George, chairman Gordon Nixon, and vice-chairs Dominic D'Alessandro and Hartley Richardson at the Toronto Club to interview candidates. In addition to the four individuals I nominated, there was a fifth who had expressed an interest in the position. Following a full day of interviews and discussions, we conducted a secret vote and a single candidate prevailed. It was John Manley, former deputy prime minister in the Liberal government of Jean Chrétien. Manley had caught my eye years before, when he was serving as a backbencher in the ranks of the Opposition. Elected to Parliament in 1988, he would go on to serve as minister of industry, minister of foreign affairs, and briefly as minister of finance. He was bright and personable, and in my books he scored highly on the integrity scale. My first contact with him was when I heard him speak in the House of Commons, reflecting a thoughtful and moderate view at odds with some Liberal Party colleagues who were bending quite heavily to the left. I remember sending him an approving note, which he confessed to me in later years he was surprised to receive. Gordon Nixon informed the board of directors of our recommended choice, and approval was quickly confirmed. Manley was to succeed me. He would begin his duties on January 1, 2010.

I took what I believed was another key step to ensure the sustainability of the Council in the years to come. After all, some one thousand CEOs and entrepreneurs had joined me in investing their faith, hopes, time, and financial resources in building the organization. I approached two members to encourage them to step up to the leadership challenge as chair of the board following Gordon Nixon's term. One was Hartley Richardson, the other was Paul Desmarais Jr. In due course, Richardson was elected chair, and later Desmarais succeeded him. I was very pleased with these governance decisions. Experienced and seasoned leaders were in place. The Council was in good hands.

In the lead-up to my succession, the board of directors had asked me for a report summing up my years at the Business Council. I responded with a paper in August 2009 titled "Three Decades of Influence: The Secrets of Our Council's Success." Here are a few of these "secrets": strict non-partisanship; membership limited to CEOs and entrepreneurs, with no substitutions allowed, and to the highest-earning companies; direct engagement and personal attendance at membership meetings; a board of directors representative of the membership and of sectors and regions, meeting at least three times a year; issues-oriented task forces made up of members as the main drivers of the Council's work; a focus on a broad range of current domestic and global issues; close cooperation with other business and research organizations; high-value intelligence; strategic advocacy; respectful engagement with government; a small but highly competent headquarters staff.

These so-called secrets were the tools and practices that guided the Council's day-to-day work. Overarching all of this was the trust and mutually rewarding relationships that developed through the pursuit of policy outcomes deemed to be relevant and important. Here, the Council's broader policy agenda comes into play. By choosing from day one to engage in issues that transcended the traditional business concerns of fiscal policy, taxation, and trade, a whole new world opened itself up to Council members. Involvement in constitutional, defence, foreign policy, and social policy issues captured the attention and the imagination of members. One of the motivations that drove us was knowing these issues really mattered. Put another way, Council members understood that a safe and well-governed country, respectful of the rule of law and with sound social and economic policy foundations, was beneficial not only to the citizenry but to business as well.

My final days at the Council were spent saying my farewells to friends and colleagues in Canada and abroad and showing my appreciation to the headquarters staff, some of whom had served the Council alongside me for over twenty years. Of those who had journeyed with me the longest, Patricia Longino, Nancy Wallace,

David Stewart-Patterson, John Dillon and Sam Boutziouvis stood out. Their loyalty, hard work and sound judgment had been indispensable to my success. My time was also occupied with briefing John Manley and fulfilling my final Council duties. Within days of the retirement dinner, I was en route to China along with Laurent Beaudoin to deliver the keynote address at the annual meeting of the mayor of Shanghai's International Business Leaders' Advisory Council. Several weeks later, I travelled to England to participate in briefings and discussions in the City of London organized by the British government on the recent financial crisis. There, I was asked to provide a Canadian private-sector perspective on how Canada had managed to navigate through the crisis better than most countries.

In the months leading up my retirement from the Council, invitations aplenty landed on my desk. I was asked to add to my list of corporate board appointments, associate myself with one of two well-known law firms, and take on teaching posts at universities. All these were designed as part-time appointments, which suited me ideally, as I wanted to preserve a high degree of flexibility and independence. There was one notable exception, a tantalizing offer that I considered seriously and which would have significantly altered my plans. I was approached by an executive recruitment firm to consider the post of chair of Barclays Canada. Following meetings in New York with senior executives of the bank in October 2009, I said I was interested but wished to retain my principal residence in Ottawa while working mainly out of the Toronto headquarters. A written offer arrived at my office, but twenty-four hours later I decided to decline. After thinking through the implications of spending the lion's share of my time in Toronto, I had real concerns about the impact on my personal life and especially the effects on Susan. Also, acceptance would have meant having to retreat from a significant number of existing commitments, which I was loath to do. Declining the offer at the eleventh hour, needless to say, was upsetting to Barclays and the executive recruiter who had pursued the search in a highly professional manner. It caused me discomfort as well, but then, in mitigation, I offered the executive recruiter an idea. I pointed out that following the conclusion of his tenure as Canadian ambassador to the United States, Michael Wilson would be an ideal candidate, given his finance background. My suggestion worked, and in May 2010, Wilson took up the post of chair of Barclays Capital Canada, where he remained in the job until his death in 2019. I justly concluded, to quote Shakespeare, that "all's well that ends well." I was pleased for Wilson and for Barclays.

With the banking option closed, the one new significant appointment I took on was to serve as senior counsel at Gowlings law firm. Headquartered in Ottawa, with a national and international practice, Gowlings seemed a good fit that would allow me the flexibility to pursue my other commitments. My colleagues there were congenial and helpful, especially my good friend Jacques Shore. After a couple of years, however, it became apparent to me that I could not in good faith serve the firm and at the same time fulfill my other obligations. I left the firm on the best of terms.

LIFE AS A BOARD DIRECTOR

Boards of directors have been an important part of my life since the early 1980s. Board activity was central to my leadership role at the Council over three decades. Council boards were composed of senior business leaders who themselves were part of their own company boards and networks of boards. Because of this, it was essential to me that Council board organization and practices be a model of excellence. Equally critical was nurturing the relationships that led to effective governance—relationships built on common purpose, trust, transparency, and collegial respect.

While leading the Business Council, I had made it clear at the outset of my mandate that I would not accept appointments to corporate boards. I simply did not have the time. I followed this self-imposed rule until the latter period of my tenure at the Council. But there was another reason for not accepting appointments: I did not wish to signal that I had favourites among member companies. And then there was always the issue of potential conflict of interest, real or perceived, a matter of great sensitivity to me.

As I passed the baton at the Council, my engagement with corporate boards formed an increasingly important part of my business life. Two publicly traded companies were cornerstones of my activity. One was Manulife Financial Corporation; the other was the CGI Group. I had joined the board of Manulife in 2005. At the time, it was the largest insurance company in North America, and it had a fascinating history. It was incorporated by an act of Canadian Parliament in 1887 as the Manufacturers Life Insurance Company, and its first president was none other than Canada's first prime minister, John A. Macdonald. Conflict of interest laws did not exist at the time, and combining the political world with the corporate was not unusual.

When I joined the board, Arthur Sawchuk served as chair and Dominic D'Alessandro as chief executive officer. Both had been members of the Council and were well known to me. My board colleagues were an impressive bunch, and they included former finance minister Michael Wilson, former Bank of Canada governor Gordon Thiessen, and Canada Pension Plan Investment Board chair Gail Cook-Bennett. Cook-Bennett was the first woman to chair Manulife's board and, in her various leadership roles in business, served as an excellent role model to other women executives.

Serving on the Manulife board tested one's intellect. The company's operations were enormously complex, with a heavy engagement in the United States via the John Hancock Financial division and a significant presence in Asia, including, among other countries, China, Japan, Indonesia, Singapore, the Philippines, Vietnam, and Cambodia. During my tenure on the company's board, I sat on committees dealing with management resources and compensation, audit and risk management, and corporate governance and nominations. When I joined the board, Manulife was in many respects the darling of the insurance world. By dint of his ambition and hard work, chief executive Dominic D'Alessandro had created a star among North American insurance companies. He had engineered the takeover of the iconic John Hancock company, headquartered in Boston, and played a key role in building Manulife's presence in Asia. I was in Beijing in November 1994 at a meeting with China's vice-premier Zhu Rongji when Zhu advised D'Alessandro that Manulife would have front row entry to operate in China. I was not a board member then, but after joining in 2005 I found the periodic visits of the board to our Asian operations extremely valuable.

With Manulife's star shining so brightly, it was a great blow when the company got caught up in the turbulence of the 2008 financial crisis. The problems that came to the fore had in fact begun several years earlier. We directors, along with observers on the street, were aware that the company had high exposure to stock market gyrations due to its large segregated fund/variable annuity business. D'Alessandro's aversion to the hedging of equity positions in the variable annuity business to cover guaranteed payouts was also widely known. Nonetheless, I, like so many of my colleagues, did not sound alarm bells, because we had faith in D'Alessandro. He had an extraordinary performance record as CEO, was an accountant by training and knew his numbers, and no one in the company worked harder that he did.

When the markets went into freefall in 2008, Manulife's net exposure due to segregated fund products soared. At that point, the Office of the Superintendent of Financial Institutions placed the company under intense scrutiny. The officials were not receptive to the defence offered by the company that segregated fund guarantees are long-dated liabilities and that once markets returned to normal, capital reserves would be restored. Our time in the "penalty box" was an uncomfortable one for directors and senior management alike. Under regulatory pressure and at significant cost, Manulife did restore its capital reserve levels with a bank debt and share issue. In addition, internal controls were buttressed. When the accounting firm Deloitte and Touche offered a reassuring report in the spring of 2009 confirming that Manulife had a "disciplined risk-management culture with a strong senior management team," my mind was eased. But significant damage had been done. When D'Alessandro bid the company farewell in May 2009, I was sad for him. I knew how painful it was for him—a proud leader who had given his all to the company—to leave under a cloud.

I continued to serve on the Manulife board until 2013 and developed a good relationship with Dominic's affable successor, Donald Guloien. The post-D'Alessandro period was a rocky one, and Guloien's most unpopular decision, reluctantly backed by the board, was to cut the company's dividend in half. While it meant savings in the range of $800 million annually, it led to a sharp fall in the share price and more questions. To provide assurances, Guloien spoke of building "fortress capital," a term not universally understood on the street. It was not an easy go for Guloien as he pursued a more conservative and cautious stance at the company. Nevertheless, he commanded the support of the board, and Manulife achieved the stability that many shareholders were craving. Today, Manulife remains a Canadian flagship company with a market capitalization of close to $45 billion, revenues in 2022 of $47.7 billion, assets under management of over $1 trillion, and some 37,000 employees. It continues to be a Canadian pioneer in Asia. Its worldwide operations are ably managed by chief executive Ray Gori.

One of Canada's most remarkable success stories is the CGI Group. In 2006, its founder, Serge Godin, called me and invited me to join the board of the company as an independent director. Godin founded CGI as an information technology consulting company in 1976. That same year, he was joined by André Imbeau, and the partners initially operated the business from Godin's basement in Quebec City. As the company grew, it moved its headquarters to Montreal and continued to offer consulting services in information technology while adding systems integration to its offerings. In due course, the outsourcing business grew as well. In the mid-1980s, the company went public and moved forward with an aggressive build-and-buy strategy. By the 1990s, it had doubled in size. When I joined the CGI board in 2006, Godin had stepped aside as chief executive and taken on the role of executive chair. His selection of Michael Roach as chief executive proved to be a brilliant move. I have seen many CEOs in action, and Roach was one of the best—smart, industrious, congenial, and a superb manager. He and Godin made a perfect pair. Annual revenue by the end of the 2006 fiscal year was $3.5 billion. With important acquisitions in the United States and Europe, CGI doubled in size again between 2010 and 2012. Today, the company employs some 80,000 people, has annual revenues over $12 billion, and has a market capitalization of over $23 billion. Success indeed!

When I joined the CGI board, one of my friends, David Johnston, was already on it. The fact that he was a director and spoke so highly of the company was attractive to me. We worked closely together until he was appointed governor general of Canada in 2010. When it became known to us that Johnston was soon to take up his new post, we came together to salute him warmly and bid him farewell. Johnston would go on to be, in my view, the most outstanding governor general of my generation.

The CGI board was composed of talented individuals, some of whom were veteran travellers on the CGI journey. One was Paule Doré, knowledgeable, intuitive, and always gracious. Another was former Alcan and Rio Tinto Alcan CEO Richard Evans. Before long, we were fortunate to have none other than Dominic D'Alessandro join us. One of the stars of the board was Quebec entrepreneur Alain Bouchard. Like Godin, Bouchard qualified as a super-achiever entrepreneur. Co-founder and chair of Alimentation Couche-Tard, he started off at nineteen working as a stock boy in his brother's milk store. At age twenty-four, he went to work for the grocer Provigo. In 1980, he founded Alimentation Couche-Tard and served as its CEO until 2014. Under his leadership, the company expanded from having one convenience store to its current presence around the world with some 130,000 employees—a stunning achievement.

I was honoured when Serge Godin invited me to serve as the company's lead director, a post that demanded equal parts skill and diplomacy. With the Godin family exercising effective control of the CGI Group, due to its dual class share structure, I became the principal interlocutor between Godin and the board. In addition, I chaired the company's governance committee. I had met very few entrepreneurs who were as driven as Godin. His passion for what he had built was formidable and heartfelt, and he demanded diligence and loyalty from his company managers and employees. He was, in other words, an alpha leader with strong views, and he commanded my deep respect. I in turn took my lead director responsibilities seriously and never shied from speaking my mind to Godin or my fellow directors. To his great credit, Godin was always ready to listen. I also never hesitated to recommend a move on a governance matter if I deemed it vital to the company's interests.

I took my leave of the CGI board in 2015 and thus concluded my board-level engagement with two of Canada's leading publicly traded companies, each with an impressive global reach. My combined experience with Manulife Financial and the CGI Group was something I will always treasure—because of the exhilarating intellectual challenge and because of the bonds of friendship and collaboration I built with fellow board members and senior management. The experience also drove home how important good governance is in the conduct of our corporate enterprises and in upholding the reputation of Canada as a rule-abiding place to do business.

WORKING WITH COMPANY OWNERS

Private family-held companies have also figured prominently in my board experience. My fascination with family enterprise goes back many decades. Early on in the life of the Business Council, I created a special category of membership called the "entrepreneur's circle." This was meant to accommodate companies that were closely held, most of them family-owned. It was also meant to provide a home in the Council's membership for those who were "owners" but did not necessarily carry the title of CEO. The roll call of past and present members of this group is closely associated with the life of corporate Canada over the past half century, among them Ted Rogers, Laurent Beaudoin, Thomas Bata, Peter Munk, Joseph Rotman, Isadore Sharp, Paul Desmarais Sr., Paul Desmarais Jr., André Desmarais, Israel Asper, Brandt Louie, Hartley Richardson, Ronald Mannix, Jimmy Pattison, Serge Godin, Michael McCain,

Prem Watsa, Galen Weston Jr., Ronald Southern, Nancy Southern, Murray Edwards, Thomas Jenkins, John Risley, Michael Audain, Donald Sobey, Hassan Khosrowshahi, and Linda Hasenfratz. Some of these individuals have passed on, but most are alive and still active. Watching them live their lives and build their enterprises was like observing a play in many acts—never boring, often touched with drama and suspense. The lesson of working with these individuals is that Canada's entrepreneurial culture is in fact rich and deep. Most who in my time made their mark were self-starters.

One privately owned family enterprise has commanded my attention as a director and adviser more than any other: the family business of Calgary-based Ronald Mannix. The board of directors of Coril Holdings, on which I served for a number of years, is a private company wholly owned by Ronald Mannix and his two sons, Stephen and Michael. Ronald Mannix is the controlling shareholder. Coril serves as the parent company of Loram Maintenance of Way (railway maintenance services); Triovest (real estate development and advisory services); and Triovest Capital (real estate ownership and management). Loram is headquartered in Minneapolis, and Triovest and Triovest Capital are headquartered in Toronto.

The Mannix family's history of involvement in Canadian business stretches back to 1898. It is an impressive story of pioneering and grit. In that year, Frederick S. Mannix purchased a team of horses and began moving earth as a subcontractor on branch lines being constructed for the Canadian Pacific Railway in Manitoba and Saskatchewan. That humble beginning laid the foundation for the development in the twentieth century of a powerful industrial force. Mannix companies were involved in some of the most challenging infrastructure projects on the continent, including the St. Lawrence Seaway, the Trans-Canada Highway, the James Bay hydroelectric project, the Toronto and Montreal subway systems,

325

the Columbia River development, and the Distant Early Warning Line radar stations built in Canada's high Arctic.

Frederick Mannix's son, Frederick C. Mannix, continued to build the family enterprise in the 1950s and 1960s, diversifying into the coal mining industry, where it became Canada's largest coal producer. Mannix companies spearheaded the construction of the Pembina Pipeline, which led to the establishment of Pembina Corporation, the largest owner-operator at the time of crude oil and liquids feeder pipelines in Canada. Fred C. Mannix went on to establish Loram Maintenance of Way, which today remains a dominant player in North America and continues to expand worldwide.

The first time I met the legendary "FC" was in Ottawa on the occasion of his induction into the Order of Canada. That was also the first time I met his son Ron. It was the beginning of a long personal and business relationship that continued as Ron Mannix took an active role in the Business Council. During the three decades in which I led the Council, Ron participated in the journey every step along the way. As a Council director, he engaged in virtually all major Council projects, giving generously of his time. As a financial contributor, he stood in a class all of his own.

I accepted Ron's invitation in 2007 to join the Coril board of directors. It was a time when he was assembling a formidable team of directors, and it was a privilege to be included. One of Ron's many admirable qualities is his strong desire to embrace good corporate governance principles. In some private companies, where the owner's word is law, corporate governance is either nonexistent or ignored. To his credit, this is not so with Ron. His respect for governance principles was strongly encouraged by his long-serving and very able chief executive, Kevin Beingessner, who recently retired from Coril Holdings. The independent directors with whom I shared governance responsibilities were Paul Wilson, Robert

Michaleski, Rona Ambrose, Carol Leaman, and Gordon Ritchie. The remainder of the board is composed of insiders who include chair emeritus Ron Mannix, Stephen Mannix, who serves as executive chair, Michael Mannix, and two outstanding executives: Loram chief executive Philip Homan and Coril chief executive Deanna Zumwalt. Apart from an excellent matrix of complementary qualifications and experience among directors, the overarching strength of the board is its intimate knowledge of Coril's operations, key managers, and, very importantly, the family shareholders.

Family businesses operate in a world of their own. No two families are alike, and intimate, family-based relationships inevitably bring into play raw emotions, questions of loyalty, and, not infrequently, conflicting visions. Succession issues, critically, are also often in play. Arguably, the most important responsibility of an independent director of a family-owned enterprise is to ensure that the business is able to perpetuate itself over many generations. The hard work involved falls not only to the directors but especially to the shareholders themselves. After observing many family businesses, I have been impressed by the amount of personal effort Ron has devoted to preparing his immediate successors and future generations of the family for the decades to come.

Among my board responsibilities over the past decades, advisory boards have figured prominently. While they do not generally assume the legal and fiduciary characteristics of a traditional board of directors, advisory boards can perform a useful function. In my case, one such advisory board provided valuable insights into the secretive world of merchant banking. In the 1990s, I served on the Canadian advisory board to London-based Schroders. Founded in 1804, Schroders was the creation of a Hamburg-based Hanseatic family that migrated to London in 1818. It grew dramatically in the 1980s under the leadership of Win Bischoff, a talented and erudite individual I first met in the following decade. When Schroders sold its investment banking division to Citigroup in 2000, I left the advisory board with other Canadian colleagues and joined the Canadian advisory board of another prominent merchant bank, Lazard. The Canadian connection was Jacques Drouin, who chaired the Schroders and Lazard Canadian advisory boards.

Lazard was founded as a dry goods business by three brothers in New Orleans in 1848. In the late 1800s and early 1900s, the firm evolved into three "houses" of Lazard, located in the United States, England, and France. In 1977, the firm came under the control of Michel David-Weill, who in 2000 united the firm. It was then that I met David-Weill, an intriguing character who in addition to his passion for merchant banking was a noted art collector. I found the work of the firm fascinating, combining Old World charm with modern investment banking methods. I always looked forward to the meetings of our advisory board, which rotated between Paris, London, and New York. Hard work went hand in hand with memorable occasions at the finest hotels in the three cities. The most memorable dinner of all was hosted by David-Weill and his wife at their historic Paris residence surrounded by their exquisite art collections. On another occasion, when I was en route to Atlanta for a Lazard meeting in the company of Lazard colleague Vernon Jordan, I asked Jordan, a close personal friend of President Bill Clinton, what had motivated the president to get involved with Monica Lewinsky. He looked straight at me and said, "Urges have a mind of their own, even for presidents."

BUSINESS COUNCIL POST-2010

Since my departure as CEO, the Business Council has continued to play a significant role in my life. I attend the Council's three annual meetings and keep abreast of its policy work. I welcome the opportunity to meet new Council members, the up-and-coming younger generation of leaders who increasingly embody the growing diversity of corporate Canada.

John Manley was fortunate to inherit an experienced headquarters team with a proven record on policy and organizational matters. The board of directors, also a source of great strength, was composed of some of Canada's finest business leaders. In its chair, Hartley Richardson, followed by Paul Desmarais Jr., the Council leadership was in exceptionally good hands. Desmarais was in turn succeeded, in 2016, by Linda Hasenfratz, the first woman to chair the organization. I was thrilled with her election. I had worked closely with Linda and admired her entrepreneurial spirit.

John Manley's term as CEO ran from January 2010 to October 2018. During this period, the Council continued to make headway on a number of important policy fronts. I welcomed the attention given to the "Pacific Century" and the need for Canada to up its game as a player in the Asia-Pacific region. In particular, I welcomed the Council's advocacy in support of the Trans-Pacific Partnership Agreement (TPP), which was signed in February 2016. The countries within this arrangement made for an impressive roll call: Australia, Brunei, Canada, Chile, Japan, Malaysia, Mexico, New Zealand, Peru, Singapore, and Vietnam. When Donald Trump was elected president, he revoked the United States' commitment. In my view, as with so many Trump foreign policy decisions, this one was wrong-headed in the extreme. I was a strong supporter of the TPP since its inception, not simply because it represented a leap forward in terms of its progressive trade protocols, but also because it created a strategic alliance in the Pacific that could counter growing Chinese power and influence. This was the rationale behind what President Obama called the "pivot" to Asia. Trump's attempts to kill the TPP did not succeed, and in 2018 it was ratified as the Comprehensive and Progressive Agreement for Trans-Pacific Partnership (CPTPP).

Also on the international front, I was pleased with the Council's support for closer relations between Canada and the European Union. As a long-time Europhile, I dared to dream of a transatlantic free trade agreement between Canada and the countries of Western Europe as far back as the 1980s and 1990s. In speeches in London, Paris, Rome, Berlin, and Madrid, and at conferences on both sides of the Atlantic, I had pitched for the idea based on the common bonds of economics, security, and culture. I also knew, given the complexities of European Union bureaucracy, that a formal trade agreement would be a long time coming. It helped that the Harper government was a strong advocate. At last, in October 2016, the far-reaching Comprehensive Economic and Trade Agreement (CETA) between Canada and the European Union was signed, subject to ratification by the European Union and national legislatures. The Business Council, along with other Canadian business organizations, was an influential player in bringing CETA across the finish line.

While Asia-Pacific and Europe have figured prominently in the international work of the Council over the past decade, Canada's relations with the United States, especially after the onset of the disruptive Trump presidency, have been centre stage. Trump's outlandish attacks on NAFTA as "the worst trade agreement ever negotiated" caused my stomach to churn and created uncertainty and anxiety among my Council colleagues. It also presented a mighty challenge for Justin Trudeau's government. We all had to get used to practising tight-lipped diplomacy for fear that Trump would lash out with some prejudicial move. Our fears were justified, as Canada was indeed punished with an unreasonable volley of tariffs. On more than one occasion, I congratulated Manley and the Council leadership for astutely supporting and helping manage the Trudeau government's negotiations leading to the Canada–United States–Mexico Agreement on July 1, 2020. My continuing deep involvement in continental affairs as Canada chair of the North American Forum allowed for a great deal of beneficial synergy between my Council work and that of the forum.

During this past decade, a special focus for me has been the Council's work on fiscal policy and competitiveness. The Council has acquitted itself well. Manley's skills and judgment as a former finance minister certainly were advantageous. Another special focus for me has been the Council's work on energy and the environment. This file at Council headquarters has remained mainly in the hands of my long-time colleague John Dillon, of whom I spoke earlier. Dillon has competently managed this often complex area of policy, which has occupied a prominent place on the Council agenda since the 1980s. Again, the synergy here between the Council's work and my role as a special adviser to the Business Council of Alberta, formed in 2019, has been fortuitous.

An area where I have seen impressive strides by the Council in the past ten years is in embracing diversity and inclusivity. The Council has moved quickly to adapt to and reflect the rapid demographic changes sweeping across Canadian society. This has not been easy in an organization that continues to draw its membership from a CEO- and entrepreneur-based leadership pool. The Council has responded with an innovative idea—the creation of a Next-Generation Business Leaders program, which extends free membership for four years at a time to a dozen or so founders or CEOs of fast-growing start-ups. It also has extended its hand in partnerships with organizations taking a leadership role in advancing the cause of diversity and inclusiveness.

Manley's successor in late 2018, the energetic Goldy Hyder, has injected new vigour into the Council. Working closely first with

Council chair Donald Lindsay, CEO of mining giant Teck Corporation, and now with chair Victor Dodig, CEO of CIBC, Hyder has harnessed to maximum effect his formidable communications skills, making him one of the most effective business association advocates on the national scene. He also has resuscitated the Council's long and successful tradition of employing members in task force groupings to advance the organization's priorities. I enjoy a close relationship with Hyder, who understands the importance of seeking counsel from leaders with long experience in business and politics. As I write, Hyder is being tested as neither Manley nor I were in dealing with the devastating effects of the COVID-19 pandemic. So far, his performance has been stellar.

SUSAN

January 2010 marked the beginning of an exciting new chapter in my life. While the pace of my activity did not diminish, I was able to exercise greater discretion in how I would spend my time and with whom. I continued with the policy pursuits that had been at the centre of my life for more than four decades. My focus on the arts intensified, and so did my philanthropic work. I was guided now by three essentials: first, whatever activity I took on had to capture my curiosity and be of genuine interest; second, it had to be intellectually satisfying; and third, I would work only with people I liked and respected. Susan figured prominently in all decisions. In 2009, she had retired from the public service as associate deputy minister of Canadian heritage and promptly took on a job as a senior fellow at the Canadian School of Public Service in governance issues related to boards of directors of Crown corporations and Crown agencies. She also put her experience to work by accepting board positions with various cultural organizations.

As I reflect on Susan's career in Canada's public service, several thoughts come to mind. First, she was fortunate to be present and open to opportunities in Ottawa at the very time that my career in business began. As she admits, beginning her journey at the Privy Council Office (PCO) was a wonderful stroke of luck and the perfect launching pad. Her seventeen years of service at the Department of Finance offered an incomparable experience in dealing with complex issues of national import. Her time at the Department of Canadian Heritage engaged her in matters touching culture that had always been close to her heart. Throughout these journeys, Susan met and worked with some of Canada's most gifted leaders. She also had the rare experience of interacting with a bevy of prime ministers, ministers, premiers, and exceptionally talented officials.

Second, to me she was an exemplar of the public servant we have been taught to respect: independent, non-partisan, professional, and discreet. As her husband, I observed her over many years as few people could. She worked in senior positions with prime ministers and ministers, Liberal, Progressive Conservative, and Conservative. She never once in that long period approached those she served or the agendas they pursued with a partisan inclination. Her loyalty to Progressive Conservative finance minister Michael Wilson was as unequivocal as her loyalty to Liberal finance minister Paul Martin. Wilson and Martin in turn responded with respect and affection. As for Susan's professionalism, she believed that Canada's public service was one of the world's finest and that to serve the nation was a privilege. And when it came to professional discretion, she was uncompromising. In her years at the PCO and Finance, she had access to top-secret meetings, conversations, and documentation, much of it touching on economic matters. Not once in all that time did she betray any confidences to me.

A final point. For the better part of three decades, from 1981 to 2009, Susan's sensitive positions in Canada's public service happened to overlap with my responsibilities as head of Canada's most influential business organization. During this period, especially while she was serving at the PCO and Finance, I was actively engaged in public advocacy on a wide variety of economic and social policy issues. There was not a single federal budget in those years that did not attract my close attention and that of my Council colleagues. Not infrequently, the government and I were at odds—sometimes sharply so. Ottawa is a relatively small place, and this did not go unnoticed. At times, I worried that Susan's position would become untenable due to a perceived conflict with my own. But as extraordinary as it seems, neither Susan nor I recollect a single occasion when our relationship became the subject of public controversy. This I owe largely to the discretion Susan exercised, day in and day out, in carrying out her public service duties.

WORKING WITH THE IVEY BUSINESS SCHOOL

In the past decade, working with think tanks and academic institutions has occupied a major part of my agenda. My association with the Ivey Business School's Lawrence National Centre for Policy and Management proved rewarding. The Lawrence National Centre was created thanks to a generous gift from my old friend Jack Lawrence, who tragically was killed when an aircraft he was piloting crashed in August 2009. His gift to Ivey was shepherded by the talented Carol Stephenson, dean of Ivey at the time, the monies to be used to advance understanding between business and government. An advisory council to the centre was established and I agreed to serve as the founding chair. In quick order, and working with the Lawrence National Centre's director Dianne Cunningham, a former cabinet minister in the Ontario government, I spearheaded the organization of a symposium in 2009 on the implications for Canada of the election of President Barack Obama. I organized a second symposium in 2010, titled "The G20: The Changing Face of Global Politics and Economics," with partners Manulife Financial and the Norman Paterson School of International Affairs at Carleton University. A third symposium followed in 2011, titled "Engaging China in a Dynamic Asia: Winning Canadian Strategies." I greatly enjoyed putting together these initiatives and calling on respected colleagues in the CEO community, government, and academe to engage in topical debates. I did not hesitate to draw on my own financial resources to help make them possible. In my view, it was putting capital to work in a productive and satisfying way. In addition, it was fun. Dianne Cunningham was succeeded at the Lawrence National Centre by Paul Boothe, a former federal deputy minister with extensive experience in Ottawa and at the provincial level. To this day, I remain involved with the Lawrence National Centre, which benefits from the strong support of the Ivey Business School's dean, Sharon Hodgson. Recently, former Bank of Canada governor Stephen Poloz agreed to serve as chair of the centre's advisory council with a stellar coterie of colleagues. Jack Lawrence's dream carries on.

CARLETON UNIVERSITY

An academic colleague I have enjoyed working with is Fen Hampson, chancellor's professor at Carleton University in Ottawa and former director of the university's Norman Paterson School of International Affairs. He and I began conversations in 2011 about a possible study that would examine Canada's role in reaching out to new and emerging markets. We were both keen to have former

Canadian ambassadors Derek Burney and Len Edwards join us in this endeavour. The four of us agreed to serve as co-chairs, set about conducting research and cross-country consultations, and ultimately settled down to the task of jointly writing our report. It was obvious to us that in cities across Canada the appetite for our inquiry was deep. There was a sense that Canada was not according emerging economies, especially countries in Asia, the priority they deserved. We had no difficulty in gaining funding from companies, law firms, and think tanks. We also were assisted by a strong national advisory council composed of CEOs, economists, lawyers, and policy specialists.

Our final report, titled "Winning in a Changing World: Canada and Emerging Markets," sounded alarm bells. We pointed out the profound shift in the global economy that the rise of emerging economies had signalled: "They have become integral to the success of new production strategies focused on global value chains, as well as important markets in their own right." "With some notable exceptions," we said, "Canadian firms have made little progress in penetrating new markets while losing market share in traditional ones. Unless Canada dramatically ups its game and changes the way it does business, it assuredly will not be a significant player in these new markets." We spoke of the inadequacy of the postwar trade and investment architecture to deal with the challenges and warned that the quasi-market nature of many of the newer global players "requires innovative approaches and different negotiating, trade and investment strategies from those Canada is now pursuing." The warning, so often repeated in recent years in public policy discourse, was once again underscored: "Before all else, Canada must defeat the culture of comfort that comes from an all-too-easy dependence on the United States."

We challenged business to aggressively market the "Canadian brand" beyond the North American continent and to pursue opportunities in emerging markets as part of a long-term strategy—a strategy that required staying power for which Canadian companies were not well known. Our fourteen recommendations included a more competitive tax base and modernized customs and regulatory regimes. One recommendation focused on the need for governments in Canada to establish clear rules for foreign investors, especially where national security interests were involved. This issue had risen in importance as Chinese investors became increasingly active, especially in Canada's resource sector.

On June 26, 2012, the day before we released our report, Burney, Edwards, Hampson, and I met with Prime Minister Harper to brief him on its contents. Harper appeared to be genuinely interested in our findings. He supported the central thesis of our report that business and governments, ideally working closely together, should pursue opportunities more aggressively in emerging markets. Not long into our discussions, the question of China came up. I expressed concerns about the growing Chinese interest in buying positions in Canada's energy sector and about the absence of clear rules to defend our country's "strategic interests," however we might define them. I advised the prime minister that, based on intelligence I was receiving in Alberta, a Chinese company was likely to make a move on a major Canadian resource producer in Calgary in the near future. In the absence of clear regulations, I said, Canada would be vulnerable to a potential stampede of acquisitions.

Not long after, my prophecy came to pass. The China National Offshore Oil Company made a friendly bid for Calgary-based Nexen Inc. in July. This triggered an intense policy discussion within federal government, business, and public policy circles.

On December 7, the prime minister approved the $15-billion take-over, as well as the $5.2-billion acquisition by Malaysia's Petronas of Progress Energy. However, to his credit, Harper made it clear that while these two transactions would be of "net benefit" to Canada under our country's foreign investment rules, new guidelines would apply in the future. The acquisition of oil sands companies by foreign state-owned enterprises would also be found to constitute a net benefit for Canada in "exceptional circumstances." Harper went on to say that these decisions marked "not the beginning of a trend, but rather the end of a trend." What was on his mind could not have been clearer when he added, "To be blunt, Canadians have not spent years reducing the ownership of sectors of the economy by our own governments, only to see them bought and controlled by foreign governments instead." The federal government also signalled that beyond the oil sands, acquisitions by state-owned companies would be reviewed to consider control or influence to be exercised on the business or the larger industry. While the prime minister's position caused ripples in free market circles, he was correct to take this stand. I had long championed open-economy principles, but I was far from comfortable with the foreign acquisition ambitions of state-owned companies operating from non-democratic countries. The Harper decision revealed the growing concerns about Chinese foreign acquisition activities in particular, concerns that understandably were to multiply in open-market economies in the years to come.

B20 ENGAGEMENT

My interest in G20 affairs began when finance minister Paul Martin first outlined the concept, and it continued in the decades to come. As CEO of the Business Council, I had made sure our organization monitored the G20 agenda. A leading Canadian authority on the G20 was professor John Kirton of the University of Toronto. In 2008, he established the G20 Research Group, which analyzed G20 deliberations and recommendations. Impressed by his work, I pledged the Business Council's support and have followed Kirton ever since.

The establishment of the G20 provided a springboard for another organization, the B20, a grouping of business leaders and business organizations meant to engage with G20 leaders at G20 leaders' summits. The first substantive encounter between the two took place in Los Cabos, Mexico, in 2012. Much credit is due to Mexican business leaders for leading the charge under the chairpersonship of Alejandro Ramírez, the head of the G20 Organizing Committee and CEO of Cinépolis, Mexico. A number of task forces were created to channel recommendations to the G20 leaders, among them task forces on food security, green growth, employment, transparency and anti-corruption, trade and investment, technology and innovation, and financing for growth and development. I was invited to be part of what Ramírez described as the B20's most important task force, concentrating on "advocacy and impact." The idea here was to improve the record of the G20 in implementing its summit recommendations, which was notoriously deficient. Kirton's meticulous work at the University of Toronto left no doubt about the G20's implementation gap.

It was a pleasure to work with my task force colleagues. They included Alejandro Ramírez; Dominic Barton, then head of McKinsey & Company; Pablo González, CEO of Kimberley-Clark, Mexico; Jean-Guy Carrier, secretary general of the International Chamber of Commerce; Thomas Donohue, CEO of the United States Chamber of Commerce; Hans-Peter Keitel, president of the Federation of German Industries; Laurence Parisot, president of the French employers' union MEDEF; and Robert Greenhill, chief business officer of the World Economic Forum. We worked hard to develop a sound report and implementation strategy, and I was pleased with the outcome.

Being part of the B20 team at the Mexico summit offered an opportunity to see international leaders in action. I had occasion to greet Mexican president Felipe Calderón, with whom I already was well acquainted. I congratulated him for hosting such an inclusive summit and for welcoming for the first time representatives of civil society. Prime Minister Harper was present, of course, as were Australia's Julia Gillard, China's Hu Jintao, France's François Hollande, Germany's Angela Merkel, India's Manmohan Singh, Italy's Mario Monti, Japan's Yoshihiko Noda, Russia's Vladimir Putin, the United Kingdom's David Cameron, and the United States' Barack Obama.

The leaders issued an eighty-one-point declaration that was heavy on rhetoric but light on concrete commitments. This was not surprising to me, as I had already had a great deal of exposure to international economic summitry. While failure to execute on a transformational scale may be normal for a summit, I believe we should expect that from time to time there will be surprises on the upside. The world had already witnessed one in the seminal role the G20 played in the 2008–9 global financial crisis. The year after Los Cabos, in 2012, the B20 met in St. Petersburg, a meeting that suffered from overbearing staging by Putin, and carried on in subsequent years in Australia, Turkey, China, Germany, Argentina, and Japan. Bottom line: the B20's track record is not terribly strong, but I believe the effort on the part of G20 business leaders continues to be worthwhile. In particular, the degree to which B20 business leaders can exert influence on G20 leaders in matters touching economic policy is of consequence.

WORKING WITH CANADA'S NURSES

In early 2011, I received a call from Maureen McTeer asking whether I would be prepared to serve on the National Expert Commission on behalf of the Canadian Nurses Association to examine the future of health and health care in Canada. I accepted her invitation, and thus began a fascinating journey in the company of a talented group of experts from across Canada. The commission was co-chaired by McTeer and Marlene Smadu. Ottawa-based McTeer, a long-time friend, a lawyer and an activist, knew how to advance important causes in public policy. Saskatchewan-based Smadu was a highly respected leader in the nursing and health fields. This team at the top of the ticket was a strong incentive for me to get involved. From the outset, it was made clear that the commission was to be independent and would operate at arm's length from the Canadian Nurses Association. My fellow commissioners were the Honourable Sharon Carstairs, Robert G. Evans, Robert Fraser, Francine Girard, Vickie Kaminski, Julie Lys, Sioban Nelson, Charmaine Roye, Heather Smith, Rachel Bard, Judith Shamian, and Michael Villeneuve. Ten of the commissioners had impressive qualifications in nursing and medicine. I was one of the exceptions but pleased to be among such a knowledgeable group. I was expected to bring business and public policy advocacy credentials to the table.

My interest in health policy went back many years through my work at the Council. In *Northern Edge*, the book I co-authored in 2001 with David Stewart-Patterson, we addressed health care as a national priority. We laid out the benefits of Canada's system plainly: "Universally accessible, publicly funded health care is central to our vision of a caring and sharing society. . . . Whatever its faults, the system as it stands achieves economies of scale by covering everyone, saves administrative costs by avoiding insurance rating and multi-stage billing and cuts financing expenses by collecting its revenue through taxation." We went on to account for the widespread feeling that the system was in a state of crisis after "years of government cutbacks . . . hurting the quality of care, causing overworked and underpaid doctors and nurses to flee the profession, and leaving patients fuming over waiting lists for treatment and lineups in emergency rooms." I also knew that with the aging of Canada's population and the growing requirements for funding and technology, much work needed to be done to bring our system up to the highest international standards and to keep pace with the best.

In the intensifying debate about the future of health care, the perspectives of knowledgeable and experienced people were vital commodities. To my thinking, who better than our nurses to help show us the way? Public trust and esteem for nurses as frontline workers was high. And their numbers say something as well. More than 268,000 nurses work with Canadians at every age and every stage of life. Licensed practical nurses and registered psychiatric nurses add almost another 90,000 to that number.

The National Expert Commission's work got under way in May 2011. We commissioned research, including assessments of health care systems in other countries; we consulted with health professionals and policy-makers; and we welcomed written submissions from the public. We also conducted public polling. It turned out to be an intensive undertaking, and I learned a great deal in the process. In June 2012, we tabled our report and a bold plan of action. We called for "a radical shift in thinking and a fundamentally new vision of health and health care" to achieve a transformation of the health care system. Our report identified nine actions. These included seeking to be among the top five nations globally in delivering key health outcomes; putting individuals, families, and communities first; implementing primary health care for all; investing strategically to improve the factors that determine health; paying attention to Canadians at risk of falling behind; urging governments to integrate health in all policies; ensuring safety and quality in care; and preparing the providers.

When we gathered in Vancouver at the time of our report's release, there was a shared sense of accomplishment, a belief we had broken fresh ground with our ideas. We were also mindful that the urgent transformation we were calling for would not come quickly. What was most gratifying to me was that a special, indeed unique, voice had been brought to the debate: that of Canada's nurses—competent, experienced, and caring health care providers.

More than a decade has passed since the tabling of our report, and the debate about the future of Canada's health care system rages on. I am disappointed that many of the report's excellent ideas and recommendations, which remain valid to this day, have failed to gain the traction they deserve. As for the nurses themselves, my work on the commission left no doubt in my mind that they are undervalued and that their expertise is far from being fully utilized. With our health care system under severe pressure, there is no justifiable reason for this, and a course correction is long overdue. Recently, through work with a private company here in Canada, I have been encouraged to see nurse practitioners being engaged in innovative ways through the application of telemedicine. For any who doubt the excellence of our nurses, the tragic COVID-19 saga tells a clear story. Their skills, courage, and empathy have been central in the battle against the virus. When the pandemic passes, I hope that a new public awareness will have developed in Canada that will drive home the need to fully recognize and empower our nurses.

THE AUSTRALIAN CONNECTION

Ever since I was a child, Australia has had a special allure for me. The Australia of my imagination was a distant land in the South Pacific made up of fascinating marsupials and expansive out-back—a land where people spoke English with a distinctive accent. My first exposure to the history of Australia at school was in the context of its place in the British Empire and the bravery of its sol-diers in the two great wars of the twentieth century. The tragic saga of Gallipoli drew heavily on my emotions, as did Vimy Ridge and Passchendaele, which were closer to home. At university, my stud-ies revealed the similarities between Australia and Canada in our parliamentary and judicial traditions. And by the time I was study-ing comparative constitutional law at the University of London, I understood in greater depth how federalism had shaped our two countries.

Despite my attraction to Australia and the tens of thousands of air miles I logged across the Pacific over the preceding three decades, it was not until 2007 that I first set foot on Australian soil. The occa-sion was the APEC Leaders' Summit in Sydney, followed by an offi-cial visit by Prime Minister Harper. I was received warmly by Prime Minister Howard, with whom I had kept in touch since our meeting in Vancouver a decade before. Nonetheless, I was startled when he seated me to his right at his luncheon in Harper's honour at Australia's parliament. In 2012, five years after my first visit, I accepted an invi-tation to serve as the Canadian co-chair of the recently established Australia-Canada Economic Leadership Forum. The Canadian co-chair at the time was Stanley Hartt, who had served as federal deputy minister of finance and chief of staff to Prime Minister Mulroney. The inaugural forum was held in Sydney in 2010, with its principal Canadian driver being Toronto lawyer Bob Onyschuk. The forum's able executive director was Toronto-based Ann Curran.

When I took on the forum responsibilities, my Australian counterpart was Bob Carr, a former minister of foreign affairs and one-
time premier of New South Wales. I respected his long experience
in Australian politics. In short order, Carr stepped down and was
replaced by the experienced and congenial Mike Rann, former
premier of South Australia. Like Carr, Rann was a member of the
Australian Labor Party. Together we co-chaired the second forum
meeting, which took place in Toronto in July 2012. The theme was
"Renewing the Partnership for the 21st Century," and it brought
together from both countries an impressive group of leaders in
business, government, academe, and the voluntary sector. Rann
and I welcomed participants with the following message:

> In the days to come, we will address a wide variety of sub-
> jects that are top of mind in both countries: approaches to
> global economic recovery following a devastating economic
> and financial crisis; competitiveness and international trade
> priorities including our joint commitment to the Trans-Pacific
> Partnership; responses to immense opportunities and trans-
> formational changes in the Asia-Pacific region; and leading-
> edge policies for harnessing technological change. Given
> that Australia and Canada are blessed with an abundance of
> natural resources, our Forum will address topical issues such
> as global food policy, the supply of minerals and energy in
> a resource constrained world, and the regulation of foreign
> direct investment.

Among the speakers were Ontario premier Dalton McGuinty,
Canadian foreign minister John Baird, and former Australian prime
minister Kevin Rudd. It was interesting to note that Baird and Rudd,
of opposing ideological persuasions, spoke as the true friends

they were. Ministerial representation at the forum was solid, with ministers Ed Fast of Canada and Martin Ferguson of Australia covering off trade and resources respectively. The CEO presence, especially from Canada, was impressive, with Mayo Schmidt of Viterra, Hal Kvisle of TransCanada Corporation, Bruce Flatt of Brookfield, and Calin Rovinescu of Air Canada serving as panellists. I was especially pleased to welcome to the forum the Australian Malcolm Turnbull, a well-known Liberal politician who would go on to serve as prime minister from 2015 to 2018.

On the eve of the Toronto meeting, I received an invitation from Kevin Rudd to meet him over lunch. He wanted me to fill him in on the political and economic context in Canada. I was equally interested in getting background from him on Australia. I especially wanted to hear what he had to say about China and the Australia-China relationship. As Rudd is a Mandarin speaker who prides himself on understanding the Chinese mindset, I listened carefully to what he had to say. The need to manage the relationship well was uppermost in his mind. There were no premonitions that China would pursue a more aggressive path in the future or thumb its nose at the liberal international order.

The 2012 forum set the course for future forums. With co-chair Rann's blessing, I shaped the forum in a way that reflected my Business Council experience: limited number of participants in the range of 125 to 150; heavy representation from the CEO community; and leader-level representation from government, academe, and the think tank community. I was also able to increase funding commitments from major corporate partners.

When the forum met for the third time, on this occasion in Melbourne, in February 2014, the same high standard set in Toronto was maintained. By then, Rann had moved on to serve as Australian high commissioner in London and had been replaced by the highly respected business executive Heather Ridout. Having served as the chief executive of the Australian Industry Group, Ridout remained active in corporate circles. She and I set out the 2014 agenda to address "global economic issues; competitiveness and international trade priorities; CEO perspectives on capital markets and global business challenges; engaging China in a dynamic Asia; achieving security and stability in Asia-Pacific; responding to resource development and infrastructure opportunities; leveraging educational advantage; and investing in arts and culture."

As in Toronto, the attendance of leaders in Melbourne was impressive. We were warmly received by the governor and premier of the state of Victoria, but it was prime minister Tony Abbott who stole the show. It was a coup to have the recently elected Abbott present the opening keynote address. He joined me and Heather Ridout at the head table, where we had a lively discussion about Australian and Canadian politics and issues we had in common.

In the coming days, our program benefited from a number of speakers presenting in tandem. Australian and Canadian foreign ministers Julie Bishop and John Baird offered views on current international affairs issues. The Australian and Canadian ministers responsible for the treasury and finance, Joe Hockey and Jim Flaherty, offered perspectives on the economic performance of our two countries. And central bank governors Glenn Stevens and Stephen Poloz addressed international finance. The impressive collection of CEOs who spoke—their companies active in the banking, insurance, pensions, construction, food, and material resource sectors—covered areas of mutual concern, including finance, trade, manufacturing, and technology. Mutual interest in higher education attracted presenters from a number of Australian and Canadian universities, including Monash, Waterloo, and Western.

In June of 2014, I performed my last duty as the Canadian chair of the forum. I hosted a CEO roundtable in Ottawa for visiting Australian prime minister Tony Abbott and joined both Abbott and Prime Minister Harper at a reception the same evening. When the three of us spoke, we shared our optimism that our two countries were destined for ever-closer cooperation.

With the Toronto and Melbourne forums having been firmly established as among the most successful bilateral leadership initiatives in the world, I decided to pass the baton as Canadian chair. It was a difficult decision for me, but I believed my mission was largely fulfilled and other demands were pressing on my time. The forum carries on to this day and serves to demonstrate what I have often said: "no two countries in the world are more alike than Australia and Canada." The ties of history, language, values, and institutions run deep, and we share common concerns in security and international affairs. I believe growing economic security challenges in the Indo-Pacific will move us toward an even deeper relationship in the future.

VATICAN SPORTS SUMMIT

In 2015, I found myself involved in one of the most fascinating projects in my life. A conclave convened in 2013 elected Cardinal Jorge Mario Bergoglio as the successor to Pope Benedict XVI. Benedict surprised the world by choosing to resign from the papacy, ceding the way for Bergoglio, a Jesuit and archbishop of Buenos Aires, who took the pontifical name of Francis. Pope Francis, a declared reformer, quickly captured the attention of the world. Many Vatican observers expected that he would introduce transformational changes to the papacy.

One of the areas that captured the attention of Pope Francis was the role of faith and sport as a positive partnership for social change and international understanding. To advance his vision of the role of the church in the cultural life of society, he appointed Cardinal Gianfranco Ravasi as president of the Pontifical Council for Culture. The erudite Ravasi became a cardinal in 2010. Prior to that, he had headed Milan's Ambrosian Library and subsequently played an important role in overseeing the cultural heritage of the church.

In 2014, Cardinal Ravasi initiated a process that would lead in October 2016 to a global conference at the Vatican titled Sport at the Service of Humanity, presided over by Pope Francis. Ravasi began by assembling an international advisory committee for the initiative. It was at this point that an old friend, Christopher Lang from Toronto, asked me if I would consider accepting an invitation from Ravasi to serve on the committee. Lang, who had over many decades played a seminal role in sports and sports policy in Canada and internationally, had been tapped by Ravasi and his team to assist in shaping the 2106 global conference. Smart, experienced, and trustworthy, and with a heart of gold, he was an ideal choice. Lang also developed an excellent relationship with Ravasi's point man on the project, Monsignor Melchor Sánchez de Toca, undersecretary of the Pontifical Council for Culture.

The international advisory committee was an impressive group composed of luminaries from the worlds of faith, sport, and business. In September 2015, we met for the first time at the Vatican. A consensus quickly developed on the goals of the conference and who should be invited. I was especially pleased that the multi-faith character of the conference was strongly endorsed.

Ravasi and I hit it off very well, in part because of my fluency in Italian, which helped us converse, given his limited proficiency in English. My saintly name, which happens to be the "most illustrious" in the history of the church, was not lost on him. He also appreciated my strong interest in the Vatican art collections, which I had visited many times over the years. I was especially touched when he gave me the book he had written on the Vatican collections. Several years later, when I would lead a group of National Gallery of Canada art patrons to Rome, he was instrumental in providing us access to parts of the collections rarely seen by outsiders.

Meetings in the heart of the Vatican can inspire a deep sense of awe. The historic setting and wondrous works of art are magnificent and inspiring. On the final day of our meetings, some of us were invited to lunch at Casa Santa Marta, the simple modern building within the Vatican walls where Pope Francis chooses to live, having declined to use the papal apartments in the Apostolic Palace. While at lunch in what is known euphemistically as the "Pope's cafeteria," I noticed across the room what looked like poorly dressed street people. When I asked Cardinal Ravasi about them, he informed me that at the request of Pope Francis such guests were often brought in for a meal. I was moved by the sight.

After a great deal of planning, we gathered in October 2016 for the first global conference on faith and sport. It was attended by some 250 delegates from around the world. Working closely with Chris Lang and his team, I was asked to help draft a declaration that would be read at the opening of the conference and serve as the foundation of the conference's deliberations. The document began with a preamble declaring a set of principles about the power of sport, its power to help others, to build trust and understanding, to include everyone, to transform lives and build character, to help us make the most of ourselves, and above all to give joy.

To these principles we added the words of Pope Francis: "I ask that you live your sport as a gift from God, an opportunity not only to bring your talents to fruition, but also as responsibility."

The conference's opening session was moving. We were seated in the Paul VI Audience Hall, designed by the Italian modern architect Pier Luigi Nervi. On the stage were the archbishop of Canterbury and leaders of various faiths, together with United Nations secretary general Ban Ki-moon and International Olympic Committee president Thomas Bach. There was a hush in the crowd as Pope Francis arrived and slowly made his way to the stage from the back of the hall. Following the reading of the declaration we had drafted, Francis rose from his chair and delivered a powerful message. He spoke of sport's challenge to us to help develop each person's God-given talents, and of its power to improve health and well-being, encourage cooperation and teamwork, and teach life lessons about winning and losing. He urged us to allow sport to become a force for inclusion that reached the marginalized and especially the young. Francis hoped that the conference would mobilize religious, business, and sporting institutions to enable all young people to play sport with dignity. Genuine sport, free from manipulation, exploitation, and distortion, should be protected and celebrated at all times, he told us. All sports people must be "amateur" in the original meaning of the word; we must live sport, and live in it and through it.

The agenda unfolded over the next couple of days with the principal themes of the declaration serving as guideposts. Athletes from rich countries and poor told their stories. So did those from the front lines of the Special Olympics movement and the Paralympic Games. So many stories were rooted in courage. I especially remember the young Pakistani woman Maria Toorpakai Wazir, who, growing up in Taliban-controlled territory, continued to pursue her career in squash at the risk of her life. We heard from Kenyan world marathon champion Tegla Loroupe, who defied authorities to pursue her remarkable running career. Business leaders did their best to argue that support of sport should be driven by ideals rather than the exclusive pursuit of profits, and yet, of the trillions of dollars embedded in organized sport, clearly only a small portion is dedicated to the goal of sport functioning in the service of humanity. Corruption in sport was universally condemned, although there was a realization that where money and sport intersect, some foul play is inevitable.

On the eve of the conference's conclusion, we gathered for dinner and a memorable performance by gifted Chinese concert pianist Lang. The setting was the courtyard of the Casina Pio IV, a patrician villa that serves as the home of the Pontifical Academy of Social Sciences, the Pontifical Academy of Sciences, and the Pontifical Academy of Saint Thomas Aquinas. The building, begun in 1558 by Pope Paul IV and completed by his successor, is one of my favourite pieces of architecture in the Vatican. As we listened to the magnificent artistry of Lang, I thought of how he must be feeling, playing in a place of such exquisite beauty under the dark blue of the Roman sky.

At the conclusion of the conference the next day, there was a sense that something greatly significant had transpired, and that athletes, sports organizations, faith leaders, voluntary associations, business leaders, and governments had an important role to play. The Vatican continues to offer moral and inspirational support to the Sport at the Service of Humanity initiative. Importantly, thanks in large measure to the leadership of my friend Christopher Lang, who sadly passed away in 2021, the ideas incubated at the global conference carry on in various forms via organizations in individual countries. It was a singular privilege to be involved.

BUSINESS COUNCIL OF ALBERTA

In the autumn of 2018, Ron Mannix and I began a series of conversations in Calgary. We aimed at coming to terms with the hard
times that were hitting the Alberta energy industry and the con-
sequent effects on jobs, investment, and overall economic activity
in the province. Our conversations were driven not only by the
economic gloom but also by the deepening chasm in the relationship between the Justin Trudeau government and the provinces
of Alberta and Saskatchewan. During those conversations, I urged
Mannix to consider the idea of creating an organization of Alberta
business leaders to engage more meaningfully in shaping economic policy and broader societal goals in the province. I suggested
an organization modelled on the Business Council of Canada that
would be CEO-based, policy oriented, and non-partisan. As Mannix
had been a long-time member of the Council and with me every
step along our journey since the early 1980s, he knew instantly
what I was talking about and responded with enthusiasm.

In November, Mannix met with me and our mutual friend and
trusted adviser David Elton, the esteemed political scientist from
Alberta, to flesh out the idea. Mannix invited Calgary executive
Adam Legge to join us. Legge had served as the head of the Calgary
Chamber of Commerce. He was bright, experienced, and hard-
working, and we looked to him as a possible recruit to our cause
and as a key staffer who might one day lead this new organization. We felt strongly that we should move forward. Shortly thereafter, Mannix reached out to senior Calgary business leaders Mac
Van Wielingen, Hal Kvisle, Nancy Southern, and Dawn Farrell to
sound them out on the idea and to establish a founding group.
Van Wielingen, a highly respected entrepreneur with a remarkable record of success in the energy domain, was an important

choice, as was Kvisle, a seasoned executive who had served as CEO of a number of major Alberta-based enterprises, including TransCanada PipeLines and Talisman Energy. Highly regarded ATCO CEO Southern, and TransAlta CEO Farrell, would add strong credibility to the undertaking. With the founding group in place, and thanks to enabling support from Mannix, Legge was retained to develop a business plan, and I agreed to serve as a special adviser on a pro bono basis. Importantly, Kvisle agreed to serve as chair of the nascent organization, bringing his immense experience and superb leadership skills to the table. I was very comfortable working with this team, especially as Kvisle, Southern, and Farrell were long-standing Council veterans.

In February 2019, the founding group convened twenty-four Alberta-based CEOs. There was unanimous agreement to move forward. In March, the new organization was incorporated as the Business Council of Alberta (BCA), and in April Legge was hired as its CEO. Importantly, the BCA was non-partisan and not for profit, and it committed itself, through its membership and policy work, to address policy issues that touched on all aspects of the Alberta economy. To me, this was vital, as there was some suspicion among the public that the BCA would be overly influenced by the energy producers. The founders and Legge worked hard to build the broadest possible base for the BCA so that it would include agriculture and food processing, finance, construction, real estate, technology, transportation, communications, mining, and manufacturing. Legge proceeded to assemble a strong team that would form the core of staff capability in research and communications. In this crucial organizational phase, I devoted considerable time to helping shape the organization to achieve optimal effectiveness. This meant working closely with the founders and Legge. It also meant close coordination with Mannix, who brought great energy and momentum to the BCA.

I counselled the founding group and Legge to reach out to Ottawa and signal the BCA's willingness to work with senior officials and relevant members of the Trudeau cabinet. On the morning of May 27, the BCA held the first of a series of meetings with Ian Shugart, the newly appointed clerk of the privy council. I turned to my old friend Joe Clark, who knew Shugart well, for help in setting up the meeting. Clark was pleased to assist and was present at a dinner I hosted with the group the evening before, where we all benefited from his advice. Legge recognized the importance of keeping channels open with Ottawa. He did not take his eye off the ball: periodic meetings in Ottawa and Calgary with Shugart and with ministers in the Trudeau cabinet followed on a regular basis.

The first formal meeting of the BCA's membership took place in Edmonton in June 2019 at the Hotel Macdonald. It coincided with the organization's public launch. A highlight of the meeting was a roundtable with recently elected premier Jason Kenney and some of his key officials. The premier was delighted that the BCA was being officially launched and pledged that his government would be happy to work with it. He acknowledged that the BCA was a nonpartisan group and said he would welcome its independent and objective contributions to the public policy debate.

Although we were not close, the premier and I had known one another for many years, going back to the late 1980s, when he served as executive director of the Alberta Taxpayers Association. Subsequently, our paths crossed in Ottawa, where he served in a variety of cabinet portfolios in the Harper government, including multiculturalism and Canadian identity; citizenship, immigration, and multiculturalism; employment and social development; and defence. As I got to know him better, my perceptions of him sharpened: he was bright, principled, energetic, ambitious, and possessed of remarkable political skills. On April 16, 2019, days before the BCA's inaugural meeting, I sat at dinner in Calgary with Mannix, Kvisle, Van Wielingen, and Legge, and we watched the coverage on television as Kenney and his United Conservative Party took the provincial election. In his acceptance speech, Premier-elect Kenney left no doubt that he was going to pursue an ambitious agenda of change.

In the four years since its founding, the BCA has progressed impressively. Its membership ranks have grown, and task forces have gone to work on a number of important policy priorities aimed at enhancing Alberta's prosperity. All this has transpired at an especially challenging time for Albertans, with the energy sector facing severe headwinds and unemployment at unacceptably high levels. Not surprisingly, political alienation in Alberta and neighbouring Saskatchewan has been on the rise. The re-election of the Trudeau government in 2019 and 2021 despite a blanket rejection of Liberal candidates by voters in Alberta and Saskatchewan has not helped. Nor has the inability of the Trudeau government to respond in any meaningful way to the exasperation of so many in the West at what they perceive as wilful neglect of Western Canada's natural resource endowment—an endowment that benefits Canada enormously. To add to my concerns, I have observed at close quarters growing separatist tendencies in the province. There are some who have been highly critical of Kenney as premier, suggesting he was fanning the flames of Alberta separatism. I do not accept this judgment of him. He is a patriot who believes in Canada and federalism. But as premier he had to deal with the considerable number of Albertans who distrust Ottawa and who believe Alberta's future is compromised by a central government that is tone deaf to what matters to the West. Some of the malcontents in his own party challenged Kenney, and perceived failures in his management of the COVID-19 pandemic led to an erosion of his popular support.

The challenges in the end proved insurmountable for him, and in 2022, failing to achieve a convincing majority vote among his party members, he resigned as premier. This was an outcome I would never have predicted of such an ambitious and experienced leader.

As I work with my Alberta colleagues, I offer advice and perspectives based on my long experience with past challenges to national unity, when the bonds of our federation were shaken by Western alienation and Quebec separatism. We survived those conflicts, and as a country we will once again prevail, but not without a great deal of work and good will. That is what healthy federalism demands. In my discussions with my BCA colleagues, I often invoke the memory and example of my friend and mentor Peter Lougheed. He reminded me often that even when clashes between Alberta and Ottawa were at their fiercest, Alberta was never prepared to give up on Canada, and he was determined to pursue the best of Alberta's ideas to strengthen the federation.

16

LEADERSHIP AND LEADERS

If there is an overarching theme of this book, it is leadership. As you've read, I have had the privilege of working with many remarkable leaders, a front row seat on what makes them tick and why they are so effective. Whether from the realm of business, government, the voluntary sector, or everyday life, they have often deeply impressed me with their stories and their example.

Forty years ago, my ideas about leadership were largely those I carried forward from my youth. As an avid student of history, it was the great soldiers, politicians, scientists, philosophers, writers, explorers, athletes, and business tycoons that fired my imagination. In my philosophical instruction, the twelve virtues of Aristotle, courage and magnanimity prominent among them, helped shape my thinking. The four cardinal virtues given to us by Saint Thomas Aquinas—prudence, justice, temperance, and courage—inspired me.

The first serious treatises on leadership I read were Niccolò Machiavelli's *The Prince* and his *Discourses on Livy*. I was about eleven years old, and my father said, "In these works there is both good advice and bad. When you have read them, tell me which is which." I can't recall whether I passed or failed the test, but I do remember thinking that being the prince was not easy! To add to the challenge, after reading these works in their English translations, my father gave me *The Prince* in its original Italian, which I read several years later. I cherish it to this day.

My mother, who was born in the heart of Tuscany, took pleasure in the thought that I was reading the works of Machiavelli, who as a Florentine was a famous son of that glorious region of Italy. The most important attribute of leadership, in her view, was summed up by the Italian word *giudizio*, which means "judgment." She often said to me, *"Il buon giudizio è indispensabile"* ("good judgment is indispensable"). Time and time again, in the decades that followed, I would apply the good-judgment test when assessing a leader and weighing my own decisions. It served me well.

In my late twenties, I had my first close look at political leadership in action. As a member of Prime Minister Pierre Trudeau's staff, I observed Canada's most charismatic leader of the twentieth century come to terms with his own meteoric rise to power and fame. I watched as he audaciously launched the unpopular Official Languages Act, crusaded for a Charter of Rights and for patriation of the Canadian Constitution, reached out to the People's Republic of China when most other Western nations dared not do so, and courageously confronted separatism in Quebec and the FLQ terrorist challenge. I also saw first-hand how this proud man responded to near electoral defeat at the end of his first term.

My experience in Trudeau's office taught me several things about leadership: that it is lonely at the top; that the physical demands of high office can be excruciating; that the buck really does stop on the leader's desk; and that the leader's hold on power can be distressingly transient. It also taught me that effective leaders, and Trudeau was no exception, often owe their successes to the wisdom they garner from competent and trusted advisers.

Over the decades, my thoughts on leadership have also been influenced by numerous theorists—often professors or celebrated gurus who write and teach on the subject. I encountered some of the largest concentrations of these theorists during my annual expeditions to the World Economic Forum in Switzerland. In the end, there is a remarkable similarity to the theories, and therefore what is especially interesting to me is what I have learned in observing how these theories are applied. When asked to list what I consider to be the most important elements of leadership, I have invariably mentioned the following.

AMBITION

I begin with where I think it all begins. Ambition is the desire to create, to build, to achieve. With some, the flame of ambition burns brightly at an early age. With others, it emerges later in life, often as a response to some challenge or provocation. Ambition is often inspired by the kind of dreams that are born of confidence and imagination, and by the belief that with hard work and good luck, those dreams can become reality. Ambition is what overcomes fear and failure and drives those who fail to try and try again. At the root of ambition lies an unquenchable desire to succeed. One of Canada's star entrepreneurs, Jimmy Pattison, puts it very simply: "I believe that *wanting* is the most important quality a person can bring to a business."

Adversity is a powerful catalyst for ambition and the creativity that goes with it. When I reflect on the Canadian entrepreneurs I know and with whom I have worked, this point is all too evident. Many have been stunning achievers despite being born into families and circumstances without privilege. In a moment of reflection, one of them said to me, "Growing up poor taught me to appreciate the value of everything around me. It also taught me there are no obstacles that hard work and determination cannot overcome."

The experience of Canadian leaders is shaped by an uncommon reality. I believe that our country is as true a meritocracy as exists, where the door to opportunity is open to virtually all who want to walk through it. Just think for a moment of the extraordinary stories of high achievers in Canadian business who immigrated to Canada and went on to command impressive organizations. Tom Bata, Peter Munk, Frank Stronach, Hassan Khosrowshahi, Prem Watsa, Frank Hasenfratz, and more recently Tobias Lütke are but a few.

Ambition is sometimes portrayed as unseemly; it is often called dangerous, because it can lead to overreach or abuse. The unease many feel about ambition has a long history. I remember as a child asking my father why Julius Caesar was killed. "Some thought him too ambitious," he replied. Shakespeare sums up the reasons for Caesar's fate in the words he gives to Brutus, the chief among his assassins: "As Caesar loved me, I weep for him; as he was fortunate, I rejoice at it; as he was valiant, I honour him; but as he was ambitious, I slew him." Think of the Greek myth of Icarus, who dared fly too close to the sun. In our own day, in politics and business, runaway ambition fuelled by hubris has destroyed many leaders. From terrible wars to massive corporate failures, we know too well what happens when the desire for power spills over the banks of reason and decency.

The potential for abuse notwithstanding, in my view ambition should be recognized as the life force that fires creativity and drives us to reach for the outer limits of our imagination. Without ambition, continents would not have been discovered, mighty cathedrals would not have been built, diseases would not have been overcome, space would not be explored. In the world of commerce, ambition has spawned innovations that have improved the lives of billions of people.

INTEGRITY

Integrity is an equal essential of good leadership. It encompasses a collection of virtues, among them honesty and authenticity. A deep sense of integrity is the most powerful check on runaway ambition. Among the leaders I have known, those who have been short on integrity have almost always in the end failed. A lack of integrity can manifest itself in myriad ways. It may appear as cutting corners or, as is often said, sailing too close to the wind. It may involve abusive behaviour, the most pernicious of which in my view is disrespect for subordinates or those least able to defend themselves. Or it may involve outright dishonesty in the form of lying, cheating, or fraud.

When it comes to integrity, there can be no compromise. I remember as a young lawyer sitting in a restaurant in the Hassler hotel in Rome and being handed by the representative of my client a briefcase full of cash for services I had rendered. When I refused to take the cash and requested that my invoice be satisfied via proper channels, my host replied, "Why not take it? No one will ever know and you will never be taxed on this." But "no compromise" means being honest even when no one is looking. The Chinese philosopher Confucius offers a stern judgment: "To know what is right and not do it is the worst cowardice."

Some argue that knowing what is right in contemporary settings can be too difficult. They would rather rely on laws and regulations. To be sure, thoughtfully conceived laws and regulations are good and useful things. But my experience over the past four decades in dealing with issues related to integrity has taught me that if a person cannot answer the question "Am I doing the right thing?" then this presents a problem. The ongoing debate about corporate ethics and accountability is a case in point. There is a tendency to view corporate ethics in the context of compliance and the inevitable tension between principles and regulation. I have often said that the chief executives who deserve the greatest respect are those who practise the highest ethical conduct not because rules or regulators demand it, but because they instinctively know it is the right thing to do.

HUMILITY

Humility is a natural companion to integrity. Proverbs 11:2 tells us, "When pride comes, then comes disgrace, but with the humble is wisdom." Having spent most of my adult life walking the corridors of power in the company of powerful people, one might rightly wonder if there is much room for humility. An honest answer is that we can only try. Humility in the first instance requires an acknowledgement of imperfection, and I am far from perfect. It requires an understanding of limitations, and I have many. It requires compassion and the ability to forgive, and in these I have fallen short. It requires understanding the fine line between forceful advocacy and boastfulness, and here again I have not always succeeded. But I have been accompanied by a saving and ever-present conviction, reinforced by the teachings of my mother. It can be explained, in part, by the Golden Rule. It also is embedded in the simple mantra that whatever our station in life, we must unfailingly show true respect for others. "Listen and learn from others," my mother would say. My father was more blunt: "Never assume you are the smartest person in the room."

In my rebellious law student days, my oft-stated belief was that no one is infallible, just as no one is above the law. Arguing as I did that this applied even to the Pope, the head of the church that had been embraced by me and my family, and by my ancestors for centuries, led me to a break with Roman Catholicism in the 1960s in favour of the Anglican Communion. Interestingly to me, the current

Pope, a Franciscan, practises an authentic humility in much of what he says and does. It is inspiring to behold, but in working with the Vatican, I have seen with my own eyes how disruptive this is to the conservative traditions of the Roman Curia. Will it in the end prove transformational? This remains to be seen.

KNOWLEDGE

A leader thirsts for knowledge—deep knowledge, relevant knowledge, up-to-date knowledge. A leader has the zeal of an inquiring mind. Harnessing this requires discipline and hard work. Plato's expectation of leaders is that they should possess deep wisdom and be learned in the art of ruling. While we cannot expect that every leader be Plato's "philosopher king," one cause of failure among leaders that I have observed is simply that they do not know enough. Having attained a leadership position, their ability to mask their deficiencies becomes increasingly difficult. Even worse, leaders with a knowledge deficit may not know what they do not know. Equally distressing are leaders who simply do not care about what they know or do not know. Canadian author Malcolm Gladwell argues that it takes some ten thousand hours of intensive practise to achieve mastery of complex skills and materials. Rest assured that Donald Trump did not have a reservoir of ten thousand hours of study of government and public policy before becoming president of the most powerful nation in the world.

The possession of deep knowledge is one thing; ensuring that one remains up to date is just as important. This requires lifelong learning. The most successful CEOs and entrepreneurs I have known are those who work hard at keeping on top of their core businesses. Those who really stand out are often, in addition, widely read and worldly in the best sense of the word.

Intellectual capital is most productive when it has deep roots, and to nurture such roots requires a lifetime of effort. The young people I mentor—some aspiring CEOs, some would-be prime ministers—hear this refrain from me: embrace education with passion; read as widely as you can; obtain a solid grounding in philosophy, literature, languages (Mandarin along with English should top the list), politics, history, and economics; and get as much practical experience outside of your intended vocation as possible. Then, and only then, can you become an accomplished player in a world that has an ever-growing supply of formidable talent.

An effective leader has a duty to share knowledge and in so doing empower others. At my offices at the Business Council, I kept the following words in my top drawer as a reminder of the importance of empowerment: "If your actions inspire others to dream more, learn more, and become more, you are a leader."

EMPOWERING OTHERS

No leader can ultimately succeed by acting alone, but some forget this reality and pay the price. The best leaders I know devote a large part of their energy to attracting and retaining the best talent they can find. Masters of the art have a number of things in common. They embrace, rather than feel threatened by, individuals who are as smart as they are, if not smarter. They foster a working environment where there is a healthy balance between freedom and control, where the highest standards are set and expectations are clearly communicated, and where creative thinking and innovation are strongly encouraged. They motivate their team as a coach would do, by urging them to exceed their perceived limits and give flight to their dreams. The advice of the German poet Johann von Goethe resonates today: "Treat people as if they were what they ought to be and you help them become what they are capable of being."

Setting an example is of paramount importance. A good leader must set an example to the organization as a whole. In business parlance, this is sometimes referred to as the "tone at the top." The most effective leaders I know are those who command respect because of their abilities and, at the same time, show genuine empathy for others, exercising courtesy in all their dealings. Add to the mix a strong dash of humility and you have a leader who will inspire both affection and loyalty.

It is one thing to empower others; it is another to consciously prepare them for leadership to ensure effective continuity and succession in the organization. I have witnessed the best and the worst of examples. Here is what I have learned.

A good leader should plan for his or her exit, and at the appropriate time the timetable should be known to the board of directors and to the would-be successors in the organization.

A good leader will know when it is time to go. Ideally, it should be when he or she is still riding high in terms of success. This gives the leader the power and flexibility to manage the exit with grace and to set a direction for the next stage in his or her life.

An astute leader, moreover, will be sensitive to the signals that an early departure is best for all. One such signal is when the leader's appetite for the daily challenge begins to wane. Another signal is when the board of directors, or the political caucus for that matter, begins to second-guess the leader's judgment. Yet another is when senior and valued members of the organization begin to jump ship.

Most leaders I know would admit that planning one's exit, especially when in a position of strength, is not an easy task. And yet to ignore its importance is to risk humiliation and possibly the tarnishing of an otherwise extraordinary career.

IVEY LECTURE ON LEADERSHIP

The stories leaders tell about themselves teach us a great deal and often inspire others on their leadership journeys. This was the impetus for the Ivey Business School's Lawrence National Centre for Policy and Management to establish an annual leadership lecture in my name in 2006 (I was both surprised and incredibly honoured when the Ivey dean, Carol Stephenson, announced this at an event with a thousand people in attendance!). The lectures over the next decade and a half by distinguished Canadians have offered up a rich variety of lessons on leadership. The primary audience is the student cohort at Ivey itself, some six hundred in all, at Western University in London, Ontario. But the annual lecture is also meant to be delivered twice, at Ivey and at an event shared with seasoned leaders from government, business, and the voluntary sector. Typically, this has taken place before a VIP audience at the Toronto Club or the National Gallery of Canada in Ottawa. In 2020 and 2021, because of the COVID-19 pandemic, the lecture was presented virtually.

The following are what I consider some worthwhile takeaways on leadership from a variety of speakers who have given the annual lecture, but they are by no means a fulsome account of the quality and depth, year after year, of these talks.

KEVIN LYNCH

As clerk of the privy council and secretary to the cabinet in 2007, Kevin Lynch underscored the leadership challenge of getting public policy choices right. A long-time public servant, Lynch was respected for his energetic work as deputy minister of finance and of industry. The principal message of this avid champion of Canadian competitiveness was how best to respond to the challenges of globalization. While rightly pointing out the importance of sound, well-led multilateral institutions to help guide the complexity of globalization at the time, he did not anticipate that the world was on the cusp of a large-scale financial crisis. For this he can be forgiven, as the suddenness and severity of the crisis caught virtually everybody unawares. He stressed what has been one of my mantras for decades: that a high-quality, merit-based public service offers Canada a comparative leadership advantage over other countries.

DAVID DODGE

At the time of David Dodge's lecture in 2008, Canada was feeling the shock waves of the great financial crisis sweeping across the world. A former governor of the Bank of Canada and deputy minister of finance, the highly respected Dodge—one of my all-time favourite public servants, whose leadership had been pivotal in reining in Canada's serious fiscal crisis in the 1990s—blamed the current crisis on a failure of leadership in governments, central banks, prudential and market conduct regulators, and financial institutions. His central message was stark: "Poor leadership got us into this mess, and now strong leadership is needed to get us out of this. The top priority of leaders is to rebuild confidence in the financial system." Dodge got it right on the money. . . . Yes, new and tougher prudential rules were essential, but as he rightly stressed, there was no substitute for competence and integrity in decision-making. It's not just about rules!

ANNETTE VERSCHUREN

A feisty Nova Scotian, proud of her Cape Breton roots, Annette Verschuren was the president of the Home Depot's Canadian and Asian operations when she presented her lecture in 2010 and in the vanguard of women leaders in Canada. In addition to being an accomplished business executive, Verschuren had a strong interest in public policy and had been an active colleague in the Business Council. The title of her lecture spoke to the theme of her remarks: "Beyond the Bottom Line: A Business Leader's Obligations to Canadian Society." She began by invoking Louis Riel: "Whether . . . a traitor or a Father of Confederation, there's no doubting his conviction for the improved treatment of the Métis nation." She continued with a powerful appeal for justice for Indigenous peoples, visible minorities, and people with disabilities. And she decried the glass ceiling, which she pointedly described as being intact. Verschuren's bottom line for business leadership included a leader's duty to promote sound public policy in the environmental domain and in innovation and skills training. The main takeaway was her conviction that in many cases business is better positioned than government to effect policy change., something with which I could heartily agree.

MICHAEL WILSON

The title of Michael Wilson's 2011 lecture was intriguing: "The Tri-Athlete: The Importance of Private, Public, and Not-for-Profit Sector Involvement." Wilson, chair of Barclays Canada at the time, attributed this idea to Joseph Nye, dean of the Kennedy School at Harvard. Nye encouraged his students to each take on leadership positions in multiple sectors—private, public service, and not for profit. Wilson was an exemplar of this. Nurtured in business, he said the first part of his career was a "slam dunk." The second part of his career was driven by a strong interest in public policy and the conviction that Canada needed a change in direction. For him, this was no slam dunk; it took courage to leave a successful Bay Street career behind and to enter into the brutal arena of politics. As minister of finance in the Mulroney government, he ushered in important reforms, notably the hard-fought Goods and Services

Tax. He also played a key role in finalizing the Canada–United States Free Trade Agreement. Not being a professional diplomat, representing Canada as our ambassador in Washington required considerable career retooling as well. Finally, Wilson became an influential advocate for dealing with mental illness. My main takeaway from the Wilson lecture was that to successfully excel in multiple domains is arguably the *summum bonum* of leadership achievement, and that leadership skills are eminently transferable to different disciplines.

MARK CARNEY

Appointed governor of the Bank of Canada in the midst of the global financial crisis in 2008, Carney was well qualified to tackle his chosen lecture theme in 2013: "Rebuilding Trust in Global Banking." He pointed out that people around the world had not only lost their savings, jobs, and houses to the crisis, they had also for the most part lost their trust in banking. Canada, he noted, was among the few exceptions where the crisis had resulted in higher rather than reduced levels of trust. He lauded the leadership of the G20 nations for enacting financial reforms but pointed out that "virtue cannot be regulated." In other words, it takes more than rules to rebuild trust. Specifically, Carney said, "five Cs" would be required: the strengthening of bank capital; clarity of reporting standards; a rethinking of "heads I win, tails you lose" capitalism; and reconnecting banking to its client roots. In the fifth of his five Cs, he called for bank leaders to embrace core values and for institutions to be guided by ethical principles. Carney presented the lecture shortly after he had accepted the appointment as the first non-Briton to lead the Bank of England as governor; he would soon leave Canada for London.

LINDA HASENFRATZ

In her 2014 lecture, Linda Hasenfratz told the fascinating tale of her journey to the top job at Linamar Corporation and how she has nurtured the culture of this outstanding Canadian success story. It is a family story. Hasenfratz's father, Frank Hasenfratz, arrived in Canada from Hungary "with nothing in his pockets" but skills as a machinist, and he started a one-man machine shop in his basement. Now that one-man shop is a major auto-parts manufacturing company with a global footprint. Hasenfratz began work as she believed appropriate—as a machine operator on the shop floor in steel boots and a hard hat. Linamar's success, she explained, has a great deal to do with core values that she, as CEO, champions: balance, entrepreneurship, respect, responsiveness, hard work, innovation, and, she emphasized, a powerful commitment to excellence.

TOM JENKINS

As the chair of OpenText, a leading Canadian software company founded in 1991, Tom Jenkins became a force in technology and public policy circles. Affable, articulate, and a powerful communicator, he was at home in government circles as well as the business milieu. Among my Business Council colleagues, few could match his ability to straddle the public policy interface with such success. He instinctively understood the importance of leadership, and spoke and wrote about it. To celebrate Canada's 150th anniversary, he and Governor General David Johnston published *Ingenious*, a book celebrating brilliant Canadian innovations that have had an impact on the world. "Technological change is advancing with stunning speed, and Canada is holding its own in the race," said Jenkins in his 2016 lecture, yet he expressed deep concerns about technology's impacts on health care, education, and jobs, and warned that we are not prepared for this brave new world. He created some dismay, particularly among students, when he pointedly warned that most of today's professional jobs may not exist in thirty years. He went so far as to raise the existential threat that machines will replace humans unless we somehow keep pace.

DOMINIC BARTON

As the long-time global managing partner of McKinsey & Company, Dominic Barton had a wealth of experience in dealing with CEOs around the world. He began his 2017 lecture, titled "In the Arena," by identifying global trends requiring strong leadership: the shift of economic gravity to Asia; the accelerating pace of technology disruption; the aging of the world's population; and the need for a new "societal deal" sensitive to the needs of those being left behind by rising inequality. He followed with an intriguing question he asked of leaders: "What do you wish you had known as a young CEO or leader that you know now? That is, what would your 'experienced self' tell your 'younger self'?" He left the audience to ponder the question. Barton identified the skills most successful leaders brandish "in the arena": they focus foremost on finding and investing in people; they set their agenda and implement it quickly; they drive change with the right levers; and they lead crises from the front. He then offered up the essential attributes of leadership as character, judgment, inspiration, and ambition. One takeaway was that the people factor matters more than anything else. It's crucial to pick the right people, invest in people, respect people, and motivate them like hell. Among the attributes of leadership he discussed, Barton's treatment of character especially resonated. Character is the foundation stone of all the leadership attributes, alongside authenticity, humility, selflessness, and resilience. Barton most recently served as Canada's ambassador to the People's Republic of

China, a challenging task given the serious deterioration of Canada's relations with that country. A defining moment in his career was the release in September 2021 of Canadians Michael Kovrig and Michael Spavor ("the two Michaels") from unjust incarceration. His knowledge of China and his consummate skills as both a negotiator and intermediary played an important role in the resolution of the Meng affair.

BEVERLEY MCLACHLIN

Having retired as chief justice of Canada in 2017, McLachlin was in a prime position in her 2018 lecture to offer her reflections on leadership. The title of her address was "Leadership and Diversity," and she opened it with a story: "The year is 1958. The place is a small town in southwest Alberta. The subject is a thirteen-year-old girl, struggling to find her identity and imagine a place for her in the world." When McLachlin's teacher told her that her destiny in life was to be a waitress or a telephone operator, she was crushed. McLachlin related in her lecture how, through grit, hard work and resilience, she would go on to shatter the glass ceiling, challenge top-down leadership, and emerge as a star in the judicial world. With her stark reminder to us that "old-style leadership" was content to exclude women as well as significant minorities—more than half the population—from leadership positions, she hit a nerve. "Modern leadership, to be successful, must do two things," she said. "It must find ways for good ideas to flow up and sideways as well as down, and it must broaden the reservoir from which ideas can emerge and allow people of all genders and backgrounds to contribute to the joint cooperative enterprise." McLachlin practised that key attribute of leadership—empowering others—in the highest court in the land: "I resolved to do whatever I could to make each Justice of the Court the best possible Justice they could be. . . . My new leadership role—such as it was—was not about me; it was about enabling the men and women I worked with, with all their differences and in all their diversity, to do the best that they could in our collective, cooperative task of doing justice for the Canadian people."

PERRIN BEATTY

Perrin Beatty's 2019 lecture was provocatively titled "Canada Adrift in a World Without Leaders." Beatty, president and chief executive officer of Canada's largest business association, the 200,000-strong Canadian Chamber of Commerce, asserted that the world he came of age in, and which favoured Canada so decidedly, no longer exists. Citing the breakdown of the world order, the retreat of the rule of law, the ravages of Trumpian policies, and the erosion of liberal democratic values, he reminded us that Canada is largely alone in this altered world. Canada must double down to hold its own in this altered world, but, he said, we can punch above our weight if we leverage our strengths. Reducing our relative dependence on the United States and developing common cause with like-minded industrial democracies should be a priority; likewise, doing all we can to bolster multilateral institutions and mutually supportive alliances should be high on the Canadian leadership agenda.

RONA AMBROSE

As a cabinet minister in the Harper governments, Rona Ambrose led no fewer than seven ministries: health, public works and government services, Western economic diversification, labour, intergovernmental affairs, president of the privy council, and environment. Focusing on her experiences as a female leader making her way in a still largely male-dominated world, she was frank, hard-hitting, and at times hilarious in her 2020 lecture. Her resilience was the main takeaway; for example, refusing to be put down when, at international meetings, her ministerial counterparts would walk past her and shake hands with her male staffer; or when she was told by a voter that she was not strong enough for the job because she was a woman. Ironically, when Ambrose left politics, having served graciously as interim leader of the Opposition after Harper's defeat in 2015, she was favoured among Conservatives to lead their party. Another takeaway: her willingness to show her vulnerabilities was a strength rather than a weakness, because it revealed her self-confidence in a disarming way. Her full lecture deserves to be read by women, of course, but also by men who want to more fully understand how a leader of Ambrose's stature sees the world of power.

HARLEY FINKELSTEIN

Who could have imagined that a modest Canadian start-up barely more than a decade and a half ago would today rank as one of Canada's largest companies. Shopify's dynamic and irrepressible president, Harley Finkelstein, presenter of the 2021 lecture, tells the story well. In 2006, Shopify's founder, Tobias Lütke, was trying his hand at selling snowboarding equipment with existing e-commerce products. Frustrated, he decided to build his own platform, and today Shopify serves 1,700,000 businesses in some 175 countries. Here are some of the insights I gleaned as I listened to Finkelstein speak.

Empowerment lies at the heart of Shopify's core operating philosophy. Finkelstein explained how his company assists small business across the world embrace digital technologies in the presentation of their products and services on Shopify's retail platforms. The low cost of participation is ideal for small businesses that otherwise would have no chance of reaching out to the world, and even more so during the ravages of the COVID-19 pandemic, when lockdowns hindered operations of bricks-and-mortar storefronts. As someone who has worked at the heart of the twentieth-century capitalist model, I listened with fascination to Finkelstein speak of this revolution in empowerment—a revolution which he and Shopify's founder, Lütke, believe is profoundly changing the core of retail business and business more broadly.

Reflecting on the valuable leadership insights and lessons offered by the Ivey-sponsored lectures in my name, my greatest satisfaction is knowing they are shared with successive cohorts of bright and eager students at Western University and beyond. I am grateful to two institutions at Ivey for organizing the lectures, both endowed by public-spirited entrepreneurs. The first is the Lawrence National Centre for Policy and Management, endowed by my late friend Jack Lawrence. The second is the Ian O. Ihnatowycz Institute for Leadership, endowed by Ian Ihnatowycz. In recent years, the opportunity to plan the lectures with the executive director of the institute, professor Gerard Seijts, and his colleague Kimberley Milani, has been rewarding. Under Seijts, the concentration on leadership at one of the world's most respected business schools offers an ideal platform for learning about such a seminal subject. Also gratifying to me is the exposure of sophisticated leadership concepts to nationals from countries around the world who have come to study at Ivey. The demand for good leaders worldwide is high. Too often, as we see, the supply of leadership training falls pitifully short. Ivey, I am pleased to say, with Dean Sharon Hodgson at the helm, has helped establish Canada as a global centre for advanced leadership training. I can think of few more important causes.

I am pleased that the 2022 d'Aquino lecture was presented by Goldy Hyder both at the Ivey Business School and in Ottawa. His passionate plea for an end to Canadian complacency in meeting urgent national challenges resonated strongly.

With His Majesty King
Abdullah II bin Al Hussein
of Jordan, Ottawa, 2007.
*(Photo courtesy of the Business
Council of Canada)*

Hosting presidential candidate Senator John McCain,
Rideau Club, Ottawa,
2008. *(Photo courtesy of the
Business Council of Canada)*

Welcoming Prime Minister
Stephen Harper to my
retirement dinner, National
Gallery of Canada, 2009.
*(Photo courtesy of the Business
Council of Canada)*

Council leaders at my retirement: Annette Verschuren, Bruce Flatt, Gordon Nixon, Paul Desmarais, Jr., Laurent Beaudoin, Richard George, and Hartley Richardson. *(Photo courtesy of the Business Council of Canada)*

Celebrating an important birthday with former prime minister and university roommate, Joe Clark. *(Photo courtesy of the author)*

With Governor General David Johnston and Bank of Canada Governor Mark Carney, Ottawa, 2011. *(Photo by Andrew Van Beek)*

Above: Hosting four Bank of Canada governors: Crow, Carney, Thiessen, and Dodge, 2013. *(Photo courtesy of Lawrence National Centre, Ivey Business School)*

Right: With one of my all-time favourite Quebecers, Jean Charest. *(Photo courtesy of the Business Council of Canada)*

With the Honorable George Shultz, leading world statesman, and Dominic Barton. *(Photo courtesy of the North American Forum)*

With the Right Honourable Beverley McLachlin, "the greatest jurist of my generation," 2017. *(Photo by Blair Gable Photography)*

Sharing a laugh with special friend, Ron Mannix. *(Photo by Andrew Van Beek)*

With celebrated Ottawa-native mezzo soprano Wallis Giunta at the National Gallery of Canada, Vigée Le Brun exhibition. *(Photo by Andrew Van Beek)*

Talking business with German Chancellor Gerhard Schroeder, Montreal, 2002. *(Photo by Marcel La Haye)*

Sharing a joke with His Majesty Carl XVI Gustav, King of Sweden, Rideau Club, Ottawa, 2006. *(Photo courtesy of the Business Council of Canada)*

Serenading our guests at the millennium gala with top hat and tails, hosted by Susan and me, with Mitchell Sharp at the piano. *(Photo courtesy of the Business Council of Canada)*

Fly-fishing for the noble Atlantic salmon on the Adlatok River in Labrador. *(Photo courtesy of the author)*

"Shooting" at Ballindalloch Castle in the Scottish Highlands. *(Photo courtesy of the author)*

Canoeing on McKay Lake, Rockcliffe Park, Ottawa. *(Photo courtesy of the author)*

Winter at our residence, Rockcliffe Park, Ottawa. *(Photo by Adrienne Herron)*

At the Vatican with Cardinals Ravasi and Bertone, and old friend Christopher Lang.

(Photo courtesy of the author)

As guests of "my favourite entrepreneur" Jimmy Pattison on the Northern Spirit.

(Photo courtesy of the author)

Left: One of the most beautiful places in the world to grow up—Nelson, British Columbia. *(Photo by Douglas Noblet)*

Below: With Australian Prime Minister Tony Abbott and Prime Minister Stephen Harper, Ottawa, 2014. *(Photo courtesy of the Prime Minister's Office)*

Above: With Ivey Business School Dean Carol Stephenson and Joseph Rotman. *(Photo courtesy of the Lawrence National Centre, Ivey Business School)*

Right: Small but mighty! The indispensable Canadian Council of Chief Executives team, 2005. *(Photo by Jean-Marc Carisse)*

17

SPECIAL MOMENTS WITH LEADERS

I have spoken of many Canadian colleagues who have travelled the leadership journey with me and who have made their mark in private and public life. The following are some very personal tales, special moments and encounters I have never forgotten.

THE RIGHT HONOURABLE JOE CLARK

"Tell me something about your new roommate," my curious mother asked. "I believe he wants to be prime minister one day," I said.

It was September 1963, and I was speaking with my mother on the telephone from the University of British Columbia. I had just started second year of law school, having returned to Vancouver from Kingston, Ontario, where I had completed my first year of law studies at Queen's University. The subject of our discussion was Joe Clark. He had completed his first year of law studies at Dalhousie University in Halifax and, like me, had chosen to continue his legal studies at UBC. A chance last-minute encounter on the UBC campus led to a decision to share an apartment.

From the moment we met, it was amply clear to me that politics was in Clark's blood. Hailing from High River, Alberta, he was a devoted Progressive Conservative and impressively knowledgeable about the party apparatus and its key operatives. While at the time I had conservative leanings, I had no affiliations with any party. We enjoyed sparring on the great political issues of the day. John Diefenbaker was prime minister, and Joe was deeply engaged in party activities—so deeply engaged he was often absent from class and failed to complete the year.

Signalling to my mother in those early years that Clark aspired to the prime ministership was not without foundation, and on June 4, 1979, Joe—then only thirty-nine—was indeed sworn in as Canada's sixteenth prime minister. Only six months later, I watched in dismay as his minority government succumbed to a vote of non-confidence. In the general election that followed, in February 1980, his party was defeated by the Liberals led by Pierre Trudeau. I have made frequent reference to Joe in earlier chapters. While his term as prime minister was brief, he remained wedded to public life for many years to come and went on to serve Canada with distinction as a senior minister of the Mulroney government. He was an outstanding secretary of state for external affairs, and his leadership role in dealing with the constitutional challenges of the 1990s gained high praise. That Clark won the prime ministership was not a great surprise to me, but that he should do so at the tender age of thirty-nine *was* a surprise. When elected, he was the youngest prime minister in Canadian history. Over the years, I can think of many special moments with Clark, sometimes in the company of his lifelong partner, Maureen McTeer, an accomplished leader in her own right. What has impressed me most about him is his deep patriotism; he has always been prepared to put country first. Also impressive is his innate ability to build bridges of understanding. Keep in mind that early on he spoke of Canada as a "community of communities," a position some of his political opponents ridiculed. But in the context of the Canada of today, I would say he was far-sighted. Later on in life, working in concert with other former heads of government from around the world, he has given generously of his time to support worthy causes, especially in Africa and other parts of the developing world. I have spoken in this book of qualities that are the hallmarks of inspiring leaders. Clark possesses many of these, but I would say that his fundamental decency, his deep integrity, and his love of country are pre-eminent—qualities found all too rarely among people in public life today.

JIMMY PATTISON

"Tom, I have this little boat out here on the West Coast . . ."

And so began a conversation with one of Canada's legendary entrepreneurs, Jimmy Pattison. It was in the spring of 2007, and Pattison was calling to say he wanted to do "a little something for a fellow British Columbia boy who has done okay in life." He was offering up to me his magnificent vessel the 150-foot *Nova Spirit* for four days with full crew to sail the West Coast wherever I would like to wander. And he asked Susan and me to bring some friends. I was deeply touched by his kindness. That July, we set out in glorious weather on our voyage north along the spectacular British Columbia coastline toward Desolation Sound. Pattison and his wife, Mary, accompanied us on the first day to get us settled in. Over dinner, we listened with fascination to his life stories and marvelled at his talent on various musical instruments. He is a demon on the trumpet!

Pattison has done more than okay himself in his storied life. Saskatchewan-born and Vancouver-raised, he began his business career as a car dealer. I remember driving past his lots when I was a student at the University of British Columbia. Years later, he proudly showed me a memento from that time: a cancelled Royal Bank of

Canada promissory note for $40,000 that helped him on his way. In his nineties, ever active, stunningly successful in many lines of business, and generous in his philanthropy, he said goodbye to me after a recent visit to his office with the words "Thanks for coming over, Tom. And we are just getting started!" Words that come to mind in summing up his leadership qualities are courage, ambition, shrewdness, generosity, and humility.

PAUL DESMARAIS SR.

"Paul . . . you have achieved a great deal in life, but in my view one of the greatest achievements of all is . . ."

It was September 29, 2003, and I was speaking with Paul Desmarais Sr. at his offices in Montreal just before a Business Council dinner I had organized in his honour. The architect of a formidable family enterprise, Power Corporation of Canada, Desmarais began his legendary career in Sudbury by rescuing a near-bankrupt bus company. He went on to create a highly successful business conglomerate with a national and international business reach. An astute visionary with an appetite for thinking big, he was for decades one of Canada's most influential business leaders. We first met when I was serving on Pierre Trudeau's staff. In those early years, he had won Trudeau's confidence and offered him support through some of the most difficult moments in Trudeau's private life. Desmarais went on to co-found the Business Council and was instrumental in selecting me as its first president.

That September evening in Montreal, I said, "Paul, we look forward to honouring you this evening, but just let me say this: you have achieved a great deal in life, but in my view one of the greatest achievements of all is how well you have nurtured the next generation and prepared them for leadership. It's hard for me to imagine a more lasting legacy." I was referring to his two sons, André and Paul Jr., co-chief executives of Power Corporation of Canada. He appreciated my point and understood better than most that preparing two sons for succession requires discipline, hard work, and an education that goes well beyond business itself.

I was present ten years later when his family and friends bid him farewell at a magnificent memorial service at Notre Dame Cathedral in Montreal. I thought to myself, "Paul's legacy is assured. Better yet, André and Paul Jr., having learned from their father, are showing the way for the generations that will follow them."

BEVERLEY MCLACHLIN
"Beverley, no need to say a word . . ."

It was early one morning in May 2014, and I was on a run through the Rockeries in Ottawa's Rockcliffe Park when I happened upon my friend Beverley McLachlin, the chief justice of Canada. She was walking her new black Labrador puppy. I had just read of Prime Minister Harper's public rebuke of McLachlin for "wrongly interfering" in the nomination of Justice Marc Nadon as an appointee to the Supreme Court of Canada. Like so many others within and outside the legal community, I found the prime minister's action surprising and inappropriate.

I said, "Beverley, there is no need to say a word, because I know you can't comment . . . but I simply want to say I believe the prime minister is out of line on this, and I believe you will be vindicated."

Always discreet, she simply thanked me and then introduced me to her puppy, Darcy. When I asked how he got his name, she replied, "Tom, I'm a Jane Austen fan. He is tall, dark and handsome."

As McLachlin confirms in her memoir *Truth Be Told*, she was deeply concerned about the prime minister's attack on her reputation.

"There is nothing more precious to a judge than her reputation," she writes. She took the unusual step of swiftly issuing a news release categorically denying any wrongdoing. The Harper government fell silent and the matter was closed. This story says a great deal about the principle and courage of the longest-serving chief justice of Canada and the most impressive jurist of my generation.

DAVID JOHNSTON

"Congratulations, Your Excellency!"

With these words, and on bended knee, I saluted David Johnston upon his appointment as Canada's twenty-eighth governor general. We were at a dinner of the CGI board in Montreal, and he was departing the board to assume his new responsibilities. All in the room agreed he was an inspiring choice. His unfailing courtesy and characteristic humility belied his credentials for his new post: a graduate of Harvard, Cambridge, and Queen's universities; president of the University of Waterloo, principal of McGill University, and dean of law at Western University; author or co-author of more than thirty books and recipient of honorary doctorates from thirty-six universities.

I had known Johnston since the late 1960s. Apart from being fellow directors of technology giant CGI, we had fly-fished for salmon together on the Sainte-Marguerite river and skied in the Laurentians. Our paths crossed often, and we both took pleasure in testing our skills as raconteurs. I could never keep up with him. Johnston offered a toast to Susan and me on the occasion of our fiftieth wedding anniversary at a magnificent dinner in the Great Hall of the National Gallery of Canada. He also demonstrated how much better he was than I at humour. I quote from his remarks:

Tom and I were directors of CGI. I chaired the compensation committee and he the governance committee, and we were jointly tasked to advise the board on "say and pay" rules. Tom and I, being great collaborators, put the two committees together, and after much deliberation produced a unanimous and lengthy joint resolution that we did not believe in "say on pay" for the shareholders. This was an essential responsibility of directors overseeing management. Tom gallantly gave me the final word on the report. And I said that while our committees were opposed to "say on pay," we are both lawyers and paid by the word, and that our report was quite long because of our professional belief in "pay on say."

PETER LOUGHEED

"Premier, where I grew up, over the mountains to the west, we considered Albertans like you as Easterners."

It was 1983. I was newly installed in my job as president of the Business Council and sitting in front of the powerful premier of Alberta, Peter Lougheed. I had just pitched the premier with a plan to have the Business Council broker an East-West compromise to help resolve the highly acrimonious energy conflict gripping the country. My rather cheeky response to the premier was prompted by his words "Why should I trust an Easterner like you to run this thing?" My reply to the startled Lougheed broke the ice and led to a highly significant policy compromise involving the CEOs of leading producer and consumer companies, the Alberta premier, Ontario premier Bill Davis, and the federal minister of energy, mines, and resources, Jean Chrétien.

This was the beginning of a long and remarkable friendship with Lougheed. In the years to come, we would collaborate closely in advancing the Canada–United States Free Trade Agreement, in North American cooperation, and in seeking to resolve thorny constitutional issues. I could not have imagined at that first encounter with Lougheed that one day, as the newly minted chancellor of Queen's University, he would choose to confer his first honorary doctor of laws degree on me.

Over the years, I have been in close contact with numerous premiers. Some were especially impressive. Jean Charest, Frank McKenna, Roy Romanow, Robert Bourassa, Gordon Campbell, and Brad Wall immediately come to mind. With the exception of Jean Charest, my relationship with Lougheed was unlike any other. He was not only a faithful friend but a deeply valued mentor who taught me a great deal about the nuances of politics. He was an accomplished leader—deeply principled, an excellent judge of people, a tough negotiator—and could read a room better than anyone. His commitment to both Alberta and Canada was never in question.

JEAN CHRÉTIEN

"By all means, Prime Minister . . ."

It was a Tuesday morning, and Prime Minister Chrétien was on the telephone. "Tom, what are you doing on Friday afternoon around four o'clock?" he said, I responded that I would be in Ottawa and asked how I could help. He said that his wife, Aline, and he would like to come and see our house. His house, like mine, had been designed by architect Hart Massey, and he wanted to compare notes. "By all means, Prime Minister," I said. We confirmed the appointment and I quickly called Susan at the Department of Finance. When I told her she needed to come home early on Friday, she said, "I can't possibly get away before seven." Then I gave her the news. She changed her plans.

When the prime minister and Mrs. Chrétien arrived, we welcomed them warmly.

"I have walked by your house many times," Chrétien said, "and always wanted to see it."

"Why didn't you simply knock on the door?" I asked.

In quintessential Chrétien style, he said, "I didn't want to disturb that big-business big shot d'Aquino."

We all had a good laugh and chatted amiably for an hour or so over a glass of wine before the tour.

Chrétien and I have more than once been sharply at odds on policy, and he takes pleasure in sticking it to elites. That said, in my view, no prime minister I have known could match him for his street smarts. He also had a canny way of communicating that won admiration and even affection. He was down to earth and unbudgingly authentic. Author Bob Plamondon captures Chrétien's strengths in his revealing book *The Shawinigan Fox*. Despite our differences, I greatly respected him, and do so to this day. I know how deeply committed he is to Canada and how passionately he fought for the unity of the country. And it was Chrétien's commitment to getting Canada out of its fiscal mess in the 1990s that empowered his finance minister Paul Martin and delivered a stunning transformation of the Canadian economy.

GORDON ROBERTSON

"I greatly appreciate the invitation, Gordon, but I don't deserve to be here . . ."

It was May 1985, and I was walking out of a luncheon in the Sir Wilfrid Laurier Room at Ottawa's Rideau Club with Gordon

Robertson. Robertson was a giant of Canada's public service. A former clerk of the privy council and secretary to the cabinet, he had served prime ministers King, St. Laurent, Pearson, Trudeau, and Clark. He had convened the luncheon to discuss creating a roundtable of eminent persons who would meet weekly to discuss matters of state.

When I had entered the room, I was astonished at what I saw. Present was an impressive number of former senior officials who had played key roles in building postwar Canada. There was Robert Bryce, distinguished economist and disciple of Keynes, who had played a seminal role at the Department of Finance; Jack Pickersgill, senior adviser to Prime Minister King and cabinet minister in the St. Laurent and Pearson governments; Louis Rasminski, outstanding governor of the Bank of Canada; and Simon Reisman, deputy minister of finance and chief negotiator of the Canada–United States Free Trade Agreement. In addition I could see, to name a few, Mitchell Sharp, Robert Stanfield, Jean-Luc Pepin, Jean Pigott, legendary diplomat Charles Ritchie, and three women who were public service pioneers, Ann Carver, Beryl Plumptre, and Pamela McDougall.

It was clear that I was significantly junior to them in age, experience, and achievement. Hence my remark to Robertson. But Robertson was insistent.

Attendance at the weekly luncheons quickly became a priority whenever I was in Ottawa. The discussions, classified as "off the record," allowed everyone to speak their minds. I often felt like a student surrounded by learned professors. I drank it all in, and I was pleased that on occasion I was invited to speak. Thirty-eight years later, the roundtable continues to meet. I am the only surviving member of the founding group, happy to be alive to tell the tale. My experience with the roundtable deepened my long-held view that

Canada's public service is among the best in the world and a powerful source of our country's competitive advantage. Robertson, for whom I had great affection, was a mentor to me for decades, and we worked closely together on constitutional issues in the 1990s. I was deeply moved when, in the winter of 2013, I was asked by his family to present a eulogy at his memorial service.

PAUL TELLIER

"Tom, you should know that the extension of the corporate surtax has been nicknamed in cabinet circles the Tom d'Aquino tax."

It was my friend Paul Tellier on the telephone, and he was chuckling. He was giving me a heads-up on the inside reaction in government to my criticism of the de-indexing of Old Age Security pensions in the Mulroney government's 1985 budget, a subject I have discussed in some detail. Tellier was clerk of the privy council and secretary to the cabinet, the most powerful of jobs in the Canadian public service. Needless to say, I did not chuckle in response. I wondered whether anyone else in the history of Canadian business had been "punished" in such a costly way.

I had watched Tellier's rise in the public service since first meeting him in the late 1960s. Our paths crossed often, and we continued to work together when he made a highly successful transition to the private sector. Smart, articulate, disciplined, and a prodigiously hard worker, he mastered every task along the way. He also had a knack for survival. Upon the arrival of the Mulroney government in 1984, he was targeted as a suspected Liberal sympathizer by Mulroney cabinet minister Pat Carney, a hard-nosed minister of energy, mines, and resources. Tellier was her deputy. In short order, he won her confidence and admiration. Mulroney's appointment of Tellier soon after to the top job in the public service confirmed in a rather spectacular way that he had made the transition from having served previous Liberal governments.

Tellier stands out for me for another reason. In my experience over the past forty years, very few public servants at the national level have gone on to become stars in business. He went on to achieve high praise as CEO of Canadian National Railway, a post he held for ten years, and subsequently as CEO of aerospace and transportation giant Bombardier. Tellier, to my mind, ranks at the top, because the seniority of the jobs he had in government matched in importance those he took on in business. There have been other notable examples of successful transitions. Ed Clark, who went on to become CEO of TD Bank Group, is one. Derek Burney, who became CEO of CAE is another. A third is Michael Sabia, who transitioned to Canadian National Railway and subsequently to the top post at the Caisse de dépôt et placement du Québec. The reality is that in Canada there are far too few examples of leadership transitions from public to private—or vice versa, for that matter. The journeys of Michael Wilson and Paul Martin from the private sector to the public domain are notable exceptions. So is that of Mark Carney.

ZITA COBB

"Zita, this is a stunning achievement. You have created something unique for Canada and the world."

It was August 2013, and Susan and I were bidding our farewells to Zita Cobb on craggy, windswept Fogo Island, the largest of the offshore islands of Newfoundland and Labrador. Cobb, a Fogo Island native, had generously hosted us for four unforgettable days, introducing us to one of the most creative entrepreneurial initiatives we had ever seen. After a remarkable career in business, Cobb had decided to give back to her community, which, like many parts of

Newfoundland and Labrador, had endured severe economic hardship going back many decades. She founded the charity Shorefast and began to pursue a vision that would bring economic development, jobs, and a renewed sense of purpose to Fogo's inhabitants, of whom there were barely more than two thousand.

Her vision led to the building of the Fogo Island Inn, an architectural marvel standing on stilts high above the rocky terrain and affording breathtaking views of the North Atlantic. She staffed the warmly inviting inn with impeccably trained locals and turned to leading designers to create furnishings based on local crafts that could be made on the island. This she coupled with the building of a number of strikingly designed studios to attract visual artists, writers, musicians, filmmakers, and designers to Fogo for quiet periods of creativity. Cobb's initiative is a model of social enterprise rooted in her concepts of community-based economic development—concepts she fiercely advocates should form the basis of a reformed capitalism. Walking the beautiful island trails with Cobb as our guide, being introduced to the locals and the visiting artists, exploring the often hard history of that special place, and listening to Zita sing local songs telling of hardship all left an indelible impression on us. I have met plenty of gifted Canadian entrepreneurs but none as electrifying as Zita Cobb.

JEAN CHAREST

"Jean, you're the total package. Go for it!"

Jean Charest had reached me on my cell phone while I was shopping at Canadian Tire. I quickly retreated to a quiet spot where our conversation would not be overheard. It was 1993, and speculation was rife that Charest would throw his hat into the ring for the leadership of the Progressive Conservative Party. Few political figures have intrigued me as much as Charest. We first met in 1986, when he was appointed minister of state for youth in the Mulroney government. At age twenty-eight, with curly hair and a youthful appearance, he was the youngest federal cabinet minister in Canadian history. I was struck by his effortless bilingualism. I was also struck by the ease with which he travelled both within and outside of political circles; no sharp elbows in evidence with this man. He also had an authenticity I found appealing.

During his time as Mulroney's minister of the environment, from 1991 to 1993, Charest came into his own. Mulroney had brought serious intent to the environment portfolio, and Charest proved to be a consummate advocate. When in 1993 Charest lost his bid for the leadership of the Progressive Conservative Party to Kim Campbell, I was disappointed. A massive electoral repudiation of Campbell and the party soon followed, with Charest being one of only two members of Parliament re-elected as Progressive Conservatives.

When in 1998 Charest left the federal politics to lead Quebec's Liberal party, I was elated. I was among those in the business community who had urged him to make the move. He did well from a standing start, but it was not until 2003 that he won a majority government and the premiership. During his nine years as Quebec premier, he managed the province well and defended Quebec's interests ably, but there was never any doubt in my mind of his loyalty to Canada. His contribution to the great pro-Canada campaigns during the constitutional turmoil of the 1990s had been profound. He also demonstrated the rare ability for a provincial leader to engage successfully in international economic affairs. We shared in a number of trade missions, and he became an early and enthusiastic proponent of a Canada–European Union free trade agreement.

As I watched Charest over the years, I remained convinced that he possessed the "royal jelly"—credentials that would qualify him as an outstanding candidate for the highest office in the land. So when he was considering taking a run at the leadership of the Conservative Party early last year, I repeated to him the identical words that I used back in 1993: "Jean, you're the total package. Go for it!" Charest indeed went for it, offering the Conservative Party a potential leader of strong character, deep experience, and moderate views. Alas, he did not win the leadership and, in my view, the Party and Canada are poorer for it. In Charest fashion, he chose courageously to challenge the odds because he wanted to build a better Canada. My admiration for him remains undiminished.

MARK CARNEY

"Mark, the public sector needs you!"

When I first met Mark Carney following his arrival at the Department of Finance in 2004, I was impressed by his command of economic and business issues. I was also charmed by his easy manner. Like me, he hailed from the West and was obviously proud of his Alberta roots. It interested me that Carney had left behind a successful thirteen-year career at Goldman Sachs to join Canada's public service. In business circles, such a move is rare—much too rare, in my view. Would he stay for long? I wondered.

I watched him learn quickly in Finance, working with Liberal finance minister Ralph Goodale and Conservative finance minister Jim Flaherty. In 2008, when Carney succeeded David Dodge as governor of the Bank of Canada, he was the youngest central bank governor in the G20. In the face of the global financial crisis that soon made itself felt, he had his work cut out for him, but he met the challenge and more. Notably, he was convinced that in the face of such a massive crisis, the state must respond overwhelmingly. He played his part with impressive sang-froid. Carney and the Bank of Canada, in concert with the Fed, the European Central Bank, the Bank of England, Sweden's Riksbank, and the Swiss National Bank, effected an emergency cut in interest rates, thus providing desperately needed liquidity when the financial sector was imploding.

Much has been written about the crucial role of the central banks in helping to blunt the devastating impact of the crisis. During those dark times, I heard Carney's name praised often in international banking circles. Canada's financial institutions fared better than their peers during the crisis, due in part to Carney and to a highly skilled team at both the Bank of Canada and the Department of Finance. Large doses of liquidity, low interest rates, and prudent regulatory practices helped save the day for Canada. The Harper government played a crucial role as well, by sensibly backing up its officials and finance minister Jim Flaherty.

When, with the blessing of the Ivey Business School, I invited Carney to present the 2013 leadership lecture in my name and he graciously consented, I did not know he was destined to become the next governor of the Bank of England. I remember saying to him at the time, "Whatever you do next, Mark, I believe national and international public service will be at the centre of it." On February 25, as governor-designate of the Bank of England, he presented the 2013 lecture. Canadians across the country took great pride that one of our own would be the first non-Briton among over 120 governors to hold the post. It pleases me that he has chosen to return to Canada, in fact to his home nearby in Rockcliffe Park, and is taking a leading role in fighting global climate change. The story of Mark Carney continues to unfold.

THE SOUTHERNS

"Ron, your Spruce Meadows vision is exciting but pretty daring . . ."

I was having a conversation with Calgary entrepreneur Ron Southern in 1981 and he was describing, with a combination of fervour and characteristic modesty, the future he had in mind for his property just outside Calgary. Spruce Meadows today is arguably the world's leading venue for international equestrian sports, the host of show jumping tournaments of unmatched quality in a uniquely welcoming environment. Southern not only realized his daring vision but exceeded it.

Hard work and an uncompromising commitment to excellence by Southern, his energetic wife, Marg, his two daughters, Nancy and Linda, and their supporting teams made it a reality. Having regularly attended sporting events at Spruce Meadows, I have always been struck by the informality and camaraderie that attracts competitors and spectators from around the world. Traditionally, equestrian sports have been considered an elite activity. The miracle of Spruce Meadows is how it appeals to the local population as well as sophisticated fans from every continent. It is cheering to see families with children in tow taking in the shows—and all in celebration of the horse. Canada has no small number of centres of excellence, and for me Spruce Meadows stands out. It is a unique story without peer for originality anywhere in the world.

The Southern vision for Spruce Meadows included a plan to attract leaders from around the world to discuss the great issues of the day in the lead-up to the show jumping. Thus was born the annual Changing Fortunes Round Table, which offers a day-long session around a marquee speaker—an event that over the years I have found remarkably valuable because of the quality of the speakers and the intimacy of the exchanges.

The Southern achievement is far from limited to sport. It extends to excellence in business—ATCO and Canadian Utilities—and to excellence in public policy discourse. Among my business colleagues, Nancy Southern never taking her eye off the ball business-wise, renowned for her passionate commitment to building a stronger Alberta and Canada—in fact, it is part of her persona. Working with her as part of the Business Council of Canada and the Business Council of Alberta continues to be a very positive experience. When in 2018 she and I were inducted as distinguished fellows at the University of Calgary's School of Public Policy, I took as much pleasure in being honoured with her as I took in the honour itself.

RONALD MANNIX

"It has been a blast."

Calgary entrepreneur Ron Mannix and I were sitting in one of our favourite Italian restaurants in Calgary and we were toasting one another with a glass of Tenuta San Guido Sassicaia 1990, one of Italy's finest. Along with a bevy of "super-Tuscans," this aristocratic red wine was a frequent companion at our get-togethers. Good and long-standing friendships are a blessing, and as I told him that night, "Through a good part of my life's journey, Ron, you've been with me every step along the way. It has been a blast. Thanks, my friend."

Mannix and I first met in the early 1980s, and I could not imagine then that he would become the most fervently engaged of my colleagues and a loyal friend. In the nearly three decades during which I led the Business Council, he participated in virtually every major policy initiative—advancing responsible fiscal policy, pushing for North American free trade, fighting for national unity, promoting tax reform and competitiveness, advocating environmental activism, and strengthening Canada's armed forces.

He was the longest serving of any director of the Council and by far its most generous financial supporter. I can also say this of Ron Mannix: over forty years, no Canadian business leader with whom I worked has matched the passion and the longevity of his commitment to advancing good public policy. Most recently, he was the prime mover in the establishment of the Business Council of Alberta, which in short order has become an influential voice in the province.

We have logged many trips with colleagues and family, to Japan, China, India, and destinations in Europe and throughout the Western Hemisphere. Special moments for me include inaugurating the village house he purchased and restored in the shadow of the Great Wall of China, sharing front row seats at the Beijing Olympics, branding cattle on his ranch in the foothills of the Rockies and eating "prairie oysters," hunting in Namibia, meeting annually at the World Economic Forum in Davos, and serving as best man at his marriage to Diane Deacon and shortly after arranging to have the marriage blessed by Cardinal Ravasi at a private reception in the Sistine Chapel. My engagement with his family enterprise, which was first established in 1898, has been one of the highlights of my experiences as a corporate director. Few business leaders have done so much to advance the education of future generations of their families in ethical enterprise. His sons, Stephen and Mike, now with successful careers of their own in the family business, are testimony to this. His philanthropy has enriched early-childhood research, the environment, and music and the visual arts. He is a man of great intensity, boundless energy, and passionate pursuits. I have known no one quite like him.

18

ADVENTURES IN THE ARTS

My first recollection of classical music was at the age of five, when my father sat me down and urged me to listen to a recording of Verdi's *La traviata*, his favourite of the great maestro's repertoire. I did not sit for long, as friends were waiting outside to play base-ball. As I began grade school and my interest in opera started to bud, I remember listening to Saturday broadcasts from the Metropolitan Opera in New York. Because of my command of Italian, I at first took a keen interest in composers such as Verdi, Puccini, Rossini, Donizetti, Mascagni, and Leoncavallo. But soon Mozart began to appeal to me, and by the time I was in sixth grade, I had discovered the majesty of Bach, Handel, and Beethoven. In those early years, the CBC was my window on the world.

Reflecting on how opera entered my life at an early age, I am reminded of one of my favourite anecdotes. As I was listening to Mozart's Don Giovanni for the first time, I asked my father who exactly was Il Commendatore (appearing as a statue early in the opera). "A gentleman of Seville with a noble title", he explained. He then added, "maybe one day you will be a Commendatore." Neither he nor I could have imagined that many years later in 2005, the President of Italy would confer on me the high honour of Commendatore!

In the late 1940s, I remember standing in front of a rather formidable woman, short in stature and stern in temperament. She was to become my music tutor. Her name was Gladys Webb Foster, the most accomplished instructor in Nelson, B.C. After carefully quizzing me, she took me on and approved of my interest in the violin. Weekly lessons and demanding exercises followed, along with the study of music theory. Her expectation was that I would practise at least one hour per day and in addition devote requisite time to the study of theory. She also demanded that I give up baseball, warning that "the violin is a jealous instrument." Much to her displeasure, I defied her edict on sports. Under Mrs. Foster's tutelage, I sat for Royal Conservatory examinations and competed in the annual Kootenay Music Festival, in Nelson's Civic Theatre. Over the years, with my proud parents looking on, I won a number of first prizes. The violin remained an important part of my life until I went off to university, and thereafter it took a back seat to other interests. However, those early years laid the ground for a lifetime of music appreciation.

I was fortunate to grow up in Nelson, the "Queen City of the Kootenays." While its prosperity was rooted in mining, lumber, and railways, its community was remarkably embracing of cultural activity. At Nelson's L.V. Rogers High, coached by talented teachers, I was active in school plays. I recall most vividly playing the role of Orestes, son of Clytemnestra and the ill-fated king Agamemnon, in Sophocles' *Electra*. Many years later, I sat in the remains of the mighty stone theatre in Syracuse, in Sicily, built by the Greeks in the fifth century bc and watched the very same play performed by consummate actors. Like music, theatre became part of my life.

Until I was eleven, my experience in the visual arts was limited to gazing at books in the school library and a few texts at home. All that changed in 1952, when my parents and I spent five months in

Italy. We docked in Genoa and went on to Florence, Siena, Lucca, Pisa, Assisi, Perugia, Rome, the Vatican, Naples, and Sicily. We travelled the length of the peninsula in a car my father had transported from Canada. The roads were terrible, as the country was still suffering from the destruction of the Second World War. We nonetheless were able to see some of the country's finest collections, museums, and churches, thanks in part to an old family friend who was a well-connected art expert. He travelled with us for most of the journey with a suitcase full of reference books. What an eye-opener this was! My parents were keen that I see as much as I could. While in Rome, my father took me to an antique instrument dealer and bought me a fine violin. When I returned to Canada, Mrs. Foster examined it carefully, put it to her shoulder, and played it for several minutes. To my great relief, she expressed her strong approval.

Years later, I lived and worked in Florence in the summer of 1964. My small apartment was a couple of minutes away from the Duomo, and my bedroom window looked out on the church of San Lorenzo. Already familiar with the history of the Renaissance, I spent countless hours taking in the wonders of that great city, free of distractions and with my Italian texts in hand. That summer, I felt deeply connected with my Tuscan roots.

In the 1960s and 1970s, I came to more fully appreciate the unique regions and diverse communities that make up the vast land of Canada. My cultural experience of the country expanded, but something fundamental was missing. While my school texts had offered me some minimal understanding of Indigenous peoples, it was far from adequate—something I did not understand at the time. I have no recollection of ever seeing an Indigenous person, let alone meeting one, in the west Kootenay region where I grew up. I knew from local history that the Kutenai people had lived and hunted in the region for thousands of years. I remember how intrigued I was to discover how the Kutenai language was unrelated to the languages of neighbouring peoples or any other language. Over the years, the Kutenai mysteriously had all but disappeared from the area. At times, when I was fishing in remote streams and lakes that I knew they must have frequented, I thought of how they must have enjoyed the exquisite beauty of these places. While at the University of British Columbia, I took a renewed interest in the diverse Indigenous peoples of the Pacific Northwest, in their complex tribal organizations and their close association with the ocean waters. But a fuller understanding of the important Indigenous legacy of Canada only began to evolve more meaningfully when I joined Pierre Trudeau's staff in 1969. Thereafter, it developed all too slowly; I continue to learn. The appointment in 2021 of Inuit leader Mary Simon as Canada's governor general is a development of great significance in the process of reconciliation with First Nations of Canada.

The seminal importance of Quebec's culture never captured my imagination in those early years. Yes, of course, I was taught about the Plains of Abraham and the heroism of General James Wolfe. That began to change in the 1960s when I married Susan, a Montrealer, and went to work for Pierre Trudeau. It continued when Susan and I in the early 1970s purchased and restored a heritage house in le Vieux-Montréal and began to read Quebec's authors and listen to the province's musicians, songwriters, and poets. Interestingly, our art collecting began modestly in the 1960s with the purchase of a fine work by Quebec's Marc-Aurèle Fortin.

My understanding and appreciation of Canadian culture was also influenced by my experience with the United States. Growing up in a community close to the American border, by the time I was in my late teens I had travelled to the majority of American states, eagerly drinking up history and folklore. I came to understand the power and allure of American culture, epitomized by the dominance of

Hollywood. Acting as an adviser to media giant Time Inc. in the 1970s and 1980s drove home how pervasive American culture can be. This awareness is what prompted me, during the free trade negotiations with the Americans, to argue strongly for the "exemption" of culture from the agreement. Canada's cultures and its cultural industries needed room to breathe—not be smothered.

Interestingly, some fifteen years later, in the face of the growing dominance of American culture through much of the world, a convention was adopted by UNESCO to permit all countries, regardless of free trade arrangements, to protect and promote their artists. It was Canada that spearheaded efforts to gain international support for this protection of what is called "cultural expression"—and Susan, then a deputy minister in the Department of Canadian Heritage, was in the thick of it, playing a pivotal role securing understanding and agreement among ministers responsible for culture from some forty countries.

Canada boasts an impressive array of cultural institutions, at the community, regional, and national levels. I have had the privilege of familiarizing myself with a good number of them. They represent far more than the bricks and mortar of their edifices. Each is a universe made up of a complex web of artists, curators, managers, and donors. Some are publicly funded, others rely almost exclusively on private support. A good number of them have to struggle to make ends meet. The COVID-19 pandemic has added to their challenges and mauled many individual artists badly. And yet, when I think about these institutions and the talented individuals that give them life, I am in awe. I have often said that the massive breadth of Canada's geography and the focus of our artists and artistic activity at the community level do not allow us to fully appreciate the impact of our cultural sector on national life. Put another way, imagine if Canada's leading museums and symphonic, opera, and theatre companies all operated within a geographical area the size of Britain. The concentration and visibility would be powerful, and our excellence would shine more vividly both within and outside our borders.

The contribution of culture to the Canadian economy is also impressive but little appreciated by Canadians. Statistics Canada reported in 2019 that the direct economic impact of cultural industries in 2017 was $58.9 billion—greater than that of agriculture, forestry, fishing, and hunting ($39 billion); accommodation and food services ($46 billion); and utilities ($46 billion). According to Statistics Canada, cultural industries have eight times more economic impact than sports and provide almost six times as many jobs. These statistics do not tell the whole story, however. The impact of government-run institutions in the culture sector is not included in these numbers, nor is the value of education and training in the sector. It has always surprised and disappointed me that our cultural industries have not been more clearly identified as an integral part of the nation's GDP.

Four national cultural institutions have figured prominently in my engagement in the visual and performing arts in Canada: the Confederation Centre of the Arts in Charlottetown; the National Music Centre in Calgary; and in Ottawa the National Gallery of Canada and the National Arts Centre. My service on the Charlottetown- and Calgary-based boards brought home to me the challenge of sustaining and growing regional institutions with a national mandate. In both Charlottetown and Calgary, despite the commitment of visionary and generous local citizens, achieving national recognition and funding was and remains a tough challenge.

Not so the case with the National Gallery of Canada and the National Arts Centre. Both are based in Ottawa minutes away from where I live and work. In this chapter, I focus primarily on the

National Gallery, which has occupied the lion's share of my involvement in the arts. But the National Arts Centre is important too. For many decades it has offered Susan and me an endless stream of excellence in music, theatre, and dance. To me it has offered even more. In observing the leadership styles and achievements of two of its towering personalities, I have been provided with insights about how complex arts organizations ideally should be run.

THE NATIONAL ARTS CENTRE

I was sporting white tie and tails, and Susan was looking splendid in a stunning golden dress. That night in June 1969, the new National Arts Centre (NAC) opened its doors to the world. Prime Minister Trudeau, barely one year in office and still enjoying broad popularity, made his appearance with his date, Madeleine Gobeil. Some 2,100 people filled the opera hall to capacity. During the weekend leading up to the grand opening, there were bands and other festivities on the terraces of the new building. Close to 50,000 people flooded Ottawa's downtown to enjoy the spectacle. Brutal though the architecture of the new building was, I actually found architect Fred Lebensold's hexagonal design intriguing. Within were the magnificently woven stage curtain in the opera hall and the massive sculptured bronze doors giving way to the salon.

That night, we were treated to the avant-garde ballet *Kraanerg*. Two weeks of ballet performances followed, including *Swan Lake* and *Romeo and Juliet*. The Toronto and Montreal symphony orchestras strutted their stuff, the Vancouver Playhouse mounted a production of *The Ecstasy of Rita Joe*, and Le Théâtre du Nouveau Monde presented a titillating performance of Aristophanes's *Lysistrata*. These early days began a journey that Susan and I travelled without interruption, except for the years we lived in London and Paris.

The NAC then and now is central to our lives in the national capital.

The NAC figures prominently in this chapter for several reasons. The first is its centrality in Canada's cultural firmament. Even with its ups and downs, it has been a success, and in many respects, with its multilingual and diverse programming, it has been a model to the world. Second, the remarkable cooperation among the NAC management, the National Arts Centre Foundation, and the trustees demonstrates clearly how much can be achieved when all interested parties and stakeholders are pulling in the same direction. Third, my own engagement in the arts, pre-eminently focused on the National Gallery of Canada, was influenced by the NAC model and in particular by Hamilton Southam and Peter Herrndorf. Their role in pursuing their dreams, inspiring others, and reaching their lofty goals is a story worth telling.

I've always been fascinated with the tale of how this great cultural institution came into being. Prime Minister Lester Pearson in 1963 recommended it to the federal cabinet. But not before visionary cultural entrepreneur Gordon Hamilton Southam had paved the way. I did not meet Southam until I arrived to work in Ottawa in 1968. I remember him telling me how he had led a group of civic-minded leaders earlier in the decade who were determined that Ottawa and Canada should have a performing arts centre of the highest excellence. What impressed me most was the intensity of his ambition. He had linked up with some visionary allies that I came to know, such as David Golden and Louis Audette. Soon after the National Arts Centre received the approval of Parliament and royal assent in July 1966, the Liberal government appointed a board of trustees, chaired by Ottawa businessman Lawrence Freiman. The board chose Southam as director general, and it was under him that the centre entered its early golden age. Southam greatly enjoyed holding court in patrician style, often in the NAC's fine restaurant.

As Southam's dream unfolded, the National Arts Centre Orchestra came into being, and so did French and English theatre at the centre. Maestro Mario Bernardi, born in Kirkland Lake, Ontario, and raised and educated in Italy, was hired to lead the orchestra. Soon after, the gifted Walter Prystawski was appointed concert master. Susan and I got to know Bernardi well and enjoyed countless performances of the orchestra under his baton.

Southam's grand ambitions appealed to me. In those early years, he saw the NAC as the logical home for an annual summer festival that took its inspiration from the Edinburgh Festival. A great fan of opera, Southam worked hard to see that high-quality performances were presented on the centre's stage, such as excellent productions of Mozart's *Marriage of Figaro* and *Così fan tutte*, enhanced by Bernardi's masterful conducting. Eventually, the summer festivals and opera productions would fade away. An institution that relied heavily on taxpayer funding faced serious challenges in times of financial restraint.

The NAC became an attractive venue for glamorous events, one of the most memorable being the January 1970 birthday celebration for the province of Manitoba. On that occasion, Pierre Trudeau arrived arm in arm with a ravishingly dressed Barbra Streisand. I was privy to the tightly held secret that Streisand would make an appearance that evening: my PMO colleague Roger Rolland, an old friend of Trudeau's, had been quietly dispatched to meet Streisand at the airport in Montreal and accompany her by limousine to Ottawa. Trudeau and Streisand caused quite a stir.

After its opening, the NAC became the venue for high profile political events. When Richard Nixon arrived in Ottawa in April 1972, he had recently paid his historic visit to Beijing, and in May he would be travelling to Moscow. At the PMO, we fully appreciated the significance of the Ottawa visit in the wake of a transformational diplomatic approach to the Chinese leadership. The president's seven-day visit to three Chinese cities marked the beginning of normalizing relations between mainland China and the United States after twenty-five years of diplomatic isolation. When I briefly met Nixon, there was a spring in his step, signalling, I sensed, the enormous importance of what had transpired. As Nixon waved from his box at the NAC, there was generous applause. This was, after all, the first American president to be hosted in Ottawa's glittering cultural palace.

My first, modest experience in organizing philanthropic support for the NAC was to head up an organization in the early 1970s we called Nine Plus; the "Nine" was meant to represent the muses of the arts and sciences in Greek mythology. Composed of volunteers, the group's main goal was to support the National Arts Centre's musical programming. Our most notable initiative was to organize a fundraising gala on the stage of the opera hall. I do not remember how much money we took in, but to my knowledge it was the first such effort drawing on private-sector support.

There are two paramount cultural leaders I associate with the NAC. One is Hamilton Southam. The other is Peter Herrndorf, who became director general in September 1999. The NAC Herrndorf inherited was in some respects a shadow of its glorious past. With his CBC background and consummate management and diplomatic skills, Herrndorf rebuilt the institution, ably backed up by the board of trustees chair, governance guru David Leighton. During the Herrndorf years, the NAC's organizational structure was tightened and programming achieved new successes. He embraced the internet as a way of reaching out to audiences beyond Ottawa. What impressed me was his determination to take the NAC to the people of Canada and to make the institution a catalyst for artistic creation across the country. One of the ways he did this was to introduce the concept of hosting regional "artistic scenes" at the NAC. In his words, he wanted to showcase the best artists from all parts of the country. Susan and I took careful note and applied Herrndorf's outreach principles to our work with other cultural institutions—most notably, in my case, with the National Gallery of Canada Foundation, which I joined as a founding director in 1997.

During the Herrndorf years, which I would describe as the NAC's second golden age, I experienced many wonderful moments, far too many to record here. In performances alone, how does one choose from the literal thousands that thrilled and inspired? We all know that the arts world is peppered with stars and great personalities. One star I came to know well was NAC music director and orchestra conductor Pinchas Zukerman, who took on his post in 1999 and remained until 2015. Zukerman took Ottawa by storm. In due course, he married cellist Amanda Forsyth and took up residence in our Rockcliffe Park community. We greatly enjoyed their company, and the National Arts Centre Orchestra performed majestically under the maestro's baton. Of Zukerman's many talents, one was his ability to attract to the NAC stage fellow international stars. Many of them came because they were friends, colleagues, and admirers of Zukerman.

If Susan and I had to choose a single most unforgettable performance of the maestro in all those years, it would be a concert at the thirteenth-century Salisbury Cathedral in October 2014. Marking the hundredth anniversary of the start of the First World War, it was a solemn and emotional salute to the Canadian soldiers who had served in that war, thirty thousand of whom had trained on nearby Salisbury Plain. We remember approaching the mighty, hauntingly lit gothic cathedral after dark. Inside, we sat in the majestic nave and listened to Beethoven's Seventh Symphony. We were overcome. We said to ourselves that the orchestra had never sounded better. Zukerman agreed.

Herrndorf's final triumph was convincing the Harper government to support his ambitious plans for the architectural renewal of the NAC building. The vision became a reality in 2017, coinciding with Canada's 150th anniversary. These few words do not do justice to this accomplishment: a challenging project completed on time and on budget. Herrndorf's success underscored another of his remarkable skills: the ability to win political support regardless of the party in office. Having spent a good part of my life reaching out to the federal government, I knew just how remarkable this accomplishment was. I said to Herrndorf at the time, "Peter, if there was an Oscar for lobbying the government, you, my friend, would win it hands down."

As he left, Herrndorf was made a companion of the Order of Canada, the highest honour that Canada can bestow. How deserving! The NAC itself continues in the able hands of its new leader, Christopher Deacon, its gifted musical director and conductor, Alexander Shelley, and the irrepressible heads of its foundation, Janice O'Born and Jayne Watson. Built to produce and present music, theatre, and dance, and designed to reflect Canada's linguistic duality and now represent Indigenous peoples, the NAC is the only performing arts centre in the world with such a complex mandate. Ever mindful of its national mandate, the NAC is now turning its focus to assisting artists and the performing arts across Canada recover and rebuild from the trauma of the COVID-19 pandemic.

THE NATIONAL GALLERY OF CANADA

It was 1998, and sitting across my board table was Montreal businessman Jean-Claude Delorme. With him was a dynamic young woman, Marie Claire Morin. Delorme was the chair of the newly created National Gallery of Canada Foundation and Morin was its founding CEO. They both made an excellent impression on me. Delorme, whom I had met once in his capacity as the CEO of Telesat Canada, had a stellar record of service in the Montreal arts world. He asked if I would join the board of the gallery foundation. Following a good chat, I agreed. Thus began a journey that was to be at the centre of my arts experience in Canada for the next twenty-five years. I was familiar with the gallery, of course, and had a profound respect for the institution, founded in the 1880s. Its incomparable collection of Canadian art was the touchstone of my education about our artists and the artistic traditions that shaped the visual arts history of Canada.

The first meeting of the newly created board took place on June 28, 1999. In the chair was John Cleghorn, CEO of the Royal Bank of Canada. Cleghorn and I knew each other well, having worked closely together in Business Council circles. That the CEO of Canada's largest financial institution would make time for the gallery foundation augured well. At Cleghorn's urging, I agreed to serve as vice-chair, and Nova Scotia business leader and noted art collector Donald Sobey came on as treasurer. With an enthusiastic Marie Claire Morin cheering us on, we were off and running. The assets of the foundation were $650,000, the result of gifts from a number of "founding partners," among them Michal and Renata Hornstein, Elizabeth and Donald Sobey, and Zeev and Sarah Vered; and corporate supporters Bell Canada, the BMO Financial Group, Power Corporation of Canada, the RBC Financial Group, and the TD Bank Financial Group.

Given that the foundation was a new creation seeking to operate where there was no tradition of organized private philanthropy, our task was not a simple one. There was a degree of instinctive wariness to us in the gallery's leadership and curatorial circles. What did we know about art? Would we share their priorities?

Would we interfere in some way? We worked hard from the outset to win the confidence of gallery director Pierre Théberge, who would go on to serve for more than ten years, retiring in 2009. Théberge was a graduate in art history from the Université de Montréal and had studied at the Courtauld Institute in London. A serious individual with a scholarly bent, his natural reserve did not make for easy conversation, but I enjoyed my chats with him. Indeed, I learned a great deal. Théberge was cast in a different mould than his respected and more affable predecessor, Shirley Thomson. Upon joining the board, I went to Thomson for advice and she counselled patience.

In those early days, despite the strong efforts of the polished and diplomatic Marie Claire Morin, reaching for synergies between the foundation and the gallery proved elusive. Cleghorn, a driven banker used to getting things done, was clearly getting frustrated. One day, he called me and said, "Tom, it's time for you to take over from me. I am stepping away from the board." Unsuccessful at persuading him to change his mind, I assumed the post of chair, certainly not imagining that I'd be there for some eighteen years.

The director of an institution such as the National Gallery of Canada has an opportunity to make a significant impact on programming and acquisitions. Théberge was responsible for acquiring the much-loved giant spider *Maman*, by Louise Bourgeois, which stands imposingly at the gallery's entrance. Among his summer exhibitions was *The 1930s: The Making of "The New Man"*, featuring more than two hundred works by artists including Picasso, Dali, Walker Evans, and Alex Colville. He was responsible for the purchase of Ron Mueck's mesmerizing outsized sculpture of a newborn baby titled *Girl* and the subsequent exhibition of Mueck works. Significantly, under Théberge's leadership, the gallery increased its holdings of First Nations and Inuit art.

Upon taking on the role of foundation chair, I identified four top objectives in close collaboration with Morin. One was for us to establish the closest possible links with Théberge and the gallery's senior management and curatorial teams; the second was to align our foundation's fundraising activities with the gallery's priorities; the third was to recruit and sustain a stellar board of directors; and the fourth was to create a pan-Canadian family of donors that would be keen to support the gallery with major gifts.

Winning the confidence of Théberge and the senior management and curatorial team took time. Along the way, we on the board learned a great deal about the institution and its collection. When it came to Canadian art, the heart of the gallery's collection, I stood in awe of veteran curator Charles Hill. By the time I met him, Charlie had been in charge of historical Canadian art at the gallery for over twenty-five years. He was associated with many groundbreaking exhibitions such as *Canadian Painting in the Thirties*, *The Group of Seven: Art for a Nation*, *Emily Carr: New Perspectives on a Canadian Icon*, and, his final *chef-d'oeuvre*, *Artists, Architects and Artisans: Canadian Art 1890–1918*. I came to recognize and respect the knowledge and experience of the many talented individuals at the gallery. I also learned that the curators were a vital pipeline to collectors across Canada and the world. Having good relations with this network served us well at the foundation.

Aligning foundation priorities with those of the gallery meant paying careful attention to the gallery's corporate plan and program planning and figuring out where the foundation's efforts could be most productive. We consulted closely with Théberge and his team. We then chose how our resources could be best deployed. This task was made easier given the high quality of the foundation board. It included individuals such as Donald Sobey, Bernard Courtois, William Teron, Zeev Vered, Jean Picard, Michal Hornstein, and

Mirko Bibic, some of whom, along with me, were among the founding directors. More than two decades later, Bibic would become the chief executive of BCE and Bell Canada.

Creating a "family" of philanthropists that would enthusiastically identify with the gallery became an obsession of mine. I saw the 125th anniversary of the gallery in 2005 as the ideal platform to give life to this idea. I believed the gallery's blockbuster summer exhibition, *Leonardo da Vinci, Michelangelo, and the Renaissance in Florence*, would serve as a powerful catalyst. With paintings, sculptures, drawings, and prints by masters such as Michelangelo, Leonardo, Bronzino, Andrea del Sarto, and Piero di Cosimo, it was certain to impress. The exhibition was imaginatively curated by art historian and Renaissance specialist David Franklin, the gallery's deputy director and chief curator.

Thus the foundation's inaugural Distinguished Patrons Soirée took place at the National Gallery in May 2005. In inviting prospective patrons to Ottawa, I asked that they support the gallery through donations of money and art and find common purpose with like-minded "collector philanthropists" in gallery activities tied to scholarship, research, art acquisitions, exhibitions, and national and international outreach. Susan and I were the first to join the newly created family of patrons. Nancy Richardson of Ottawa, Michael Audain and his wife, Yoshiko Karasawa, and Donald and Elizabeth Sobey quickly followed. The gift level for joining our new "family" was $100,000.

The soirée was a smash, with nearly five hundred people in attendance. Believing that an impressive guest list adds to the lustre of a party, I invited a who's who of well-known Canadians from the worlds of the arts and politics to join with the business leaders, entrepreneurs, and philanthropists who were generously offering financial support. We welcomed Pierre Théberge and his senior curators, the brilliant architect of the National Gallery, Moshe Safdie, as well as former prime ministers Joe Clark and Jean Chrétien, a clutch of cabinet ministers, senior government mandarins, members of the Senate and judiciary, and a host of ambassadors. Prime Minister Paul Martin was the evening's centre of attention, and minister of Canadian heritage Liza Frulla offered her blessings as the government's senior culture representative. The extraordinary culinary offerings, the overflowing floral works, and the very fine wines added to the memorable occasion.

The story of the wine deserves a special mention. Given the Renaissance theme of the soirée, I had invited one of Tuscany's leading noblemen and arguably Italy's most celebrated winemaker, Marchese Piero Antinori, to be our guest and donate one of his finest wines in support of the soirée. I had known Antinori for some years. When he and I spoke, he said other commitments kept him from joining us. He then asked which of his wines I had in mind. "Twenty cases of Guado al Tasso," I replied. He chuckled and said, "Tom, you have chosen one of my best. You shall have it." The Guado al Tasso, which came to us through the good offices of Italian ambassador Marco Colombo, created quite a buzz. It was of exceptional quality and boasted a lineage going back to the seventeenth century.

The soirée netted a stunning $1 million plus—a national record for the year in cultural giving. But there was also a great surprise in the wings. Minister Frulla, who was impressed with the success of our foundation, had decided in the weeks leading up to the soirée to support the gallery with a matching gift of $1 million from the Canadian government. Tipped off in advance, Marie Claire Morin and I went to the podium and invited the elegantly-gowned Frulla to come forward. With great aplomb and to thunderous applause, she stepped up to the podium clutching a giant replica of the one-million-dollar cheque. Prime Minister Martin, who was seated at our table along with his wife, Sheila, turned to me in surprise. "How in the hell did you pull this off? I know nothing about this one million dollars!" I responded that the government's gift was serving an excellent cause and was hugely appreciated on the 125th anniversary of the gallery. He smiled and, with tongue in cheek, said, "If you arrange to have another bottle of that magnificent wine we're drinking brought to the table, I won't create a fuss." Needless to say, I did.

The distinguished patrons would go on to form the core of the gallery foundation's philanthropic family for decades. What began with some fifty families now stands at over one hundred, and they are by far the largest source of private funding for the gallery. Their love of art is the binding force, and many are serious collectors in their own right. Looking after them became my top priority. As a donor myself, I knew I had to be in regular contact, to be sure. But in addition, working closely with our foundation CEO and the gallery director and curators, we had to interest them in the gallery's collection, scholarship, and exhibitions. Connecting them with the curators was important. One of the reciprocal benefits tied to their philanthropy was the opportunity to consult with curators on their own collections, something Susan and I have occasionally done.

While most leading gifts to the gallery from the foundation are channelled to designated purposes, the foundation on occasion has set out to acquire an important work of art for the national collection. One example is Canadian Prairie artist Joe Fafard's stunning *Running Horses*. When in 2008 Susan and I first set eyes on *Horses*, which was on loan to the gallery, we knew immediately it should be part of its permanent collection. I consulted with the gallery and we got the green light. Susan and I kicked off the fundraising drive, and then I began to work the telephones, reaching out to fellow members of the distinguished patrons family. Before you knew it, we had raised some $650,000, enough to purchase the work and provide an endowment that would allow for it to travel in Canada. On May 2, 2008, we saluted a greatly appreciative Fafard at the gallery in the presence of his family members. *Running Horses* now occupies a privileged position in front of the east face of the gallery, overlooking Sussex Drive. For this acquisition, I shall remain forever grateful to the generosity of fellow patrons Michael Audain and Yoshiko Karasawa, Laurent and Claire Beaudoin, Dominic and Pearl D'Alessandro, André and France Desmarais, Murray Edwards, Fred and Elizabeth Fountain, Hartley and Heather Richardson, Donald and Beth Sobey, and William and Jean Teron.

In December 2008, Marc Mayer succeeded Pierre Théberge as the director and chief executive officer of the gallery. A Franco-Ontarian from Sudbury, Mayer was an art historian who had served as director of the Musée d'art contemporain de Montréal and of the Power Plant in Toronto and as deputy director at the Brooklyn Museum. Imbued with energy and an infectious passion for art, he quickly began to make his presence known beyond the walls of the gallery. At the foundation, he was well received and I took a liking to him.

One of the most important jobs of a gallery director is to recruit an outstanding chief curator. With the departure in 2010 of deputy director and chief curator David Franklin, Mayer appointed as his successor Paul Lang, an experienced, trilingual Swiss-French art historian. Lang had been chief curator of Geneva's Musée d'art et d'histoire and had mounted impressive exhibitions. Some critics wondered what the new chief curator, a specialist in neoclassical European art, had in common with the gallery's Canadian collection. A consummate professional, Lang readily understood the importance of embracing Canadian art and connecting with Canadian artists. He also saw in the post an opportunity to work in a purpose-built North American institution that possessed, by the way, a fine collection of European art. For the foundation, he would prove to be a trusted ally. I learned a great deal from him and we became good friends.

Given the importance of the distinguished patrons to our foundation's philanthropic aspirations, I wanted to establish an annual event, tied to a leading exhibition, that would recognize and celebrate them. Thus, was born the aforementioned Distinguished Patrons Soirée, an idea that sprang from the 2005 event that established the distinguished patrons family. In June 2011, with the gallery's lavish exhibition *Caravaggio and His Followers in Rome* as the backdrop, we assembled in the gallery's Great Hall. I welcomed dignitaries and guests. Governor General David Johnston spoke at the reception, as did the soirée patron, chief justice of Canada Beverley McLachlin, and Michael Audain, chair of the gallery's board of trustees. We delighted our guests with a musical concert by maestro Julian Armour. It was important to me that music be an integral part of our soirées to offer up what I called a "full cultural experience." The main event of this soirée was a preview tour of the Caravaggio exhibition led by co-curator Sebastian Schütze. Amiable and knowledgeable, Schütze was professor and chair of the art history department at the University of Vienna. He and David Franklin had collaborated closely in shaping the exhibition. Based on their impeccable scholarship—a hallmark of National Gallery exhibitions—the exhibition added greatly to the respect in which the gallery is held around the world.

In 2012, the signature exhibition was the popular *Van Gogh: Up Close*, co-curated by the gallery's Anabelle Kienle Poňka and Van Gogh specialist and guest curator Cornelia Homburg. I took pleasure in welcoming to the soirée that year the Harper government's minister of Canadian heritage, James Moore. The importance of his presence was not lost on anyone.

In 2013, the signature exhibition was *Artists, Architects and Artisans: Canadian Art 1890–1918*, the creation of the gallery's long-time curator of Canadian art, Charlie Hill. This was Hill's last major exhibition prior to his retirement, and Susan and I were mightily impressed by his scholarship and his insights into the Canada of the period. When I welcomed the patrons to the 2013 soirée, two important developments had taken place in gallery and foundation circles. Calgary businessman Michael Tims had been appointed chair of the board of trustees, and museum professional Karen Colby-Stothart had become the foundation's CEO. Tims, a respected figure in the Calgary oil patch with an excellent record of charitable engagement, was a collector and clearly committed to his new role. Wise and measured in his approach, Tims would go on to honour the tradition of excellence established by his predecessors Donald Sobey and Michael Audain. Like Sobey and Audain, he took an active interest in the work of the foundation and agreed to serve on its executive committee.

I led the search efforts leading to the recruitment of Karen Colby-Stothart. I was assisted closely by several foundation board colleagues, especially by investment banker Michael Adams, who, during our lengthy period of collaboration at the foundation, would make an outsize contribution. Colby-Stothart was an insider who had joined the National Gallery in 1992 having acquitted herself well in positions at the Montreal Museum of Fine Arts and previously at the Art Gallery of Ontario. When I first approached Colby-Stothart, she was serving as deputy director in charge of exhibitions and installations. I cleared the way, of course, by consulting with Marc Mayer in advance. I knew that she was not a professional fund-raiser, and to some on the foundation board my courtship of her for this reason seemed risky. I proceeded in the belief that the foundation would benefit greatly from the engagement of someone who knew the National Gallery inside out and who had deep experience working with artists, collectors, and donors. I also believed we could counsel Colby-Stothart in the art of fundraising. My gamble paid off handsomely. She would become a highly successful leader of the foundation and would go on to serve from 2013 to 2019.

In the meantime, in May 2013 the gallery mounted the groundbreaking exhibition *Sakahàn: International Indigenous Art. Sakahàn*, meaning "to light a fire" in the language of the Algonquin peoples, was billed by director Marc Mayer as the largest-ever survey of contemporary Indigenous art. Indeed, it was a historic initiative featuring more than 150 artworks by some eighty artists from sixteen countries in six continents. The exhibition was co-curated by the gallery's Audain curator of Indigenous art, Greg Hill, associate curator Christine Lalonde, and guest curator Elizabeth Simonfay. Mayer announced, "We plan to make a quinquennial habit of bringing you the finest examples of new work by modern exemplars of the world's ancient cultures." Mayer, in my view, showed his stuff in the *Sakahàn* project and won the financial support of the RBC Foundation, which went on to play an important role in the philanthropic tradition being fostered by the gallery foundation.

During my tenure as foundation chair, I sought opportunities to link the appreciation of art with important events in history. So it was, on the eve of Remembrance Day in 2014, that I invited distinguished patrons and guests to a "special World War I commemorative evening." The evening started with a panel I moderated involving Dean Oliver, director of research at the Canadian Museum of History, and distinguished historian Desmond Morton. Oliver's participation had special relevance, because the Canadian War Museum falls within the purview of the Canadian Museum of

History and houses an impressive collection of war art. A private tour of the moving exhibition *The Great War: The Persuasive Power of Photography*, the creation of Ann Thomas, senior curator of the gallery's photographs collection, followed the panel. At dinner in the Great Hall, remarks were presented by Lt.-Gen. Guy Thibault, vice-chief of the defence staff, and by my good friend Blake Goldring. A prominent Toronto business leader, Goldring also served as an honorary colonel in the Canadian Army and was a fellow distinguished patron. Suffice to say, there were moments of high emotion at the gallery that evening, as there was a recounting of Canada's staggering sacrifices in that bloody conflict. Marc Mayer, never still, lightened the mood following dinner by providing us all with a tour of the Jack Bush exhibition that was about to open to the public in the following days.

The year 2015 offered up some transformative developments in the gallery-foundation relationship. Karen Colby-Stothart was quickly grasping the dos and don'ts of fundraising and was winning the respect of the board and donors. Board of trustees chair Michael Tims, who sat with us as a foundation board member, ensured that we were connected to the trustees. Trustee vice-chair Harriet Walker was always helpful and constructive. Continuing a tradition that had been initiated by Michael Audain, Colby-Stothart and I attended the meetings of the trustees to update them on foundation work. And to complete the process that connected us all so successfully, Marc Mayer was present at all meetings of the foundation board. We were well on our way to achieving what to me was the holy grail of philanthropic engagement with the National Gallery: "seamless cooperation."

In 2015, a decision was taken to create the Canadian Photography Institute (CPI) as a department within the gallery. The CPI was built on an important partnership between Canadian art patron David

Thomson, the gallery, and the foundation. Thomson's generous gifts of photographs combined with those of the gallery to create, in the words of Marc Mayer, "one of the greatest and most comprehensive photography holdings worldwide—an internationally acclaimed collection of the history of photography from its origins to its present day." The CPI presented the gallery with an opportunity to establish an incomparable centre of excellence based in Canada, with endless possibilities involving research, scholarship, partnerships, and more. One of the special attractions to me was that the Thomson gift would include the photo archives of the *Globe and Mail*, providing a unique and invaluable record. I found the prospect of working more closely with David Thomson in the decades to come tantalizing. I had never met a collector more erudite and learned. I knew that his commitment, like that of his father, Ken, to the advancement of Canada's visual arts collections and scholarship was deep and sincere. My affection for Thomson has grown over the years, and I continue to learn from his experience as one of the world's pre-eminent collectors.

The Thomson gift to the gallery in support of the CPI was a powerful enabler of the largest corporate gift in the gallery's history. Mayer, Tims, and Colby-Stothart joined me in a call on Brian Porter, the CEO of Scotiabank. A supporter of the arts, Scotiabank had already demonstrated an interest in photography. I suggested to my colleagues that we ask the bank to consider a gift of $10 million. They believed the sum was too ambitious. The pitch we made to Porter was that Scotiabank would be an ideal partner in the CPI venture and that with Canada's 150th anniversary in 2017 fast approaching, the timing was perfect. Having received us hospitably, Porter listened intently and after some fifteen minutes nodded his approval. He would strongly recommend this gift to his board. The four of us left his office elated. There was no doubt in my mind that Thomson's involvement in the partnership was a decisive factor in our favour. Scotiabank's support of photography programming at the gallery endures to this day, and in recognition of the bank's philanthropy, the gallery's Great Hall bears the bank's name.

On December 8, 2015, I had the great privilege of chairing a historic foundation event. We welcomed my friend and colleague Ash Prakash to a special soirée in his honour in recognition of his donation to the gallery of his collection of works by the iconic Canadian artist James Wilson Morrice. In my journeys through the arts world, I have met some remarkable individuals, and Prakash ranks high among them. Having emigrated to Canada from India as a young man with little in his pocket, he served in Canada's public service early in his professional life. He went on to become a seminal player in Canada's art world. A dealer in art and a collector, scholar, author, and philanthropist, he has served as an adviser to some of our country's leading collectors and institutions. Fortunately for the National Gallery of Canada, he decided, through the A.K. Prakash Foundation, to donate his impressive Morrice collection to the gallery, but not before giving other Canadian arts institutions an opportunity to voice their interest in this $20-million gift. In the face of this competition, I declared, "This is a collection our foundation cannot afford to lose. Let's go to work!" At the soirée in his honour, I saluted Prakash's extraordinary generosity, his devotion to collecting and scholarship, and his enthusiasm in helping others build their own collections. He is a rare individual in the world of art.

On that memorable evening, former governor general Adrienne Clarkson, Marc Mayer, Mike Tims, and Prakash's daughter Sangeeta spoke warmly before the gathered guests. To the surprise and delight of everyone, David Thomson offered a particularly glowing tribute. Such an appearance by Thomson is rare. The gallery's very able senior curator of Canadian art, Katerina Atanassova, presented perspectives on the Morrice collection and guided us through the A.K. Prakash Gallery, the newly established home of the fifty rare and beautiful paintings. Given Atanassova's key role in organizing and mounting the collection, we listened carefully to her every word.

The highlight of 2016 at the National Gallery was doubtlessly the stunning exhibition Élisabeth Louise Vigée Le Brun (1755–1842). Curated by the gallery's Paul Lang and by collaborators Katharine Baetjer, of the Metropolitan Museum in New York, and international expert on Vigée Le Brun Joseph Baillio, the exhibition shone a light on this fascinating but not well-known French artist of the eighteenth century. Her life as a celebrated portrait painter before and after the French Revolution was filled with drama. Having found favour with Marie Antoinette, she became the darling of French aristocrats but had to leave the country quickly as the revolution advanced. Gamely, she travelled Europe and found favour and opportunity to continue her career across the continent, including in Russia.

Just before it opened to the public, the exhibition formed the backdrop of our 2016 Distinguished Patrons Soirée. It was an enormous hit, and I was not surprised. Several months before, Susan and I had attended the exhibition's opening at the Metropolitan Museum in New York in the company of Paul Lang. The scholarship behind it was deep and impressive, and the exhibition added to the great respect the National Gallery of Canada has gained over the years. Our soirée that special evening was made complete by a performance by one of my favourite mezzo-sopranos, the internationally acclaimed Wallis Giunta. Giunta was performing in Germany at the time, but I was able to persuade her to travel to her native Ottawa for the occasion. Her family was thrilled, as were our patrons and guests. I have a great photo with Giunta in her dazzling red gown at the entrance to the exhibition.

An immensely satisfying outcome of this exhibition and of the dedication of Paul Lang was the anonymous donation to the National Gallery of Canada of the outstanding portrait by Vigée Le Brun of the Russian countess Anna Tolstaya.

At the foundation, we believed that Canada's 150th anniversary presented us with unprecedented opportunities. When I invited distinguished patrons and guests to gather at the gallery on June 13, 2017, it was to view the "reimagined" Canadian and Indigenous galleries—the culmination of an ambitious project that wove together for the first time the gallery's Canadian and Indigenous art. Some eight hundred paintings, sculptures, prints, photographs, silver, and decorative objects were beautifully and imaginatively presented. I was proud of the team responsible for this historic undertaking: Marc Mayer, whose vision had driven the project; curators Katerina Atanassova and Greg Hill; and the talented deputy director of exhibitions, Anne Eschapasse. Mayer and his team consulted closely with Indigenous advisers in developing the highly acclaimed outcome. As I walked through the galleries, I felt that the story of Canada's Indigenous past and of the creativity of First Nations and Inuit peoples was now being told in a way that would make new connections and resonate powerfully with viewers.

At dinner that evening, I interviewed architect Moshe Safdie. Guests were engrossed by the story he told of standing on the exact spot where we were speaking and envisaging a beautiful edifice perched on the cliffs high above the Ottawa River, overlooking the heart of our nation, our Parliament Buildings.

Canada's 150th anniversary was a catalyst for another remarkable initiative that was to open the next day: the Canada 150 Art for the

Nation Summit. It was the product of an idea that had motivated my work at the foundation for some time. Simply put, I believed that the foundation's role should extend beyond fundraising and that leveraging the deep experience of the foundation board on matters touching art, collecting, scholarship, and exhibitions was an important way for us to assist the gallery. It helped, of course, that our foundation CEO, Karen Colby-Stothart, was herself an art historian and experienced museologist.

The summit got under way early in the morning with the patronage of Governor General David Johnston. Graham Flack, deputy minister of Canadian heritage, provided an excellent and provocative review of Canadian cultural policy. I had known Flack for quite some time and respected his strong intellect and command of his subject matter. A panel on art collecting and the market followed, with insights from Mayer, Canadian James Bradburne, who was serving as director general of Milan's Pinacoteca di Brera, David Heffel, president of Heffel Fine Art Auction House, and philanthropist Rob Sobey. A second panel brought to the stage Simon Brault, CEO of the Canada Council of the Arts, and artists Edward Burtynsky and Geoffrey Farmer. Senator Patricia Bovey, herself an art historian, moderated the discussion. Their perspectives on the place of Canada and Canadian artists in the international art world were well received. Over lunch, I welcomed remarks by finance minister Bill Morneau. A strong supporter of the arts, along with his wife, Nancy McCain, Morneau clearly felt at home with us. Given the central role of the Department of Finance at the apex of federal government policy, I took comfort in knowing that Morneau understood the arts and the pre-eminent position of the National Gallery of Canada.

The summit concluded with a session focusing on art, innovation, and philanthropy. Again, it was a privilege to welcome three heavy-hitters: entrepreneurs, art collectors, and philanthropists Michael Audain and Pierre Lassonde, and Canadian art historian Emily Braun. All brought perspectives that few others could. Braun was the New York–based curator of the outstanding Leonard A. Lauder collection. Audain had built the splendid Audain Art Museum at Whistler, British Columbia, and Lassonde had built the equally splendid Pavillon Pierre-Lassonde at the Musée national des beaux-arts du Québec. When we brought the summit to a close, I knew that much had been accomplished. The importance of the visual arts in the mix of Canada's public policies had been affirmed; the vibrancy of Canada's art market was clear for all to see; Canadian artists were making their mark on the world; and art philanthropy in Canada was alive and well.

When I welcomed distinguished patrons to Ottawa in May 2018, the focal point was a fine exhibition titled *Impressionist Treasures: The Ordrupgaard Collection*. Chief curator Paul Lang, who was largely responsible for attracting the show to Ottawa, was not with us. To my great regret, he had left the gallery to take up senior museum responsibilities in Strasbourg. The exhibition came to us from the state-owned Ordrupgaard museum in Denmark and featured masterpieces from the golden age of European Impressionism. Among the paintings were works by Monet, Matisse, Gauguin, and Hammershøi. Following a tour of the exhibition, we travelled a few minutes away to the French embassy, where we were received by the highly respected French ambassador, Kareen Rispal. A splendid dinner awaited us in the embassy's grand salon. Marc Mayer, Karen Colby-Stothart, and senior gallery staff joined with distinguished patrons and guests in the evening's celebrations. Built in art deco style by the French government in the 1930s and prominently situated on Sussex Drive adjacent to the prime minister's residence, the embassy building makes a powerful impression.

———

The ambassadors of the United States, France, Italy, Germany, Spain, Austria, the Netherlands, Mexico, Japan, and China and the high commissioner of the United Kingdom were among our frequent guests at Distinguished Patrons Soirée events. Apart from my business dealings with them, I made a point of connecting them with the foundation and the gallery, as cultural diplomacy forms part of their responsibilities. These connections were most helpful in dealings with museums abroad and mounting the annual distinguished patrons art tours we were later to begin.

I witnessed diplomacy and art woven together in a significant way in 2016. I was approached by Mexican ambassador Agustín García-López with a proposal that the National Gallery host an exhibition of works by the Mexican modernist artist Rufino Tamayo. The ambassador's interest in art was deep, and he and I had been discussing how we might connect Canada and Mexico in some form of creative partnership. Over lunch at the Rideau Club in Ottawa, we concluded that the ideal moment would be to host a Tamayo exhibition during the summit of North American leaders scheduled to take place in Ottawa on June 29, 2016. The summit would bring together presidents Barack Obama and Enrique Peña Nieto and Prime Minister Harper, the "Three Amigos." I saw a unique opportunity here to promote the National Gallery of Canada as the summit venue, and I pushed hard for it behind the scenes. The Harper government indeed did choose the gallery and we were all set. Now I had to convince Marc Mayer to mount the Tamayo exhibition on extremely short notice—something that curators abhor. It was a tough sell, but the Mexicans could not have been more helpful. The well-connected García-López arranged for an excellent selection of Tamayo paintings to be assembled, engaged a variety of Mexican art museums and curators to support the venture, and with the support of the Mexican government, which covered most of the costs, the Tamayo exhibition was on its way. On June 24, together with Mayer and García-López, we opened the exhibition, titled *Tamayo: A Solitary Mexican Modernist*. The three leaders met at the gallery with the Tamayo exhibition as backdrop. I saw President Peña Nieto during the visit and received a fond embrace from him. He told me how proud he was that this cultural connection was made at such a propitious moment.

Another such linking of art and diplomacy was the spirited initiative of Vicki Heyman, wife of American ambassador Bruce Heyman, an appointee of President Obama. Partnering with the American embassy in Ottawa and the State Department's Art in Embassies program, Vicki Heyman launched the highly successful "Contemporary Conversations" speaking series at the National Gallery to craft discussions on issues such as social justice, the environment, and identity. Susan and I saw a great deal of the popular Heymans during their posting in Ottawa. The lion's share of my dealings with the ambassador related to Canada–United States issues; he was exceptionally effective in applying what he called "the art of diplomacy." As for the Heyman husband-and-wife team, I was impressed not only by their enthusiasm for Canada but also by Vicki's creative embrace of her role as cultural envoy.

Being engaged in international affairs throughout my career, I have hosted many foreign business leaders and, occasionally, political leaders. My first choice of venue in Ottawa was always the National Gallery of Canada. I could not think of a better place, given the majesty of its architecture and incomparable position facing Canada's Parliament Buildings and the historic Ottawa River. My guests were also able to view the national collection, a fascinating window on Canadian art and history.

—

Little did we know when I welcomed distinguished patrons to the gallery on May 22, 2019, that this would be the last in-person gathering for some time. We could not have anticipated the havoc that the COVID-19 pandemic would wreak. The backdrop of the soirée was the fine exhibition we were previewing, *Gauguin: Portraits*, expertly co-curated by Gauguin specialist Cornelia Homburg and Christopher Riopelle from the National Gallery in London, the gallery's esteemed partner in this collaboration. Riopelle, a Canadian and senior curator at the National Gallery in London, was well known to Susan and me. On more than one occasion, he had graciously hosted us at the gallery in London and guided us through the collections at that magnificent institution.

Riopelle is one of a number of respected Canadian museologists and curators serving beyond our borders who I believe would be enthusiastically welcomed to fill leadership positions at Canadian museums. But one major obstacle stands in the way: our public institutions such as the National Gallery of Canada are not offering salaries remotely competitive with their offshore counterparts. Approaches by myself and others to public authorities to remedy this disadvantage have not borne fruit. Some of my colleagues and I, acting privately, continue to press the government on this issue.

Our May gathering ushered in some profound changes at the gallery. Sasha Suda had recently been appointed to succeed Marc Mayer, and I and other patrons warmly welcomed her. To my great regret, we were also bidding au revoir to foundation CEO Karen Colby-Stothart. During her six years as our CEO, she had achieved extraordinary results. The bet that I and the board had made on her—that her lack of fundraising experience would be trumped by her deep understanding of the visual arts and long experience with the National Gallery—paid off handsomely. Working closely with me, fellow patrons, and the board, she quickly learned the ropes and connected very well with donors and potential donors. Erudite, thoughtful, and respectful, she won their trust and confidence. Once she had signalled she was leaving the foundation, I moved quickly to win support from my colleagues for her election to our board. It was a wise decision, as her contributions have been invaluable.

The art world is, of course, universal. It has lured me to destinations both familiar and unknown. Thus was born my enthusiasm for one of the most significant innovations embraced by the foundation: the annual distinguished patrons art tour in the company of and facilitated by the gallery's director and chief curator and the foundation's CEO. It began with a trip to Russia organized by chief curator Paul Lang and newly appointed foundation CEO Colby-Stothart. Lang was seeking a number of loans from the Hermitage and the Pushkin Museum in St. Petersburg for the National Gallery's upcoming Vigée Le Brun exhibition. Ottawa-based Canadian Robert Kaszanits, president of the State Hermitage Museum Foundation of Canada, was recruited to assist with the planning. Kaszanits had been on the staff of the National Gallery of Canada for almost ten years in the late 1980s and had come to the attention of the Hermitage authorities for his deep knowledge of how museums run. He went on to win their confidence by showing them how to protect their art from theft and ultraviolet light and assisting them with upgrading their seriously dilapidated infrastructure and support systems. Dramatically illustrating the role that art can play in diplomacy, President Putin bestowed on Kaszanits the Presidential Award for Distinguished Service for the years he spent helping to modernize the Hermitage's operations.

In the autumn of 2013, with the incredibly well-connected Kaszanits at our side, Lang, Marc Mayer, and Colby-Stothart departed for Russia with a small entourage consisting of gallery trustee Harriet Walker and patrons Reesa Greenberg; Michael O'Brian and his daughter; Anne Stanfield; and Susan and myself. The eleven-day journey, which included St. Petersburg and Moscow, was a spectacular success, with private access to Russia's pre-eminent museum leaders and the country's most important collections. Of the many wonderful moments, I shall treasure most the memory of being given access to the Hermitage for a full day on our own. This included being taken to a room in the basement where we were shown a Vigée Le Brun portrait with a tear in it. On the spot, we agreed that our foundation would pay for the restoration. Lang succeeded in arranging the loan by Russia of their Vigée Le Brun masterworks, and thus a vital aspect of gallery business was accomplished.

The success of the Russian visit led to the art tour becoming an annual event, starting with London in 2014 and followed by Venice in 2015, Paris in 2016, Berlin in 2017, Rome and the Vatican in 2018, and Amsterdam in 2019. So rich have these tours been, they deserve much more than the snippets I offer here, but they give the flavour. I took a direct interest in the planning of each tour, working with Colby-Stothart and Lisa Turcotte, a superb events planner on Colby-Stothart's team, as well as Cheryl Eadie in my private office. Typically, each tour would take place over four days, involve some twenty patrons, feature private access to leading museums and museum directors and curators, and include both a music and diplomatic dimension.

In London, over the course of four days in October, we were privileged to be received by David Thomson at his Archive of Modern

Conflict, followed by private visits to Sir John Soane's Museum, the National Gallery, the British Museum, the Imperial War Museum, and the Wallace Collection. One highlight was rare private access to Her Majesty's state apartments and the royal collection at Buckingham Palace, arranged at my request by long-time friend high commissioner Gordon Campbell. Campbell also received us at his residence and offered some perspectives on the Canada–United Kingdom relationship. Bank of England governor Mark Carney hosted us at breakfast at the bank and chaired a roundtable focusing on the great financial issues of the day. When Carney and his wife, Diana, first went to London, I asked if they would serve as patrons of our foundation in the United Kingdom. This they did with grace, and continued in the role until their return to Canada.

The commitment of the National Gallery and our foundation to the Venice Biennale and the Canada Pavilion was the driving force in selecting Venice for the October 2015 art tour. Over the course of five days, our private visits included the Gallerie dell'Accademia, the Peggy Guggenheim Museum, the Ca' Rezzonico, and briefings at the Venice Biennale headquarters, the Ca' Giustinian, led by Paolo Baratta, president of the Biennale. A long-time colleague of mine, Canadian ambassador to Italy Peter McGovern, joined us for dinner at the historic Palazzo Albrizzi. Over the years, Susan and I have often lost ourselves in the Byzantine splendour of the Basilica di San Marco. On this tour, it was arranged for our group to enter the church on our own late at night and to see the ancient mosaics and sculptures by candlelight, as they would have been seen for centuries prior to electrification. It was a stunning experience. On these art tours, so many masterpieces evoked strong emotions—often awe and at times, I confess, even tears. One such moment in Venice was when Mayer, Colby-Stothart, and I, together with Susan and a couple of patrons, were ushered into a small, dimly lit room at the Galleria dell'Accademia, where we quietly gazed upon a fragile masterpiece they had brought out for us: Leonardo da Vinci's *Vitruvian Man*. Seeing the famous pen-and-ink drawing up close was breathtaking.

Music, of course, was not forgotten. We listened by candlelight at the Palazzo Contarini Polignac to a majestic piano concert by Russian-Italian artist Alexander Gadjiev. As in all our tours, great care was taken to select the most knowledgeable and respected of curators and art historians to guide us.

Paris followed Venice in 2016. The five-day tour began with a visit to the Palace of Versailles on a day when it was closed to the public. Curators at the Musée national des châteaux de Versailles et de Trianon took us in hand. With Paul Lang, we focused on a number of works by Vigée Le Brun. What a pleasure for us to see Lang at work and so demonstrably attracting the respect of his French colleagues. At lunch that day, I sat next to the president of the museums complex at Versailles, Catherine Pégard, and was staggered to hear of the annual cost to the public purse of maintaining this immense cultural monument, one of so many in France. In comparison, I reflected, the public cost of supporting Canada's principal cultural institutions are minuscule. In the days that followed, we were received by senior curators at the Musée d'Orsay and the Musée du Louvre, again with the advantage of private access to select parts of their immense collections. En route from one part of the Louvre to another, our host curator had us pause in front of Leonardo's *Mona Lisa*. While not a favourite of mine or Susan's among Leonardo's great paintings, for our small group to stand quietly before the great masterwork in a room free of throngs of tourists was extraordinary. We all knew it was most unlikely to ever happen again. Later, at the Palais du Luxembourg, home to the Senate, Lang, a specialist on Eugène Delacroix, offered insights on the artist's works. As our small group took our seats in the Senate chamber, I reflected on some of the historic moments that this room would have seen. A bonus of our Paris tour was the opportunity, again arranged by Lang, to visit private collections in the homes of two Parisian families. We all remarked on the pleasure of sipping coffee in the intimate company of our hosts, who received us so cordially. For the lovers of modern art and architecture among us, a visit to the Fondation Louis Vuitton provided great excitement. Fortunately for us, the spectacular museum was hosting *Icons of Modern Art: The Shchukin Collection*, a rare opportunity to appreciate one the world's greatest private collections.

The music offering on this tour was Offenbach's opera *Les contes d'Hoffmann*, at the Opéra Bastille, the home of the Paris Opera. Before leaving Paris, we visited "Paris Photo," the world's top photography fair, housed in the Grand Palais. To our delight, none other than Canada's celebrated artist Edward Burtynsky was there to greet us. Immensely stimulated by all we had experienced over the preceding days, we went off to Lapérouse for our closing dinner and toasted to our next art tour, Berlin in 2017.

With a great deal of anticipation, in 2017 Susan and I returned to Berlin and our favourite hotel, the historic Adlon, overlooking the Brandenburg Gate. While art is the focus of these tours, our hotels were selected because of the great comfort they offered, usually in historic settings—the Grand Hotel Europe in St. Petersburg, the Metropol in Moscow, the Savoy in London, the Gritti Palace in Venice, and the Meurice in Paris—places where the patrons could come together and relax at the beginning and end of long days. Berlin, home to more than 170 museums, had more than enough to offer. Again, benefiting from careful planning and excellent curatorial guidance, we selected judiciously. We saw exquisite works on paper at the Kupferstichkabinett, Old Masters at the Gemäldegalerie, and a fine collection of nineteenth-century paintings at the Alte Nationalgalerie. In Potsdam, the recently opened Museum Barberini featured Old Masters and works by Impressionists. Schloss Sanssouci was on the agenda—less because of its art and more because of its historic importance as the residence of Frederick the Great. The celebrated military commander and statesman was also an impressive man of letters who understood the importance of the arts. In keeping with my desire to infuse our art tours with a diplomatic element, I invited an old friend, Canada's ambassador to Germany and special envoy to the European Union, Stéphane Dion, to join us in Potsdam. Over an enjoyable lunch, Dion briefed us on Canada-Germany relations and offered timely perspectives on political developments in the European arena. The Berlin arts scene is incredibly vibrant and has attracted no small number of Canadian artists. One of them, General Idea co-founder AA Bronson, has a studio in Berlin, where he and a number of other artists received us. (Neither Bronson nor I knew that in 2022 a General Idea exhibition would open at the National Gallery of Canada.) Another Canadian artist studying in Berlin at the time, cellist Brian Cheng, played beautifully for us late one evening. In keeping with tradition, the musical offering on the Berlin tour was the Deutsche Oper Berlin production of Richard Wagner's *Lohengrin*. At our concluding dinner, I announced that the 2018 tour would take us to Rome and the Vatican.

Ever since taking on the chair of the National Gallery of Canada Foundation, I had wanted to connect it in some way with the great museums of Rome and the Vatican. The distinguished patrons art tour of 2018 provided the opportunity. How does one begin in five days to savour the exquisite offerings that lay ahead? Again, with judicious planning and exceptional curatorial assistance. The Canadian ambassador to Rome, Alexandra Bugailiskis, got us under way with a briefing on Italy's socio-cultural context. Eric Reguly, long-time Rome resident and correspondent for the *Globe and Mail*, provided political and economic context. Visits to San Pietro in Montorio, Villa Farnesina, and Palazzo Colonna followed. Palazzo Colonna, one of Rome's most splendid, was known to Susan and me; we had attended receptions and concerts there. We were friends of one of the branches of that ancient family, which had produced a pope and a number of powerful statesmen and military commanders.

Rome, so infused with the ancient world, has a lively contemporary scene. This became clear with our visit to MAXXI Museum, Italy's first purpose-built art institution, serving as a cultural hub and laboratory for cultural experimentation. The Rome visits included the Galleria Borghese and the Borghese Gardens, Palazzo Doria Pamphilj, the Trinità del Monte convent, and the rarely seen Villa Madama, designed by Raphael and used exclusively by the Italian government to host foreign dignitaries. Thanks to my friend Kareen Rispal, the French ambassador to Canada, we were hosted at the Palazzo Farnese by France's ambassador to Italy, Christian Masset. The palazzo housing the French embassy is considered one of the most magnificent high Renaissance palaces in Rome. Masset graciously offered insights on the paintings and decor, beginning with his own office.

A good part of two days was dedicated to the Vatican Museums, founded by Pope Julius II in the sixteenth century. It helped that I had been working as an adviser on the Sport at the Service of Humanity initiative, a project inspired by Pope Francis and led by

Cardinal Gianfranco Ravasi, the president of the Vatican's Pontifical Council for Culture. The immensely erudite Ravasi and his under-secretary, Monsignor Melchor Sánchez de Toca, quietly paved the way for us to see rarely accessible parts of the Vatican rooms and collections. Standing on our own in the company of our curators in the Sistine Chapel, the Sala Regia, and the Cappella Paolina, study-ing the stunning ceilings and walls painted by Michelangelo and Raphael, filled us with awe. It did not matter that I was no stranger to these rooms. As in times past, I was overwhelmed.

The Vatican is not known for its contemporary art collections. Micol Forli, curator of the contemporary art collection, briefed us on these, and we were surprised at their extent. The second day at the Vatican included visits to the Cortile Ottagono, the Galleria degli Arazzi, and the Scala del Bramante. Especially informative was a briefing by Vatican Museums director Barbara Jatta, the first female director in the history of the Vatican Museums, who explained how the Vatican collections are managed and financed.

The musical offering on the tour took place at the Palazzo Doria Pamphilj, with counter-tenor Raffaele Pé singing excerpts from works by Handel composed in Rome. Handel's music of the period is among my favourites. I was swept away.

Art is a prized target of thieves, and the international black mar-ket in art is extensive. The Italian authorities have sought to counter this criminal activity with a special branch of the country's national police force, the Comando Carabinieri Tutela Patrimonio Culturale. On our last morning in Rome, we were given a fascinating briefing at the police headquarters by its head, Brig.-Gen Fabrizio Parrulli, and a tour of confiscated art—quite a collection! Interestingly, the reach of this special unit covers many countries, including Canada.

I have not dwelt on the many excellent restaurants and exqui-site culinary experiences of our tours to various countries. I will make an exception in mentioning our closing dinner in Rome at the Casino dell'Aurora Pallavicini Rospigliosi. A summer pavilion originally built for Cardinal Scipione Borghese, its grand dining room is a marvel, decorated by Guido Reni, among others. There were many toasts that memorable evening as we enthusiastically pledged to continue our art tours. Next on the list, Amsterdam!

When Christine Sadler, Karen Colby-Stothart's successor as foundation CEO, greeted the distinguished patrons on arrival at Amsterdam in November 2019, she said to us, "Welcome to a city of nearly a million bicycles, 1,753 bridges, almost 7,000 sixteenth-, seventeenth-, and eighteenth-century buildings, and 165 canals, 100 kilometres of fascinating waterways wending their way through this eye-pleasing and culturally rich city." Amsterdam was on my preferred list of European art capitals to visit because of its rich visual arts heritage but also for another reason. The National Gallery of Canada was to host a major Rembrandt exhibition in 2020, and we patrons knew the importance of nurturing partnerships between our gallery and our Dutch counterparts. I was delighted that the chair of the gallery's board of trustees, Françoise Lyon, was able to join us as well as Stephanie Dickey, Bader chair in northern baroque art at Queen's University. A Rembrandt specialist, her participation in the tour was invaluable and her connections superb, as she was engaged at the time in the demanding work of curating the National Gallery's forthcoming Rembrandt exhibition.

As in previous tours, our program gave us private access to the leading collections of the country and to its most respected directors and curators. This included the Van Gogh Museum, the Frans Hals Museum, the Teylers Museum, the Rembrandthuis, the Mauritshuis, the Rijksmuseum, and the Kröller-Müller Museum. The richness of the collections defies description. The tour began with a private visit to the hugely popular Van Gogh Museum, where we were received by the head of exhibitions and by Willem van Gogh, the artist's great-grandnephew. Van Gogh joined us for dinner that evening, and we chatted late into the night. Deeply engaged in the museum's mission, he was both knowledgeable and charming. We exchanged views on the challenges of curating major collections, and it was helpful to learn that even such a famous museum as the Van Gogh, which accommodates some six thousand visitors a day, is not free of problems. Clearly, attracting visitors is not one of them. The following morning, Ann Demeester, the director of the Frans Hals Museum, in the nearby thirteenth-century walled city of Haarlem, impressed us with her command of the works of Hals. At 11 a.m. that day, we stopped where we stood in her museum for a moment of silence to commemorate the end of the First World War. She was startled. The Dutch, who were non-combatants in the First World War, do not commemorate the armistice as we do. The visit the following morning to the Rembrandthuis, the home of Rembrandt from 1639 to 1656, was memorable, in part because the knowledgeable Stephanie Dickey was at my side. Enjoying our morning coffee and pastries in the original kitchen, I wondered what the great master might have had for breakfast in his day. A highlight of the Amsterdam tour for me was being received at the historic Jan Six House by a member of the Six family and seeing the family collection. Jan Six, Rembrandt's most important patron, began the collection in the seventeenth century.

I always enjoy meeting entrepreneurs who love art. So it was in The Hague, an easy drive from Amsterdam, where we were received by industrialist Joop van Caldenborgh at his remarkable Voorlinden Museum. The building, a superb piece of modern architecture located in beautifully landscaped gardens, was very much our host's creation. As we sat together at dinner that evening at the

Mauritshuis, Van Caldenborgh explained how he had conceived of the museum and built his collection. Before we dined, we had the thrill of seeing exquisite Vermeers and Rembrandts in the rooms a few metres away, a sharp contrast from the exciting modern and contemporary Van Caldenborgh collection.

The highlight of the tour in many respects was our two visits to the Rijksmuseum, which was marking the 350th anniversary of Rembrandt's death. After seeing so many fine works so expertly explained by accommodating curators, a great surprise was in store. We were ushered into the grand room where Rembrandt's famous *The Night Watch* was being restored behind a glass partition. Our host invited us to enter the space behind the glass to see the giant work up close in its most minute detail. I was told later that this never happens—but somehow it happened to us. Dickey certainly did not complain. Nor did any of us.

The concluding candlelight dinner at the Museum Van Loon was an appropriate finale. Home to one of Amsterdam's oldest families, co-founders of the Dutch East India Company, it is beautifully preserved—an oasis of objets d'art, silver, porcelain, and fourteen generations of family portraits. Tenor Charles Daniels and lutist Fred Jacobs performed music of the seventeenth century, transporting us back to the Dutch Golden Age. I had met Daniels during one of his performances in Ottawa and was again impressed by his voice. As we walked to our hotel along the famous Keizersgracht canal, I thought, Once again, mission accomplished! Little did any of us know that in the months ahead a dreaded pestilence would descend upon the world and all plans would have to be put on hold.

During my time as chair of the National Gallery of Canada Foundation, one of the most extraordinary projects undertaken by the gallery with the indispensable assistance of the foundation was the restoration of the Canada Pavilion at the Venice Biennale. Opened in 1958, the pavilion has ever since offered a permanent exhibition space to artists selected to represent Canada at the famous exposition, established in 1895. Every two years, the Biennale hosts exhibitions of the best of contemporary art from around the world.

Architecture exhibitions were introduced in the off year at the Canada Pavilion in 1991. But by 2008, the pavilion and Canada's engagement at the Biennale, which for the better part of five decades had been the responsibility of the National Gallery of Canada, was facing a crisis. Public funding had dried up, government support waned, and the pavilion itself had fallen into disrepair. To the great credit of gallery CEO Marc Mayer, a rescue mission was launched in 2010. It was clear that in the absence of strong gallery and philanthropic support, the mission was likely doomed. At the gallery, Colby-Stothart, in charge of exhibitions and subsequently as foundation CEO, played a leading role in pulling together a coalition of supporters, initially including the Canada Council, led by CEO Simon Brault, and RBC Wealth Management and the RBC Foundation. I pledged my enthusiastic support and rallied my foundation colleagues to do likewise.

One of my foundation board colleagues who required no persuasion was Reesa Greenberg of Ottawa. An art historian and philanthropist with a special interest in contemporary art and architecture, she led the way by generously agreeing to finance all research and construction costs for the restoration of the pavilion. In addition, the foundation launched the Canadian Artists in Venice Endowment Fund, and it attracted financial support from the Donald R. Sobey family, the Michael and Sonja Koerner family, and the Jack Weinbaum Family Foundation. Over fifty families, private foundations, and smaller government agencies have also donated to the foundation's biannual exhibition campaigns. Foundation colleague

Michelle Koerner has been working tirelessly to raise money in support of Canada's presence in Venice, and foundation chair Ann Bowman has been an indispensable enabler of RBC support.

Meeting the goal of restoring and officially opening the Canada Pavilion and its gardens in May 2018 was no small accomplishment. It required skilful handling of the Biennale authorities in Venice and officials of the cultural arm of the Italian government. Importantly, it required close cooperation with the Italian architectural firm responsible for the restoration. I pitched in wherever I could, my fluency in Italian being an advantage. Canada's ambassadors in Rome provided a great deal of help—first Peter McGovern and subsequently Alexandra Bugailiskis. Their Italian counterparts in Canada, especially my good friend Ambassador Gian Lorenzo Cornado, were particularly adept at providing guidance through the various government approval processes.

Following the November 2018 distinguished patrons tour to Rome and the Vatican, a small group of us, led by Marc Mayer and Karen Colby-Stothart, travelled on to Venice. Susan and I were seeing the completed pavilion for the first time. In addition to the superb restoration of the building, carried out under the watchful eye of Milanese architect Alberico Belgiojoso, I was impressed by the creative landscaping surrounding it. None other than legendary landscape architect Cornelia Hahn Oberlander had a hand in this, and it showed. The restoration of the Canada Pavilion at the Venice Biennale was a triumph of vision and will on the part of many. It reaffirms the importance of projecting Canada's cultural influence beyond our borders and offers Canadian artists and architects a vital channel and place to display their creativity. Marc Mayer and his team at the gallery led with the vision. Without the passion and commitment of numerous philanthropists, pre-eminent among them Reesa Greenberg, and the unflinching support of the foundation, led by Karen Colby-Stothart and donors from across Canada, a successful outcome would not have been possible. The Canadian government engaged with enthusiasm, as did its important cultural agencies. Most gratifying to me was to see the complex network of national and international partnerships that have been forged—partnerships that will sustain our country's presence at the Venice Biennale for years to come.

I have always believed that the world should know more about Canada's art and artists. The Venice Biennale has done a good job of showcasing our top contemporary art and artists for over sixty years, but other efforts have been few and sporadic. So to me one of the most impressive undertakings during my time with the foundation was the first major exhibition beyond our borders of works by Canadian Impressionists. It opened in Munich in July 2019 and returned home to the National Gallery in February 2022. Titled *Canada and Impressionism: New Horizons*, the exhibition featured 121 masterworks. It travelled from Munich to the Fondation de l'Hermitage in Lausanne, and subsequently to the Musée Fabre in Montpellier. Organized by the National Gallery of Canada and curated by the gallery's senior curator of Canadian art, Katerina Atanassova, the exhibition contained works by thirty-six Canadian artists, a good number of them women.

From the first moment my friend and Impressionist scholar and author Ash Prakash spoke to me about the idea of this undertaking, I was hooked. I promised the foundation's vigorous support. Prakash was keen that these Canadian works be meticulously curated and seen by discerning audiences beyond our borders. High on our list of potential foreign hosts were institutions in Germany, Switzerland, and France. Once Marc Mayer had given his blessings to the project, a group of us went to work. Anne Eschapasse, deputy director of exhibitions and outreach at the gallery, began to scout for partner institutions, and Ash and I began to sound out potential donors. Prakash himself took the lead by arranging for the A.K. Prakash Foundation to serve as the exhibition patron. The hero of this story, in my view, is Katerina Atanassova. She and her team wasted no time in imagining the architecture of the exhibition and identifying specific works of interest as well as possible lenders. In her office one day, she laid out for me pictures of many of the works she had in mind. The task of assembling such an exhibition is enormous and complex. Curatorial networks have to be activated, loan agreements need to be negotiated, insurance coverage has to be put in place, a catalogue has to be written. Normally, this takes many months. Atanassova accomplished miracles in record time. In her words, the exhibition presented "the untold story of the dissemination of Impressionism and the role of Canadian Impressionists in the development of modern art in Canada. Equally, the exhibition challenges the monolithic notion of Impressionism which is wedded to the art of the French Impressionists. It reveals the visual differences between their work and the contributions of Canadian artists who adapted its philosophy to a specific time and place."

Loans from the National Gallery, from other Canadian museums, and importantly from private collectors formed the core of the exhibition. Among the private collections, we were fortunate to be able to count on loans from, among others, Ash Prakash, the Lassonde and Schaeffer families, and Power Corporation of Canada. Among individual loans, Susan and I were pleased to contribute one of our own, David Milne's *The Blossom Pickers*. Friends and colleagues did likewise. Throughout the preparatory process, Prakash contributed hugely with his ideas and advice as well as with generous financial support. Other financial supporters included the Donald Sobey Family Foundation, the Pierre Lassonde Family Foundation, the Heffel family, Michael and Renae Tims, and Kanta Marwah—all members of our distinguished patrons family.

Canada and Impressionism: New Horizons was launched at the Kunsthalle Munich in July 2018. The gallery's director, Roger Diederen, was as surprised as I was to see long queues of people on the street waiting to see *Kanada und Impressionismus* and the unique interpretation Canadian artists brought to this period. The looks of pride among all the Canadians there who had supported the exhibition said it all. Canada was making a big hit in one of Germany's sophisticated art capitals, and this was only the beginning. Attendance in Munich widely exceeded expectations, and the exhibition attracted critical acclaim in Germany, Switzerland, and France, despite complications arising from the COVID-19 pandemic.

I would like to see more of these international exhibitions originating from our museums. The Venice Biennale is a vital channel, and we are well positioned there. We have rich collections, unique art perspectives, talented curators, and a philanthropic community with a growing capacity and desire to support the arts. As *Canada and Impressionism: New Horizons* demonstrates, vision, ambition, and leadership can make a difference.

Throughout my life in business, politics, and the voluntary sector, I have been drawn toward people who stimulate and inspire and whom I respect and trust. Marc Mayer is such a person. During the twenty-five years I served on the board of the National Gallery of Canada Foundation, I had the privilege of travelling the journey for a full decade with him. It was a creative period, exciting and at times tumultuous. Every new gallery director understandably wishes to make an imprint of their own. The fluently bilingual Mayer came to his post with deep experience and respect for the history of the gallery and for those who have laboured to build it since 1880.

As he once said to me, "At the gallery, we stand on the shoulders of those who came before us." I could see this in him when he organized an event at the gallery to celebrate the contributions of its past director Jean Boggs. Mayer's strong career before joining the gallery included serving as head of visual arts with cultural services at the Canadian embassy in Paris, curator of the Albright-Knox Art Gallery in Buffalo, deputy director at the Brooklyn Museum, director of the Power Plant in Toronto, and director of the Musée d'art contemporain de Montréal.

When Mayer was appointed director and CEO in December 2008, his early encounters with our foundation were a bit tentative. But he quickly saw the value and potential of the foundation, and we began to work closely together. Articulate, passionate, and a good storyteller, he left his mark on our donors, and I was always pleased to introduce them to him. There was not a single occasion when he did not respond enthusiastically to an invitation to participate in a foundation function. He attended all our board meetings. In addition, he worked constructively with his board of trustees and with board chairs Michael Audain and subsequently Michael Tims. I, in turn, did all I could to assist him. This included hosting him on one occasion at a meeting of the Australia-Canada Economic Leadership Forum in Melbourne. As the Canada chair of the forum, I had organized a panel on the role of culture in our respective countries. Mayer impressed the participants and took advantage of his visit to Australia to connect with leading museums. While travelling with our distinguished patrons to the art capitals of the world—to New York, St. Petersburg, Moscow, London, Venice, Paris, Berlin, Rome, and the Vatican—I saw him in action, a most effective cultural ambassador. Always game for some good fun, in Rome, at a restaurant called Il Pagliaccio, he joined me in standing up to sing the great aria "Vesti la giubba" from Leoncavallo's tragic opera—to the astonishment of those around us.

On December 5, 2008, an enthusiastic crowd of well-wishers assembled in the Great Hall of the National Gallery to bid farewell to Mayer. Several months before, over lunch, I committed the foundation to take the lead in organizing a salute to him. He was richly deserving of the honour by any measure. But he had also taken a beating in the press over the past year over the "Chagall-David controversy." At the root of the controversy was Mayer's decision to auction a work by Marc Chagall in order to ensure that a painting by eighteenth-century French artist Jacques-Louis David, owned by a Quebec City parish church, did not leave Canada. A public furor ensued. The actors in the play were the gallery, the foundation, the Montreal Museum of Fine Arts and its outspoken director, Nathalie Bondil, the Roman Catholic Church, the Vatican, the government of Canada, the government of Quebec, and Christie's auction house in New York. I became closely involved in the behind-the-scenes discussions in National Gallery and foundation circles aimed at resolving the dispute. I argued that for the gallery's sake, the sale of the Chagall should be rescinded. When Mayer, under pressure, reversed his position and withdrew the Chagall from auction with Christie's, there was relief, but there was also fallout. It helped Mayer's cause greatly when an old friend of mine and a long-time gallery donor called me to say he would satisfy the outstanding financial obligation to Christie's and spare the National Gallery any expense. I served as the intermediary between the donor, who wished to remain anonymous, and Christie's. Problem solved, but to this day I marvel at the swift generosity of the donor. In the meantime, Mayer was wounded, and I wanted as best I could to help him heal.

The elegant soirée honouring Mayer was heartwarming. His many contributions over the decade were saluted by me, by board of trustees chair Françoise Lyon, and by Michael Audain. Mayer himself, surrounded at his table by members of his family, spoke with humility and emotion: "No words can express how deeply rewarding it has been for me to serve in this role; the life-defining honour of having been given it will be my solace always."

At the conclusion of the evening, Karen Colby-Stothart announced, to a standing ovation, that "in conjunction with the celebration of Marc Mayer's leadership and his accomplishments at the gallery," the gallery foundation was announcing $3 million in gifts. The financial support came from our distinguished patrons. The first to volunteer were Arni Thorsteinson and Susan Glass of Winnipeg. In addition, two special gifts of art were offered to the gallery in Mayer's honour: *The Last of the Hurons*, by Antoine Plamondon, a gift of distinguished patrons Fred and Beverly Schaeffer of Toronto; and *Parade, Party or Protest*, by Geoffrey Farmer, a gift of Gilles and Julia Ouellette of Toronto. As an emotional Mayer looked out at his well-wishers, he exclaimed, "It has been a grand journey. Thank you!"

Today, in penning this memoir, let me say that for me as well, my time with the National Gallery of Canada has been a most exciting and satisfying grand journey.

One of the most precious gifts I was given in my time with the foundation was my engagement with fellow philanthropists dedicated to the National Gallery, the enrichment of its collections, and the celebration of Canadian art and artists. Early on as foundation chair, I began to press for the recognition of major donors by the naming of specific spaces at the gallery. With the arrival of Marc Mayer, this conversation picked up momentum, and eventually the gallery's board of trustees put a naming policy into effect. Today, the named spaces tell the story of these remarkable people: the Donald R. Sobey Family Gallery, the Audain Gallery, the Michael and Sonja Koerner Atrium, the A.K. Prakash Gallery, the Ronald Mannix Boardroom, the Fred and Elizabeth Fountain Garden Court, the Lacey Family Gallery, the Weinbaum Family Gallery, and the Rennie Gallery. In addition, and for the first time in the gallery's history, a space was named in recognition of a generous corporate donor: Scotiabank. Together with trustee chair Michael Tims, Marc Mayer, and Karen Colby-Stothart, I was proud to open the Scotiabank Great Hall in the presence of Scotiabank CEO Brian Porter, a $10-million gift to coincide with Canada's 150th birthday celebrations. In the years to come, when I visit these spaces, I will take great satisfaction in being able to say, I know these families and was privileged to share a unique philanthropic journey with them. No doubt, as new namings take place, I will recall with satisfaction that these early pioneers helped lead the way.

May 18, 2022, was one of those evenings I shall remember all of my days. Some 250 people gathered in the ballroom of the Château Laurier to honour my twenty-five years of service to the National Gallery of Canada Foundation. I was pleased beyond words that the elegant black-tie soirée was coupled with the homecoming at the National Gallery of the magnificent *Canada and Impressionism: New Horizons* exhibition.

I was surrounded by friends and colleagues from across Canada many of whom had accompanied and inspired me during my twenty-five-year journey. The moving tributes of Michael Audain, Michael Adams, Marc Mayer, Karen Colby-Stothart, and foundation chair Ann Bowman hit home with me. At our table, Susan and I sat with three individuals and their spouses who had honoured me and the foundation with their patronage and support over the years: former governor general David Johnston, former chief justice of Canada Beverley McLachlin, and former prime minister Joe Clark. The gifted Katerina Atanassova was also with us, helping to mark an evening of warm reminiscences and camaraderie.

I saluted the artists, collectors, philanthropists, curators, and cultural and business leaders who had been such loyal contributors and who had given life to the foundation.

I saluted fellow foundation directors whose wisdom and support were indispensable to whatever I might have achieved over the years, notably Michael Adams, Michael Audain, Linda Black, Bernard Courtois, Fred Fountain, Reesa Greenberg, Michelle Koerner, Ash Prakash, Julie Lassonde, Don Pether, Hatty Reisman, Paul Genest, Pierre Laporte, John Doig, John Mierins, Sandra Pike, and the late Donald Sobey.

I saluted Ann Bowman, who succeeded me as foundation chair in 2020 and leads the foundation today with purpose and devotion.

I saved the last of my plaudits for two "largely unsung heroes": Lisa Turcotte, the foundation's executive director and long-time faithful colleague, and Cheryl Eadie, my executive assistant, who, in addition to assisting me with my daily business responsibilities, devoted literally thousands of volunteer hours to assisting me with my foundation work.

My final words that memorable evening were simple and heartfelt: "Dear friends, I will step away from the foundation board this September. But one can never walk away from our National Gallery. For Susan and me, this cultural gem is part of our lives, part of our souls. So are the bountiful memories and friendships we share with so many of you. They will live on and give us constant joy and satisfaction. So too will our great National Gallery live on and, God willing, be a source of pride to Canada and the world for centuries to come."

Love of art rarely diminishes with age. So it was that following twenty-five years of involvement with the National Gallery, I was ready for a new and exhilarating adventure. The telephone rang and Michael Audain asked if I would co-chair, along with France Chrétien Desmarais, the Jean Paul Riopelle centenary celebrations. Audain, an avid collector of Riopelle, wanted to celebrate the life of Canada's best known international artist and ensure that his work would continue to be recognized nationally and beyond our borders. To achieve this end, he created the Jean Paul Riopelle Foundation in Montreal and established a board of directors. Among those he invited to join the board were André Desmarais and Pierre Lassonde, like himself enthusiastic Riopelle collectors. Fortunately for us, the day to day work of the Foundation is led by a consummate organizer and advocate, Manon Gauthier.

The Riopelle celebration, which will culminate in 2023, the hundredth anniversary of the artist's birth, is unmatched in its ambition to shower recognition on a single Canadian artist. The celebration is to include a Riopelle retrospective at the National Gallery of Canada in 2023, the building of a magnificent "Espace Riopelle" in Quebec City housing the artist's works, and a play inspired by his life and work written by Robert Lepage.

I accepted Audain's invitation without hesitation. While far from being an expert, I saw Riopelle as a fascinating figure—innovative, bold, and uncompromising. He had first caught my eye as a man of revolutionary fervour. He had signed the "Refus Gobal" in 1948—a stinging rebuke of Quebec's political, religious, and social order. Interestingly, one of his co-signatories was fellow artist Paul-Émile Borduas. I also wanted to be of help to my fellow British Columbian Audain, who had been a stalwart supporter of my work at the National Gallery Foundation. But there was more. Here was a man from Vancouver reaching out into the heart of Quebec with his financial support and donations of art to celebrate a great Québécois artist. In my eyes, he was proving that the true spirit of giving knows no boundaries. A final and important reason is motivating me. By elevating Riopelle to greater national and international recognition, we are creating the template for doing likewise with other deserving Canadian artists. It would help remedy a sad situation: simply put, Canadian artists are too little known and appreciated beyond our borders. The Riopelle initiative in my view serves as a powerful counterpunch that will motivate Canada to do more—hopefully, much more.

EPILOGUE

REACHING FOR GOLD

Writing this memoir has been a rewarding experience. It has prompted me to reflect deeply on the people, issues, and events that have shaped me and my world. It has helped me to discover myself. That I am writing in the autumn of my life has also helped; my journey has been long and rich. It is from this vantage point, drawing from lessons learned from the past, that I dare arrive at some conclusions about the now and the future.

Let me begin with Canada. I express an unbridled love of country in much that I have written. Indeed, when I began this memoir, I had proposed to my publisher that my book be titled *For Love of Country*. Unsurprisingly, it was dismissed as bordering on the "maudlin." I remain unrestrained in my enthusiasm, nevertheless.

What then does Canada represent to me? A vast and beautiful land I have travelled east and west, north and south, that is home to people of all races and creeds. A welcoming land to immigrants and to refugees from war-torn countries which this year alone will attract over 400,000 new arrivals. A safe country that in the past two centuries has been free from attack or invasion. A country hewn out of the wilderness and bound together by bands of steel into one of the most advanced societies on earth, democratic and respectful of the rule of law. A nation with an identity forged in war and sacrifice in the defence of freedom. A country laden with talent and achievement in the arts and sciences, in entrepreneurship and business, committed to providing the best education in the world. A caring country.

But my Canada is not perfect. As I have acknowledged, my full awareness of Indigenous peoples, their history and their plight, came relatively late to me and to the vast majority of my generation, including our leaders. Truth and reconciliation must pave the way for them to live with justice and dignity in their chosen ways among us.

My Canada suffers from complacency. In far too many areas of endeavour, we satisfy ourselves with bronze and silver rather than aspiring to gold. While we benefit from a federalist system of government, regional divisions persist, and Western alienation has risen to disturbing levels. Extremism and hate have made their debut in our political discourse, and respect for individuals and institutions is in retreat. In the critical area of policy-making, essential to the shaping of sound laws and regulations, we tend to be quite inventive and creative, but we are not so adept at execution—at getting things done. We were once a country renowned for its great construction achievements: railways, dams, pipelines and seaways. Now we seem to have lost our capacity to think big and deliver even bigger. The exciting idea of great national projects seems to have faded away. More than two decades ago, I boldly stated that we should shape a Canada that is "the best place in the world to live, to work, to invest and to grow." We are not there yet.

Our standards of living have risen spectacularly since we were largely an agricultural society, but relatively low levels of growth have been the norm—far short of our potential. We boast of advanced social programs and yet our health care system is struggling badly.

This was the case even prior to the assault of the COVID-19 pandemic. Poverty, especially in our cities, is too much in evidence. In harnessing technology and the advantages of the Fourth Industrial Revolution, we are leaving too many of our citizens behind. Our huge endowment of natural resources carries an obligation for us to protect our environment. Once, I aspired to Canada becoming an energy and environmental superpower. Today, I see a country bitterly divided and sparring, seemingly oblivious to the fact that the progress of our country and humanity requires a symbiotic relationship between environmental and energy policy. Our ability to meet our net-zero carbon emissions targets by 2050 currently stand significantly in doubt. Internal trade barriers with Canada persist. International trade, a cornerstone of our prosperity, is threatened by a protectionist America, and yet we are laggards at diversifying our global markets, especially in the Indo-Pacific region.

Nowhere is Canada's complacency more evident and potentially more consequential than in our defence posture. Over the past century, Canada demonstrated again and again a remarkable readiness to marshal impressive military forces to counter aggression. Over a million and half served in Europe alone in the two world wars. But over the past four decades, our armed forces have suffered from serious neglect, and our combat readiness to defend our skies and shores is hopelessly inadequate. The brutal attack of Russia on Ukraine has served as a wake-up call for Canada, the NATO alliance, and the democratic world. The stark reality is that we now share an Arctic border with an aggressive nuclear power willing to flagrantly challenge the international order. In addition to an aggressive Russia, a powerful and autocratic China under the leadership of Xi Jinping has the intent and the means to achieve global superpower pre-eminence. Democratic countries around the world collectively are scrambling to meet this challenge. Canada, among them, can no longer delay or equivocate. We need a clear and sensible China strategy.

For the better part of a century, Canada could count on the protective security offered by the United States. This remains a lifeline and we must do all we can to enhance our joint contribution to continental defence. But as a life-long friend of America, I am deeply concerned about the malaise and divisions plaguing the Great Republic and the proliferation of America-first populism. Prudence dictates that we build a much more effective and resilient defence posture of our own to deal with come what may.

There was a time when Canada's voice in the world was among the most respected; it was often said that we "punched above our weight." This is no longer the case. In projecting and practising soft power, our lofty words have not been matched by deeds. We are less effective in part because we have failed to match soft power with credible military capabilities. In trying to be all things to all people, our foreign policy lacks focus and a clear set of priorities. Sadly, serious consideration of foreign policy issues is absent in our public debates—a failure that our political leaders have devoted precious little time to addressing.

In the domain of culture and the arts, our achievements in literature and the performing and visual arts are extraordinary. But as a country we have not matched others in bringing our creativity to the world.

So, what is to be done? Let's begin by unapologetically celebrating our successes as a nation. At the beginning of this epilogue, I sought to articulate what that success means to me. And throughout this book, I have not hesitated to point to countless examples of Canadian excellence, both in the past and the present. But I am deeply troubled by the waves of denial and cynicism I see in our public discourse, especially by those who offer the construct of the Canadian state as a failure, as an affirmation of a destructive colonialism. My simple response is contained in a few words I carry in my wallet: "O Canada, accept my gratitude for what you offer me. A country built on the courage, sweat and sacrifices of the generations that have come before me. A great nation, envy of the world, the True North Strong and Free! Give me the strength to contribute in some small way."

While acknowledging our weaknesses and failures, the journey of building and improving must go on. Values have a seminal role play here, values that have helped create who we are: hard work, honesty, compassion, humility, tolerance, respect, and a sense of fair play. Let's work harder at finding common ground to bridge our differences. Let's reject the sharp elbows, nastiness, personal insult, and even hateful rhetoric that are sadly tarnishing more of the political debate in the country.

The most powerful means to sustain our values that have helped create who we are as a people is sound education. In the ranking among nations, we score relatively highly. But we also know that parts of our educational system, including colleges and universities, are under stress. Striving for excellence often takes second place to the politics surrounding funding and political correctness. One of the overarching goals of education surely must be to shape present and future generations to think rationally, to understand the past and prepare for a future in a time of accelerating change. We must prepare an informed, responsible, and engaged citizenry. An equally vital goal of education is to prepare the leaders of tomorrow. Leadership and the role of leaders is a subject that goes to the very heart of this book.

Where do we go from here? The answers will be delivered by a new generation of Canadians—young, energetic, idealistic, committed to change, and wanting to make their mark. As I observe young people across Canada—in our schools, in our institutions of higher learning, in our workplaces, in every sphere of endeavour—I would say we are blessed. We have good reason to feel confident.

When students have asked me what it will take to make Canada the best place in the world in which to live, to work, to invest, and to grow, my answer has always come down to three essentials: good public policy, leadership, and the will to act.

Good public policy is a cornerstone on which a great country is built. Done well, it creates the conditions for fresh thinking, what today we call innovation. It helps generate an educated workforce, well-paying jobs, fiscally responsible economic growth, equality of opportunity, sound health, a clean environment, and public security. Good public policy can germinate only where the rule of law is respected and where leaders are genuinely dedicated to the public good, and where strong values are embraced. It cannot be created on the fly. It requires knowledge and hard work. It requires arduous, evidence-based research. It requires collaboration and consultation. We are exceptionally adept at shaping the ideas and the analysis that form the basis of good public policy—among the best in the world, I would say—but we are less effective in transforming policy into action.

I know we can do better. Ambitious and public-spirited individuals of strong character striving for excellence can be found in the tens of thousands across Canada, in our governments, in our courts, in our armed forces, in our industries and workplaces, in our hospitals, in our universities and schools, in our arts and sports organizations, and in our communities. All are contributing in their own way toward nation-building, and the Canada we know today is a reflection of their efforts. The primary responsibility for the attainment of national goals lies with our elected officials in Ottawa and the provinces, territories and our cities. The vast majority who serve in public office are hard-working and well-intentioned. But their efforts are often stymied by partisan conflict, opportunism, and short-term thinking dictated by short election cycles. Their efforts are also increasingly affected by a public service falling behind in the use of advanced digital technologies. Making complex change happen is hard work. Nation-building on a grand scale requires focus and big ideas and ambition to match. It also requires collective effort, often over a long period of time. In the face of formidable challenges in the past, Canadian leaders have risen to the occasion brilliantly. In the wake of a terrible pandemic, and with rising inflation, exploding public debt, and threats to global peace, now is the time to set fresh and ambitious priorities and get on with the job.

In this book, I have chronicled my small part in nation-building—sometimes successful, sometimes not, but always believing that no opportunity should go unanswered. As a young boy sitting with my Latin tutor, I was taken by two words from the writings of the Roman poet Horace: *carpe diem* ("seize the day"). They have guided me along the way. May these words guide Canada in the journey ahead. To all my fellow Canadians, I say *carpe diem*!

ACKNOWLEDGEMENTS

I owe special thanks to scores of people for the genesis of this book, beginning with my parents who gave me life and the privilege of being born and raised in this great country. In my early life, family members, schoolmates, and teachers helped shape who I am. University professors challenged me to read deeply. They taught me how to think. More than any discipline, the study of the law prepared me for what was to come.

My four-year experience on Parliament Hill serving a member of cabinet and, subsequently, the prime minister taught me a great deal about politics and the exercise of political power. Elected representatives of all political stripes, by their example and their actions, helped me understand the complexity and the preciousness of democratic government. While on Parliament Hill and long after, my interactions with the public service proved to be enormously enriching. There I met countless individuals who serve our country with great skill and selflessness. Working with gifted politicians and public servants taught me why good public policy—an enduring theme of this book—is the holy grail.

With the launch of my private business career in Europe and in Canada, I took to entrepreneurial life with gusto and imbibed the ethos of those driven by a desire to build and succeed—in whatever walk of life. Throughout the seventies and eighties, running my own business, it was high octane all the time. Daring was fun. It was also profitable. Exceeding client expectations was the name of the game. Going at it with the help of a carefully recruited and talented team made the seemingly impossible, possible.

The energy generated and the lessons learned stayed with me as I began my three-decade involvement with Canada's CEO-based business association known today as the Business Council of Canada—formerly the Business Council on National Issues and, later, the Canadian Council of Chief Executives. My recollections remain vivid of the over one thousand chief executives and entre-preneurs, and dozens of loyal staffers, with whom I worked over this time. A good number shared unforgettable moments in my life. Many became friends. My gratitude to them for their wisdom, example, and support is profound.

Threaded throughout my adult life and experiences in business, politics, and the arts, the role of the academy has been seminal in shaping my thinking. I have worked with many dozens of scholars and researchers in the domains of the law, political science, eco-nomics, international trade, the environment, constitutional stud-ies, foreign policy, and defence. Canadian universities have been an important source of expertise as have been independent think tanks. My time teaching in the university classroom was enor-mously stimulating and rich with discovery. My time on the boards of Carleton University and the University of Ottawa helped me understand the complexities of governing a modern day university.

The arts have been part of my life from the beginning, leading me to deep and enduring engagement with arts organizations and philanthropy. The artists, scholars, curators, museum directors, col-lectors, and philanthropists with whom I worked along the way have inspired me beyond words. Among the institutions I have supported and continue to support, the National Arts Centre and the National Gallery of Canada stand out. Through them and in them, they have helped shape who I am as a Canadian.

My work on this memoir has been facilitated significantly by a large archival collection which includes my correspondence, meeting notes, speeches, published papers and articles, photographs and media mentions. I have chosen to forego endnotes and author's notes in the knowledge that all these materials are in the possession of Library and Archives Canada for anyone wishing to carry out research on any of the subjects I have addressed. Also, upon publication, complementary materials of relevance to my memoir will be available on my website, www.thomasdaquino.ca.

The pages of this memoir tell the story of the people who have influenced my life. This book is a homage to them. With gratitude, I now turn to those who assisted me in preparing my manuscript—Cy Strom, who edited early versions, and Jim Mitchell, Dwayne Wright, Goldy Hyder, Jack Hughes, Perrin Beatty, Fen Hampson, Marc Mayer, and Michael Adams who read select chapters.

I am especially grateful to Stephen Poloz for reviewing an early version of my manuscript and to Andrew Cohen who, in addition to reviewing a late stage of the manuscript, offered invaluable advice and comments throughout the writing process.

At Penguin Random House Canada, the assistance of Doug Pepper, my editor and the publisher of Signal/McClelland & Stewart, was constant and indispensable. A master of his métier, I benefitted greatly from his commentary and suggestions.

Words alone will not suffice to thank my executive assistant, Cheryl Eadie Maloney. It was she who suggested that I write the memoir in the time of the COVID-19 pandemic and that I think of it as a gift to myself for my eightieth birthday. She prepared countless drafts with patience and good cheer—always encouraging me to press on despite numerous distractions. I could not have crossed the finish line without her.

As in all important things in my life, the work and support of my wife Susan was fundamental to this undertaking. She was present every step along the way offering precious advice. She never hesitated to question and to challenge. Her good judgment—and her memory—were indispensable. For these reasons and many more, it is with gratitude and humility that I have dedicated this book to her.

Many hundreds of individuals can rightly claim credit for having enabled me to write this book. That said, I accept full responsibility for any errors, omissions, or other deficiencies that may appear in these pages. Having tried my best, of this I am certain—the quest for perfection has eluded me. For this I hope I may be forgiven.

INDEX